PATTERN OF
REDEMPTION

PATTERN OF REDEMPTION

· · ·

THE THEOLOGY OF
Hans Urs von Balthasar

EDWARD T. OAKES

CONTINUUM · NEW YORK

1994
The Continuum Publishing Company
370 Lexington Avenue, New York, NY 10017

Printed in the United States of America

Library of Congress Cataloging-in-Publication Data

Oakes, Edward T.
   Pattern of redemption : the theology of Hans Urs von Balthasar /
Edward T. Oakes.
     p.   cm.
   Includes bibliographical references and index.
   ISBN 0-8264-0685-8 (alk. paper)
   1. Balthasar, Hans Urs von, 1905–1988. 2. theology, Doctrinal–
–History—20th century. 3. Catholic Church—Doctrines–
–History—20th century. I. Title.
BX4705.B163025 1994
230′.092—dc20
                                          94-28336
                                             CIP

Imprimi potest: E. Edward Kinerk, S.J., Provinical, Missouri Province, 22 April 1994

Excerpts from "Choruses from 'The Rock'" and "Ash Wednesday" in *Collected Poems
1909–1962* by T. S. Eliot, copyright 1936 by Harcourt Brace & Company, copyright ©
1964, 1963 by T. S. Eliot, reprinted by permission of the publisher.

Excerpt from "A Dialogue on Dramatic Poetry" in *Selected Essays* by T. S. Eliot, copyright
1950 by Harcourt Brace & Company and renewed 1978 by Esme Valerie Eliot, reprinted
by permission of the publisher.

Excerpts from "Burnt Norton" and "East Coker" in *Four Quarters*, copyright 1943 by T.
S. Eliot and renewed 1971 by Esme Varerie Eliot, reprinted by permission of Harcourt Brace
& Company.

*To my father and mother,
and sister and brother*

Contents

Acknowledgments

Pascal says somewhere that in speaking of their works, authors will usually say: "My book, my commentary, my history, etc." They would do better, he thinks, to say: "Our book, our commentary, our history." In working on the book now before the reader, I have more than once felt the justice of this observation, and so I would like on this page to thank all of those who made this "our" book.

First of all, to the Director and Board Members of the Marguerite Eyer Wilbur Foundation for two consecutive grants that freed me from teaching duties when I began this project. Second, a research grant from the German Government's *Deutscher Akademischer Austauschdienst* (German Academic Exchange Service) enabled me to travel to Frankfurt, Germany where I was able to consult some important unpublished or otherwise inaccessible documents, as well as secondary literature not available in this country, at the Philosophisch-Theologische Hochschule St. Georgen, to whose Rector, Dr. Werner Löser, S.J., and librarian, Dr. Georg Miczka, I owe a real debt of gratitude for their unfailing hospitality.

To Professor Löser as well as to Prof. Dr. Medard Kehl, S.J., I am also indebted for their willingness to offer the assistance of their expertise in Balthasar's thought. Specialists in twentieth-century theology who are already acquainted with their work know how thoroughly steeped they are in Balthasar's thought, and I happily made abundant use of that expertise in my stay there.

Both Professors Avery Dulles, S. J., of Fordham University and Louis Dupré of Yale read the first draft of this book and together helped to transform it from a lumpy, indigestible encyclopedia into what I hope resembles a sustained and flowing argument. Portions of the later drafts were also read variously by Professors Alfred Ivry, David Leahy and F. E. Peters, all generous colleagues of mine at New York University. I have not in every instance followed their respective suggestions, so the usual disclaimer is doubly valid in this case: the flaws that remain are my own.

My editor at Continuum, Frank Oveis, is one of those dreams come true: an editor who not only supports and understands an author but can wink at his oft-expressed anxieties and cure them with his own joy at life.

And speaking of which, it is also to Professor Peters and his wife Mary that I owe occasional residence at their summer estate, a kind of Casa Bellagio for junior faculty, always an occasion to restore my own joy at life.

And of course finally to my family, to whom this book is dedicated, and who no longer have to wait for the answer to That Question: "When is your book coming out?"

Edward T. Oakes, S.J.
Peter-Faber-Kolleg
Berlin, Germany
31 July 1994

Table of Abbreviations

TL I–III   *Theologik:* Volumes I, II, III
TP   *Thessalonicher- und Pastoralbriefe des hl. Paulus*
UA   *Unser Auftrag*
W   *Weizenkorn: Aphorismen*
WC   *Wer ist ein Christ?*
WF   *The Word Made Flesh: Explorations in Theology:* Vol. 1

Note to the reader: the abbreviation *TD* stands for both the German and the English versions, an anomaly. Roman numerals refer to the German, Arabic to the English volumes. Note also that the German distinguishes two parts to Volume II, a distinction not made in the English publication. Therefore 1 = I; 2 = II/1; 3 = II/2; 4 = III; 5 = IV. *TD* 4 & 5 have not yet appeared at the writing of this book. I have taken my English quotations from existing translations whenever possible (with minor silent changes). The German is cited only if the text is scarce and unlikely to appear in English anytime soon. The *TL* is not yet out in English, but to avoid future confusion I have used Roman numerals for it too, as all citations will necessarily be from the original.

I also follow the standard abbreviation system for the Bible and for the following oft-cited secondary works:

CD   *Church Dogmatics,* by Karl Barth
DS   *Enchiridion symbolorum: Definitionum et declarationum de rebus fidei et morum,* ed. H. Denzinger & A. Schönmetzer, S.J. (Freiburg im Breisgau: Herder, 1963
ER   *The Epistle to the Romans,* by Karl Barth
KD   *Kirchliche Dogmatik,* by Karl Barth

Except for those four works, all secondary works of literature that are abbreviated are always abbreviated internal to the chapter itself and are cited in full at the first instance. All other works are cited in full. English works of Balthasar's are generally from Ignatius Press (San Francisco), German from Johannes Verlag (Einsiedeln, Switzerland, and lately from Trier, Germany).

Full bibliographic information on the works of Hans Urs von Balthasar, including lists of all translations in whatever language, may be found in: Carnelia Capol, *Hans Urs von Balthasar: Bibliographie, 1925–1990* (Einsiedeln: Johannes Verlag, 1990); and for Karl Barth in the two-volume *Bibliographie Karl Barth,* ed. Markus Wildi (Zurich: Theologischer Verlag, 1984, 1992).

Introduction

Pious scholars are rare.

Pascal

When set against the wider background of twentieth-century theology, the figure of Hans Urs von Balthasar comes across as rather isolated, even lonely. This is largely, though not entirely, due to the accidents of his biography: born in Lucerne, Switzerland, on 12 August 1905 of an upper-middle class family of noble stock (hence the *von* in his name), he quickly became known for his precocious talents in music and literature. After exploiting to the full the wonderful schooling available in that Golden Age of Swiss education (first at the Benedictine, and later the Jesuit *Gymnasium:* commensurate, at least chronologically, with our "high school"), he was then matriculated into the University of Zurich, where he pursued doctoral studies in German Language and Culture (note: and *not* in theology!).[1]

---

[1] Balthasar had little interest in his own biography, and this work introducing his thought has even less. Fortunately, his cousin has usefully summarized all the biographical details that are necessary for our purposes: "He came from an old patrician family in Lucerne which had given his hometown army officers, statesmen, scholars and churchmen—abbots and abbesses, canons, and a Jesuit provincial of Mexico. His father, Oscar Ludwig Carl Balthasar (1872–1946), was the canton *Baumeister,* responsible, among other things, for the St. Karli Kirche, one of Switzerland's pioneering modern church buildings. Through his mother, née Gabrielle Pietzcker (d. 1929), co-foundress and first general secretary of the Swiss League of Catholic Women, he was related to the Hungarian martyr-bishop, Apor von Györ, who was shot by Russian soldiers in 1944 for harboring some women refugees in his house. His younger brother Dieter served as an officer in the Swiss Guard. His sister Renée (1908–1986) was Superior General, from 1971 to 1983, of the Franciscan Sisters of Sainte Marie des Anges. He spent much of his childhood at the Pension Felsberg run by his grandmother, where cosmopolitan attitudes and trilingualism (German, French and English) were taken for granted. . . . As Balthasar himself has testified, his childhood and youth were pervaded by music, for which he had quite an extraordinary talent" (Peter Henrici, "Hans Urs von Balthasar: A Sketch of his Life," *Communio* 16/3 [Fall 1989]: 306–350; here, 307–308). There is a book-length biography in Italian by Elio Guerriero, *Hans Urs von Balthasar* (Milan: Edizione Paoline, 1991), also translated into German by Carl Franz Müller (Einsiedeln: Johannes Verlag, 1993).

When he was nearly finished with his dissertation, he made a retreat under a Jesuit renowned for his fervor and preaching skill; and in a walk through a forest one day, Balthasar felt a powerful call to the Catholic priesthood in the Society of Jesus, entering the order on 18 November 1929.[2] Because the Jesuit order was not a legally recognized entity in Swiss law at the time (and in fact would not become so until the 1970's), he made his novitiate and did his philosophical studies in Germany, where the standard curriculum was that notorious "sawdust Thomism" of the infamous neo-scholastic manuals. Even late in his life, Balthasar would speak of that time—with considerable lingering bitterness—as a desert; and this alienation from the standard training of that time is probably the first sign of what would later become his acute sense of isolation. He certainly leaves no doubt how severely marked he was by this steady diet of scholastic gruel:

> My entire period of study in the Society of Jesus was a grim struggle with the dreariness of theology, with what men had made out of the glory of revelation. I could not endure this presentation of the Word of God! I could have lashed out with the fury of a Samson. I felt like tearing down, with Samson's own strength, the whole temple and burying myself beneath the rubble. But it was like this because, despite my sense of vocation, I wanted to carry out my own plans, and was living in a state of unbounded indignation. I told almost no one about this. [My teacher Erich] Przywara understood everything; I did not have to say anything. Otherwise there was no one who could have understood me.[3]

Interestingly enough, Balthasar's decision to devote his life to theology did not even take place when he went to the Jesuit theologate in Fourvière

---

[2] Actually, the call to the priesthood and the Society of Jesus was secondary to the fact of being called at all, and this would no doubt prove crucial to his later decision to leave the Jesuits: "Even now, thirty years later, I could still go to that remote path in the Black Forest, not far from Basel, and find again the tree beneath which I was struck as if by lightning. . . . And yet it was neither theology nor the priesthood which then came into my mind in a flash. It was simply this: you have nothing to choose, you have been called. You will not serve, you will be taken into service. You have no plans to make, you are just a little stone in a mosaic which has long been ready. All I needed to do was 'to leave everything and follow,' without making plans, without wishes or insights. All I needed was to stand there and wait to see what I would be needed for" (Hans Urs von Balthasar, *Pourquoi je me suis fait prêtre* [Tournai: Editions Centre Diocésain de Documentation, 1961], 21).

[3] These revealing remarks are to be found in the course of an Introduction Balthasar wrote to Adrienne von Speyr's *Erde und Himmel: Ein Tagebuch. Zweiter Teil: Die Zeit der großen Diktate* (Einsiedeln: Johannes Verlag, 1975). It is also interesting to note that what kept his soul together at that time was the project of rewriting his dissertation for publication, which,

(near Lyons, France) to study the prescribed pre-ordination theology. Although he fell in love with the Church Fathers under the tutelage of his great teacher Henri de Lubac and wrote some of his first works in patristics there, he still spent a large part of his free time outside the lectures by reading and translating some of the great contemporary French literary figures like Paul Claudel, Charles Péguy, George Bernanos and Paul Valery.[4]

His first full-time assignment after his ordination to the priesthood on 26 July 1936 was to work at the distinguished Jesuit monthly, *Stimmen der Zeit,* in Munich. But the sounds of war, literally audible from Balthasar's room in the form of goose-stepping soldiers and the blare of Nazi propaganda on the loudspeakers, meant he would have to leave. His superiors gave him an interesting choice: to go to Rome to be a professor of theology or to return to Switzerland to be a student chaplain at the University of Basel, and we are not surprised that he chose the latter.[5]

It was there that he met the twice-married Protestant physician, Adrienne von Speyr, who converted to Catholicism under his auspices and who was the recipient, almost upon their first encounter, of a series of mystical graces so intense that it eventually prompted him, under her encouragement, to leave the Society of Jesus. This was done so that the two of them could then found a "secular institute"—which is, roughly speaking, a form of life that seeks to follow the inner essence of religious life (vows, celibacy, etc.) but in an entirely hidden way, without external supports, while being fully engaged in the secular world of work.

It was this encounter, more than any other event in Balthasar's life, that no doubt led to his isolation from the wider guild of professional theologians, for as he has made clear on more than one occasion: "I want to try to prevent anyone after my death from undertaking the task of separating my work from that of Adrienne von Speyr. This is not in the least possible, either theologically or in regard to the secular institute now underway" (*UA,* 11). If this judgment is true, and I think it must be

---

he adds in a fascinating aside, he was resolved to do "whatever the cost, in order to *rebuild the world from its foundations*" (ibid; my emphasis).

[4] Note once more the motif of isolation: "Fortunately Henri de Lubac was in residence, and he referred us beyond scholasticism to the Church Fathers, generously making his notes and excerpts available to us. So it came about that while the others were out playing soccer, I studied with Daniélou, Bouillard and a number of others and wrote books on Origen, Gregory of Nyssa and Maximus" (*Test Everything, Hold Fast to What is Good,* an interview with Hans Urs von Balthasar by Angelo Scola, tr. Maria Shrady [San Francisco: Ignatius Press, 1989], 11–12).

[5] "Everything at that time was running true to course . . . but the boots of the SS sounded ever more loudly from the nearby Ludwigstrasse, and no ear could escape the loudspeakers that were set up everywhere in the city. The area around the old Hofbräuhaus became eerie and terrible, and I was glad to be offered the position in Switzerland that transferred me to direct pastoral work" (*MW,* 13).

conceded on all sides, then we have before us the single most telling factor responsible for Balthasar's isolation from the rest of twentieth-century theology; for Adrienne von Speyr struck (and still strikes) many people as, if not bizarre, at least alienating and too intense for their taste; even those who approach her story with the best will in the world find her life so startlingly unusual and disconcerting that they are often put off by her. And no doubt eyebrows were raised in the Gossip Brigade when Balthasar moved into the Kaegi household in Basel in order to be her spiritual director full-time (Werner Kaegi was von Speyr's second husband and a professor of history at the University of Basel).[6]

But there are other factors to consider as well. For one thing, one of the first apostolates of the secular institute was to establish its own publishing firm, under the patronage, like the institute itself, of St. John (hence the name Johannes Verlag); and two of the first books to come out from that press were Hans Küng's famous dissertation *Justification* and Karl Rahner's *Das freie Wort in der Kirche* (*Free Speech in the Church*), famously "liberal" books that did nothing to allay the suspicions of a revanchist Rome.[7] Moreover, Balthasar's own famous book on Karl Barth had just appeared, which happened to arrive at the bookstores just after Pope Pius XII had condemned the so-called "nouvelle théologie" of the faculty of Fourvière in his 1950 encyclical *Humani Generis*. The upshot of all these developments was that after leaving the Society of Jesus, Balthasar could find no bishop to incardinate him in a diocese, a development which had the canonical effect of turning him into a kind of sacerdotal Ishmael: forbidden by canon law to celebrate Mass publicly, to preach or to hear confessions, Balthasar had to struggle at that time in real poverty, subsisting on the generosity of the Kaegis, on the meager earnings of a fledgling publishing house and on retreats and conferences he would give from time to time in Germany.

Eventually, in 1956 the bishop of Chur in Switzerland allowed him to be incardinated there (though he would always live in Basel), which finally dispelled the canonical cloud under which he had been working for so long. But his relations with the Swiss bishops were never so smooth or mutually admiring that he would ever have been considered for nomination as a *peritus* (expert theologian) to accompany them when the Second Vatican Council was convoked. So, not untypically, he had to sit out the most epochal event in Roman Catholicism of this century, quietly and patiently writing, editing, translating and publishing.

---

[6] Adrienne von Speyr died in 1967; her husband in 1979; and Balthasar himself on 26 June 1988, two days before he was to be elevated to the College of Cardinals.

[7] It is hard to recapture the atmosphere of those times, but readers who would like some sense of what theologians had to face at that time who fell under suspicion should consult Joseph A. Komonchak, "Theology and Culture at Mid-Century: The Example of Henri de Lubac," *Theological Studies* 51/4 (December 1990): 579–602.

In a way, the Council represented the complete vindication of all that he had fought for as a theologian: the abandonment of a top-heavy rationalism in favor of the more symbolic and aesthetic approach of the patristic period and the dismantling of the "bastions" of a "fortress mentality" Church in favor of a greater openness to the world—precisely what he had recommended in the very title of one of his earliest books.[8] But that is not how matters turned out. Soon after the conclusion of the Council, Balthasar grew worried about the trends that were being justified in its name, and he set his reputation on the line within a few years by adamantly and openly opposing the majority trend in theology, especially as represented in the international journal *Concilium,* which he countered with his own foundation, the journal *Communio.* And so the battle-lines were drawn.

The upshot of all of this is easily imagined: working in isolation, yet immensely learned and energetic; under suspicion first by Rome and then by his own national bishops, yet now regarded with almost equal suspicion by most theologians in the wake of Vatican II; the full-time spiritual director of a woman who seems, at least by *his* claim, to be the recipient of mystical graces not equalled since Teresa of Avila, yet whose own theology is not so much mystical (in the technical and specific sense of that word) as "aesthetic" and humanistic—how does one come to terms with such a theologian? What box does he fit in and how might he be pigeonholed? Well, obviously he can't.[9] But perhaps that too is one part his continued isolation: what is not familiar and categorizeable is ignored.

It is the purpose of this book to heal that isolation. Admittedly, the task is daunting, primarily because of Balthasar's almost crushing erudition. As he himself says of the seventh-century Church Father, Maximus the Confessor: "He had undoubtedly read a great deal." True enough, and for both men! In fact, I have often discovered that Balthasar frequently gives an unconscious portrait of himself when he is ostensibly describing another theologian. In any event, I have taken his description of Maximus'

---

[8] *Schleifung der Bastionen: Von der Kirche in dieser Zeit* (Einsiedeln: Johannes Verlag, 1952).

[9] Thomas O'Meara makes the same point: "He is not as well known in the English-speaking world as Yves Congar, Henri de Lubac, or Hans Küng. Moreover, he is known through fragments—works only partially translated—or through small essays. What complicates his reception even more is his recent critique of certain directions in theologians such as Rahner and Küng and his consequent appropriation by an intellectually conservative minority. One hears he is a Barthian, a mystic, a papalist. The true Balthasar, however, is not an integralist but a cultural theologian ... whose career began with a study of religion in German idealism. His major works are collages of culture and Christianity. The systematician ... is a patrologist, a competent historian of Greek and German philosophies, a pioneer in the rediscovery of Maximus the Confessor, a translator of Paul Claudel" (Thomas F. O'Meara, O.P., "Of Art and Theology: Hans Urs von Balthasar's Systems," *Theological Studies* 42/2 [June 1981]: 272).

theology as my clue to how to structure this book: "But, despite his vast reading," Balthasar continues, "[Maximus] built his spiritual house on just a few well-chosen pillars: those that permitted him to look beyond all the spectacular cross-beams and mock-ups, past the distracting façade of the past, and win back once more the true form of the living tradition. Maximus's genius was that he was able to open up five or six spiritual worlds that apparently had come to seem irreconcilable and to interrelate them. Moreover, he was then able, from each of these worlds, to find an inner light to illuminate all the others and to set them in a new relationship with one another, from which the most unexpected reflections and relations would arise."[10]

In many ways, the true greatness of Hans Urs von Balthasar as a theologian is rooted in this same charism: setting aside for a moment all of his own extraordinary reading and prodigious scholarship—the laborious struggle to keep the Church's tradition alive and vibrant in his work as both publisher and translator—we can see that he too was able to look beyond all of that immensity and build his own house as well on just a few "well-chosen pillars." The present book proposes to guide its readers through this rather vast and intimidating mansion. Well-founded, it well might be; grounded in a few simple but sturdy pillars that reach all the way down to the bedrock of the Christian proclamation, it well might be. But this house is also extraordinarily large, astonishingly so considering how few laborers took part in its construction. And so the guide is faced with the painful choice of deciding which of the many rooms of this mansion must be ignored, which are too detailed in their embellishments to spend time on in one day's tour, and which must regretfully be postponed for another day.

But even when the tour guide has thoughtfully worked out his plan of action for the day's tour, how can he ever give his charges any idea of the sheer architectural *simplicity* of the house? How to convey the excitement of the designer's first drafts, the quickly conceived but slowly realized blueprint that in fact, miraculously enough, attained final completion before the architect's death? For us, the building is complete, and we are free to walk about it at leisure and sample whatever part of it might please us at the moment. But what is the significance of the whole? Why is it

---

[10] Hans Urs von Balthasar, "Mittler zwischen Ost und West: Zur 1300. Jahrfeier Maximus' des Bekenners (580–662)," *Sein und Sendung* 8 (1962): 358–361: "Maximus hat zweifellos viel gelesen, aber sein geistiges Haus hat er auf ein paar wenige wohlgewählte Säulen gestellt, jene, die ihm erlaubten, über alle spektakulären Galgen und Strohpuppen hinweg die wahre Gestalt der lebendigen Tradition wiederzugewinnen. Das Geniale an Maximus ist, daß er fünf oder sechs scheinbar unter sich beziehungslos gewordene geistige Welten in sich selber gegeneinander zu öffnen vermochte und aus jeder ein Licht zu gewinnen verstand, das alle übrigen erhellt und in neue Zusammenhänge rückt, wodurch die unerwartetesten Spielungen und Bezüge entstehen" (358–59).

there, and what does it mean for the Church? For it is the totality of the work that is significant much more than the many parts that make it a whole.[11]

That is why this book does not wish to be taken merely as a guide book, a *vade mecum* or Baedeker, through the maze of a complexly constructed building. Beyond that, it hopes to convey a sense of the architecture of the plan. When Malcolm Miller gives his tours of Chartres Cathedral,[12] he does more than point out the innumerable facts or the almost infinitely many details that one could learn about the construction of this extraordinary example of Gothic architecture; he also conveys his love for the place, and the tourist is left feeling not so much like a tourist but like an incipient catechumen invited to join in the worship for which the cathedral was designed in the first place.

Balthasar once made a remark about his theology that might well grate on some ears but which I think, rightly understood, goes far to explain the architecture of his thought. He said that he wished to pursue a "kneeling theology" and not one that produces its work at the writer's desk.[13] This, as I say, might strike some ears as either unctuous piety or as the equiva-

---

[11] This is always the dilemma facing his interpreter: "In considering the work of Hans Urs von Balthasar, the question arises: is it not really just an assemblage of all-too disparate elements, so much so that we cannot really expect a clear and direct answer to the question of what Balthasar really wanted to say? And in fact Balthasar's work *is* characterized by his selection of the linguistic and expressive forms which he uses for presenting this variety of content. Thus the impression could arise that he has only a heterogeneous conglomerate of things to say—one day this, the other that. If that were true, then the reader really interested in finding out whether our author set much store in expressing one thing over all else—doing so in a quite special and in fact entirely unique way—would finally set aside these many books, justifiably disappointed. But this impression does not correspond to reality. For Balthasar, the 'one thing necessary' was always crucial, and the immense variety of things he said and wrote only has meaning insofar as it brings this 'one thing necessary' to ever new expression. This 'One' can be summarized in its pithiest form in the sentence: 'Being and love are co-extensive'" (Werner Löser, "Being Interpreted as Love: Reflections on the Theology of Hans Urs von Balthasar," *Communio* 16/3 [Fall 1989]: 475–490; here, 475–476). I agree with this assessment, but because Balthasar understands "being" analogously, that "one thing necessary" soon gets complicated and metaphysical. This is why I have had to introduce the theme of analogy of being so early, which I hope will not intimidate readers innocent of metaphysics. But however complex, the issue is essential if one is to understand the ultimate simplicity of Balthasar's thought..

[12] Malcolm Miller is a tour-guide famous among English-speaking tourists in France: he has devoted most of his adult life to giving tours in the summer months of the Cathedral at Chartres, and his knowledge, love and enthusiasm for the place is legendary.

[13] "Hans Urs von Balthasar, as he himself once put it, wants 'a kneeling, not a sitting theology.' Basically, theology is 'adoration and sanctity, or love of God and neighbor,' even if, as he admits, 'between these two poles something is inserted that can be called a theoretical concern with the Word'" (Jakob Laubach, "Hans Urs von Balthasar," *Theologians of Our Time*, ed. Leonhard Reinisch [Notre Dame, IN: University of Notre Dame Press, 1964], 146–147).

lent of the Pharisee in front of the synagogue congratulating himself for kneeling during the service while the pedantic scribe is sitting in a pew at the back, scribbling mere "academic" theology.

But this would be to misunderstand both the remark and his theology. Theology is always a *construction,* but one that is meant to symbolize or to point to a reality of which it is only the response. Balthasar has, in other words, constructed his building for a purpose. Museums contain relics of the past, but churches are built for worshippers, however much they might in the course of time also become tourist attractions. Perhaps the best way of interpreting Balthasar's remark about a "kneeling" theology is to recall those signs one often finds in famous Gothic and Baroque churches throughout Europe: "This church is built for worship. During services, please respect the dignity of the place."

Of course, tours are permitted in these places, but only during "off hours," so to speak. And so this book will make bold to be soberly descriptive, giving a merely "off hours" tour, but it will be a description of a theology that at all times is meant to point to God and to God's revelation, the response to which must always be first, not theology, but worship.

But of course, even in books that are written with only the tourist (or even potential convert) in mind, things can get technical, and this book is no exception. As I said before, I feel under no obligation to be complete, to cover all aspects of Balthasar's thought; but he has made major contributions to the theological debate in the twentieth century, and it is impossible to understand the *significance* of his thought without first understanding the nature of his contribution to contemporary theological debate. And that demands that a considerable amount of space must be devoted to the course of that debate. Consider Karl Rahner's extraordinarily effusive, but entirely accurate, appreciation of Balthasar's achievement:

> He writes minute patristic monographs on ancient Church Fathers (basically, he is *the* discoverer of Evagrius of Pontus), and with the same scrupulousness does a commentary on an almost forgotten section of Thomas's *Summa* and makes a part of the theology of Aquinas comes alive again; but he can also sketch out magnificent collective portraits of the Fathers (on Origen, Gregory of Nyssa, Maximus the Confessor, etc.) as hardly anyone else can do. . . . He writes an intellectual history of the nineteenth century. . . . He is also a systematic theologian: he writes a *theological* aesthetic, the only one that has ever been written, a work that makes the bold claim of pointing out to theology its unique and definitive center; what he says about Christian eschatology, about the relationship between nature and

grace, about the Catholic position on that modern Protestant Church Father, Karl Barth, about the theology of history, and much more: . . . all that has become an integral part of contemporary systematic theology. He is a spiritual writer who writes about contemplative prayer, unlocks the Scriptures for meditation, gives a Christian interpretation to existential angst, praises the heart of the world in a Christ-book of hymnic flight, and who says something important to the German-speaking world about the nature of modern secular institutes. He is an apologist in the best sense of the word who answers the God-question in a way that makes sense to a person of today. He is a philosopher not only in his interpretation of German Idealism in his *Prometheus* but also in his work *Wahrheit*. He is a translator of rank not only for Origen, Augustine, Gregory of Nyssa, Ignatius of Loyola, but also for Blondel, Péguy, Bernanos and, above all, Claudel, for whom he has become *the* decisive mediator to Germany.[14]

This appreciation is especially valuable, I think, because it comes from a man who has often been considered his chief rival for the mantle of "most influential Catholic theologian in our century," a rivalry that became especially pointed during their common tenure on the Vatican-sponsored International Theological Commission. But I mention Rahner's summation of his achievement not so much to snare wary readers who might be approaching Balthasar for the first time with a cautious reserve that comes from his supposedly "conservative" reputation, but more so that they will not get deterred by the opening chapters, which attempt to come to grips with this vast range of influence so aptly and succinctly described by Rahner.[15]

Nonetheless, as I say, it is not my intention that this introduction to Balthasar's works should be a mere catalogue of achievement, with numbered plates keyed to specific works in the manner of museum catalogues tied to special exhibits. For behind this teeming array of material that Balthasar has been able to marshall, there is in fact an important organizing structure, and that is what we shall be trying to describe in the opening chapters. For in reading through the vast number of pages that comprise his complete works, it became increasingly clear to me how important

---

[14] Karl Rahner, S.J., "Hans Urs von Balthasar," *Civitas* 20 (1964/65): 602; author's emphasis. *Prometheus* is the published version of the first part of Balthasar's dissertation for the University of Zurich (originally entitled *Die Apokalypse der deutschen Seele*), and *Wahrheit* became the first volume of Part III of the Trilogy.

[15] The philosophical background to the tension between these two men will be the focus of Chapter 3, and Chapter 12 will discuss its implications for contemporary Catholic life.

the debate is in theology regarding what is called "the analogy of being" and how, whatever its wider importance in theology generally, it forms one of the central avenues of access to Balthasar's thought in particular. I do not wish to maintain that this doctrine controls his thought (in fact, just the opposite is the case). But I do think that those who are not familiar with the importance of this debate on the analogy of being will also miss the wider significance of Balthasar's thought, and so the next chapter will have to discuss this issue in general terms first, to set the stage for a later discussion of Balthasar's own version of this doctrine.

If I might return once more (but finally) to the image of Chartres: one can certainly appreciate the beauty of the place without any prior aesthetic or religious background. But one's appreciation and understanding of the building immeasurably improves when one understands both why Gothic architecture arose in Europe when it did, and why Chartres is so peerless an example of the form. And a full appreciation of that insight demands at least some acquaintance with the technicalities of flying buttresses, high vaulting, etc. Similarly, I would like to encourage readers unfamiliar with the arcana of metaphysical theology to persevere through the first two chapters on the analogy of being. As soon as one sees the inevitability of the debate and what hinges on it, Balthasar's thought will take on not just new dimensions, but, I hope, new excitement as well.

As the above cited quotation on Maximus the Confessor so well shows, a not insignificant feature of Balthasar's thought is his work as mediator of the thought of others—or perhaps it would be better to say, as a conversation partner with the great thinkers and saints of the past: from Origen and Augustine, through Maximus and Anselm, and down to today, where such influences include Karl Barth, Thérèse de Lisieux, and Adrienne von Speyr. At times the influence of these people is so strong and the mark they stamped on him so evident that his very description of these men and women will, as we have already seen, end up being an unconscious portrait of his own thought. Thus the first part of this book will be devoted to specifying how the greatest of these figures have influenced his life: Erich Przywara, Karl Barth, the German Idealists, Origen, Maximus, etc.

I have, however, decided to postpone a consideration of the greatest influence on his life, Adrienne von Speyr, to the end of the book, where I finally attempt to step back from the edifice and make some critical evaluations and assessments of my own. I must admit that such a stance might not have met with the approval of the master of the house, were he still alive and able to hire and fire tour guides at will, for in his later years he had often expressly insisted that his and her work are two parts of one whole (and of which his is indeed the more insignificant contribution). But for the purposes of this book, at any rate, I shall be insisting on the opposite: that his is a building that not only can stand on its own, but does. There is, to be sure, a perhaps initially intimidating manor next door, the one built by Adrienne von Speyr, but its relationship to the edifice we shall be visiting in this book will be taken up only at the end of the tour.[16]

After discussing the most important influences on Balthasar's thought, we shall then proceed to a treatment of the famous Trilogy, both its significance as whole and its various outworkings and implications. The "deep backgrounding" necessary for a right understanding of this immense work is not easily gained, and it can be no part of the purpose of this book to provide it.[17] While it aims to go as deeply into his thought as a one-volume work will allow, it cannot substitute for that sensibility that only comes from the combined influences of faith and experience. This is a matter of maturity, of patience, of slowly letting-be and letting-grow what has already been planted. There is only one parable in Mark that is not found in either Matthew or Luke, and I am often reminded of it when I think of what a reader must bring to the appreciation of the work of this extraordinary man of the twentieth century:

> Jesus also said, "This is what the kingdom of God is like: A man scatters seed on the ground. Night and day, whether he sleeps or gets up, the seed sprouts and grows, though he does not know how. All by itself the soil produces grain—first the stalk, then the grain, then the full kernel in the grain. As soon as the grain is ripe, he puts the sickle to it, because the harvest has come." (Mark 4:26–29)

Appreciating the significance of the achievement of Hans Urs von Balthasar takes time. My only hope for a work like this is that it will make that task be more inviting and seem less intimidating than a quick glace at his collected works might make it seem. To borrow an image that first crops up in the legends that clustered around the life of St. Augustine, writing a one-volume book on Balthasar has often been for me like trying to fit the Mediterranean Sea into a child's water pail.[18] I have accordingly,

---

[16] And even if one concedes that Balthasar is right—that their respective works really are two parts of one whole— this too dictates the decision to take up her influence at the end. Otherwise, we would be anticipating most of the themes of the rest of the book, which seems both pedagogically unwise as well as impossible to encompass in just one chapter. But once we have become acquainted with his own thought in some detail, it will be much easier to summarize the nature of her influence and bring them into a single perspective for a final, though tentative, evaluation.

[17] Some reference to this background is of course inevitable, however brief; and this will entail a certain amount of *geistesgeschichtlich* generalization, for which I beg the patience of the expert.

[18] It was also said of St. Augustine, by the librarian at the monastery of Seville, in an inscription over the bookcase that housed his complete works: "Whoever claims to have

for the sake of economy, arranged the material in clusters, according to the structure of the Trilogy itself. Thus I have treated Balthasar's views on the relationship between the Old and New Testaments in the section on his Aesthetics, for it is there that he devotes two volumes to this theme; and I take up his Christology in my treatment of his Theodramatics; and his theology of the Trinity I reserve for the last part of the Trilogy, the Theo-logic, where he is at his most speculative. Of course, Balthasar's theology is trinitarian and christological from beginning to end, but only by clustering the topics in this way have I been able to convey both the structure of his thought and the major motifs that characterize this vast building as distinctively Balthasarian, and to do so in the limited space available.[19]

But before we can reach these apartments, we must first examine how his design was influenced by the great visionaries and teachers who shaped his life so markedly, and so it is with an examination of these influences that we will first begin our tour.

---

read all these books is a liar." I shall not make myself a liar by claiming that I have done the same for all of Balthasar's writings either, though a foraging trip to Germany allowed me to track down a number of pieces that for some reason never appeared in his books of collected essays. For the benefit of readers who will be unlikely to have access to these works, I have cited the original German in the footnotes whenever the translations are both my own *and* have come from works that are not likely to be translated anytime soon or are otherwise hard to track down. In all other cases, I use either my own translations of texts still available only in German or existing translations, making the occasional silent emendation against the German original.

[19] Every author writes with an imaginary audience in mind. Mine is not so much the professional theologian (who I hope will still find this book of interest) as the student and general reader curious about this man much rumored about but little known. Hence I have tried to avoid as much as possible such "in house" topics as: fundamental theology, inspiration, the *actus fidei*, etc., or other topics whose treatment is usually confined to the technical literature. The single great exception to this strategy is, of course, Chapter 1.

Part I

TRIBUTARIES OF INFLUENCE

• • •

In my beginning is my end. In succession
Houses rise and fall, crumble, are extended.,
Are removed, destroyed, restored . . .

Houses live and die: there is a time for building
And a time for living and for generation.

T. S. Eliot
"East Coker," *The Four Quartets*

· 1 ·

Erich Przywara
and the Analogy of Being

The detail of the pattern is movement.
Desire itself is movement
Not in itself desirable.

T. S. Eliot
"Burnt Norton," *The Four Quartets*

"In short, I believe that where *many* others have just been blowing hot air, I have managed in my book to put everything firmly in place by being silent about it." This remark, startling in its bluntness, appears in a letter that Ludwig Wittgenstein wrote to a friend explaining the purpose and intent of his *Tractatus Logico-Philosophicus;*[1] and it could well serve as a warning fit to terrify anyone who dares to be a theologian. For what resort do we have but, with Wittgenstein, to "pass over in silence those things of which we cannot speak"?[2] The alternative seems clear: either we apply human language to God and thus fall victim to the idolatry of anthropomorphism, labelling God with human terms and thereby making God like unto ourselves, or we claim that our terms mean something entirely different when applied to God, thus making theology little more than runic tablets that have no way of finding anchor in the world we actually do know.[3]

It is the claim of the theory of analogical relations to have resolved this

---

[1] Letter to Ludwig von Ficker, quoted in Paul Engelmann, *Letters from Ludwig Wittgenstein with a Memoir* (Oxford: Basil Blackwell, 1967), 143.

[2] "Wovon man nicht sprechen kann, darüber muß man schweigen," *Tractatus*, section 7 (London: Routledge & Kegan Paul, 1922), 188.

[3] "If all our terms derive from earthly experience, how can any of them be applied to God? If theologians use words in their ordinary sense, their theology will be anthropomorphic. If on the other hand a term is to mean something quite different when applied to God, then theology is incomprehensible" (Humphrey Palmer, *Analogy: A Study of Qualification and Argument in Theology* [London: Macmillan, 1973], xv).

seeming contradiction. According to this theory, language can be used in many senses which, while not utterly divergent, are yet clearly related in meaning. It is true that in language the same word can have totally different meanings (as, in English, the noun "mail" can mean a suit of armor or the day's allotment from the post office, or the verb "to lie" can mean either to deceive or to be at rest). This is an accident of language that is called "multivocation" or, more frequently in the literature, "equivocation." On other occasions, two different words can be used virtually interchangeably, a convergence of meaning called "synonymity." (Because it shares Teutonic and Romance ancestry equally—in its vocabulary, if not its grammar—English teems with such synonymous overlappings, such as the words "freedom" and "liberty.") But when the *same* word is used of two different things but still means the same thing (for example, the "mail" of both King Arthur's and Prince Valiant's suit of armor, or "dog" applied to a fox terrier and a German shepherd), this is called "univocation."

But there are other occasions when the same word can refer to different things that are neither utterly divergent nor identical, but are *related* somehow to each other, a relatedness which can be graded according to a certain proportionality of reference, that is, according to the fullness of the object to which the term refers. The standard, and perhaps thereby the rather overworked, example (deriving from Aristotle) is that of "health" applied to a person, to a facial complexion, or to one's diet. Under this schema, "healthy" is a term that primarily applies to a living organism, after which the term can then be legitimately applied to other phenomena, but only insofar as they are keyed to the primary referent (the way a rosy complexion indicates, and a nutritious diet promotes, good health).

This ability of language to apply to related things but in different ways is then taken to show that this same flexibility can apply to language about God: just as health applies primarily to the body and only secondarily to what indicates or promotes it, so too terms like "good" and "just" refer primarily to God, and only secondarily to us and to the universe, who serve to "indicate" true goodness: the goodness that is God's. Unfortunately, the matter is not that simple. For to complicate the issue, this analogy (whereby "health" might apply to different phenomena but only to one entity, the body, primarily) can only be used of God *analogously* (!), since God is God and not an object in the world proportional to other objects in that world. Presumably we are justified in calling diets, complexions, etc., "healthy" because we *already know* both what it means for an organism such as the human body to be healthy and how other phenomena either indicate or promote such health. But this we cannot claim of God. The *standard* by which we might judge the appropriateness of applying various terms to God is precisely what is lacking in the case of theological language and indeed must be lacking if we are to confess that God is God, who remains ever incomprehensible to us.

Nonetheless it is the claim of the doctrine of the analogy of being that it can give legitimate and true reference to God, however "analogous" the application *of* the analogy. This claim, however, cannot be taken in isolation, for it entails a whole series of complexities that are not easily kept in view at one and the same time: does, for instance, the application of analogy to God (which, after all, we have drawn from the world and applied to God) involve the same anthropomorphism it was the intent of analogy to avoid? Is it, as Karl Barth claims, *the* invention of the anti-Christ—meaning *the* ultimate attempt by man to seize hold of God—who cannot be grasped? Can analogy truly claim finally to have developed a language that can really say something meaningful of God without presuming thereby to have grasped him?

There is the further and related issue of faith and reason, or—to put the issue in more historical terms—of Hebrew and Hellenic thought patterns, of Biblical imagery versus Greek dialectics: "analogy" is a term invented by the Greeks in their science of mathematics and later expropriated by their philosophers to explain non-numerical proportions. But the Bible is quite innocent of such concerns and stakes its claim to be the medium of God's revelation blissfully unaware of such philosophical scruples. What does that mean? Does the doctrine of analogy force us to do interpretive violence to God's revelation in the Bible, or is it precisely the way to rescue it from what is alleged to be its tribal obscurantism and primitive naïveté?

And then there is finally, and perhaps most importantly, the issue of the credibility of the Christian proclamation in the face of modern skepticism and secularism: vast numbers of people in the advanced industrial societies of the world either cannot bring themselves to believe in God or they find the whole issue so disengaged from their lives that God is, in effect, functionally dead. Is that *due* to the fact that religions have been chattering on about God for so long that verbal inflation has set in and the words applied to God have lost their cash value, or is it the other way around: that language about God can once again give modern men and women renewed access to the living God if only such language could be rightly understood?

Erich Przywara devoted a large part of his labors as a philosopher of religion to this issue of analogy, and his influence on Balthasar both as teacher and mentor was considerable. In this chapter we shall examine the contours and implications of this doctrine of analogy and Przywara's role in the twentieth century as its advocate and defender. By the nature of his influence on Balthasar and because this doctrine had such an important methodological influence on Balthasar's entire work, this chapter can hardly do more than specify the implications of this theory of analogy:

exactly how Balthasar then made use of the theory can only be made clear as we are introduced into his work as a whole. Nor is this book a work on Przywara specifically, and so much of his own refinements on the theory as well as his wider work as a modern interpreter of Augustine and Kierkegaard (among others) will have to be ignored. The focus of this chapter, in other words, will be on the theory itself more than on the vagaries of its fate in this century among both its advocates and its attackers. But after outlining the essentials of the theory, we shall then try to specify, as much as space allows, the specific contribution that Przywara made to this debate and what of this contribution Balthasar himself took over into his own thought. This chapter, accordingly, shall be divided into three sections, the first outlining the general contours and motivation of the doctrine of analogy, the second specifying Przywara's contribution to the debate, and the third discussing, in a very general way, what Balthasar drew from his teacher and mentor.

I

As mentioned above, the theory is not only rather complex on its own terms but involves other related issues that must also be kept simultaneously in view. But such simultaneity can only be attained after one has become familiar with the separate issues. Accordingly, this section will focus on the following six issues related with analogy of being: a) first, we shall examine the role and presence of analogy in *human cognition* (that is, analogy as a mental ordering process and phenomenon of language); and then b) we shall look at the sheer fact of analogy and proportionality *in the world* as such, independent of human cognition (that is, analogy as the innate proportionality of worldly being); and c) because Christianity is so historical a religion, we shall then look at the issue of *history* and the way analogy plays a role in historical knowledge; then d) we shall deal with the Greek doctrine of *the Great Chain of Being* and the way the Greek philosophers after Parmenides insisted that the term "being" must be understood as entailing gradation and proportionality— that is, must be understood analogously; then in e) we shall discuss how the Christian doctrine of *creatio ex nihilo* altered this scheme while adopting for its own uses the conceptual insights of Greek philosophy; and in the last subsection f) we will discuss the important question of how Christians come to subscribe to this doctrine of creation: *through faith or reason?* This concluding subsection will then set the stage for discussing Przywara's own contribution to the discussion and then for providing a brief overview of what Balthasar learned from Przywara.

a. Human Cognition.
Let us begin then with the first of our six subheadings: analogy in human cognition. Consider first the way a child grows into its native language:

by adapting its limited vocabulary to many different, though analogous, situations. Although its vocabulary is still necessarily minimal, the child instinctively learns how the same word can be applied to different settings: Daddy will *fix* you; *fix* my wagon; *fix* my pants; *fix* my dinner; or: *make* my bed, *make* a sandwich, *make* a mistake, *make* time for, *make* a plane, *make* an appointment. On the basis of such vocabulary studies, linguists have determined that children learn to speak by comprehending the same word with multiple meanings, and indeed that they learn their native language far more easily this way than they would if they had to learn a different word for each new context and each new restricted zone of use.[4] Language learning is therefore inherently analogical; that is, it takes the same word and applies it to different, but related contexts. But for the child to be able to learn a language this way, the language must itself be open to this multivalency.

b. Analogy in the World.

But analogy exists in the world too and is not merely a function of human cognition or semantic fluidity. To draw once more on an example first coined by Aristotle, a bird and a fish are not the same, but they do share certain commonalities. Both are animals that move in a medium suited to each respective species: air in the case of the bird, and water in that of the fish. And both have analogous organs for such movement—wings and fins, respectively—appendages which clearly differ but whose structural similarities are such as to permit us to extrapolate from such proportionalities (wings are structurally similar to fins, but differ as air does to water) and to imitate such structures by this same act of extrapolation, as in the invention of airplanes and submarines.

And the same applies when we encounter a new reality that as yet has no name. For example, Greek has a term both for "wing" and for "fin." But Aristotle was frustrated that only "lung" could serve to describe the organ for the reception of oxygen. But with what organ do fish oxidize and replenish their cells? All Aristotle could say was that what the lung is to some animals is in other animals something which is *like* a lung. Or, while some animals have blood, others have something else that has the same effect as blood.[5] This example of Aristotle's in fact is an instance of

---

[4] See J. F. Ross, *Portraying Analogy* (Cambridge: Cambridge University Press, 1981), from whom I have drawn these examples. Ross's conclusion is an important one: "So the child has *already* mastered response to some semantic structure by which distinct senses for the same word are determined in context" (5).

[5] "It will be remembered that I have said already that there are many attributes which are common to many animals, either identically the same (e.g, organs like feet, feathers and scales, and the passions too), or else common by analogy only (i.e. some animals have a lung, others have no lung but something else to correspond instead of it); again, some animals have blood, while others have its counterpart [ἀναλογίαν] which in them has the

both kinds of analogical insight that we have encountered so far: on the one hand, the analogy really exists in the real order, though it is not yet reflected in the language; and its shows how the human knower always assimilates new experiences in terms of its analogies with the past, using the same term for analogous entities.

c. Analogy and Historical Knowledge.

While language is multivalent and polysemous in any case, flexible *because* past experiences must assimilate new knowledge, there is the further epistemological issue of the way language and imagination are used to give access to *history,* which I shall contend is an inherently comparative and thus an analogical process. This issue is particularly important in Christian theology, which not only must meet the challenge of how we speak about God meaningfully in general but also about how we can assert that God has revealed himself in the events of history. But before taking up the specific challenge of revelation, we shall first treat the issue of every form of historical knowledge as such via this same multivalency of language that is present in all acts of knowing and communication.[6]

Historical knowing is inherently an act of the imagination, and requires for its success the application of language to referents that are by definition

---

same value as blood in the former," (*De Part. anim.*, 6453b, tr. A. L. Peck, The Loeb Classical Library). It is fascinating to see how Aristotle will take this same schema used in his biology and apply it to metaphysical abstractions. In fact, his central disagreement with Plato can be simply put this way: Plato thought that such abstractions as "good" and "just" had an ultimate *univocal* meaning that was its true use, whereas Aristotle thought that such terms could not be reduced to one common denominator: "When Aristotle asks in what sense the concept of good is used, he replies that it is *kat'analogian* (*Met.* 1048 a35-b9). He opposes the Platonic thought that 'good' is a general term corresponding to a single idea— the idea of good. He says that, on the contrary, it designates many things of quite different natures. It is, however, not used in a multifarious sense, but designates something which is analogously common to several things. The examples given by Aristotle enable us to go a little more closely into what constitutes this analogy: as vision is a good in the body, so is intellect a good in the soul, and some other thing in something else. . . . The good, when said to be analogous, states that certain terms have like functions. The analogy consists not only in the statement of like relations of different things, but the concept is said to be analogous because the members on the one side of a number of similar proportions can be designated good" (Hampus Lyttkens, *The Analogy Between God and the World: An Investigation of its Background and Interpretations of its Use by Thomas of Aquino* [Uppsala: Almqvist & Wiksells Boktryckeri AB, 1952], 49). This insight might remind the reader of Wittgenstein's famous notion of "family resemblances" in ordinary language.

[6] This applies, by the way, no less to science than it does to history: "The language of natural science is irreducibly metaphorical and inexact, and formalizable only at the cost of distortion of the historical dynamics of scientific development and of the imaginative constructions in terms of which nature is interpreted by science" (Mary Hesse, *Revolutions and Reconstructions in the Philosophy of Science* [Brighton: Harvester Press, 1980], 172). Nonetheless, there are crucial differences between scientific and historical knowing, which we shall draw out in the next paragraph.

beyond the ken of the present knowers, who must supply the narrative of history with their own life-understanding, which they then apply to the historical situation *analogously,* that is, by using terms drawn from their primary experience in the present and applying them to the correspondences of the past.[7] And if we are willing to follow the argument of the literary critic Erich Auerbach, there is even a sacral dimension to all historical knowing as mediated by the interest the imagination takes in historical narrative: "The thing represented [in historical narrative] must be something very important and holy for those concerned, something affecting their whole life and thinking, and this something is not only expressed or imitated in the sign or symbol, but is considered to be itself present and contained in it."[8]

But once more, we move into a whole new realm of complexity when dealing with the historical narratives of the Bible, which claim a different kind of holiness than Auerbach sees in all historical narratives as such. And within the Bible the New Testament is especially exceptional, for it claims to be narrating the very story of God incarnate: "That which was from the beginning, which we have heard, which we have seen with our own eyes, which we have looked at and touched: this we proclaim as the Word of Life. This life appeared: we have seen it and testify to it" (1 Jn 1:1–2). So once more, we are forced to admit that it is quite one thing to see the ubiquity of analogous use of language in historical knowing, but quite another to say that this fact alone resolves the issue of how the New Testament refers! Wittgenstein, for one, was certainly aware of how startlingly different the issue of New Testament narrative is in comparison with other stories:

> Christianity is not based on a historical truth; rather it offers us a (historical) narrative and says: now believe! But not, believe this narrative with the belief appropriate to historical narrative, rather: believe, through thick and thin, which you can only do as the result of a *life. Here you have a narrative, don't take the same attitude to it as you take to other historical narratives!*

---

[7] This is a point that the poet and literary critic W. H. Auden was especially shrewd in spotting: "Temporal events may be divided into two classes: natural events and historical events. A natural event is recurrent, i.e., a member of a class of similar events and occurs necessarily according to law. An historical event occurs once only, i.e., the unique member of a class of one and it occurs not necessarily according to law but voluntarily according to provocation; and it is a cause of subsequent historical events by providing them with a motive for recurring. Natural events are related by the principle of Identity; historical events by the principle of Analogy" (W. H. Auden, "Nature, History and Poetry," *Thought* 25 [1950]: 412–422; here, 412).

[8] Erich Auerbach, "Figura," *Scenes from the Drama of European Literature: Six Essays* (Glouster, MA: Peter Smith, 1973), 56.

Make a quite different place for it in your life. There is nothing paradoxical about that![9]

Well, perhaps not paradoxical, but certainly analogical. For what Wittgenstein means by believing through thick and thin is: take this narrative as a pointer to God. Believe that God is manifesting himself in this narrative. But how can that be? How can God both manifest himself in history and yet remain ever the Incomprehensible? This question shall constitute the central preoccupation of Part III of this book, our analysis of Balthasar's theodramatics—that is, his understanding of how God can involve himself in human history and yet still remain hidden: truly revealed and yet ever inaccessible. For the moment it is enough to note how all historical knowledge is rooted in analogical forms of reasoning and imagination. The further question of how God may be said to be revealed in this historical medium will be the focus of later reflections.

d. Analogy and the Great Chain of Being.

But before presuming to treat so difficult a theme, we must first deal with the prior question of *being* itself. This is not simply because history and historical revelation are but subsets of the wider problem of existence itself, though of course they are. But more crucially, that very revelation proclaims that the universe itself owes *its very existence* to God's free decision to create it out of nothing. And this above all is what brings us to the final crux of the doctrine of analogy: the theme of the being of the universe itself. For an essential part of the Christian message is that the very "being there" of the universe is *derivative*. But to assert this is already to slip, however unawares, into analogical language. For the very concept of derivation requires that one draw a comparison: first there was God, the Uncaused Cause; then came the universe derivatively, created by God *ex nihilo*.

But how can such a comparison be drawn when the principle of the comparison remains ever inaccessible to us? The doctrine of creation implies that the universe has its being "on loan," so to speak: existence is not the universe's possession, rather it owes its being-there to God. But the complexities of such a statement enter the picture immediately, for even this "loan" of existence is not a direct one, as if God had something called "being" in his store, a portion of which he lent out to his creation like money in a bank account. For a bank loan is still an impartation of substance (which is then meant to accrue!). But the being of the world does not share in God's being in this way.

The Greek philosophers after Parmenides were of a different opinion.

---

[9] Ludwig Wittgenstein, *Culture and Value*, tr. Peter Winch (Chicago: University of Chicago Press, 1980), 32e (author's emphasis).

Not working with a doctrine of creation, they saw the world as emanating from God in a more direct way. How Greek philosophy came to terminate in such a doctrine of emanationism (in Neoplatonism) is a complex story, but for our purposes we need only see how the notion of *gradations* in being arose in Greek thought. We all admit that the universe exists, and ourselves within it. Even in moments when the world seems like a phantom without any ontic weight whatever ("we are such stuff as dreams are made on, and our little life is rounded with a sleep"), we have to ascribe to that phantom a phantom being. And this seemingly innocent distinction in the grades of being marks the beginning of the career of Greek metaphysics. For even to claim a merely apparent being in contrast to "real" being is to begin to admit distinctions within being itself, leading in short order to a doctrine of analogy of being.

But before such a doctrine could mature, it had to emerge out of the contradictory theses of the pre-Socratic philosophers Heraclitus and Parmenides. Heraclitus simply began with what was so obvious to his senses, and indeed one of his extant fragments says, "I honor more those things which are learned by sight and hearing."[10] And the testimony of those senses was that of constant change and strife: "Cold things grow hot, the hot cools, the wet dries, the parched moistens. . . . One should know that war is universal, that justice is strife, that all things come about in accordance with strife and with what must be."[11] But if such coincidence of opposites is *all* that there is to the universe, then nothing is stable, and Becoming is all. But if that is the case, then when it comes to the question of Being, only paradoxes can reign: "Gods are mortal, humans immortal, living their death, dying their life. . . . We step and do not step into the same rivers, we are and we are not."[12]

But to Parmenides this made no sense; he insisted that the seeming tautology "being is" excluded gradations in being and that it is philosophically incoherent to admit that being might have various "levels." Either something is or it is not. Parmenides is thus the Founding Father of all other subsequent thinkers who have denied the legitimacy of an analogical discussion of being, and his example is thereby quite instructive. His philosophy is one vast thought experiment on the dilemmas of discussing the topic of "being" without admitting gradations. He was, for one thing, the first to notice the deficiencies among the pre-Socratics who tried to find a common substrate in the universe (which would be air, or fire or water or whatever). For Parmenides, the common element was simply being: all

---

[10] Diels-Kranz, B 55; quoted in *Early Greek Philosophy*, tr. and ed. by Jonathan Barnes (London: Penguin, 1987), 103.

[11] Barnes, 115, 114; Diels-Kranz, B 126, 80.

[12] Barnes, 117; Diels-Kranz, B 62, 49a.

beings share by definition in just one common characteristic: being itself. But Parmenides' real importance arises because of his definition of being.

What then is being? For him the answer was equally obvious because equally required by his tautology: it is the very definition of being that all that which shares in it *is*, whereas that which does not share in it *is not*. In other words, between Hamlet's two alternatives "to be or not to be" there can be no third alternative. All rather smooth reasoning apparently, and it led equally smoothly to the conclusion that *being can have no cause*. For in order to cause being, that cause would have first to be, which means that since being is the only conceivable cause of being *it has no cause*, and therefore no beginning. Nor can it ever come to an end, for any conceivable cause of its destruction would also have *to be* before destroying it, and thus being has no end: it is eternal. But that also means that it is essentially foreign to change: being cannot include becoming. Change, therefore, simply does not exist.

The only way out of this impossible contradiction is by positing a gradation of being, either through a distinction between reality and appearance, prototype and copy, as in Plato, or by a distinction between act and potency, which was Aristotle's innovation over Plato. But in either case, the issue of analogy has been forced out into the open, as Przywara well notes: "Behind the problematic of analogy in Plato there lurks the same [motivation] as in Aristotle: the criticism of the two extremes of absolute change and absolute identity, and from this comes the basic stress on the *meson* [the midpoint] between the two."[13]

Analogy thus appears, in this question of being, as the only alternative between two impossible conclusions: for Parmenides, the conclusion was that being could have no other cause than itself, and what seemed to be caused—motion, generation, life-forms, etc.—could not participate in being; while for Heraclitus the tautology "being is" meant just the opposite: only motion is. Becoming is all. There is no stability, and all impressions of identity are illusory. To avoid these two apparent absurdities, both Plato and Aristotle were forced to admit an *intermediate level of being*, lest the mutual exclusivity of being and non-being lead to impossible conclusions.[14]

---

[13] Erich Przywara, *Analogia Entis: Metaphysik* (Einsiedeln: Johannes Verlag, 1962/1938), 143: "Im Hintergrund der Analogie-Problematik Platons steht das gleiche wie bei Aristoteles: die Kritik der Extreme des absoluten Wandels und der absoluten Identität, und hieraus die grundsätzliche Betonung des *meson* zwischen ihnen." Abbreviated henceforth as *AE*.

[14] Przywara strikes a characteristic note when he discusses this dilemma faced by Plato and Aristotle in their efforts to deal with the awkward legacy of Heraclitus and Parmenides: he stresses how analogy generates *movement* that is born out of pondering these strange antinomies: "And so we see what this presentation is aiming at: how the principle of non-contradiction is grounded, as it were, in the crucial minimum of the constant back-and-forth movement between these two deepest contraries of thinking. . . . *Analogia entis* has

Out of this admission of (at least one) intermediate level of being came the later Neoplatonist doctrine of the Great Chain of Being, itself a synthesis of Platonic and Aristotelian elements.[15] It was Plotinus (A.D. 205–270) who took the Platonic and Aristotelian heritage of gradations in being and fused this idea with the notion of a non-jealous (and otherwise unnamed One); and so he came to postulate a Great Chain of Being that emanates from the One down to the lowest forms of being in the scale of the universe: atomic matter. According to Plotinus,

> the One is perfect because it seeks for nothing, and possesses nothing, and has need of nothing; [but] being perfect, it *overflows,* and thus its superabundance produces an Other. Whenever anything reaches its own perfection, we see that it cannot bear to remain in itself, but generates and produces some other thing. . . . How then could the Most Perfect Being and the First Good remain shut up in itself, as though it were jealous or impotent—itself the potency of all things? . . . Something *must* therefore be begotten of it.[16]

e. Being and the Creation of the World.

This assertion that the One "must" create the world highlights the great difference between a Christian doctrine of analogy and the view that was derived from the Greeks—a point often missed by those who accuse analogical theologians of importing a false Hellenizing category into revelation.[17] As we pointed out earlier, the universe exists, but it does not

---

been developed precisely to the extent that it is founded both in the principle of noncontradiction as well as in the way it defines itself on this basis against (pure) logic and dialectics" (Przywara, *AE*, 111, 142). We shall return to this theme of analogy-as-movement in the second section of this chapter.

[15] "Though the ingredients of this complex of ideas came from Plato and Aristotle, it is in Neoplatonism that they first appear as fully organized into a coherent general scheme of things," (A. O. Lovejoy, *The Great Chain of Being* [Cambridge, MA: Harvard University Press, 1936], 61).

[16] Plotinus, *The Enneads* V, 2, 1; V, 4, 1; cited in Lovejoy, 62; my emphasis.

[17] The Anglican theologian E. L. Mascall is one of the few commentators who have noticed how much the doctrine of analogy *undermines* rather than draws upon the Greek heritage of the Great Chain of Being: "While in one sense [the doctrine of analogy] postulates between God and the world a distinction than which none could be more ultimate and unconditional, in another sense it brings them into a relation more intimate than any other doctrine has ever postulated. In its unqualified assertion that God is self-existent and that every other being depends entirely upon him, it leaves no room for any semi-divine intermediaries between God and the world. No system of hierarchically graded aeons cascading down in a series of steadily diminishing divinity, no *nous* or World-Soul neither fully divine nor yet exactly finite, no Arian Logos near enough to God to be able to make a world and yet far enough from God to demean himself to so lowly a work, nothing whatever to bridge the gulf between Being that is self-existent and being that is altogether dependent, except

draw its existence from that of God *substantially,* as if the existence of the universe were a portion of God's existence, "carved out," so to speak, so that we might be. This is quite different with the assumptions of the eternal existence of the world within which the Greek philosophers did their thinking. According to this world view, the universe shares its existence as the progressively diminishing emanation of God's being, radiating outward into the world, until finally, like the cold rays of the sun reaching the outer planets, the light of Being fades away before the ultimate recalcitrant prime matter that served as the raw material for the forming power of the Demiurge. But the doctrine of analogy arose in Christian theology as an outgrowth of its meditations on the doctrine of creation, which in one swift stroke establishes God's utter transcendence to worldly being and yet postulates a much closer intimacy between God and the world than was possible in the Neoplatonic doctrine of the Great Chain of Being. The universe, in other words, is derivative in a much more radical sense than the word "emanation"—or even the word "derivation"—might imply.[18]

When Christian theology, based on the doctrine of creation, claims that the being of the universe is analogous to that of God's, it does so because it is forced by the doctrine of creation to claim that, as God's *creation,* the universe must have some connection to God (for the inevitable reason that no cause can bring about an effect at utter variance with itself), and yet as *God's* creation, it cannot be God but entirely finite, dependent and created. That is, because God created the world, it must share some similarities with God's being only in the sense of not being utterly variant from God, but the world is also far more unlike God's being, and this

---

the sheer omnipotent fiat of God himself" (E. L. Mascall, *Existence and Analogy* [London: Longmans, Green and Co., 1949], 124).

[18] It is essential to see how all-governing is the doctrine of creation in relation to the efforts to *explain* creation by means of analogy. This is particularly true because of Thomas Aquinas' heavy borrowing from Aristotle, which has often given the false impression of what is at stake here. We must recall that, for Aristotle, "the analogous concept *sums up* what is common to several. *It is superior to the things of which it is said.* Applied to the knowledge of God, this would imply an attempt to summarize in general concepts what is common to God and creation" (Lyttkens, 52; my emphasis). This is what has led so many critics of analogy astray, Barth in particular: thinking that because *Aristotle* was trying to establish a conceptuality "superior to the things of which it is said," they assert that the same must hold for a Christian theologian. We shall see later how Przywara and Balthasar deal with this challenge, but at this juncture we need only recall a point stressed time and again by St. Thomas's most important twentieth-century interpreter, Étienne Gilson, "Here again St. Thomas departs from . . . even the most authentic Aristotelianism" (*The Philosophy of St. Thomas Aquinas,* tr. Edward Bullough [New York: Dorset, 1929], 120). This judgment has also been seconded by Mascall: "The fundamental principle of St. Thomas's metaphysics—his existentialism—while it completely revolutionized Aristotelianism, did not come from Aristotle at all, however necessary it may have been if Aristotle was to be made really coherent" (*Existence and Analogy,* xviii).

precisely because it is created being and not divine being! This is the motivation behind the decree of the Fourth Lateran Council that "between Creator and creature no likeness can be discerned without a greater unlikeness having to be discerned as well."[19]

But obviously, since the terms "similarity" and "dissimilarity" are being applied over against the standard of God's being, they too must be understood analogously (since, after all, our whole experience of similarity and dissimilarity is derived from our experience of and in the world). This might sound once again like we are running into the danger of falling into an infinite regress, but we can show how this danger can be avoided provided we follow the only path open to us: *by starting with creaturely being*. A theology based on the doctrine of analogy avoids the danger of infinite regress by beginning at the only place where it can begin: with an analysis of the only being accessible to us: our own. And what that analysis testifies to is simply the inexplicability of the world's being on its own terms. Mascall has aptly summarized the gist of this doctrine when he asserts: "God is, of course, given to us in a concept, *but not in a concept of God*. He is given to us in the concept of finite being, which declares its dependence for existence on a transfinite cause."[20]

f. Knowledge of Creation: Through Faith or Reason?

But even here there is the danger of misunderstanding, of starting off with a fatal misstep: for if creaturely being is the only being that is accessible to us, how do we know that it is precisely *creaturely*? Is revelation required for us to recognize our creatureliness or is it evident from an analysis of worldly being as such? This raises one of the most complex aspects of the issue of analogy, one we only alluded to above but which now must be given full treatment and which will be of decisive importance in the coming chapter on Karl Barth: that of faith and reason. Historically speaking, acknowledgment of creation "from nothing" comes from the Bible and was never a part of Greek metaphysics. Is this a mere accident of history or does the impact of God's revelation of himself in Exodus as "I am who am" mark an absolutely decisive moment in the definition of being which could never be arrived at otherwise but through God's own gracious disposition?

First of all it is crucial to recognize that, purely as a matter of history, the Greeks (or any other pagan culture, for that matter) did *not* come to

---

[19] Denzinger, no. 432: "*inter Creatorem et creaturam non potest tanta similitudo notari quin inter eos major sit dissimilitudo notanda.*.

[20] Mascall, *Existence and Analogy*, 88. This same insight, by the way, is echoed in Przywara: "*Analogia entis* bespeaks not the construction of a concept of God by the creature, but simply the understanding of the creature by means of a consideration of God" (Przywara, *Polarity*, 86).

an insight into creation *ex nihilo* from their own analysis of being. On the contrary, the results of research into the history of philosophy force us to acknowledge that metaphysical thinking was fundamentally altered and restructured when Christian theologians in their encounter with the Greek metaphysical tradition first began to reflect on the meaning of the word "being" prompted by Exodus' "I am who am." Unless this historical point is admitted, the subsequent debate between Przywara and Balthasar against Barth on the one hand and the neo-Scholastics on the other will make no sense.

But to answer the question we must turn first, not to the history of Christian philosophy (which developed only slowly), but to the Bible itself and to its consistently held polemic against paganism. For inside this polemic there lurks the decisive difference between Greek and Christian metaphysics and therefore between the two versions of analogy of being in the two systems.

The biblical polemic against idolatry is a motif in the Scriptures that can be easily misunderstood, with its rhetoric of a "jealous God," and its seeming contempt for Israel's neighboring religions, a polemic which ever since has seemed to give to monotheistic religions a rather fanatical and inhuman air. But this rhetoric grew out of Israel's experience of her God, that is, out of her experience of the transcendence of God over against his creation in comparison to the *emergence* of the pagan gods out of the pre-existing universe. Biblical polemic against paganism makes no sense until we first understand the deep structural incompatibilities between the Greek and biblical understanding of being.[21]

The best way of understanding this contrast is to consider the issue of theogony, that is, the "genealogy of the gods." Throughout the entire world of non-biblical religion one will encounter stories of the birth of the gods, how they came to be out of a *pre-existing universe,* one that is simply understood to have always been (as in Aristotle's eternally existing universe). These stories betray innumerable surface variants: cosmic eggs, confluence of world rivers, the tree at the center of the world, etc., all of which served as the proto-natural womb out of which the gods of mythology are born. But as the great Israeli historian of the Old Testament, Yehezkel Kaufmann, points out,

> all of these embodiments involve one idea which is the distin-
> guishing mark of pagan thought: the idea that there exists a

---

[21] In attributing an understanding of "being" to the Bible, I am of course speaking implicitly. In fact the rest of this chapter is will seek to establish the truth of Claude Tresmontant's statement that "if we analyze the material which is offered us by the history of religion at the present day, we find that all religions possess a metaphysical content in themselves. And we see, too, that the philosophies strictly so called are much more dependent than has hitherto been realized on metaphysical beliefs implicitly contained in the religions out of

realm of being prior to the gods and above them, upon which the gods depend, and whose decrees they must obey. Deity belongs to, and is derived from, a primordial realm. This realm is conceived of variously—as darkness, water, spirit, earth, sky, and so forth—but always as the womb in which the seeds of all being are contained. This is to say that in the pagan view, the gods are not the source of all that is, nor do they transcend the universe."[22]

The structure of the universe is entirely otherwise in the view of Israelite religion. This is not to say that pagan religions are "mythical" while the religion of Israel is by contrast a "demythologized" Semitic variant, for mythological expression is an important feature of biblical narrative. But what these narratives lack is a *theogony:* "Israel's God has no pedigree, fathers no generations; he neither inherits nor bequeaths his authority. He does not die and is not resurrected. He has no sexual qualities or desires and shows no need of or dependence upon powers outside himself."[23] Two passages in the Old Testament crystallizing this world view

---

which these philosophies have in fact emerged" (Claude Tresmontant, *The Origins of Christian Philosophy,* tr. Mark Pontifex [New York: Hawthorn Books, 1963], 9–10).

[22] Yehezkel Kaufmann, *The Religion of Israel: From its Beginnings to the Babylonian Exile,* tr. and abridged by Moshe Greenberg (Chicago: University of Chicago Press, 1960), 21–22. And Tresmontant once again rightly insists that all etiological myths contain an implicit metaphysic, one which we will show in a moment is quite other than the biblical view: "Thus, when the cosmogonic Egyptian and Assyro-Babylonian mythologies (adapted by Hesiod) suppose as the principle of all things a watery chaos from which come the gods, the world and man, this amounts to saying, if put explicitly, that in these religions the chaos is the absolute, and the gods are not. There is a coming into being of the divine element as there is of the world. The divine element is not, strictly speaking, the absolute. These religions also teach that man was made from the spittle, the blood or the seed of a god, and this too involves metaphysical teaching. It means, in abstract terms, that according to these religions man was made from the god's substance, that he is consubstantial with the god" (Tresmontant, *The Origins of Christian Philosophy,* 9–10).

[23] Kaufmann, 60–61. It should be noted that in drawing on Kaufmann we are trying to stress the ultimate influence of biblical monotheism on the debate about the nature of being in later Christian metaphysics, for it is this debate that will furnish the key, I argue, to Balthasar's thought. Thus it is unnecessary here to take any position about when and how Israelite religion developed into full-fledged monotheism, although I agree with Baruch Halpern that arguments for the *lateness* of explicit monotheism argue in a circle: "To argue P is late because it assumes centralization, as Wellhausen did, is identical to arguing the United States of America's Bill of Rights must be late because it assumes the manumission of the slaves. It can be done, but the argument bases itself heavily on a conjecture as to what lay between the lines of a document whose overt intentions still defy our psychologizing" (Baruch Halpern, "'Brisker Pipes Than Poetry': The Development of Israeli Monotheism," *Judaic Perspectives on Ancient Israel,* ed. Jacob Neusner, Baruch A. Levine, and Ernest S. Fredrichs [Philadelphia: Fortress Press, 1987], 77–115; here 108, note 17). Later philosophical reflection by Christian theologians will introduce a new element of self-consciousness into the plot, but the basic world view of monotheism was there, *and uniquely so,* from the beginning,

were virtually all-determining for later Christian speculation: Isaiah 45 and Exodus 3:

> I am the Lord, there is no other. I form the light and create darkness, I bring weal and create woe; I, the Lord, do all these things (Is 45:6–7).

> Moses said to God, "Suppose I go to the Israelites and say to them, 'The God of your fathers has sent me to you,' and they ask me, 'What is his name?' Then what should I tell them?" God said to Moses, "I am who am. This is what you are to say to the Israelites: 'I AM has sent me to you'" (Ex 3:13–14).

Because of the accidents of history, the impact of this perspective on a doctrine of the analogy of being was late in coming and only began to form an explicit part of Christian reflection after the rediscovery and translation of Aristotle's texts in the 11th and 12th century (Aristotle's logic of analogy is much more explicitly treated than Plato's, who tended to sketch his analogies with a merely implicit logic). At this point, as Aristotle was for the first time becoming the intense object of Christian reflection, the juncture of the Bible's definition of God's name as "I AM" and the Aristotelian view of being as an act or an energy created a revolution not just in Christian metaphysics, but throughout the whole history of western philosophy from that moment on, primarily through Thomas Aquinas. But Thomas did not simply fuse or overlap these two points of view; he necessarily had to *restructure* the Aristotelian doctrine of the eternity of the world. Because of this assumption of Aristotle's that the world was eternal (drawn of course from the presuppositions of the pagan world view), his stress was on the *substance* of being; but Thomas, building on the revealed doctrine of creation, put the stress on the pure *act* of being. That is, because of the influence of biblical revelation, it finally dawned on the human mind that the act whereby a substance *is* must belong to another order than does the act whereby a substance is a substance. A lion is a *lion* because its essence or form dictates it to be such; but a lion *is* because of an act of *being* that is separate and not to be identified with the idea of its lionhood. As Gilson says,

---

as Halpern rightly insists: "From the time she entered history, Israel seems to have been monolatrous and henotheistic, that is, unselfconsciously monotheistic" (101). What remains crucial is how the biblical world view eventually broke the spine of the Greek world view, which in retrospect we see was *the* underpinning for all Greek philosophers of whatever school: a belief in the eternity of the world *out of which* the gods sprang: "The Greek situation was less conducive to the application of a monotheistic program, and the result was the development of a sort of meta-theological discourse the offspring of which would later style itself science" (104).

the form, then, is the very act whereby a substance is what it is, and, if a being is primarily or, as Aristotle himself says, almost exclusively *what* it is, each being is primarily and almost exclusively its form. This, which is true of the doctrine of Aristotle, will remain equally true of the doctrine of his disciples, otherwise they would not be his disciples. The distinctive character of a truly Aristotelian metaphysics of being lies in the fact that it knows of no act superior to the form, not even existence. . . . [But] if anyone posits, above the form, an act of that form, he may well use the technical terminology of Aristotle, but on this point at least he is not an Aristotelian.[24]

And Thomas, in this sense, was not an Aristotelian. For to him we owe what has hereafter been known as "the real distinction between essence and being." What this means is that the act of existing that inheres in each individual is distinct from what that individual is. Each actually existing individual is, *qua* existing, a thing distinct from its own essence. Not only does it not have to be, it owes its existence to an act of being, an *esse*, that is itself not derived. This distinction is absolutely crucial, for from it comes the development of the analogy of being which in turn gives us access to the whole structure of Balthasar's thought. What the so-called real distinction implies is that "to be" is the supreme act of all that is. The real distinction tells us that the form of a lion makes it to be *a lion* but it does not make it *to be:* for that is owed to the act of *esse* itself, and *nothing in the essence of a thing can make an inherent claim on being.* The being of all essences is a received being, bestowed upon the forms by virtue of no claim that inheres in the essence of the thing.

But God's essence *is* to be. Here there is no case of a "definition" that "happens" to be instantiated in being. In God we cannot think of a distinction between his essence and existence. "Tell them I AM sent you." But what does this "I AM" mean? Precisely that *it is beyond conceptualization,* for only essences can be conceived, *and being is not an essence!* All of this might seem unnecessarily subtle, but on it hinges the whole justification for the analogy of being inside Christian thought. Because of its importance, we shall let Gilson set out the subtleties of the doctrine and from that foundation establish the inevitability of the notion of analogy:

What is here at stake is not mere formal correctness in logical reasoning; it is an option between two radically different metaphysics of being. In fact, what is at stake is the metaphysical realization of the autonomous character of the order of exis-

---

[24] Gilson, *Being and Some Philosophers* (Toronto: Pontifical Institute of Medieval Studies, 1952), 47.

tence, and this is a realization which is impossible to anyone who approaches being only by way of conceptual representation. As a concept, "to be" is indeed a pseudo-concept, but "to be" might well escape representation in virtue of its very transcendence. When we say that God is only *to be* (*Deus est esse tantum*), we are not falling into the error of those who said that God was that universal being (that is, "being" taken as a mere universal) owing to which each and every thing should be said to be as through its form. Quite the reverse: the only instance in which "to be" is absolutely pure of any addition or determination is also the only instance in which being is absolutely distinct from all the rest. God does not owe His *esse* to His own individuality; rather, supreme and unique individuality necessarily belong to Him, and He *is* He, precisely because He alone is "to be" in its absolute purity: "*Unde per ipsam suam puritatem est esse distinctum ab omni esse.*"[25]

If the reader can follow this argument and see what Thomas has done here, the inevitability of a doctrine of analogy will directly follow. For creatures are not only a mixture ("*per ipsam suam impuritatem,*" we might say) of *esse* and *essentia,* but are that mixture not in the sense of ingredients being differently mixed, but in a way that makes their very being analogous. What this means is, first of all, that they are contingent with respect to their cause, that is: they might not exist. But even further, *in* and *by* existing, creatures are analogous to God. Erich Przywara, who stamped Balthasar's thinking so deeply on this issue, puts it this way:

> In this form the creaturely realm is the "analogy" of God. It is similar to God through its commonality of unity between its "being-what-it-is" [*Sosein:* that is, its essence] and its "being-there-at-all" [*Dasein:* that is, its existence]. But even in this similarity, it is essentially dissimilar to God because God's form of unity of essence and existence is an "essential unity" while that of the creature is a "unity in tension." Now since the relation of essence and existence is the essence of "being," so God and creature are therefore similar-dissimilar in "being"—that is, they

---

[25] Gilson, *Being and Some Philosophers,* 177. The quote from Thomas occurs in *De esse et essentia,* Chapter VI, section 4 ("Wherefore, in its purity [God's] 'to be' is distinct from all other [acts of] 'to be'").

are "analogous" to one another: and this is what we mean by *analogia entis,* analogy of being.[26]

II

Przywara's whole life was deeply affected by this notion of analogy. At the heart of all religious thought, he claimed, one could detect an implicit metaphysics of the God-world relation, and one which presented insoluble problems unless illuminated and corrected by a doctrine of analogy. Perhaps the best access to the world of Przywara's thought is with the word "polarity."[27] This word expresses the tension that must always exist between God's transcendence (God above us) and God's immanence (God in us). Only by maintaining this tension can we avoid the collapse either of the being of the world into God (theopanism) or of God into the world (pantheism). In other words, neither extreme—God in us or God above us—can be maintained without the other, and this at all times:

> *The* primordial metaphysical fact is the tension of the analogy
> of being or, expressed differently, the tension between "God in
> us" and "God over us," or once more, the tension between the
> self-reality and self-spontaneity of the creature and the universal
> and total reality and spontaneity of God, between the universe
> of creatures as the visibility of God and the invisibility of the
> selfsame God over the whole universe of his creation.[28]

This position enabled Przywara to see how much the history of philosophy could be interpreted as the pathos of this tension. For example, both Plato and Aristotle thought of the first principle of being as pure spirit—either as the supreme Idea of the Good (Plato) or as the Self-Thinker

---

[26] Erich Przywara, *Religionsphilosophie katholischer Theologie* (1926), reprinted in *Religionsphilosophische Schriften* (Einsiedeln: Johannes Verlag, 1962), 403: "In dieser Form ist das Geschöpfliche die 'Analogie' Gottes. Es ist Gott ähnlich durch das Gemeinsame einer Einheit von Sosein und Dasein, aber es ist in eben dieser Ähnlichkeit Gott wesenhaft unähnlich, weil Gottes Einheitsform von Sosein and Dasein 'Wesensidentität' ist, des Geschöpfes Einheitsform aber 'Spannungseinheit.' Da nun das Verhältnis von Sosein und Dasein das Wesen von 'Sein' ist, so sind Gott und Geschöpf also im 'Sein' ähnlich-unähnlich, d. h. 'analog' zueinander: *analogia entis,* Analogie des Seins."

[27] This was indeed the word used to translated the title of his *Religionsphilosophie Katholischer Theologie.* See *Polarity,* tr. A. C. Bouquet (Oxford University Press, 1935).

[28] Przywara, *Weg zu Gott* (1926), reprinted in *Religionsphilosophische Schriften,* 92–93: "Die metaphysische Urtatsache ist die Spannung der *analogia entis,* oder anders ausgedrückt, die Spannung zwischen 'Gott in uns' und 'Gott über uns,' noch anders gesagt, die Spannung zwischen Eigenwirklichkeit und Eigenwirksamkeit des Geschöpfes und Allwirklichkeit und Allwirksamkeit Gottes, zwischen dem All der Geschöpfe als der Sichtbarkeit Gottes und der Unsichtbarkeit desselben Gottes über allem All der Schöpfung."

(Aristotle). And yet for Przywara this inkling of transcendence is not decisive because of the legacy of Greek mythical (that is, theogonic) thought, whereby the gods emerge out of and are born into a pre-existing universe. Thus as James Collins says, in describing Przywara's subtle position:

> [In the Greek view according to Przywara] God is scarcely envisioned apart from His exemplar or dynamic relation to the world. Furthermore, the world of sense experience contains an ultimate surd that removes it from direct and effective divine knowledge and providence in Aristotle. Matter is a *counter-power* [to the divine], while natural events are submitted to the inexorable law of *moira,* of fate. Hence Greek religion experienced alternative excesses of puritanical formality and dionysiac carnality, especially in its later phases. The natural rhythm of religious and ethical life was vitiated by a basic inconclusiveness concerning the extent of divine immanence and transcendence.[29]

The same could be said of the career of Western metaphysics since Descartes, and Przywara insisted on this point with considerable vigor, for what he did was to take the formulas of Augustine and the precision of Aquinas and then reinterpret all of modern philosophy in the light of this doctrine—perhaps the single most important part of his thought that most influenced Balthasar, as we shall see in Chapter 3. But if we were to characterize the most crucial feature of his doctrine, independently from his historical analyses, we would have to say that what analogy really means is that the *self-manifestation of God in his creation is never*

---

[29] James Collins, "Przywara's 'Analogia Entis,'" *Thought* 65 (1990): 265–277; here, 271 (this article is a reprint from the March 1942 issue of the same journal). Mascall seconds this view while extending its reach beyond Greek religiosity to its notorious failure to nurture the empirical sciences: "In the view of the world as an artefact any element that is contingent must be ascribed either to bad workmanship on the part of the Artificer or to recalcitrance in the material upon which he works. Now the divine Demiurge cannot be accused of bad workmanship; hence the character of contingency in natural objects must be ascribed to the material element in them. But matter is the object of sensation, as form is the object of intellection. Hence the contingent character of the natural world, which arises from its materiality, cannot be understood; it can only be sensed. It cannot be the object of knowledge, and so the absence of an empirical element in Greek natural science is accounted for. . . . [But] in a world that is *created* and not merely *manufactured,* contingency is not an imperfection in the embodiment of form; it is precisely that which constitutes the creature as a creature. And since the contingent is, as we have seen, the object of the senses, it follows that sensible experience is indispensable to the science of nature, and, moreover, indispensable not merely in the sense that it is necessary stage on the way to real knowledge, but in the more radical sense that the very element in the creature which constitutes it as a creature, namely its contingency, cannot be an object of the intellect but only of the senses" (Mascall, *Existence and Analogy,* 7).

an exhaustive one: although there is some similarity between the world and God, *in* this very likeness there is even greater dissimilarity. But this can only be recognized in an inner dynamic that recognizes, in faith, the self-manifestation of God within creation and then *in* that act of faith recognizes that it must "deny itself" and go beyond what it had just then seized.

If one had to select out one word that captures Przywara's unique contribution to the discussion of analogy it would, in my opinion, be the word "dynamic." However legitimate is the complaint that Greek categories are too static to fit the inner dynamism of the Bible, with Przywara at least, this does not hold true. For analogy is a moment in the life of faith, and what that faith sees in analogy is the demand to go beyond itself, and it does so precisely in its own legitimate act of recognizing the world as God's creation. "Constant change" (*stetige Wandlung*) is a phrase that repeatedly occurs in Przywara's writings, and not by accident.[30]

The crucial point to recall in this regard is that the moment of analogical thinking begins inside the act of faith: "For the principle of *analogia entis,* it is an unassailable axiom that all striving towards and all experience of God must *assume rather than prove* the relationship to God. . . . Scientific doctrine about God is always something which *ensues* in the practical life of religion."[31] And this is a faith that demands a constant act of self-denial, both of the heart as well as of the mind. This lends to Przywara's writings an intense emotionality that we will also soon encounter in Balthasar too. There is, in other words, an emotional correlate to the doctrine of analogy, because this doctrine arises out of the tensions of the act of faith itself. Now the emotional correlate to God's transcendence is "the fear of the Lord," while love and intimacy are proper to God's interior relation to the world. Yet neither one can abolish the other; the former alone would result in mere servility, the latter in cloying sentimentality.[32]

---

[30] Collins rightly points to Newman's manifesto "My unchangeableness here below is perseverance in changing" as Przywara's own motto as well ("Przywara," 268). This is a dynamism that not only goes all the way back to Paul but is itself a constant mark of authentic theology: "That our knowledge of God is, compared to its object, no knowledge at all, in the sense that we cannot comprehend him, does not mean that creation provides no indirect way to meaningful language about its cause. In Cusa's phrase, our ignorance of God is a learned one, and Dionysius would hardly deny that we are better off after the efforts of affirmative and negative theology than we were before. It is a matter of some importance to note that not even Scripture, which is God's revelation to man, transcends the human mode of naming, which is to apply to God names of perfections best known to us in creatures" (Ralph M. McInerny, *A History of Western Philosophy: Philosophy from St. Augustine to Ockham* [Notre Dame, IN: University of Notre Dame Press, 1970], 51).

[31] Przywara, *Polarity,* 36, 45.

[32] The distinguished Anglican theologian John Macquarrie has noticed this same inflated sentimentalism and praises Balthasar for his reluctance to appeal to that over-invoked word

Przywara particularly reacted against Max Scheler's overemphasis on love as the key to the religious life, wondering how much such wishful thinking masked an unacknowledged fear, and so he recommended Augustine's formulation of "a fearing love and a loving fear."

This direct alignment between Przywara's religious feelings and his metaphysical views not only generated an emotional life of great intensity, this emotionally keyed-up life redoubled his commitment to a life of hard labor in the cause of Christ. Because of the inner dynamism that is always at work in the doctrine of analogy—forcing us never to be content with concepts already gained, with work already achieved—, the Christian will always feel drawn to and inspired by the example of St. Paul, whose labors in the cause of Christ were unremitting (1 Cor 9:24–27). And this same life of unremitting labor particularly characterized Przywara's life and goes far to explain Balthasar's own unusual capacity for work: "There is a basic law in the life of grace," said Przywara, "deflating for the lazy, uplifting for the tireless: however much grace we have received, that is how much work we must yet accomplish."[33]

But beyond this personal implication of the doctrine, the discovery of the inner riches in the doctrine also gave Przywara the perspective to see how and where modern philosophy slipped from its rails, and this constitutes, as we have said, perhaps the most signal contribution Przywara made to the shape of Balthasar's thought: *for he taught Balthasar to interpret the pathos of modern philosophy according to how it reacted to the doctrine of analogy.* He made him see, in other words, the dilemmas that human thought runs into when it abandons the tensions represented in analogy. According to Przywara, the history of modern thought may be interpreted as the inability to hold together the polarity between God's transcendence and immanence; that is, as running aground either in the pathos of stressing God's omnipotence, thereby robbing the world of its own reality by overwhelming it with God's transcendence, as in Luther, or by the world absorbing God into itself through a pantheistic identification with him, as in Spinoza.

"love" rather than to a direct encounter with the living God: "[Balthasar's book] is truly radical because the author is willing to acknowledge not only the questionableness of the idea of God in our time, but the questionableness of some of the substitutes that get advocated in place of God. We are told perhaps that in place of God we should give our allegiance to Jesus or even to love. But for [people] of today, these alternatives are hardly likely to be any more meaningful, for not only the word 'God' but Christian language as a whole has deteriorated. Balthasar asks: 'Must we really keep on using this word "love," which has gradually become unbearable, and continue to tear it to shreds?'" (John Macquarrie, "Introduction" to: Hans Urs von Balthasar, *The God Question and Modern Man*, tr. Hilda Graef [New York: Seabury Press, 1967], xi).

[33] "Es gibt ein Grundgesetz im Gnadenleben, niederschmetternd für den Trägen, emporhebend für den Unermüdlichen: soviel Gnade wir empfangen, soviel Arbeit müssen wir leisten"

But more than displaying the pathos of individual thinkers who were unable to hold the two poles together, Przywara was also able to see how the whole of philosophy was the story of this unfulfilled passion for wholeness. He could see how *all* philosophy was continually running aground, both because of the almost inevitable failure of every individual person to harness the tensions in the human soul and because those tensions are but the psychological reflection of the inner structure of the universe's relation to God.[34]

Przywara lived out this dynamism to a high degree, recognizing with Thomas that analogy is not a mere doctrine, a "that," but a whole way of life, a "how," that demands the fullest commitment of the soul to transcend itself: "Considered as objective fact [*Dass*], the How of *analogia entis* is already revealed as a principle. Inasmuch as the *analogia entis* is founded on the contradiction [between God and creature], it shows itself to be the most radical principle. But inasmuch as it shares in this principle's method of a 'negative-reductive formality' and 'movement in *actu primo*', it displays itself as the most open principle."[35]

Radically intense yet the most open of all: this marks Przywara's most signal contribution to the debate in the 20th century on analogy of being. More than any other thinker of this century, he was able to take the insights of analogy and harness them into a critique of modern philosophy that was both radically severe and yet fundamentally open: "Creation, in spite of its innermost dependence upon God is endowed with its own separate essence and separate existence. God is wholly real, and yet the creation is in its own way real also. God is Universal Value, and yet creation has value of its own."[36]

There are extraordinary benefits to be gained from such a perspective, benefits which reach down even to the most practical attitudes of the believer. Take, for example, the issue of petitionary prayer. How can God be influenced by prayer or moved by what we ask? According to Przywara, a right understanding of the relationship between God and world clarifies

---

(Przywara, "Eucharistie und Arbeit" [1917], reprinted in Przywara, *Frühe religiöse Schriften* [Einsiedeln: Johannes Verlag, 1962], 3).

[34] "As against all flight from the comprehensible into the incomprehensible, the Catholic type of evidential reasoning proceeds from the inward meaning of the comprehensible itself, to direct the adoring gaze at the incomprehensible. Here is the reason why the Catholic basis of religion attracts to itself a double reproach: the reproach of rationalism and yet also the reproach of the submission of science to irrational piety. . . . [But] the *analogia entis* is *above* both rationalism and irrationalism" ("Polarity," 47).

[35] Przywara, *Analogia Entis*, 205: "In dieser Weise des Daß offenbart sich aber bereits das Wie der *analogia entis als Prinzip*. Indem die *analogia entis* im Widerspruchsatz sich begründet, zeigt sie sich als das radikalste Prinzip. Indem sie aber eben hierin seine Weise einer 'negativ-reduktiven Formalität' und 'Bewegung in *actu primo*' teilt, enthüllt sie sich als das offenste Prinzip..

[36] Przywara, *Polarity*, 54.

this always painful pastoral issue: "It is primarily in this complete 'surrender' as Newman says, in the adoring unrestrained abandonment to the greatness of God who is beyond all need of his creatures, that the saving meaning of the relationship to God is fulfilled. God is not measured according to his power for the saving of souls, but the saving of souls is confidently enfolded in the mystery of his inscrutable ways."[37]

Thus "to pray in confidence" as commanded in the Gospels (Lk 11:1–13) is an aspect of our complete trust in God who creates and redeems, but "God is not measured according to his power *for* the saving of souls." On the contrary, our confidence is salvation is enfolded in the mystery of God's transcendence:

> This phenomenon expresses itself most clearly in the tension between naïve Catholic petitionary prayer and the somewhat astringent piety of surrender that we find in Francis de Sales and Ignatius Loyola. The God of the former is the Mild Patriarch, whom one petitions for fine weather and food and drink as His free gifts; the God of the latter is the Divine Majesty whose will is inscrutable and who fulfills His purpose in every event as by Divine Decree. In congruity with the first aspect, the laws of the universe appear as the non-legalistic governance of free love; in congruity with the second, Deity appears almost like the personification of the fateful power of the law. This rhythm [hovers] between trustful love and trembling reverence, which in accordance with the *analogia entis* expands itself within the soul; . . . [and] because of that we see here more clearly than ever the ultimate meaning of that rhythm: surrender to a God is who open.[38]

---

[37] Przywara, *Polarity*, 46. One might well recall in this context Aquinas' remark that "it does not belong to God to bewail the misery of others, but it does most properly belong to him to dispel that misery" (*ST*, I, 21, 3c). And Mascall also notices this same connection between analogy, God's transcendence, his compassion and his power to save: "When we reflect upon the fragility and tenuosity of the beings that compose this finite world of ours and upon the ephemerality of all in it that we hold most dear, we shall see that the God who can meet our deepest needs will not be one who is himself entangled in its contingencies—not merely 'the great companion, the fellow sufferer who understands"—but one who, while his loving care extends even to the least of his creatures and while he knows them in their weakness and need better than they know themselves, is himself unchanged and unchangeable, the strength and stay upholding all creation who ever doth himself unmoved abide, a God in whom compassion and impassibility are reconciled in the union of omnipotence and love: 'I the Lord change not; therefore ye, O son of Jacob, are not consumed' (Mal 3:6)" (142–143)..

[38] Przywara, *Polarity*, 71.

Or as Przywara says in perhaps his most lapidary summation of the whole meaning of analogy: "In the whole expanse of Catholic teaching from creation to super-nature and on to the incarnation, the one foundational axiom prevails: *creation as directed upon God but not God as a supplement to creation.*"[39]

III

Unless one chooses to include Balthasar's work as a whole (always possible when taking the broad view of Przywara's influence on his thought), there are two places in Balthasar's large *oeuvre* where one can ascertain what specifically he drew from Przywara and where he distanced himself from his first great mentor in the Society of Jesus: in his introductory essay to a complete bibliography of Przywara's works edited by Leo Zimmy[40] and in his book on Karl Barth. The former is, as suiting its occasion, more appreciative in style and approach, while the latter shows, as clearly as one is likely to find, where Balthasar expressed his reservations toward the positions of his teacher. This is because Barth's own polemics against analogy of being were primarily directed against Przywara and indeed were occasioned by their conversations in Germany while Barth was still professor there in the early 30's.

Thus in his book on Barth, Balthasar is at pains to insist, before moving on to address Barth's objections directly, that Przywara's stance (on any open issue, not just analogy) need not be taken as determining *the* Catholic position on these questions. This then affords him the opportunity of distinguishing his own position from that of Przywara before he comes to Barth himself. But because his formulation of his differences with Przywara are so intertwined with his interpretation of Barth, we must postpone a full-scale treatment of Balthasar's position on analogy until the next chapter, and content ourselves here with Balthasar's acknowledgment of his debt to his mentor.

First of all, we can see perhaps the greatest affinity between Balthasar and Przywara in their common antipathy to system and in their shared insistence on harnessing theology to what Balthasar calls "the yoke of relativity" *so that* the true universality of the mystery of Christ might shine through. This highly lyrical testimony could also read as a description of Balthasar himself, so strong is Przywara's influence in this regard:

For everyone who has been placed before the living God and is called to speak of Him, Przywara is more than just a "thinker."

---

[39] Przywara, *Polarity*, 46.
[40] Leo Zimmy, *Erich Przywara: Sein Schriftum, 1912–1962* (Einsiedeln: Johannes Verlag, 1963).

If with the one half of his being he was as sharp and as relentless a thinker as scarcely any other of his time, his only purpose as a thinker was to discharge the Pauline office of "demolishing strongholds with weapons fashioned by God, stripping away every argument and pretension that sets itself up against the knowledge of God, taking captive every thought to make it obedient to Christ" (I Cor 10:4–5). The passion with which he cleared away and broke down every possibility for constructing a system and harnessed it to the yoke of relativity only makes sense when this passion knows that it must obediently serve the mystery that could not be made transparent without this clearing away.[41]

Coupled with this deep aversion to systematization, Balthasar also appreciated the deep pathos that marked Przywara's life, not only personally but also in his intellectual apostolate—perhaps never more so poignantly than in the fate of the term "analogy of being" in twentieth-century theology. For Przywara advocated it precisely because he saw it as a way of breaking through the closed horizon of modern consciousness and its nearly exclusive concern with either the world or man-in-the-world. Yet Karl Barth accused Przywara (and, because of his encounter with this lonely Catholic priest, all of Catholicism as well!) of precisely bringing about what it had been Przywara's intention of avoiding! But the whole thrust of Przywara's thought was to let God be God, making all the more ironic his separation from Barth on the question of terms:

Erich Przywara was placed in a time that devoted all of its powers to its interest in the world and man; he lived in a philosophical and speculative era when "world and man" was the great reality and theme, when God was at most a "horizon" of the world's being, a boundary concept of thought, a cipher of existence. But thinking, whether theoretical or practical, logical or dialectical or intuitive, is always sure of and has a firm grasp of precisely this always-constituted boundary concept, as the condi-

---

[41] "Erich Przywara," in the Zimmy Bibliography (henceforth: Zimmy), 6: "Wie jeder, der vor den lebendigen Gott gestellt wird und von ihm künden soll, ist Przywara mehr als nur ein 'Denker.' Wenn er mit der einem Hälfte seines Wesens ein so scharfer, so unerbittlicher Denker war, wie kein anderer seiner Zeit, so hat er als Denker doch nur das paulinische Amt versehen, 'mit für Gott mächtigen Waffen Festungen umzulegen, Sophismen zu entlarven und jede hochfahrende Burg, die sich wider die Erkenntnis Gottes aufreckt, zu schleifen, jeden Gedanken in den Dienstgehorsam Christi gefangenzunehmen' (2 Kor 10, 4–5). Die Leidenschaft, mit der ab-und aufgeräumt, jegliche Systemmöglichkeit gebrochen und in das Joch der Relativität gebeugt wird, hat ihren Sinn nur daher, daß sie sich selber als Dienstgehorsam an dem Mysterium versteht, das ohne diese Auskehr nicht ansichtig werden konnte."

tion of its own possibility and reality. Przywara's center is accordingly not the immanence of world and man but rather the ungraspable point of encounter with the living God. . . . Przywara has christened this point the "analogy of being"—admittedly a term that does not have much life to it but which still must be the term of choice. The word is now being bandied about in the general vocabulary of the educated without its true pathos ever being understood or truly adapted to our age. How can a pathos be systematized? In the scholastic manner of scholars who manage to render everything harmless, the doctrine of analogy of being takes on a form hardly distinguishable from its opposite, so that Karl Barth could brand it "*the* invention of the anti-Christ," whereas the truth of it is that it was precisely what was most closely related to Barth's own pathos: both stand against Kantianism and Hegelianism, against the methods of immanence of either Schleiermacher or Modernism, against every form, whether pious or impious, of trying to get control over the living God. Przywara's radicalism clearly shows that this inter-confessional struggle was a misunderstanding—presupposing that his analysis of the original Protestant dialectic as theopanistic is recognized as being right.[42]

The pathos of Przywara's life, however, goes deeper than such terminological misunderstandings, for he also suffered the pain of misfired communication, first because of his rather murky and Teutonic style (no doubt evident in some of the cited quotations from him in this chapter), and later because of mental illness. But whatever inherited personality traits were involved (either in causing his mental breakdown or in throwing up severe communication barriers between him and his readers), Balthasar could also see the underlying tensions at work in Przywara's almost impossible intellectual challenge:

---

[42] Zimmy, 5–6: "Erich Przywara wurde in eine Zeit gestellt, die sich mit allen geistigen Kräften für die Welt und für den Menschen interessierte, in eine philosophische-spekulierende Zeit, für welche Welt und Mensch die Wirklichkeit und das Thema war, Gott aber höchstens ein 'Horizont' des Weltseins, ein Grenzbegriff des Denkens, eine Chiffre der Existenz; gerade dieses wie immer beschaffenen Grenzbegriffs aber ist das Denken, theoretisch oder praktisch, logisch oder dialektisch oder intuitiv, als der Bedingung seiner eigenen Möglichkeit und Wirklichkeit versichert und habhaft. Przywaras Mitte ist demgegenüber nicht die Immanenz von Welt und Mensch, sondern der unfaßbare Punkt der Begegnung mit dem lebendigen Gott. . . . Przywara hat diesen Punkt, an dem sich nicht leben läßt und der doch gewählt werden muß, Analogia Entis getauft; das Wort ist ins allgemeine Vokabular übergegangen, ohne daß sein wahres Pathos verstanden und mitübernommen worden wäre. Wie ließe sich ein Pathos systematisieren? In dieser schulhaft verharmlosten, nicht mehr unterscheidbaren Gestalt konnte die Analogia Entis von Karl Barth als '*die* Erfindung des Antichrist' gebrandmarkt werden, während sie in der damaligen Gegenwart doch wohl das

It is the inner mystery of every soul to be a new and unique tapestry of two basic tendencies—power and love, surmounting and surrender, domination and humility. In the case of the theoretical thinker this tension has the special form of a positioning between the poles of the most universal theoretical domination of the knowable in a systematic totality and a surrender to the immense variety of the empirically knowable world (rationalism vs. empiricism). All thinkers incline to the one pole (rationalist and systematic) or to the other (irrational and unsystematic). In rare cases the passion for thinking might be intensely drawn by both poles. And Przywara belongs to this type. His dynamic thinking arises in the extreme tension between two contraries of the thinking process.

As a matter of content this means the interpenetration of an unconditioned will to make everything transparent to its core, almost with a rationalistic abhorrence of all philosophies of experience that dispense with structure and substance. This is a type of thinking that "penetrates everything, until soul and spirit, bone and marrow are cut apart from each other." But on the other hand, this tension demands the interpenetration of a no less radical knowledge of the *inconclusiveness* of every movement of thought, an anti-rationalism at its most extreme, an absolute mistrust of every principle, whether located in a system, in thinking, or in being itself, a being from which supposedly anything could be deduced or systematically constructed.[43]

---

war, was seinem eigenen Pathos am verwandtesten war: beide standen gegen Kantianismus und Hegelianismus, gegen schleiermachersche oder modernistische Immanenzmethode, gegen jede Form, unter welcher der Mensch, unfromm oder fromm, sich des lebendigen Gottes bemächtigt. Der Radikalismus Przywaras läßt diesen interkonfessionellen Kampf als ein Mißverständnis erscheinen, vorausgesetzt, daß seine Analyse des ursprünglich Protestantischen (als theopanistische Dialektik) für richtig anerkannt wird." How Barth might still remain exposed to the charge of theopanism will the subject of the next chapter.

[43] Zimmy, 7–8: "Wenn es das innerste Geheimnis jeder Seele ist: eine neue einmalige Verflechtung von zwei Grundtendenzen zu sein: Macht und Liebe, Bewältigung und Hingabe, Beherrschung und Bescheidung, dann hat diese Spannung für den theoretischen Menschen die besondere Form eines Stehens zwischen den Polen allgemeinster theoretischer Beherrschung des Wißbaren in systematischer Totalität, und Hingabe an die unschießbare Vielfalt der empirisch-wißbaren Welt. Alle Denker neigen dem einen, rationalistisch-systematischen, oder dem andern, irrationalistisch-unsystamatischen Pol zu. In seltenen Fällen mag die Denkleidenschaft gleich intensiv von beiden angezogen werden. Diesem Denkertyp gehört Przywara an. Sein dynamisches Denken entsteht in der äußersten Spannung zwischen zwei Gegensätzen des Denkprozesses. Inhaltlich besagt das ein Ineinander einerseits eines unbedingten Willens zur Durchleuchtung bis ins Mark, mit einer fast rationalistischen Abneigung gegen all unsachliche, gerüstlose Erlebnisphilosophie, eines Denkens, das 'durchdringt, bis es Seele und Geist, Gelenk und Mark voneinander scheidet,'—anderseits eines nicht minder radikalen Wissens um die Unschließbarkeit jeder Denkbewegung, eines Antira-

The demands of loneliness on such a life would have to have been considerable, and in Przywara's case they were, but in pausing to appreciate the costs such efforts demanded, we must also not fail to appreciate what Przywara has given us thereby: "The *result* is a philosophy in the Archimedean point: which means simultaneously the most radical formality and the most radical suspension of all systematics, finding the formula to annihilate every formula by pointing out the fault line in the creaturely to its very ultimate."[44] In this Przywara assumes his rightful role with all the others who have worked out a theory of analogy—not to grasp at God but to explain why God cannot *be* grasped! Not to claim God but to explain why God can, and does, claim us! And this is why his work will remain of lasting importance:

> The prophets whom the angels seized up into heaven and brought before the Throne of Glory to experience how much they had "to suffer for His Name" could only remain alone. Alone in the fullness of mission-determined communication, distant in the confusion of close-order battle with friend and foe, with one's own people and with foreigners, forced into the distance for the sake of discerning the spirits as commanded, but only by virtue of first having been touched with the all-consuming fire that would mark them henceforward and which they would never forget. Their Word burns: it does not baptize in water but in spirit and fire. Zeal for God's house consumes them. They themselves are certainly fire. And when—misunderstood and rejected of men, despised, mocked and betrayed by family and neighbors—they give their soul, fatigued unto death, back to God, then it can be that He Who Consumes with Fire will send them his fiery chariot to call them home.[45]

---

tionalismus bis ins Letzte, absoluten Mißtrauens gegen System-wie Denk-und Seinsprinzipien, aus denen irgend etwas deduziert oder systematisch ausgebaut werden soll."

[44] Zimmy, 9–10: "So *resultiert* eine Philosophie im archimedischen Punkt, der zugleich radikalste Formeinheit und radikalste Aufhebung aller Systemeinheit bedeutet, die Formel findet, jede Formel zu vernichten, indem sie den Riß im Kreatürlichen bis ins Letzte hinab aufzeigt und anerkannt."

[45] Zimmy, 5: "Die Propheten, die an den Haaren von Engeln hinwegentrückt und vor den Thron der Herrlichkeit geschleppt wurden, um dort zu erfahren, wieviel sie 'für Seinen Namen leiden' sollten, sie konnten nur Einsame bleiben. Einsame in der Fülle auftragsbedingter Kommunikation, Ferne im Nahkampfgewühl mit Feind und Freund, mit Volk und Nichtvolk, in die Distanz gezwungen um der befohlenen Geistunterscheidung willen, aber kraft der ersten, nie mehr zu vergessenden, nie zu überholenden Berührung mit dem Verzehrenden Feuer. Ihr Wort brennt, es tauft nicht im Wasser, sondern in Geist und Feuer, der Eifer für Gottes Haus verzehrt sie, Flamme sind sie sicherlich. Und wenn sie, unverstanden, unaufgenommen, von den Eigenen und Nächsten geringgeschätzt, verachtet, verhöhnt und verraten, ihre todmüde Seele Gott zurückgeben, dann kann es sein, daß der Verzehrende ihnen sein Feuergespann schickt, sie heimzuholen."

We are not surprised that to learn from this passage that one man's isolation—born of his passion for God's cause—could so deeply appreciate the achievements of another man whose whole adult life as thinker and priest was marked by a much more severe loneliness.

· 2 ·

The Dialogue with Karl Barth

Not only do we know God by Jesus Christ alone, but we
know ourselves only by Jesus Christ. We know life and death
only through Jesus Christ. Apart from him, we do not know
our life, nor our death, nor God, nor ourselves. Thus without
the Scriptures, which has Jesus Christ alone for its object, we
know nothing, and see only darkness and confusion in the
nature of God, and in our own nature.

Pascal
Pensées (B 548)

"Not since Luther and Calvin has Protestantism had a single theologian of the stature and importance as Karl Barth." This is the
judgment of a French Protestant theologian at the University of Paris,[1]
but it is one that will surely be echoed by anyone with even the slightest
acquaintance with contemporary theology. It is true that for the most part
in the last three decades Protestant theologians have abandoned Barth's
method and have largely outgrown his influence, which used to be so
massive. But even today he still towers over his lesser successors, not least
because he remains *the* major Protestant theologian who has both seen
the weaknesses of, and undermined from within, the Kantian and Schleiermacherian foundations of liberal Protestantism and yet has not fallen
victim to its (apparently only) alternative, fundamentalism—while yet remaining entirely faithful to his Protesting forefathers Luther and Calvin.
And that is why, for Balthasar, "we must choose Karl Barth for our partner because in him Protestantism has found *for the first time* its most
completely consistent representative. He embodies a Protestantism that
can only be reached by going back to its roots, its deepest sources: to
Calvin and Luther; in other words, past all subsequent 'developments,'

---

[1] Georges Casalis, *Portrait of Karl Barth,* tr. Robert McAfee Brown (New York: Doubleday, 1963), 3.

deformations and etiolations of liberal Protestantism until we reach that moment where Barth purifies and radicalizes those sources."[2]

This chapter proposes to examine the nature of Barth's influence on Balthasar's thought, their disputes with each other, the results of their dialogue together, so happily facilitated by their common residence in the city of Basel.[3] But "influence" is perhaps not quite the right word in this case, at least if it implies a passive reception of one thought form upon another. For the encounter between Barth and Balthasar was mutual, that is, a true instance of dialogue, marked by a constant effort to let the other be other and to meet him precisely there. Perhaps we can glean some idea of the effort and labor such dialogue took by looking at Balthasar's portrait of dialogue's opposite number: a triumphalism that thinks it already knows the answer and thus has no need to listen across the table, for the partner has already been "answered":

> Such condescending attitudes are to be found not only among the stubborn and rigid revanchists who think that time has suddenly stood still for them because, after all, everything necessary

---

[2] *KB,* 22. Not that Balthasar was very concerned with the ups and downs of Barth's reputation in post-war Christian thought, for he never was one to fuss too much over trends, currents, reputations, etc. In Barth he had clearly found someone who would transcend such ephemera for the rest of time: "We shall not be conversing with Barth because he is the head of a strong current in contemporary Protestantism. Schools of thought are transient phenomena that ebb and flow with the times. And not few are the voices that claim, perhaps rightly and not without a certain satisfaction, that Barth's influence is already waning. But then there are also times when it is no bad sign for a person to be losing influence. . . . But [that] shall not prevent the Catholic from still asking for a dialogue, all the more so when one supposedly cannot hear any answer coming back. One should still try to further the conversation all the more when the *cause* no longer seems to be something personally desired by the other party" (*KB,* 21, 9).

[3] Barth's biographer Eberhard Busch relates several amusing but highly revealing incidents occasioned by their geographical proximity to each other, especially when they met in a Basel tavern called "The Charon": "In Amsterdam Barth had made no bones about his disappointment over the failure of Rome to join in the ecumenical movement. During the next months, however, he was surprised by a new and hopeful possibility of conversation with Catholicism which opened up so to speak at his very door, in Basel itself. In the winter of 1948–49 Hans Urs von Balthasar gave ten much discussed lectures on Barth, resulting later in his book *Karl Barth,* published in 1951, which attracted even more attention. When possible Barth went to the lectures—'to learn more about myself.' Afterwards, there were post-mortems with a very small group including Balthasar at the Charon. . . . On hell, Balthasar remarked (first of course at the Charon): 'The dogma is that hell exists, not that people are in it.' At any rate, on these evenings Barth discovered to his amazement a Catholic theologian who, he said, 'envisioned a kind of reformation of the Catholic Church and of Catholic theology from within. And now I was to be introduced like a new Trojan horse to bring it about (against Thomas and also against Augustine!)'" (Eberhard Busch, *Karl Barth: His Life from Letters and Autobiographical Texts,* tr. John Bowden [Philadelphia: Fortress Press, 1976], 361–2).

has already been thought and said with such exhaustive suffi-
ciency that nothing new need be generated even to the end of
the world. But such smugness is also to be found among many
of the most nimble and agile minds; these are controversialists
who can fight with all the weapons of the opponents, can get
inside the skin of anyone and know how to use any philosophical
system. Through such skill they think that they have thus already
attained superiority. Faced with such a debater, who can so nim-
bly penetrate, distinguish, and classify his opponent before he
has even begun to open his mouth, is it any wonder that the
Protestant representative would lose his sense of humor? We
might well ask ourselves whether such a representative of the
cause of Catholic *universality* truly realizes what division in the
Church means: the yawning chasm over which no dialectical or
analogical method can leap, the bloody wound that cannot be
healed with the plaster of theological formulae. (*KB*, 11)

But this willingness to hear the other and be influenced by him is not
the only reason that makes the conversation between Barth and Balthasar
so fruitful. For neither one elevated "dialogue" to an end in itself, as if
the divisions prompting the dialogue were not as important as the act of
dialogue itself. Both men knew that divisions in the Church are not willed
by Christ, that separation between Christians is a matter of guilt and
personal responsibility, demanding first confession of sin and then an
effort to attain the truth, the only true end of any dialogue. But this
must be a truth that cannot be attained by papering over differences, or
pretending they are not there, or assuming that dialogue itself is so overarching a value that it will of itself resolve the differences.

What made the conversation so fruitful between the two theologians
was that it took place within a faith that they both perceived to be inherently dynamic. We have already seen in Chapter 2 that the doctrine of
analogy of being must subserve the wider truth that faith is always dynamic. Analogy is not just a way of expressing the doctrine that the being
of the universe is a created being, but it is also a way of insisting that our
faith in God is but partial and therefore needs the supplementation that
only dialogue can bring. It is because faith is dynamic that dialogue becomes imperative:

And so Catholics with any sense of flexibility—those, that is,
who appreciate the infinity of revelation, the vibrancy of both
Scripture and tradition, and the development of dogma—should
have no trouble in realizing how partial is their own position
and even how imperfect is the contemporary Church's interpretation of the faith. Such Catholics will keep an alert ear for all

those who are searching for an authentic faith. ... And what could be more Christian than to hear out what one's fellow Christian has to say? This readiness is an integral part and an important sign of a living faith. Just as true love of God is shown in love of neighbor and cannot be divorced from it, so too a willingness in faith to accept God's truth cannot be separated from an openness to the word and truth of one's neighbor. (*KB*, 16)

Because Balthasar's book on Barth is so peerless an example of such mutuality,[4] it is really impossible to isolate those elements that Balthasar might have learned or "borrowed" from Barth, if that should be our definition of influence. Perhaps, then, it would be better to draw on Goethe's term and speak of "elective affinities," a convergence at the depth and along the implicit structures of Christian thought that make their disagreements all the more illuminating for us. And among these many affinities that these two men share none perhaps is of greater importance than the artistic, or more specifically, the musical temperaments they bring to the craft of theology. As one of Barth's interpreters rightly says, "Barth is an artist, not just a dry reasoner. He creates a world, and the reader has to accept it while he is within it; the more he learns to move freely about in this world, the greater satisfaction he will derive."[5]

Another point that made them true brothers in dialogue was their common assessment of liberalism in theology and Church life, especially the dangers to theology represented by a cult of academic objectivity. This is perhaps an even more marked feature of Balthasar's life, who never held an academic post, than it was of Barth, who, though he never got a doctorate (except of course honorary ones), was named a professor of dogmatics at the University of Göttingen by virtue of his epochal commen-

---

[4] Perhaps it would be well at this point to record Barth's own judgment of Balthasar's book on him: "the well-known book which Hans Urs von Balthasar addressed to me ... is incomparably more powerful than most of the books which have clustered about me" (CD IV/1, 768). This same passage contains Barth's response to Balthasar's criticism of his "christological narrowness" to which we will return toward the end of this chapter.

[5] William Nicholls, *The Pelican Guide to Theology*, Vol I: *Systematic and Philosophical Theology* (Harmondsworth: Penguin Books, 1969), 119. One might also think of adding the affinity of sheer prolixity to the list, but if so Nicholls' judgment on the vast length of Barth's work will hold true of Balthasar too: "What I have said so far might suggest that Barth's work might be better for pruning. This may perhaps be true, but it is nothing like so true as one would suppose if one had not read him at length. The extreme extent of the *Church Dogmatics* is not just a consequence of his having so much to say. It is a result of his method. He wishes to be responsible to his sources, Scripture itself, and the writings of past theologians, including the confessions of faith of ancient and more recent times. All these must be honored, in accordance with the commandment 'Honor thy father and thy mother'" (118).

tary on Romans. But Barth too was deeply suspicious of the subtly corrupting influence an academic post could have on the purity of theology. Indeed it was the very sycophancy of his German (state-employed) professors at the onset of World War I that made him question their liberal approach to theology:

> One day in early August 1914 stands out in my personal memory as a black day. 93 German intellectuals impressed public opinion by their proclamation in support of the war policy of Wilhelm II and his counsellors. Among those intellectuals I discovered to my horror almost all of my theological teachers whom I had greatly venerated. In despair over what this indicated about the signs of the times, I suddenly realized that I could not any longer follow either their ethics and dogmatics or their understanding of the Bible and history. For me, at least, 19th-century theology no longer held any future.[6]

This shock forced Barth to reconsider the entire set of presuppositions on which he had heretofore based his theology. What he saw at work in Protestant theology of the 19th century was an attempt to tailor the Gospel to academic norms of respectability so that theology could be seen to take a fitting place in the firmament of the university's faculties. But to do that, theology had first to concede a neutral ground whereby revelation could be judged against wider norms accessible to all academic debaters. But under the shock of August 1914 and the appalling bloodshed of the next four years, Barth felt compelled to reach out to revelation on its own terms, and not always be transposing it into its correlate in human consciousness. And out of that search for new foundations came his epochal commentary on Romans, a book which Karl Adam rightly describes as falling like a bombshell in the playground of the theologians.[7]

And well it might fall like a bomb, for it was written, not in the usual manner as a commentary on an ancient document needing the decoding labors of a philologist, but as an explication of the words of an apostle who had been *sent*, and whose mission was to preach a message of *revelation*.[8] It is not, of course, as if this had not been recognized before, for it

---

[6] "Evangelical Theology in the 19th Century," in *The Humanity of God,* tr. Thomas Wieser (Richmond, VA: John Knox Press, 1960), 14.

[7] Barth's own description of its impact is even more telling: "As I look back upon my course, I seem to myself as one who, ascending the dark staircase of a church tower and trying to steady himself, reached for the banister, but got hold of the bell rope instead. To his horror, he had then to listen to what the great bell had resounded over him, and not over him alone" (*Die christliche Dogmatik im Entwurf* [Munich: Kaiser Verlag, 1927], ix).

[8] "A truly historical and critical reading of the Bible will take seriously Scripture's self-understanding as a testimony to revelatory events. Barth always had a taste for irony: it

had; but the revelatory message itself tended to get bracketed by the academic framework, and this is the real reason that this teeming, turbulent work from a pastor in a Swiss village hit with such impact on the "playground of the theologians":

> Barth's doctrine of revelation . . . challenged liberal theology at a point very dear to it, the point at which it tried to ground theology in an objective academic method. If liberalism had been right, analysis of the problem of religion would have provided a basis for talking about God objectively and publicly, in spite of the collapse of the philosophical demonstration of his existence. Thus theology could remain in the community of learning in the university. But if Barth were right, theology could only arise from specifically Christian faith. It must be an activity of the church, oriented to preaching, not a public activity open to anyone willing to think objectively about religious problems. Barth seemed to the liberals to be putting the clock back, to be undercutting the ground on which they considered they had made progress in rendering theology intellectually respectable in the modern world. No wonder that charges of reaction and obscurantism were levelled at him.[9]

And yet paradoxically enough, far from seeking to privatize theology, insulating it from corroding academic influences and making it the sole

---

was the historical critics, not he, who were insufficiently critical because they would not risk an interpretation of the biblical words' central claim to be a faithful attestation to the divine Word. As in the *Romans* commentary, Barth argues that a thoroughly radical historical-critical approach will not stop with the Bible as merely a collection of history-specific words but will seek to uncover the meaning of these words as witnesses to revelation" (Mark I. Wallace, "Karl Barth's Hermeneutics: A Way beyond the Impasse," *Journal of Religion* 68/3 [1988]: 396–410; here 399).

[9] Nicholls, 96. Again without asserting anything like a direct influence, we may still notice the same "elective affinity" in Balthasar's ironic attitude toward historical-critical exegesis in the Catholic Church, which is perhaps even more sharply phrased than Barth's strictures: "The turn toward the Word of God has been praised in today's Catholic world as the loveliest and clearest sign of hope; and we cannot doubt that this is so. Here we clearly have a case where all curtains have been drawn aside that once clouded our vision of the Christian source (the curtains would be all the later ecclesiastical, catechetical and dogmatic formularies of revelation) so that we may go directly to the truth of God and Christ. . . . We stand dumbfounded before the dark past when so many barbed-wire fences had been drawn around the holy text, when even touching it could bring down the electrical shock of excommunication. . . . The joy occasioned by this breakthrough must not be dampened, but it does need to be chastened by the realization that the emergence of the modern Catholic Biblical Movement is not due primarily, as was Luther's battle-cry of *sola Scriptura,* to an elementary longing for God's original Word behind all scholasticism and Church doctrine, but essentially to the growing realization of informed exegetes that Catholic biblical science

province of the Christian preacher (a kind of Sunday school with foot-notes), Barth stressed more than any Protestant theologian of his time the *objectivity* of theology. In the wake of Schleiermacher theology had managed to gain access to the academy by paradoxically stressing what made it most inaccessible: subjectivity, or the personal experience of each believer. But Barth insisted that the content of theology is "out there," that what determines theology is not an initial choice of method but the content of revelation, which must determine the method of theology, and this is no doubt what Balthasar found so appealing:

> Like Calvin and unlike Luther, Barth turned away from the disposition of faith and focused on its content. Indeed Barth writes well *because* he strictly adheres to theological objectivism ("Faith lives from its object") and because he so sharply veered from the liberal Protestantism of Schleiermacher. That is why he is so readable and why we need not fear mushy piety or empty pastoral edification from him. The subject matter does its own edifying, builds its own edifice. (*KB*, 25)

This stress on the all-determining object of revelation accounts for two features of Barth's theology that we will also in the course of this study discover in Balthasar as well: an insistence on the objectivity of aesthetic form (meaning: its power to enrapture) and a polemic against all those trends in contemporary theology which so rapidly slip into subjectivism and soon leave one feeling exhausted and spent. How this comes to expression in Balthasar's theology would best be left to the rest of the book to describe, but the affinity between these two men in the question of the aesthetic form of theology becomes especially clear in Balthasar's description of Barth's method, which is one of the most lyrical passages in his book on Barth:

> Who but Barth has gazed so breathlessly and tirelessly on his subject, watching it develop and blossom in all its power before his eyes? One would have to go back to Thomas Aquinas to find a similar spirit, one free from the constraints of every tenseness and narrowness, combining superior gifts of understanding with goodness of heart. In Barth this graciousness occasionally takes the form of a tinge of humor; but more often we see it displayed in his extraordinary sense of timing, of just the right tempo, a sense of due rhythm. Barth really makes us believe that for him Christianity is a radiantly triumphant opportunity. He managed

could no longer continue to set up its shop selling antiquated wares without becoming the laughing stock of the whole scientific world" (*WC*, 33–34).

this not so much because he possessed the gift of style, or wrote well, but because he bore witness, sober witness, to a reality that epitomizes style, since God is its author. Barth is the very antithesis of Kierkegaard here, who sharply divided the aesthetical from the religious and ethical. But for Barth the religious sphere is aesthetical *because* it is religious, because it is in itself the most authentic. (*KB,* 26)

The rejection of Kierkegaard's thesis is significant here, for it will provide us later with an important clue to why Balthasar begins his own theological trilogy with a fully developed, seven-volume aesthetics. According to Kierkegaard, the aesthetic sphere is a closed-off sensual world that ultimately terminates in despair.[10]

The result of Kierkegaard's influence was to bring to Christian theology a certain aversion to style and rhetoric, a vague and often implicit feeling that beauty is, if not something foppish, at least dispensable and extraneous. But this is not the case, for revelation has an attractive beauty of its own, so that, as Balthasar points out, once one becomes fully absorbed by revelation on its own terms, *style takes over the author.* The prejudice is that style is some mannered addition to what one is trying to say (as of course in many authors it is); but a powerful style is merely the reflection that one has been seized by a power greater than one could have anticipated. And this for Balthasar eminently characterizes Karl Barth:

If we are not to misunderstand Barth's purpose, we must see it as an expression of the final purpose of the martyrs and saints. How else can we explain this steadfastness of theme, the tireless variations he weaves around this theme, the certainty in ecstasy,

---

[10] Kierkegaard's analysis of the aesthetic sphere in fact actually shows much more sympathy for the values of this dimension of existence (especially in his treatment of Lucretius and Epicurus) than he is often given credit for. William Barrett has effectively captured these combined moments of sympathy and critique in this summary: "The child is the perfect and complete aesthete, for the child lives solely in the pleasure or pain of the moment. Some people do grow up retraining something of this childlike immediacy of response, this capacity for existing in the moment. They are sometimes beautiful to watch, these immediate ones, says Kierkegaard, as they glow in the moment responding to some simple and beautiful object with all the grace of their nature and their blood. ... Kierkegaard explores the aesthetic attitude with great subtlety and sympathy; but, he says, in the end it must collapse into despair. ... The most beautiful Epicurean poems of the Greeks and Romans are always haunted by sadness: there is a grinning skull behind the flowers. ... The man who has staked his whole life on its pleasurable moments has to become desperate in his search for them, as Don Juan becomes desperate in his search for new loves. The aesthete is driven into a panicky flight from the prospect of boredom, and this flight—which is in fact a flight from himself—becomes his form of desperation and therefore of despair" (William Barrett, *Irrational Man: A Study in Existential Philosophy* [New York: Doubleday, 1958], 163–164).

this magnetic power for ordering all things to their center, this relentless submission of everything that has meaning and value to the throne of God, to whom belongs all worship and love? . . . Even in his later writings, however, there is an almost Old Testament pathos that pervades all his work. Here is a Jeremiah, consumed with the fire of zeal, surrounded by misunderstanding and becoming more and more restricted in his influence. Here is Job, suffering the dialectical shifts from judgment to love and back again. Here is the sardonic Preacher of Ecclesiastes, the skeptic for God's sake, weighing all earthly values in his scales of judgment and finding them wanting. (*KB*, 169).

This passage perhaps gives some inkling of the other affinity with Balthasar we mentioned above: their polemical stance toward most contemporary schools of Christian theology (and thus their common isolation from contemporary trends). Once again it must be stressed that in the case of both men this is no case of simple revanchism or a pessimistic nay-saying to everything that has happened in the modern world. Nor has their thought been besotted by its opposite number: a willingness to replace the hope given to us in the Good News with a naïve hope that the modern world, or History, or the Future, or some such abstract figment of our idolatrous imagination, will deliver us from our plight. As we have already seen, before World War I Barth was fairly content with his training in liberal theology up to that time, but the implosion of his naïve hopes and easy assumptions on the battlefields of the Marne changed his views forever and gave him a retrospective insight into what was wrong with Protestant theology in the 19th century, one which has clearly influenced Balthasar as well:

But this much is clear: why Barth has rejected liberal Protestantism: in all of its main doctrines it has moved farther and farther away from revelation. While Catholicism indeed is a "distortion, but nonetheless a distortion of a substance it has not lost" but has preserved, Protestantism—at least in its final phases—has now moved so far from authentic Christianity that all that remains is the name itself. God's revelation coming to us from outside and above in order to elect, save, sanctify and redeem man, has been replaced by a growing interest in subjectivity. Pietism was the first, if veiled, expression of this trend. Idealism further prepared the way, and then in Feuerbach we have the fullest enunciation of the theory of the "religious" person's self-redemption, the reduction of faith to the "highest possibility" of reason, and of revelation to the "highest possibility" of history. And from there it is but a short and inevitable step to interpreting Jesus's "awareness of God" as but the highest possibility of human religiosity. (*KB,* 34)

Barth was only confirmed all the more in these views with the advent of National Socialism in Germany. In fact, the close student of Barth will notice in the course of his work (which came to its full maturity during the Nazi period) a subtle change in his analysis of the 19th-century roots to the crisis of Europe in the 20th century. At first, World War I caused Barth to see in retrospect the *inadequacies* of the past century's theology. But as he became increasingly involved in the struggle against the Nazi regime, and especially against the collusion of the German churches in this new order, his logic intensified, almost to the point where he seemed to be saying in the heat of battle that Schleiermacher had *caused* National Socialism—or at least if Protestant thought had not taken the Schleiermacherian turn, the churches would never have been enticed by the vicious pseudo-Aryanism of the "Deutsche Christen."

This might remind the reader of those simplistic attempts of certain intellectual historians who claim that, for example, Nietzsche "caused" World War I, or Hegel "led to" Hitler, or, more prejudicial still, that there is something innate in the German character that makes a Hitler inevitable. The connection between the history of events and the history of ideas is a complex one, and the link between German thought and the disasters of the 20th century as Balthasar sees it will be the focus of our next chapter, but this much must be said: for Barth, at any rate, there was a deep inner connection (even if cause-effect proves to be not the best way of describing that connection) between the abandonment of theological norms to subjectivity and the inability of the churches to withstand the firestorm of fascism:

> For Barth, this whole river empties out with total inexorability into the idolatry of the "Aryan Christians" and into neo-paganism in general. If Schleiermacher is already the "Niagara Falls over whose rim the main rivers of theological thought for at least two centuries come roaring down with frightful relentlessness," then the later transposition of Christianity into a version of nationalism and racial idolatry is but the "last stop" on that "halting journey" that began with Schleiermacher and coursed through the whole of the 19th century. Barth could summon the German churches to the struggle against liberalism with such vehemence precisely because these connections were so perfectly obvious to him. This was why he pronounced his "unconditional and unhesitating No to the spirit and letter of this doctrine [of religious subjectivity]" and thought that "it would be better for the evangelical churches to become tiny remnants

hiding out in the catacombs than that they should make peace, even from afar, with this doctrine." (*KB*, 35)

To assert this connection and then to go on to establish it are of course two entirely different matters. Here, however, it is sufficient simply to note the connection Barth saw between the turn toward subjectivity and the later inability of the churches to say No to the *Zeitgeist,* even in its most demonic forms. To discover how much Balthasar also shared this "elective affinity" with Barth entails analyzing his own encounter with German culture, the subject of our next chapter. But in both cases we are dealing with theologians whose starting point has given them a perspective for a fascinating and full-scale diagnosis of the ills of a lamentable period in history.

• • •

But dialogue for both men, as we have seen, is scarcely a matter of mutual self-congratulation, an opportunity to see how much their minds have converged at various points. What do we make of their *disagreements* and what do they tell us of the general contours of Balthasar's own achievement?

There are of course substantive disagreements, as one would expect from, respectively, the quintessential Protestant and Catholic theologian of this century, and there is no point in belaboring the more obvious issues that immediately separate the two religious bodies and, *a fortiori,* these two thinkers. What is much more crucial, and what emerges so strikingly in Balthasar's book on Barth, is the *formal* nature of their disagreement. Often Barth's distance from Catholicism on substantive issues centered more on the secondary dogmas (sacraments, papal authority, the role of Mary in the economy of grace, etc.) than on the primary dogmas of God and Christ. But as Balthasar pointed out, that did not necessarily mean that rapprochement was near: "Barth positioned his *Church Dogmatics* between two flanks: on the left he rejected the *content* of liberal Protestantism while admitting its formal principle; and on the right he rejected the *formal* structure of Catholicism while showing a deep appreciation for the content of many of its doctrines."[11]

---

[11] *KB*, 36. Barth often expressed this distinction by playing with the verbal contrast between the two Latin words "alia" (different things) and "aliter" (in a different manner). And as Balthasar points out, a too-hasty concentration on the *alia* at the expense of the *aliter* in ecumenical discussion will only be a waste of energy: "If anyone for instance wants to jump into the heat of battle without due consideration of these realities in order to do fight over the set of *alia* (the distinctive doctrines separating us), he will certainly have his work cut out for him; but in the end perhaps it will all have come to naught. It could well be that the primary problem still stands untouched because in the whole dispute it has never been thematized. According to Barth the primary problem is a formal one, or if one prefers, a 'modal' problem (that is, the *aliter* is more decisive than the *alia*)" (*KB*, 47–48).

And what precisely is that formal principle? Being purely formal, it is of course hard to describe without also introducing the concrete issues they determine. But briefly put, Barth accuses the Catholic principle of insisting that dogmas, and by extension revelation itself, must be fitted into a prior framework established by natural theology, *upon which* revelation is then meant to sit like the capstone to a building. Catholics, in other words, take the word "supernatural" too literally, and see it as something added "on to" (= Latin's *super*) nature. In a shrewd remark, Balthasar describes Barth's approach as an attempt to reverse the Hegelian project: "What Barth has in fact done is to invert the Hegelian intent but in the Hegelian manner: as Hegel tried to absorb the assertions of theology into a more comprehensive philosophy, Barth ordered all of the paths of human wisdom, philosophical and religious, around the central core of a purely theological point of view."[12]

Catholicism for Barth of course is not the same as Hegelianism, which rejects the need for revelation,[13] something impossible in the Catholic religion. But by admitting revelation only in the sense of being a completion of a structure already in the process of being built (however imperfect that structure would remain without its superstructure), Catholicism in Barth's view is being unfaithful to revelation in principle. And this is at the root of his whole disagreement with the doctrine of the analogy of being, the objection to which is effectively summarized by Balthasar:

> By now Barth's objection to Catholicism should also be clear: he accuses it of possessing an overarching systematic principle that is merely an abstract statement about the analogy of being and not a frank assertion that Christ is the Lord. This principle presupposes that the relationship between God and creature can already be recognized in our philosophical fore-understanding (of natural theology). This means that God's revelation in Jesus Christ seems to be merely the fulfillment of an already existing knowledge and reality. Perhaps this need not imply a metaphysics that sets itself above faith itself, but Christ's place as the fulfillment of salvation history is still reserved "in advance": in an ontology that exists prior to the order of revelation and which cannot be shattered by it. (*KB*, 37)

---

[12] *KB*, 36. See also Balthasar's remark that "Barth's exposition of Hegel's philosophy in his history of Protestant theology is written with such verve and conviction that one can hardly miss a kind of inner congeniality between the two thinkers" (*KB*, 208), a suspicion that also occurs to the reader on more than one occasion in reading Balthasar.

[13] "According to the traditions of metaphysical idealism, we are not dependent upon a revelation to apprehend the truth. The metaphysics of idealism finds man's own spiritual nature to be the fullest expression of that which is to be taken as basic in reality" (Maurice

We know that Barth's disagreement here with Balthasar (or more exactly with Przywara, in whom Barth first encountered the doctrine of analogy of being as a principle of contemporary Catholic thought) is genuinely a formal one because of the almost mirror-image way the Catholic responds back: for Przywara, Barth was doing the same thing with his famous dialectical method: subsuming revelation under some broader and more overarching concept! Both sides, then, are accusing the other of weaving a scheme and constructing a Procrustean bed into which revelation must fit. So which is *the* invention of the anti-Christ, analogy or dialectic? And how to decide? This was Barth's dilemma and Balthasar was already posing it to him as early as 1944:

> Barth obviously (and justifiably) sees in [analogy] a formal structural principle that pervades everything: but ultimately [it is also] the anti-Christian attempt of man to place himself on a common level with God, to "grasp after" God, which grasping is precisely the very meaning of sin. Now it is significant, however, that Erich Przywara in his analysis of the Barthian dialectic raises the very same objection against *it:* dialectic is for him the titanic attempt to leap over the boundary—a boundary that can only be guaranteed by the principle of analogy!—of creaturely distance to God. This highly paradoxical situation in the discussion, in which both opponents hurl the same objection at the other, and in fact defend the same underlying intent, must provoke us to test once more these two formal principles.[14]

In testing these two clashing principles in the course of his book-length study, Balthasar traces a gradual evolution in Barth's thought away from

---

Mandelbaum, *History, Man & Reason: A Study in Nineteenth Century Thought* [Baltimore: The Johns Hopkins University Press, 1971], 6).

[14] "Analogie und Dialektik: Zur Klärung der theologischen Prinzipienlehre Karl Barths," *Divus Thomas* 22 (1944): 171–216; here 171–172: "Barth sieht in ihr offenbar (und mit Recht) ein alles durchherrschendes formales Strukturprinzip: letztlich den widerchristlichen Versuch des Menschen, sich mit Gott auf eine gemeinsame Ebene zu stellen, nach 'Gott zu greifen,' welcher Griff eben das Wesen der Sünde enthüllt. Nun ist es aber bedeutsam, daß Erich Przywara in seinen Analysen der Barth'schen Dialektik ihr gegenüber genau denselben Vorwurf erhebt: Dialektik ist für ihn der titanische Versuch, die—allein im Prinzip der Analogie gewährleistete—kreatürliche Distanz zu Gott zu überspringen in eine Art von theologischen Pantheismus. Diese höchst paradoxe Lage der Diskussion, in der sich beide Gegner letztlich den gleichen Vorwurf entgegenschleudern, also offenbar ein gleiches Anliegen verteidigen, muß uns zu erneuter Prüfung dieser formalen Prinzipien anregen." In his preface to his Barth book, Balthasar says that the book supersedes all his earlier essays on Barth, which is true, but I have drawn from them when the views expressed therein have remained the same as the book and when the formulation of the issues is pithier, as if often the case with the essay format.

dialectics and toward analogy, with "dialectics" representing the approach best typified by his commentary on Romans and "analogy" emerging in the period when he was writing the *Church Dogmatics* (although Barth called it the "analogy of faith" to distinguish it from its malign twin, the analogy of being). Admittedly, "dialectics" is a notoriously slippery term in any case, and especially so in Barth's *Romans* period, when his style was expressionistic to the point of being openly contradictory. Perhaps the best way we can understand both the term and how it affected Barth's polemic against the analogy of being is through the following description of Balthasar's:

> [For the early Barth] the sharp blade of the absolute cuts through everything and thus cannot be expressed in a neutral concept of being, applicable to both Creator and creature alike. On the contrary, through the event of revelation it invades the world and seizes and overpowers man. Simultaneously, the other edge of the blade reveals man is a sinner, totally alienated from God and thereby and to that extent deserving of damnation. Whatever he may have in the way of worldly goods and property, all of his pluses and minuses stand, to the extent he is a sinner, within the bracket of the most important minus sign of all: the fact of his unbelief, disobedience and divine condemnation. (*KB*, 81)

As we see in this passage, "dialectic" refers to the total opposition between man and God, in which revelation "overpowers" man, who is defined as being "totally alienated" and before whose entire existence there stands a minus sign: himself!—defined as the negation of God. So dominant is this theme in Barth's commentary on Romans that almost any passage chosen at random can illustrate the power of this dialectic at work, but perhaps the following assemblage best illustrates both the expressive power and the thoroughness of Barth's dialectical method here:

> There is no fragment or epoch of history which can be pronounced divine. The whole history of the Church and of all religion takes place in this world. There are no saints in the midst of a company of sinners; for where men have claimed to be saints, they are thereby marked as not-saints. Their criticism and invective and indictment of the world inevitably place them— unless they themselves be the object—within the course of this world and betray that they too are of it. Their indictment springs not from their capacity to help but from their own distress! . . . This is as true of Paul, the prophet and apostle of the kingdom of God, and of Jeremiah, as it is of Luther, Kierkegaard and St.

Francis, who far surpassed Jesus in "love," childlikeness and austerity. Everything human swims with the stream either with vehement protest or with easy accommodation, even when it appears to hover above it or to engage in conflict with it. . . . Since power belongs only to God, it is the tragic story of every man of God that he has to contend for the right by placing himself in the wrong.[15]

The style here is obviously powerful, almost intoxicatingly so, and one can easily imagine why it had so immense an impact on the theological world after the devastation of World War I. But within its powerful thunder there lurks an inner contradiction that cannot be resolved by the dialectic itself, and one that Barth later in the evolution of his thought would admit was its undoing. The reason for the contradiction is that the dialectic so contrasts the difference between God and creature that the event of revelation has the paradoxical effect of abolishing the status of the creature as a creature, as Balthasar explains in this careful dissection of Barth's commentary:

> First, God is identified (in all his aseity!) with his revelation. Then the creature is defined as the pure opposite to God and thus is identified with nothingness. And finally, when the creature is retrieved by God through revelation and brought back to God through a dynamic movement (which is an absolute, because divine, movement), creation is then equated with God himself, at least in its origin and goal. (*KB,* 84)

The truth of this charge exposes Barth's dialectic to an extremely painful bind: it is hardly the point of revelation to espouse a pantheism (or more exactly a theopanism[16]), and yet it is into just such a foreign mold

---

[15] Karl Barth, *The Epistle to the Romans,* tr. Edwin C. Hoskyns (London: Oxford University Press, 1933), 57.

[16] Technically, pantheism says that the universe, all that is, is God; whereas theopanism says that God is everything, interpreting Paul's statement that at the end of time "God will be all in all" to mean that God will overwhelm all the rest of being and only the divine will remain. In a sense they both mean the same thing, since both versions assert God = nature; but it is still more useful to call Spinoza a pantheist, as he begins with nature and equates God with this primary substrate (nature), while the theopanism of Luther begins with God and sees nature only in terms of its final absorption in God. This is Balthasar's description of how theopanism has undermined the project of Barth's commentary on Romans: "The best way of characterizing this ideology is by describing it as a dynamic and actualist *theopanism,* which we define as a monism of beginning and end (protology and eschatology): God stands at the beginning and the end, surrounding a world-reality understood in dualistic and dialectical terms, ultimately overcoming it in the mathematical point of the miracle of transformation. As we have seen, this monism of the Word of God, which invades the hostile

that Barth has cast his commentary on Paul! *Barth,* then, is the one imposing an alien form on revelation!

> These equations, identifications, levelings, are to be found in
> both editions of *The Epistle to the Romans.* The irony is that at
> the very place where Barth wants to do pure theology, where
> human thought has no more room for maneuver unless it be
> dialectical and "superseded," here we encounter the unexpected
> (but also unavoidable!) irruption of a very unbiblical philosophi-
> cal pantheism (or more precisely, theopanism). This ultimately
> becomes evident in Barth's use of dialectics itself: its very exclu-
> sivity necessarily serves to be its own undoing. "The dialectical
> way is by far the best," says Barth. And yet a few pages later he
> goes on to aver that "the dialectician is as such no better than
> the dogmatician or the critic."[17]

Such outright contradictions could not be borne for long, and the recognition of this began the movement that led to the *Church Dogmatics.* In
retrospect, we are now able to see that Barth's theological development
was marked by three important transitions: the first of course was the
outbreak of war in 1914 when he abandoned the liberalism of his teachers
in Germany; the second occurred in the 1920's when his study of Anselm's
principle *credo ut intelligam* (I believe in order that I might understand)
convinced him that *in* the act of faith true knowledge was possible and
that faith need not be understood merely as the dialectical opposite of
knowledge;[18] and the third occurred when Barth abandoned the first vol-

---

world and is expressed in such Idealist categories as mediacy and immediacy, object and
objectlessness, threatens time and again to swallow up the reality of the world. Though the
world (which does after all stand in relation to the Word of God) is certainly something
and not nothing, it looks so forlorn and hopeless under this harsh glare that one might just
as well wish it did not exist" (*KB,* 94).

[17] *KB,* 84. Such an admission on Barth's part leaves him open to the same kind of thunder-
ous treatment to which he submitted Francis of Assisi, Paul, Jeremiah, etc., an opportunity
Balthasar does not fail to exploit: "*The Epistle to the Romans* is the very thing against
which it itself raged and thundered: a pinnacle of human religiosity. Its insistent cry of 'Not
I! Rather God!' actually directs all eyes on *itself* instead of on God. Its cry for distance gives
no room for distance. Perhaps, shuddering at the dreadful pain of its flagellations, we could
admit that it is right—a hundred times right! But the very blow tells us of its guilt. The real
scandal is the mystery of God, which cannot be evaluated in language, even indirectly. There
is no suitable method for describing 'the infinite qualitative difference between God and
man,' even if only negatively. Dialectic cannot replace theology. It must be content to serve
merely as a corrective. As the moment of indirection, it can itself only be indirect" (*KB,* 94).

[18] Expressed in his monograph *Anselm: Fides quaerens intellectum, Anselm's Proof of the
Existence of God in the Context of his Theological Schemes,* tr. Ian W. Robertson (London:
SCM Press, 1960). One of the great merits of Balthasar's study of Barth is that it was the
first (and still one of the few) to recognize the important methodological shift represented

ume (the so-called *Prolegomena*) of a projected dogmatics bearing the title *Die Lehre vom Wort Gottes,* and in its stead brought out in 1932 a completely revised first volume of a new dogmatics, this time to be called *Church Dogmatics.* Barth's theological public was alert to the change of title and what it implied:

> Again Barth had scandalized the theological public. Not only would he write dogmatics, he would now write *ecclesiastical* dogmatics, dogmatics linked to the church and to its confession, instead of to the academic community and to free inquiry. In the preface to the new volume . . . he says that his aim in revision had been to remove from his writings any trace of dependence upon existentialism or any other philosophy. Theology is to depend wholly on the Word of God. . . . Thus it necessarily becomes an activity of the church. But this repudiation of philosophical support should not mislead us. Barth now intends to speak *more* rationally than before, not less so. Theology is defined as science, in the sense that it has an object by which it is determined, and a discipline which renders it critical in its attempts to conform its own utterance to the given nature of its object.[19]

And in this progressive movement toward an ever greater recognition of the inherent rationality in theo*logy* (in Greek "logos" means reason), we can see Barth being more and more forced to acknowledge the place of ana*logy* in theological language. This in fact, according to Balthasar, is the single most important reason why Barth abandoned his first draft of a dogmatics and started anew: he realized he was still too influenced by dialectics, and so he still saw God and creation too much as contrasting, even contradictory terms:

---

by this short monograph, as Barth himself generously acknowledged in the Preface to the second edition: "Only a comparatively few commentators, for example Hans Urs von Balthasar, have realized that my interest in Anselm was never a side-issue for me or . . . realized how much it has influenced me or been absorbed into my own thinking. Most of them have completely failed to see that in this book on Anselm I am working with a vital key, if not *the* key, to an understanding of that whole process of thought that has impressed me more and more in my *Church Dogmatics* as the *only* proper one to theology" (11; my emphasis). William Nicholls has also seen the significance of this crucial shift and expresses its implications in this useful summary: "Barth had now taken a crucial step beyond the position of his early work. Faith can, in his view, admit to rational knowledge of the object of faith. It gives rise to rational propositions about God, and these bear on the being of God, in this case on his necessary existence, though not yet on his essence. Barth has moved in principle beyond a dialectical theology to a positive theology" (Nicholls, 106–107).

[19] Nicholls, 108–109; my emphasis.

[And so] certain motifs or accents from *The Epistle to the Romans* still crop up in the *Prolegomena* and are the reason why Barth withdrew it to start anew. . . . Barth does not yet state clearly and emphatically that creation is not a contradiction in itself but rather is first of all a legitimate, good and divinely willed *counterpart* to God. It is characteristic for Barth that he came to a balanced christology earlier than he did to a balanced doctrine of creation. It is from Christ himself that he will eventually learn that it is a good thing to be a creature, that not to be God is not a disaster or a contradiction in terms but a good in and of itself. (*KB*, 90–91)

Nonetheless, the *Prolegomena* (the name by which the first volume of the projected, but later abjured, dogmatics is generally known) represents a real development in the evolution of Barth's thought, for finally Barth has come to admit that the term "nature" does not mean that which stands in contradiction to God. One particularly eloquent passage from an essay of Barth's at that time marks this shift in his thinking with startling and irrefutable clarity:

For sin has not destroyed God's image in man to such an extent that man has ceased being a person created and loved by God. Sin does not turn man into a stone or a torso of his former self. Even as a sinner, man is still man; and God speaks to him in Jesus Christ. Thus humanness is Promise. And man is capable of sharing in this promise. The human race has been restored to life through God's active reassertion of his claim in Jesus Christ.[20]

Thus when Barth came to reject all of the extraneous philosophical forms that had previously constricted his theology by scrapping the *Prolegomena* and starting afresh with the *Church Dogmatics*, we find an inexorable movement toward a doctrine of analogy. True, it is in the Preface to the first volume of the *Church Dogmatics* that Barth first said his famous line about the doctrine of analogy being the invention of the anti-Christ, but the gravitational pull of his new Anselmian logic was nonetheless irresistible, so much so that as Balthasar says in one of the more penetrating remarks in his book:

Over and over again Barth will be forced to develop his theology "at a hair's length nearness to Catholic theology," fully alive to

---

[20] Karl Barth, *Die Theologie und die Kirche* (Munich: Christian Kaiser Verlag, 1938), 376; the book appeared in 1938 but the essay from which this quote is drawn first appeared in 1928.

"the danger of meeting up with certain false statements of Roman Catholicism." For example, he will often draw his portrait of the analogy of faith in a way that will scarcely be distinguishable from that of the analogy of being, so that it will be exceedingly difficult for him to stop at the border he has drawn and call the one formal principle "Christian" and the other as belonging to the "Antichrist." (*KB*, 53)

This of course does not mean that the differences between what Barth meant by analogy of faith and what Balthasar means by analogy of being are without further significance, nor does Balthasar claim this, either in this passage or elsewhere. Nonetheless, it is clear that Barth is moving closer to a substantial or ontological understanding of analogy, so that the differences between the two will come down to epistemology: do we come to see the simultaneous similarity/dissimilarity between God and us *in* the act of faith alone, or can philosophical analysis contribute to our understanding of analogy? And if so, is that analysis propaedeutic to faith or only subsequent to it? In any case, it is clear that Barth has finally realized the inevitability of analogical language: "The relation [between God and creature] must be described as a *middle ground* lying somewhere *between* two extremes, and this we call analogy. This middle term cannot for its part be transposed to another level or reduced to a 'partial identity' and a 'partial dissimilarity.' . . . Analogy is an ultimate relation-term: it cannot be explained by any more fundamental identity or nonidentity."[21]

This is certainly a remarkable step forward for Barth, but it should not deceive us: the epistemological issue of how the believer arrives at this insight is still crucial, for Barth wants to insist that the reason that analogy truly expresses the actual relationship between God and creature is not because they can both be subsumed under some wider category called "being" but because *God* has created the creature and therefore *God* has established the truth of the relationship, a point concisely summarized by Balthasar's formulation of Barth's position:

But the words that we use of God are not independent of the relationship *which God establishes*. Therefore, it is not something one already finds present in nature as part of its innate laws but is a relation founded on revelation. The truth contained in our concepts is—corresponding to their objects—a created, relative, finite truth. To pertain to God, *God* must produce from

---

[21] *KB*, 109; these are Balthasar's words but they are located in a passage summarizing Barth's doctrine of the analogy of faith.

within himself the relation between temporal truths and his divinity. He chooses our truth to express his truth.[22]

There is nothing in this approach that Balthasar finds objectionable, and indeed we have already seen that the doctrine of analogy draws its legitimacy from the attempt of faith to understand what it means to be a creaturely being, which obviously implies that God both establishes the being and the truth of what he has created, and precisely by creating it. Where Balthasar disagrees with Barth, and indeed where the disagreement becomes quite pointed, is how one comes to ground the doctrine of analogy. At this juncture it becomes unimportant whether the term used be analogy of "faith" or of "being," because the real issue centers on Barth's wish to ground a doctrine of analogy in christology exclusively. We should recall Balthasar's earlier observation that "it is characteristic for Barth that he came to a balanced christology earlier than he did to a balanced doctrine of creation. It is from Christ himself that he will eventually learn that it is a good thing to be a creature, that not to be God is not a disaster or a contradiction in terms but a good in and of itself" (*KB,* 91). Balthasar has considerable sympathy for this insistently christological focus, as one might expect from a thinker noted for his consistent christocentrism, and so he notes with approval Barth's gradual movement away from a focus on the doctrine of the Word of God to one that stresses the historical, fleshly and therefore *created* nature of Jesus Christ:

> As Barth continued to publish succeeding volumes of the *Church Dogmatics,* he gradually and without fanfare, but no less inexorably, replaced the central notion of "the Word of God" with that of "Jesus Christ, God and man." What emerges as this great Summa unfolds is the insight that "God's Word" is not the most comprehensive term for the essence and content of revelation. Word is in fact but *one* designation for the Son, and it is the Son himself in whom God has decided to unite everything in heaven and on earth. But because the Son himself becomes man in the midst of his creatures, creation already has an essential connection to him, just as he has to creation. . . . It is already justified. And from the very outset of God's decision to create it is appropriate for God to choose man for his partner. . . . However much *sin* may be a total contradiction of grace, *nature* cannot possibly be such because it is founded on Christ. (*KB,* 114, 116)

This represents a remarkable advance on the attitude toward nature in traditional Protestantism, and in fact Barth openly avers that he has not

---

[22] *KB,* 109; second emphasis mine.

followed "the usual practice in theology of first denigrating human nature as much as possible in order then to make God's grace working in man all the more effective" (*CD* III/2, 274). In fact, based on his insight that "sin indeed wreaks inconceivable havoc, but precisely because human nature is so good," Barth will move on to make a most remarkable assessment of Greek culture, praising it for understanding—more than any culture before or since—the inherent goodness of human nature:

> A certain agitation among theologians in the past few decades against Greek culture has not been a good thing. With their emphasis on Eros, the Greeks understood that man is a free, open-hearted, willing, spontaneous, cheerful, bright and social being. . . . No other nation of antiquity, not even the chosen people of Israel, was granted the privilege of displaying so fully what humanity as an unbroken continuum means. . . . Much of the theology of the New Covenant is painted not in Israelite but in what are doubtless Greek shades of color, redeemed in the light of true love but fundamentally undisturbed. . . . The *agape* of the Christian would not be what it claims to be if it remains hidden to the transparency of Greek Eros; when a person schooled in Hellenic culture encounters the Christian, he should feel a sense of solidarity to the very roots of his erotic being.[23]

Clearly, in Karl Barth Protestant theology has moved a long way from the censorious attitudes of Luther and Calvin, yet without falling into the trap of later liberal Protestantism of subsuming the majesty and sovereignty of revelation under a more controlling humanistic category. Nonetheless, and despite his thoroughgoing approval of the direction Barth was taking his thought, Balthasar has nonetheless accused Barth of still being too beholden to the old Protestant narrowness regarding the independence and goodness of nature. The reason for this is because, ac-

---

[23] *KD* III/2, 340–343; ET: *CD* III/2, 283–285; my translation, which differs to some extent from the Bromiley translation. Three points should be mentioned about this remarkable passage: 1) Barth insists that his views on Hellenic culture have scriptural warrant in Paul's admonition that "whatever is true, whatever is noble, whatever is right, whatever is pure, whatever is lovely, whatever is admirable—if anything is excellent or praiseworthy—think on these things" (Phil 4:8), all of whose adjectives are drawn from the standard terminology of Greek philosophy. 2) Balthasar has cited this passage with complete approval, making clear he had adopted it as his own. 3) It is no secret that one of the major reasons for the secularization of civilization in formerly Christian lands and for the alienation so many people feel from Christianity stems from its perceived hostility to precisely the view that Barth defends here (Nietzsche's critique of Christianity would make no sense had post-Reformation Christianity—both Protestant and Roman Catholic—not been perceived as so hostile to the eros of life). Clearly this is a resource lurking within the treasury of neo-orthodoxy that has yet to be fully exploited.

cording to Balthasar (and it is crucial to remember that this is *his* interpretation), Barth reads the relationship between Christ and creation too one-sidedly. In a way, this dispute is rather reminiscent of the old debate between Thomists and Scotists on the reason for the incarnation: did the Son of God become man *because* Adam and Eve sinned, or would the incarnation have taken place anyway, independent of the event of sin?

Barth's position is reminiscent of Scotus in this sense: clearly Christ could not have become man had not the universe been created; for him to become flesh there must first be flesh to assume. That is why Barth calls creation the *presupposition* for the incarnation, an extremely important term in his theology.[24] But apparently, the value of creation is what we might call a Scotist value: that is, it stems solely from its potential for making possible the incarnation. Barth of course never says that creation would have had no value whatever had not the incarnation occurred, but according to Balthasar by refusing the term analogy of being except in terms of the analogy of faith, that is in effect what he is doing:

> Protest though he will and despite the "open-ended" use he makes of the transcendental categories, a tendency toward constraint and system is unmistakable in Barth. Indeed, this constraint clings to the whole project of the *Church Dogmatics,* so much so that it affects its articulation at every limb and joint. It is not so much a matter of Barth omitting some crucial doctrine as it is a distortion of nuance, an inappropriate coloration to the whole. In Catholic terms, we may call it an exaggeration, an overstatement, a failure of balance. We are referring to Barth's christological starting point. Such a starting point is quite legitimate—indeed if we want to take the Bible seriously, it is absolutely essential. But it is a big step from there to the *narrowing* of everything to that one point. The priority of Christ over creation and sin in no way requires that the whole work of creation has to be so painfully forced to occupy the Procrustean bed of Barth's christological schema. . . . Barth ends up talking about Christ so much as *the* true human being that it makes it seem as if all other human beings are mere epiphenomena. (*KB*, 241–242, 243)

Barth, who had a fascinating way with metaphor, chose two images to express how the creature is related to his christological starting point. The first is of the hourglass, where two contiguous vessels (God and

---

[24] The German word for presupposition is *Voraussetzung,* which conveys to the German ear much more than it does to the English the act of "positing" or "establishing" (*Setzung*), which God must first (*voraus*) do to make possible the incarnation.

creature) meet only at the narrow passage through the center, where they both encounter each other in Jesus Christ. The purpose of the image, of course, is to show that there is no other point of contact between the two chambers: as the sand flows only from top to bottom, so too is God's revelation one-sided, flowing from his gracious decision alone. But as Balthasar points out, the image can undermine Barth's point, for as the sand flows down into the other chamber, there is really is an increase in the creature—a counter-movement in the other chamber, which to be sure is only the result of the movement in the first chamber (*KB*, 197).

Barth's other image is that of the reflector lights on the back of automobiles whose only ability to radiate a light comes from the headlights of the car behind them. To which Balthasar replies not by exploiting the weakness in the image itself (such passivity!) but by responding with a more biblical image: the true image that expresses the relationality between Christ and disciple is not that of hourglass or reflector light but that of vine and grape. It is of course true that the principle of life flows entirely from the vine to the grape, but that does not deny the mutuality between the two but rather confirms it, for who, Balthasar asks, could conceive of a grapevine without grapes?

> This image of the vine and its branches could help to dispel the final differences that divide Catholic and Protestant concepts of the Church. For it expresses two things: grace, like the vine, is the exclusive principle of fruitfulness, but nature, like the branches, can bring forth much fruit when united to the vine. While the Catholic stresses this latter point, the Protestant will stress the exclusive source of life. But the parable categorically expresses both at the same time: "You shall bear much fruit." But: "without me you can do nothing." Catholic theology has always tried to do justice to both aspects, although to be sure it has too often understood the aspect of cooperation under the forensic, and not directly biblical, concept of "merit." Because this term "merit" conjures up the idea of a claim of the creature upon the Creator, Protestant theology has shunned it. But one can make the fact of authentic creaturely cooperation with grace less abrasive and yet no less urgent through the Lord's preferred image: the branch of the vine bearing fruit. The principle of fruitfulness is the vine, not the grape, and yet who could conceive of a grapevine without grapes? (*KB*, 387–388)

So it is not Barth's christological focus *per se* that Balthasar finds objectionable, only the way Barth exaggerates the communication between Christ and believer so that it really only goes in one direction and true mutuality is lost. Because of this exaggeration, Barth has a hard time explaining how the life from the vine enters into the innermost depths of the believer with a *transformative* power. In his attempt to preserve grace as truly grace without any taint of merit, Barth has transposed its trans-formative power into a purely eschatological reality. But for Balthasar, "God's grace is a participation in his inner divine life. As such it raises the creature above and beyond any claims or longings it might possess. This participation is neither purely forensic nor purely eschatological, but is real, internal and present. It is an event that effects a transformation of the very being of the creature" (*KB*, 377).

But if this is true, then we must allow for a certain *distance* between God and creature so that the creature can gradually grow in grace. Trans-formation of a creature is an idea whose correlate is that of time: it takes time to be transformed, just as grapes do not emerge suddenly in full bloom from the vine. Redemption, since it was effected by the incarnation, by definition must respect our incarnate lives. That is why Balthasar can say that

> because of this character of grace (to be an event of transforma-tion), it leaves room for all real events and phases that make up man's way to God: conversion, progress, backsliding, coopera-tion and obstacles. Redemption is not effected "in one lump," so to speak, as if all the petty details of daily life were ultimately meaningless (since in this view they have been relegated to a dead past under the gaze of eternity). Redemption comes to us respecting our incarnate lives in time, leaving room for us to continue to change as we follow in the footsteps of the incarnate Lord. The steps we take in this discipleship have their own inher-ent meaning and weight. God takes our decisions seriously, working them into his plans by his holy providence.[25]

According to Balthasar, this is what the doctrine of analogy is meant to say; far from collapsing God and creation into a wider and more-controlling schema, analogy of being is meant to put into conceptual terms the distance that inheres in the relationship between God and creature— a distance which, in Barthian terms, is the presupposition for the transfor-mation that gives us a share in the divine life. That is why Balthasar can conclude with a certain trenchancy:

> The attempt by Karl Barth and his disciples to bind the distinc-tively Catholic doctrines with (a philosophical) doctrine of *ana-logia entis* at any price has failed. . . . Whether we are discussing

---

[25] *KB*, 377–378. This passage, which occurs quite early (1951) in the chronology of Baltha-sar's works, succinctly establishes the foundation for his later Theodramatics.

church structures (e.g., an infallible magisterium or the objective grace "contained" in the sacraments) or Christian's "cooperation" with grace (e.g., "merits," "holiness" and especially the doctrines of Mary's own holiness), we are really talking about God's free use of the human world he created in Christ. And God is free enough even to use the human condition and the natural world or to endow an analogous form of himself in one of his created natures. (*KB*, 387)

By allowing for such a distance, we also make room for a real drama, for only this perspective lets there be real significance in the response of a human being to the word of revelation. This is an important point, because it will have direct bearing on Balthasar's own theology of dramatic forms, which constitutes the middle part of his trilogy. So crucial is this to his thought and so central is this notion to his entire vision of Christianity that it leads him to make what is probably the most effective criticism of Barth ever leveled and which his own later work will try to resolve:

> Too much in Barth gives the impression that nothing much really *happens* in his theology of event and history, because everything has already happened in eternity: for example, . . . he rejects the Catholic and Lutheran doctrine that the sacraments effect and cause real change. [Moreover] he transposes time [in such a way that] sin is ever-past and justification ever-future, and rejects all talk of growth, progress—even of a possible lapse and loss of grace and of faith. In short, Barth rejects all discussion of anything in the realm of the relative and temporal that would make for a real and vibrant history of man with his redeeming Lord and God. (*KB*, 371)

And this gives to Barth's theology of the Church a strangely pale cast; not only is it hard to see the Church as genuinely the Body of Christ but the image of Bride is even harder to justify, because in the image of marriage we finally *do* have a metaphor entailing a genuine partnership! Nothing more undermines Barth's whole polemic against analogy of being, nothing so deeply challenges his view of the one-directional flow of grace, nothing gets closer to the legitimacy of Balthasar's accusation of christological "narrowness" in Barth, than the biblical doctrine that the Church is the Bride of Christ. For here we have the clearest assertion in the Bible that Christ means for the Church—and by extension, each believer—to be a self-subsistent being, with an autonomy and a power to say Yes on her own that cannot be taken from her. Perhaps there are aspects of revelation and of the economy of divine grace where the image of the hourglass and of reflector lights *might* be appropriate, but they completely break down when we come to appreciate the meaning of the mutuality between Christ and his Church expressed in the biblical image of the Bride.[26]

In the course of this book, we shall come to see how important these issues have proved to be for Balthasar. Out of his encounter with Barth, he came to have a new appreciation for the nature of event, both in the positive sense that Barth gave it, but also in the fuller sense that he himself came to give it in his disputes with Barth. This he attempted to develop in his five-volume theodramatics. But also in his more direct encounter with this great *magister* of 20th-century Protestantism, Balthasar came to appreciate with a new depth the importance of understanding the Church as the Bride of Christ, an insight that shaped his ecclesiology from that moment on. And both of these legacies come together in perhaps what is the single most important contribution of Balthasar to contemporary theology: his concept of mission. Mission for Balthasar is both a moment in the individual's drama with God but is also inherently ecclesial. These are themes whose implications can only emerge in the course of this study, but their development owes a lot to the encounter with Barth, both in the sense of what he learned from him and in the sense of what he developed in response to perceived deficiencies in Barth. But in both cases, he was able to grow in finding his own voice and his own convictions from his early and intense encounter with his fellow Basler. And out of this engagement would emerge positions which he would fully develop only later on but which even in the Barth book had already been present with a powerful articulation:

> What the Protestant considers to be human overreaching in the Catholic Church is for her the sign of the most extreme condescension of divine grace, which is at the same time, then, the very high point of grace's power. And here the Catholic would

---

[26] This also leaves in tatters Barth's rather annoying habit of associating all theological viewpoints opposed to his own with the Nazis; he had even been willing, at least for a short period after the war, to link the Roman Church with National Socialism. Balthasar is too serene and confident in his own faith to take too much umbrage at this odd pose. But he is willing to see it, and shrewdly so, as part of Barth's wider difficulties with Christ's incarnation in his Church: "And here we can finally see the common roots to his opposition both to Romanism and National Socialism. However different they both are, Barth has to say No to both of them, because in both, however differently they each conceive it, there is a claim made by an institution that will not admit of being relativized. Of course, in Nazi ideology this claim is sheer effrontery, whereas the claim of the Roman *ordo* bears on the truth. But Rome still makes a worldly and total claim on the spirit and conscience of man, whereas such a claim can only be raised in the name of Christ. The point here, though, is to see that in both cases what Barth sees is Institution writ large" (*KB*, 246).

do well to bear in mind that what at first sight seems like a case of grace elevating nature is really due to grace descending into nature: it is grace itself that assumes hierarchical and institutional forms in the Church in order the better to lay hold of man, who is of course a being bound by nature, structure and law. But it is also grace itself that takes shape in the most personal aspects of a believer's life through the charismatic mission of a vocation in order to transform the unique talents and traits of the individual into what grace alone can envisage. (*KB*, 387)

· 3 ·

Goethe, Nietzsche and the
Encounter with German Idealism

Vergebens werden ungebundne Geister
Nach der Vollendung reiner Höhe streben.
In der Beschränkung zeigt sich erst der Meister,
Und das Gesetz nur kann uns Freiheit geben.

In vain do unfettered spirits aspire
To the pure heights of all perfection.
Only in limits can we become the master,
And the law alone frees as manumitter.

Goethe
"Natur und Kunst"

In a revealing interview Hans Urs von Balthasar once mentioned that the best way of understanding the differences between himself and the renowned Karl Rahner, his great rival in 20th-century Catholic theology, would be to see them as each representing one of the two major—and contradictory—strains of German culture: those represented, respectively, by Goethe and Kant. According to Balthasar, Rahner has adopted the Kantian view, whereas he, Balthasar, appeals for his methodological starting point to Goethe:

> First I would like to say that I consider Karl Rahner to be, on the whole, the strongest theological power of our time. And it is evident that he is far superior to me in speculative power. In 1939 we worked together on a plan for a new work in dogmatics ... which later became *Mysterium Salutis*. But our starting points had actually always been different. There is a book by [Georg] Simmel called *Kant und Goethe*. Rahner has chosen Kant, or if you prefer, Fichte: the transcendental starting point. And I—as a Germanist—have chosen Goethe, [who stressed] the

figure: this indissolubly unique, organic, self-developing form (I am thinking of Goethe's *Metamorphosis of Plants*). This form [is] something that Kant, even in his aesthetics, never really dealt with.[1]

This remark goes far to explain the source of the tension between these two great theologians—but only if one first understands the tension in German culture represented by Kant and Goethe. An understanding of German culture is important, however, in a presentation of Balthasar's thought for reasons that go well beyond his polemics against Rahner: for Balthasar's doctoral degree was not in theology but what is known as "*Germanistik,*" a term not easily translated but roughly referring to a literary and cultural study of the great classic texts written in German, a kind of interdisciplinary degree established well before interdisciplinary studies became all the rage in North America.[2] What makes a study of Balthasar's work with the German classics so important is the issue of interpretation: for it was from his study of the German classics that Balthasar first received his training as a scholar and thus first came to his method of textual, and even theological, interpretation. And thus an examination of his encounter with the greats of German culture constitutes an indispensable moment in understanding his theology.[3]

What most distinguishes the treatment of a classic text in the field of *Germanistik,* as opposed to how that same text might be treated in, say, a philosophy department in the English-speaking world, is that it is, especially in Balthasar's hands, "literary" or "mythical." These terms must

---

[1] "Geist und Feuer: Ein Gespräch mit Hans Urs von Balthasar," *Herder Korrespondenz* 30 (1976): 72–82; here 75–76.

[2] "Hans Urs von Balthasar was by no means well known for divulging autobiographical details. He was sparing in the use of such information. . . . Nevertheless, in private conversation, he occasionally liked to point out with some irony that he was really a professional scholar of German literature and not a theologian, . . . a tension that was to shape not only von Balthasar's theological work, but especially his work in German literature" (Alois M. Haas, "Hans Urs von Balthasar's *Apocalypse of the German Soul:* At the Intersection of German Literature, Philosophy and Theology," *Hans Urs Von Balthasar: His Life and Work,* ed. David L. Schindler [San Francisco: Communio Books/Ignatius Press, 1991]: 45–57; here 45). This same point emerged in the above cited interview: "You address me as a theologian or a theological writer," was Balthasar's reply to one question, "but I never got my doctorate in theology; by nature and upbringing I am a Germanist" (73).

[3] "With the dissertation and his final oral examination . . . that Balthasar completed on 27 October 1928 at the University of Zurich, he concluded his study of *Germanistik.* But because he decided not to get another doctorate but only went so far as to get a Licentiate in the course of his philosophical and theological studies as a member of the Society of Jesus, his doctorate in *Germanistik* is an especially important moment in Balthasar's intellectual formation" (Johannes Gesthuisen, *Das Nietzsche-Bild Hans Urs von Balthasars: Ein Zugang zur "Apokalypse der deutschen Seele* [Rome: Pontifical Gregorian University Press, 1986], 15).

be used with some trepidation, for the potential for misunderstanding is great. Balthasar's own preferred term for his method of analysis in this work is "mythical," which we shall define in a moment, but in describing his work also as "literary" I am trying to highlight a central fact: the inclusivity of the texts brought under consideration. "Literary," therefore, is meant not to restrict the kind of texts studied (fiction as opposed to fact, for example, which is what the word most connotes in English) but to contrast it with either a purely analytic approach or with the historical-critical method to which it is to some extent a rival.[4] Texts, that is, are taken on their own terms and not as defective testimonials to the past out of which they came. This is partly due to the fact that many of the texts studied *are* literary in nature and mean to create their own world, but it is also because the habit of pigeonholing the study of texts into various specializations and departments has never been as pervasive in the German university system as it has been here, as the distinguished tradition of *Germanistik* itself attests.

Once we get into the later parts of this book, we shall notice at various points how centrally the issue of the interpretation of texts will continue to recur and how much Balthasar's own unique voice as a theologian is due to the distinctive approach he takes to this hermeneutical issue, including especially the issue of interpreting the Bible. But a full appreciation of these interpretive methods requires that we first see what he gained from his encounter with the classical texts of German culture, culminating in his three-volume study *The Apocalypse of the German Soul*.[5] It should

---

[4] In other words, by calling his study "literary" we are referring neither to the texts selected for treatment (works of the imagination as opposed to historical, philosophical or theological texts) nor to the kind of methods that were once taken for granted in most literature departments in the English-speaking world when the New Criticism held sway. The term is somewhat hard to define until one sees it in action ("cultural" as opposed to "historical," or "synchronic" as opposed to "diachronic" might be other ways of giving an initial description). Perhaps the best way of characterizing his approach to texts is to note first the wide net he casts, hauling in texts from nearly all genres, and secondly his insistence that they be taken above all on their own terms. There are rather interesting parallels in his methods with those of the so-called postmodern school; see Jeffrey Kay, "Hans Urs von Balthasar: ein nachkritischer Theologe?" *Concilium* 7 (1981): 86–90.

[5] *Apokalypse der deutschen Seele: Studien zu einer Lehre von letzten Haltungen;* Vol. I: *Der deutsche Idealismus* (Salzburg: A. Pustet, 1937); Vol. II: *Im Zeichen Nietzsches* (1939); Vol. III: *Die Vergöttlichung des Todes* (1940). These three volumes are a considerably expanded version of his doctoral dissertation, *Geschichte des eschatologischen Problems in der modernen deutschen Literatur* (University of Zurich: unpublished dissertation, 1930). Because of its central thesis, that the German soul was especially prone to the lure of nihilistic utopianisms, the work ran afoul of the book-burning frenzy of the Nazis and copies of it are quite scarce. The first volume was later published as *Prometheus: Studien der Geschichte des deutschen Idealismus* (Heidelberg: F. H. Kerle, 1947), but Balthasar felt that this work needed further revision and that his more definitive views regarding these thinkers were best distilled in his two volumes on metaphysics in *Herrlichkeit* and therefore he refused to

be said at the outset that the texts chosen for treatment are inclusive and the method, while explicitly theological, is neither purely apologetic nor philosophical. Balthasar's method is both "intertextual" in the sense of ranging across a wide spectrum of texts (including all the seminal works of German culture from the advent of the language in the Middle Ages to the poetry of Rilke in the 20th century) and in the sense of refusing to categorize texts into neat subsections (literature, history, poetry, Bible, theology, etc.), each with its own special method. We might sum up his method in a very preliminary way by saying that every text must be taken on its own terms and none are to be excluded by reason of its genre.[6]

Nor is "literary" to be understood in opposition to "theological," a frequent implication of the word in its current usage. Balthasar's own term for his method, as we have noted, is "mythical"—a label which is open to more potential misunderstanding than even "literary" is. What Balthasar is seeking to establish, however, is that the dominant eschatological myths of German thought (Prometheus, Dionysus, twilight of the gods, etc.) arise from the refusal to make the (analogical) distinction between God and world. This results in either an attempt to effect a complete transfiguration of the world and a divinization of the earth (Marx) or a pure collapse into nothingness and nihilistic despair (Nietzsche). These myths thus arise out of a distention which is *in fact* an aspect of the distention of the arms of Christ on the Cross: "In this way all the myths of German intellectual history find themselves in a *reductio ad crucem*."[7] Or in Balthasar's own words at the conclusion of the third volume:

---

have the *Apokalypse* republished. Accordingly, we shall also be continually drawing on the judgments located there as well in analyzing Balthasar's attitude to Kant, Goethe, Hegel and Nietzsche.

[6] In his consistent demand that texts should always be first taken on their own terms, Balthasar's method here is deeply indebted to a remark Karl Barth made after the initial publication of his epochal commentary on Romans caused such a storm. When accused by his academic peers of violating the standards of the historical-critical method in his commentary on Paul's greatest letter, Barth insisted that he was not at all being "biblicist" (roughly, the equivalent of the term "fundamentalist" today) or obscurantist, or trying to isolate the text of the Bible in some esoteric bubble immune to the corroding acid of historical scholarship, as if the Bible "dropped down" from heaven like some UFO. On the contrary, the text was there as a text and needed to be interpreted as such: "It is my so-called 'biblicism' that forbids me to allow the mark of competent scholarship to be that of the critic disclosing fragments of past history and then leaving them—unexplained. I have, moreover, no desire to conceal the fact that my 'biblicist' method—which means in the end no more than 'consider well'—is applicable also to the study of Lao-Tse and of Goethe. . . . When I am labeled a 'biblicist' all that can rightly be proved against me is that I am prejudiced in supposing the Bible to be a good book and that I hold it to be profitable for men to take its conceptions at least as seriously as they take their own" (Karl Barth, *The Epistle to the Romans*, 12).

[7] Haas, 5.

The distention of existence between "life" and "spirit," between "Prometheus" and "the goddess soul," between existential and ideal truth, between earth and heaven, this distention of existence, which imparts to it its final attitude and its full truth, is a crucifixion. The "contradiction" of the entire dialectic of Idealism, like the "contradiction" between nature and spirit is *mythically* and concretely the crossing of the beams of the Cross. . . . This is why even "Prometheus bound" and "Dionysus crucified" find their enlightenment here.[8]

Perhaps the key to Balthasar's method in this teeming and fascinating work is to be found not in the labels he or we choose to give it but in the title: apocalypse—the Greek word for "unveiling." In an article written after the publication of the first volume of the *Apokalypse* for a Catholic magazine in Austria, Balthasar explains the purpose of this work in precisely these terms: "[I am attempting] to dig down into the wellspring of living water surging up in the souls of the great Germans from Lessing, Herder and Kant to Nietzsche, Rilke, Heidegger and Barth, in order to 'unveil' (*apo-calypse*) their innermost religious essence, which will itself reveal to us the souls of the great Germans and thus also the German Soul itself in its attitude toward the Last Things."[9] A perhaps even more indicative manifesto of his program comes at the beginning of the *Apokalypse* itself, where Balthasar avers:

> Our first task will therefore be to search for the ultimate stance of the German spirit using the guiding motif of the eschatological mythic. This is a constellation of myths which this spirit has created for itself as the reflection and expression of its self-understanding. The verbal essence of an era should be revealed

---

[8] *A* 3, 434–435: "Die Ausdehnung des Daseins zwischen 'Leben' und 'Geist,' zwischen 'Prometheus' und der 'Göttin Seele,' zwischen existentialer und idealer Wahrheit, zwischen Erde und Himmel, diese Ausdehnung des Daseins, die ihm allererst seine Letzthaltung und seine volle Wahrheit gibt, diese Ausdehnung ist eine Kreuzigung. Der 'Widerspruch' der ganzen idealistischen Dialektik wie der 'Widerspruch' zwischen Natur und Geist ist *mythisch* und konkret das Sich-Kreuzen der Kreuzbalken. . . . Hier finden deshalb auch der 'gefesselte Prometheus' und 'der gekreuzigte Dionysus' ihre Aufklärung."

[9] "Apocalypse der deutschen Seele," *Schönere Zukunft* 14 (1938):57–59; here 57: "[den Versuch] in den Seelen der großen Deutschen von Lessing, Herder, Kant bis zu Nietzsche, Rilke, Heidegger und Barth nach den Quellen lebendigen Wassers zu graben, jene 'Enthüllung' (Apo-kalypse) ihres innersten, religiösen Wesens zu vollziehen, welche uns die Seelen der großen Deutschen und damit auch die Deutsche Seele selbst in ihren letzten Haltungen offenbart." In light of these remarks it is difficult to decide whether Balthasar is being serious or ironic when he said that he changed the title of Volume I of the *Apokalypse* (to *Prometheus*) in 1947 "because of the American declaration at the time that 'a German soul' had in the meantime ceased to exist" (*MW*, 104).

clustered around the eschatological mythos of its period in history: and the soul of each epoch should be more clearly reflected in the Image than in any abstract theory.[10]

In other words, this work is *not* an exercise in that kind of "theology of literature" that tends to baptize whatever it reads and sees Christ symbols in every protagonist. While the work is frankly theological,[11] it is in no way an imposed interpretation, for according to Balthasar, "the history of the eschatological problem [is] a history of myths."[12] And thus his method is one in which the eschatological myths of German thought are brought to light and seen for their true implications:

This is our immediate justification for taking up above all the image-history [*Bildwerdung*] in the literary-eschatological parable. But by this literary and humanistic inquiry we encounter at the same time a deeper question: What causes an era to make use of precisely *this* mythos as its self-expression (for example, why does German thought so often revert to Prometheus, Faust, Don Juan, and especially the eschatological myths of the Twilight of the Gods, the Anti-Christ, the returning of Christ, the immolation of the world in fire, etc.)?[13]

In this chapter, we shall follow the same method employed in Chapter 1 and first discuss in general terms the nature of the debate between the

---

[10] *A* 1, 8–9: "Unser erste Aufgabe wird es also sein, die Letzthaltung des deutschen Geistes am Leitfaden der eschatologischen Mythik zu suchen, welche sich dieser Geist als Spiegel und Ausdruck seines Selbstverstehens geschaffen hat. Um eschatologischen Mythus einer Zeitspanne soll sich das eigentliche Wesenswort dieser Zeit offenbaren, im Bilde sich, klarer als in jeder abstrakten Theorie, die Seele der Epoche spiegeln."

[11] And why not? This hardly does violence to the text but simply sets it in its proper context: "I tried [in this work] to show that Being and the subject in their phenomenal dimension are always richer and deeper than what the surface shows. . . . Naturally this implies that an indirect light from Christian revelation descends upon the object of philosophy. But before the encounter with Christianity [took place], all philosophy that had any vitality was at the same time a kind of theology. And once it encounters Christianity, philosophy can maintain its vitality only in a passionate conversation with the theology of revelation—indeed in the readiness to let its hidden theological implications be illumined by the latter" (*MW*, 21).

[12] *Geschichte des eschatologischen Problems* (the unpublished dissertation that was later expanded into the three-volume *Apokalyspe*), 3.

[13] *A* 1, 9: "Dies rechtfertigt es unmittelbar, daß die Bildwerdung im dichterisch-eschatologischen Gleichnis uns besonders beschäftigen wird. Aber durch die literarisch-geisteswissenschaftlichen Fragen . . . dringen wir sogleich zur tieferen: Was veranlaßt eine Zeit, sich gerade *dieses* Mythus (etwa Prometheus, Faust, Don Juan, und spezieller eschatologisch: Götterdämmerung, Antichrist, wiederkehrender Christus, Weltbrand, usw.) als ihres Selbstausdrucks zu bedienen?"

Kantian and Goethean streams in German culture and above all why the eschatological theme is so dominant in German thought, then in the second section we shall describe Balthasar's own position in this debate. In this presentation, we shall be drawing primarily on his work *Apocalypse* (and contemporaneous essays) but also on his later formulations in *Herrlichkeit*, especially where these have superseded his earlier views.[14]

I

After the recent collapse of Communism in Eastern Europe and the reunification of Germany, the esteemed editor of *Die Welt* and the author of a famous biography of Adolf Hitler, Joachim Fest, published a book called *The Shattered Dream*, which said that only now, near the turn of the millennium, has Europe in the 20th century finally been given the chance to shake off the two utopian visions of Karl Marx and Adolf Hitler . . . with the great question remaining what history would do with the opportunity.[15] The remark was startling in its juxtaposition of two men who would hardly seem to have much more in common than their native language, but it does point up, in its own macabre sort of way, a number of points worth keeping in mind in our subsequent discussion of German culture: first, the extraordinary influence that ideas hatched in Germany have had on world culture and history, reshaping maps and destinies with a power unmatched by any other culture the past two centuries; and second, the place that Utopianism (itself a form of eschatology with its own mythology) held in the imagination of so many German minds—and from them, the minds of so many people inside and outside of Europe.

My point in noting the outcome of such utopian influence is not to make invidious comparisons with other supposedly less utopian cultures (vast numbers of the human race, after all, have subscribed in this century to one or the other version of the Utopian vision), nor to say that these two men represent some putative "essence" of German culture, but to ask, in general terms: what was the ultimate source of energy that made German culture and ideas so influential and why did it issue, at least in these two instances, in such a malign utopianism? What kind of vision(s) animated German thought?[16] Are there counter-currents to these trends

---

[14] Thus this chapter will be a comprehensive treatment of Balthasar's encounter with German thought, encompassing all of his writings—a strategy which will avoid repeating the same themes when the time comes to present the trilogy.

[15] Joachim Fest, *Der zerstörte Traum: vom Ende des utopischen Zeitalters* (Berlin: Siedler/Corso Books, 1991).

[16] At the outset of this chapter, I wish to clear up several potential misunderstandings from this attempt to establish the extraordinary weight that ideas, and in this case, German ideas especially, can have in history. First, in the course of this work I shall not be "blaming," for example, the Nazis on Nietzsche or the Gulag on Marx—still less on Utopianism. Nor

and if so, how are they to be interpreted? And can the clashes within the German thought world still be understood as expressions of some other overarching and more unifying vision (much like Plato and Aristotle still share something identifiably Greek despite their evident differences)?

Utopianism gains its power, as Hegel well knew, from man's "unhappy consciousness," a crucial term in German Idealism.[17] Hegel inherited from Descartes and Kant a philosophical tradition that stressed the substantial difference between knowing subject and known object. But so radically bifurcated were these two realms of *res cogitans* and *res extensa* that consciousness itself was bound to feel alienated, a stranger in the world

---

do I see a direct connection between ideas and certain turning points in history: too many accidents and chance constellations came together in the take-overs of Lenin and Hitler to claim a cause-and-effect connection between ideas and the seizure of power by the Communists in Russia and the Nazis in Germany (such accidents would include Lenin's ability to get a safe passage on the train from Zurich to Moscow in 1917, or Hindenburg's acquiescence in Hitler's assumption of the Chancellorship despite the fact that the Nazis had lost seats in the Reichstag in the election of 6 November 1932). And it is farthest from my intention to see something opaquely but really present in that hypothetical specimen "the German character" which led" to Marx, or Hitler, or . . . anybody. For one thing, at least in the case of the Nazis, I do not think their ideology would have possessed whatever meager plausibility it did have on men's minds without the prior influence of social Darwinism as one element in its lethal mixture. The following citation does not come from *Mein Kampf* or from the overheated paeans to the Blond Beast in Nietzsche's writings, but from the pen of Charles Darwin: "Looking at the world at no very distant date, what an endless number of the lower races will have been eliminated by the higher civilized races throughout the world" (Letter of 3 July 1881 to W. Graham, *The Life and Letters of Charles Darwin*, ed. Francis Darwin [London: J. Murray, 1888], Vol. I: 316). Fest himself has an interesting essay on precisely this theme of the connection between national character and national guilt. He points out that, ironically, this attitude of so-called "national guilt" stems from the same Utopian imagination that has so influenced German thought: "The condemnation of society, vague and undefined as that concept is used, is ultimately an attempt to free oneself from society: by accusing the generality of injustice and weakness, one simultaneously announces one's responsibility while also getting rid of it" (Joachim C. Fest, "Die Schuld der Gesellschaft," *Aufgehobene Vergangenheit* [Stuttgart: Deutsche Verlags-Anstalt, 1981], 147–149; here 148).

[17] This is because in German Idealism, "consciousness" denotes not a mood or a feeling but a total sense of self-in-the-world, defining all one's relations to world and self; and therefore the "unhappy" consciousness is rooted in the structures of that world: "Hegel starts the dialectic of self-consciousness with the famous dialectic of the master and slave. The contradiction underlying this is the following: men strive for recognition, for only in this way can they achieve integrity. But recognition must be mutual. The being whose recognition of me is going to count for me must be one that I recognize as human. . . . The contradiction arises when men at a raw and undeveloped stage of history try to wrest recognition from another without reciprocating. . . . This leads to armed struggle. And necessarily so, says Hegel" (Charles Taylor, *Hegel* [Cambridge: Cambridge University Press, 1975], 153). And Marx continues the same analysis, at least on the formal level: "The suppression [*Aufhebung*] of self-estrangement follows the same course as self-estrangement" (Karl Marx, "The Third Manuscript," *Economic and Philosophical Manuscripts of 1844*, ed. and intro. Dirk J. Struik [New York: International Publishers, 1964], 132).

set over against it. And this Hegel set out to cure through a descriptive analysis ("phenomenology") of the knowing subject (*Geist*). We get some idea of the almost religious power of his healing vision in some remarks by the American philosopher John Dewey on the lessons he drew from his reading of Hegel:

> But the sense of divisions and separations that were, I suppose, borne in upon me as a consequence of a heritage of New England culture, divisions by way of isolation of self from the world, of soul from body, of nature from God, brought a painful oppression—or, rather, they were an inward laceration. My earlier philosophic study had been an intellectual gymnastic. Hegel's synthesis of subject and object, matter and spirit, the divine and human, was however no mere intellectual formula; it operated as an immense release, a liberation. Hegel's treatment of institutions and the arts involved the same dissolution of hard-and-fast dividing walls, and had a special attraction for me.[18]

Dewey's pathos is clearly a religious pain and the cure that he sought was equally so; and the same may be said of Hegel too. One of the significant lessons Dewey had drawn from Hegel was the belief that all philosophical doctrines are not just historically located but also contextually determined ("the distinctive office, problems and subject matter of philosophy grow out of the stresses and strains in the community life in which a given form of philosophy arises"[19]). What then made Hegel's philosophy both so religious and yet also so therapeutic of the divisions which religion had come to express? And why did such therapy yield so easily to utopian hopes? To answer this question, we shall trace these issues back to their real context: to Kant and Goethe, and then see Hegel's response together with the collapse of his synthesis in Nietzsche. Then we

---

[18] John Dewey, "From Absolutism to Experimentalism," *John Dewey on Experience, Nature and Freedom,* ed. Richard J. Bernstein (New York: Liberal Arts Press, 1960), 10. Dewey wrote this essay to explain his eventual rejection of Hegelianism in favor of a more Anglo-Saxon empiricism, but he never kidded himself about the loss this entailed: "The chief intellectual characteristic of the present age is its despair of any constructive philosophy—not just its technical meaning, but in the sense of any integrated outlook and attitude. The developments of the last century have gone so far that we are now aware of the shock and overthrow in older beliefs. ... Skepticism becomes the mark and even the pose of the educated mind. It is more influential because it is no longer directed against this or that article of the older creeds but is rather a bias against any kind of far-reaching ideas, and a denial of systematic participation on the part of such idea in the intelligent direction of affairs" ("What I Believe," *John Dewey: The Later Works, 1925–1953,* ed. Jo Ann Boydston [Carbondale: Southern Illinois Press, 1984/1930] 5:276–278; here 276).

[19] John Dewey, *Reconstruction in Philosophy,* in *John Dewey: The Middle Works, 1899–1924,* ed. Jo Ann Boydston (Carbondale: Southern Illinois University Press, 1982) 12:256.

will conclude by seeing what Balthasar drew from the resources of these four thinkers.

a. Kant and Goethe:

Neither Kant nor Goethe can be understood except in terms of the Newtonian world view they both inherited and which they both struggled to humanize. Isaac Newton's *Principia Mathematica* (1687), with its mathematical specification of the law of gravity and its subsumption of all motion under this one law, caused an immense crisis to the European mind almost upon its publication. This is because it seemed to mechanize the entire physical universe, leaving only one apparent exception: the knowing subject that could recognize such a mathematically rule-governed mechanism. But this lone exception had then to look out on a world without value, one it could no longer call home: "Because of the mechanistic principle of the natural sciences, reality seemed to be placed in complete contrast to all that previously had seemed to give meaning to this reality: it had no more room for ideas, values, purposes, for religious meaning and moral freedom."[20]

Immanuel Kant's (1724–1804) solution was fundamentally one of juxtaposition, indeed outright dualism: subject over against object, mind over against matter, the freedom of the moral subject over against the law-governed behavior of physical bodies, the *subjective* perception of beauty over against the *objective* sterility of the Newtonian universe (which, because of entropy, was dissipating into complete uniformity and sameness). These juxtapositions were set forth in his three Critiques: *The Critique of Pure Reason* (1787), *The Critique of Practical Reason* (1788), and *The Critique of [Aesthetic] Judgment* (1790). The order of their publication is crucial, for this ranking implied not only that the theoretical reason of the first Critique can be neatly divided from the practical reason of the second and from the appreciation of beauty discussed in the third Critique, but that practical reason and aesthetics will always be subordinate to and reliant on the discoveries of pure reason. In this as in so much else of his philosophy, Kant adopted as his own the very Newtonian assumptions it was the intent of his philosophy to undermine.

Because the Newtonian universe was so relentlessly mechanical, the question immediately arose: did the human mind also obey these same mechanical rules? If the answer were proven to be Yes, then obviously free will was an illusion as was the belief in the immortality of the soul.

---

[20] Georg Simmel, *Kant und Goethe: Zur Geschichte der modernen Weltanschauung* (Leipzig: Kurt Wolff Verlag, n.d.), 9: "Durch das mechanistisch-naturwissenschaftliche Prinzip scheint die Wirklichkeit in völligen Gegensatz zu allem gestellt, was dieser Wirklichkeit bis dahin Sinn zu geben schien: sie hat keinen Raum mehr für Ideen, Werte, Zwecke, für religiöse Bedeutung und sittliche Freiheit."

Kant set out not only to fight these implications but more crucially to do so *in terms of the reigning Newtonian paradigm,*[21] and his solution was ingenious: in Newton's world, space and time are "absolutes," that is, abstract grids or coordinates within which bodies careen and can be located. But in Kant's interpretation, space and time are "constituted" by the human mind; that is, the sensations of the physical world bombard the mind, but the mind *structures* these sensory data according to its own categories of understanding, the primary ones being the forms of space and time. In other words, the mechanical world view of Newton is true but is itself constituted by the human subject's categories of understanding, which impose on the sense data the absolutes of space and time.

This "Copernican turn" of perspective, as Kant called it, at once alters the terms of the problem, for no longer is the subject enmeshed in the cause-effect nexus of the physical world but is rather the constituting foundation of it.[22] But there was a price to be paid for such a finessing of the problem. First of all, any literally *meta*-physical speculations regarding God, freedom or the immortality of the soul were ruled out, because pure reason could only reliably function when it had sensory data to work with: the categories of understanding were meant to impose form and intelligibility upon sense data, without which they had no legitimate speculative function. But secondly, we could reach a *practical* certainty of such matters as the existence of God and the immortality of the soul through the practical action of leading moral lives; that is, we could come to an experience of freedom only by the defiant assertion of that freedom in spite of the deterministic world revealed by Newton.

But the price to be paid lies in the raw and unassimilated juxtaposition of the sovereignty of the subject's freedom over against the relentless determinism of the physical universe. Simmel, already cited by Balthasar in this regard, neatly summarizes the implications of this Kantian method and why it would prove so unsatisfactory to Goethe and Hegel:

> First, there is the juxtaposition of subject and object, which modernity has worked up into the sharpest contrast. The thinking

---

[21] "It is not going too far to suggest that [Kant's] most basic problem was: *How are autonomy and free will possible in a deterministic Newtonian universe?*" (Walter Kaufmann, *Discovering the Mind*, Vol. I: *Goethe, Kant, Hegel* [New York: McGraw-Hill, 1980], 86; author's emphasis).

[22] As Kaufmann points out, Kant's choice of metaphor leaves something to be desired: "Kant claimed to have accomplished a Copernican revolution. Actually, his appeal is inseparable from the fact that in his *Critique of Pure Reason* he brought off an *anti*-Copernican revolution. He reversed Copernicus' stunning blow to human self-esteem. Before Copernicus the Western world had believed that man was at the center of the universe and that the sun revolved around our earth. Copernicus's doctrine involved what Freud liked to call a 'cosmological mortification' of man's self-love. . . . [But Kant] restored man to the center of

"I" feels itself sovereign in relation to the whole world present before him. The sentence "I think, therefore I am (and therefore the world also is)" becomes the single indubitable feature of existence, however much that sentence is reconfigured or further developed. But on the other hand this objective world still has a merciless facticity; and precisely after this division the "I" appears as the objective world's product to which its powers have been interwoven no less than with the case of a plant or a cloud. And so not only the world of nature but also that of society lives on, split in two. In this world of society the individual demands the right of freedom and uniqueness, while [nature] wants to recognize the individual only as an element that is subordinate to its supra-personal laws. In both cases, the self-mastery of the subject is in danger of being swallowed up by an objectivity foreign to it or of falling prey into an anarchistic arbitrariness and isolation.[23]

Johann Wolfgang Goethe (1749–1832) rejected this approach—meaning not just the Kantian attempt to finesse the problem of Newton but the whole of Newtonian physics as well—with a visceral and almost bodily revulsion. For him, "measurements, numbers and signs do not constitute a phenomenon."[24] Virtually the whole of his professional life was spent trying to fight off the implications of Newtonianism, whether in his theory of colors, his botanical researches, and even in his poetry; and not to understand his objections to philosophical Newtonianism is in effect not to understand Balthasar's theological methodology. So consistent was Goethe's polemic against Newton and so high is the repute of Newton in the history of the Western mind that his consistent rebellion against Newtonian science has caused considerable embarrassment among his advocates and interpreters, who generally relegate his scientific activities

---

the world and actually accorded even greater importance to man than the Book of Genesis had done. He tried to prove that it is the human mind that gives nature its laws" (87–88).

[23] Simmel, 7–8: "Zunächst ist es das Gegenüber von Subjekt und Objekt, das die Neuzeit zu schärfstem Gegensatz herausarbeitet. Das denkende Ich fühlt sich souverän gegenüber der ganzen, von ihm vorgestellten Welt, das 'Ich denke, und also bin ich—und also ist auch die Welt'—wird, wie umgestaltet und weiterentwickelt auch immer, zur einzigen Unbezweifelbarkeit des Daseins. Aber andrerseits hat diese objektive Welt doch eine unbarmherzige Tatsächlichkeit, gerade nach dieser Trennung erscheint das Ich als ihr Produkt, zu dem ihre Kräfte sich nicht anders als zu der Gestalt einer Pflanze oder einer Wolke verwebt haben. Und so entzweit lebt nicht nur die Welt der Natur, sondern auch die der Gesellschaft. In ihr fordert der Einzelne das Recht der Freiheit und Besonderheit, während sie ihn nur als ein Element, das ihren überpersönlichen Gesetzen untertan ist, anerkennen will. In beiden Fällen droht die Selbstherrlichkeit des Subjekts entweder von einer ihm fremden Objektivität verschlungen zu werden oder in anarchistische Willkür und Isolierung zu verfallen."

[24] Goethe, *Dünndruckausgabe*, ed. G. Ipsen, 2:678.

to the charming and edifying spectacle of an amusing hobby indulged in by a genius whose real talents lay in other directions.

So embedded is this view that it has become something of a cliché which can only be overcome with effort. In an important testimonial, T. S. Eliot once described how much this same spell had on his mind as well: "For most of my life I had taken it for granted that Goethe's scientific theories . . . were no more than the amiable eccentricities of a man of abounding curiosity who had strayed into regions for which he was not equipped."[25] This same essay describes in fascinating detail how Eliot came to suspect he might be wrong, a journey that he felt had proven to be liberating ("And antipathy overcome, when it is antipathy to any figure so great as that of Goethe, is an important liberation from a limitation of one's own mind"[26]). What made Eliot especially suspicious of his prejudices was the sheer unanimous weight with which Conventional Wisdom had rendered its verdict on Goethe's scientific efforts: "It was, first, the unanimity of ridicule and the ease with which the learned in these matters appear to dismiss Goethe's views, [that] impelled me to wonder whether Goethe may not have been right, or at least whether his critics might not be wrong."[27]

The distinction is perhaps subtle but crucial: if we insist that an appreciation of Goethe's scientific (and highly polemical) views must entail a rejection of the mathematical law of gravity, for example, then of course his science must be rejected. But it is precisely on the basis of such easy (and lazy) disjunctions that so many have been led to dismiss Goethe out of hand without seeing what he was driving at.[28] For Goethe cannot be understood unless we see him as trying to get beyond the disjunctions represented by Newtonian mechanism, Kantian dualism and the Romantic sentimentality that came in reaction to both Newton and Kant.[29] In other

---

[25] T. S. Eliot, "Goethe as the Sage," *On Poetry and Poets* (London: Faber and Faber, 1957): 207–227; here 214.

[26] Ibid., 210.

[27] Ibid., 215. Another important scholar of the German mind puts it similarly: "It may have become clear by now that Goethe's physics, though anti-Newtonian in motivation, is in fact not anti-mathematical, but as it were a-mathematical, which is as much as to say that it is not physics at all—at least not in the now accepted sense of the word. Newton's and Goethe's theories never meet, except at some points of confusion on Goethe's part" (Erich Heller, *The Disinherited Mind: Essays in Modern German Literature and Thought* [London: Bowes & Bowes, 1975/1952], 24).

[28] Eliot's careful formulation, all the more careful for being formulated as a question, puts it this way: "Is it possible that Goethe was wrong only in thinking the scientists wrong, and the scientists wrong only in thinking Goethe wrong?" ("Goethe as Sage," 218).

[29] "Goethe's diagnosis of the 'universal sickness of the age' corresponds exactly to his fierce criticism of the shallow subjectivity of the romantics: they are incapable of divesting themselves productively of their subjectivity and of venturing into the world of objects" (Karl Löwith, *From Hegel to Nietzsche: The Revolution in 19th Century Thought*, tr. David E. Green [New York: Holt, Rinehart and Winston, 1964/1939], 6). Substitute Balthasar's name for Goethe's here, and one comes close to an exact description of the motivation of

words, even though literary historians of German culture freely speak of the "Age of Goethe," he cannot be understood except as a figure who, like some Titan fighting off a host of lesser gods, tries to overcome all of the dichotomizing pathologies of his age, a point which Eliot for one saw as the true mark of Goethe's genius:

> Is it not possible that Goethe, without wholly knowing what he was doing, was to assert the claims of a different type of consciousness from that which was to dominate the 19th and 20th centuries? If so, then Goethe is about as unrepresentative of his Age as a man of genius can be. And perhaps the time has come when we can say that there is something in favor of being able to see the universe as Goethe saw it, rather than as the scientists have seen it: now that the "living garment of God" has become somewhat tattered from the results of scientific manipulation.[30]

If we approach Goethe from the kind of openness Eliot recommends rather than with the naïve assurances of an allegedly more exact science, we can see how farsighted and prescient he was. This comes out most especially in a short piece Goethe wrote in 1817 on "The Four Ages of Man," which demonstrates an unusually perceptive power to anticipate the place that faith (that tattered "living garment of God") would be forced to occupy in contemporary civilization. In this essay, Goethe displays a prophetic faculty that could never have developed without his transcendence—his isolation, if you will—from the prejudices of his age. In this short but astonishingly perceptive work of only three pages, Goethe divides history into four ages: the Age of Poetry, the Age of the Holy (or Theology), the Age of Philosophy (Rationalism or Enlightenment), and finally the Prosaic Age.

The Age of Poetry describes that earliest period in history when the spirits of myth and poetry emerged out of the primeval chaos (the "*tohu webohu*" of Genesis) and wielded their undivided power over a community in which stories, naïvely narrated, constituted the very heart of the community and the poet reigned as supreme "legislator" of the tribe or clan: "For [at this time] the empire of poetry had thrived, and only he was a poet who possessed this popular faith (or knew that he had to

---

Balthasar's polemic against so much contemporary theology, especially of the transcendental school.

[30] Eliot, "Goethe as the Sage," 218–219. As Eliot warns in a remark that will be crucial when we come to Part II of this work: "We must remember that we tend to think of an Age in terms of the man whom we take as representative of it, and forget that equally a part of the man's significance may be his battle with his Age" (219).

adapt himself to it). The character of this epoch was a free, virtuous, serious and noble sensibility, exalted through its imaginative powers.[31]

But man soon finds himself thrown into new perplexities and the poetic imagination realizes that it is being beset by new terrors and apprehensions which can no longer be placated by poetic fancies and tapestries of the imagination but by a new activity of the Spirit. It is in this era, and only in this era, that God can be revealed, purifying the fear and terror of the poetic stage into a reverence that is simultaneously love and awe:

> But since man knows no boundaries in his self, even when trying to be noble, and since even the clear region of human existence does not speak to him in all circumstances, he still strives to go back into the mystery and seeks a higher source for what appears before him. And just as poetry creates Dryads and Hamadryads over whom the higher gods exert their presence, so too does theology bring forth daemons [that is, lesser gods] which it has been subordinating to itself for so long that they can finally be thought of as completely dependent on *one* God. We may call this epoch [the era of] the holy.[32]

But it cannot last, for reason will insist on doing to God what theology had done to the gods and daemons: subordinating them to a notion of the One. Only this time, the notion of the One is an abstract concept, not derived from the revelation of a living God but from reflection upon the meaning of religion as such. Goethe's description of this period is a remarkable summation of both Kant's and Hegel's philosophy of religion:

> In its greatest energy and purity, the understanding honors its earliest beginnings and rejoices in the poetic faith of the people, highly esteeming this noble need of man to recognize a highest realm. The only trouble is, the man of understanding strives to appropriate everything thinkable to terms of *his* clarity and to

---

[31] Goethe, "Geistesepochen, nach Hermanns neusten Mitteilungen," *Goethes Werke* (Hamburg: Christian Wegner Verlag, 1953) 12:298–300; here 299: "Das Reich der Poesie blüht auf, und nur der ist Poet, der den Volksglauben bestizt oder sich ihn anzueignen weiß. Der Charakter dieser Epoche ist freie, tüchtige, ernste, edle Sinnlichkeit, durch Einbildungskraft erhöht." A complete English translation of this piece is available in Volume 54 of The German Library, entitled *German Essays on Religion* (New York: Continuum, 1994).

[32] "Da jedoch der Mensch in Absicht der Veredlung sein selbst keine Grenzen kennt, auch die klare Region des Daseins ihm nicht in allen Umständen zusagt, so strebt er ins Geheimnis zurück, sucht höhere Ableitung dessen, was ihm erscheint. Und wie die Poesie Dryaden und Hamadryaden schafft, über denen höhere Götter ihr Wesen treiben, so erzeugt die Theologie Dämonen, die sie so lange einander unterordnet, bis sie zuletzt sämtlich von *einem* Gotte abhängig gedacht werden. Diese Epoche dürfen wir die heilige nennen" (*GW* 12, 299).

dissolve even the most mysterious of phenomena. This in no way means that the faith of the people and the priests has been rejected, but behind that same faith what the man of understanding assumes is something conceivable, commendable, useful. He seeks for the meaning and transforms the unique into the general, deriving from all things national, provincial and even individual something that can pertain to mankind in general. One cannot deny to this epoch a noble, pure, and clever striving, but it suits much better the individual of talent than the people as a whole.[33]

But this too cannot last. For one thing, the people as a people can never reach such a level of sophistication—although they soon come to feel the demythologizing effects of these "individuals of talent," the philosophers of religion. And so, under the powerful influence of the Age of Philosophy, the masses visit on their own culture a terrifying revenge, swamping it in a sea of vulgarity (Goethe's prescience here should be obvious):

> Instead of instructing its age with its understanding and serenely sinking its roots into the past, the people of this age randomly strew good seed and bad in all directions. There is no center of gravity any more from which perspective can be gained. Every individual steps forth and sets up shop as teacher and leader and purveys the most utter nonsense as if it were the well-rounded perfection of the whole. In this way, then, even the value of each individual mystery has been destroyed, and the faith of the people desecrated.[34]

This analysis, unusually accurate in its prophetic power, brilliantly anticipates the later career of German thought, with Hegel representing the Age of Philosophy and Nietzsche frantically warning against the pathetic misery that awaits man in the 20th century—the most Prosaic Age of all.

---

[33] "Dieser, in seiner größten Energie und Reinheit, verehrt die Uranfänge, erfreut sich am poetischen Volksglauben und schätzt das edle Menschenbedürfnis, ein Oberstes anzuerkennen. Allein der Verständige strebt, alles Denkbare seiner Klarheit anzueignen und selbst die geheimnisvollsten Erscheinungen faßlich aufzulösen. Volks-und Priesterglaube wird daher keineswegs verworfen, aber hinter demselben ein Begreifliches, Löbliches, Nützliches angenommen, die Bedeutung gesucht, das Besordere ins Allgemeine verwandelt und aus allem Nationalen, Provinzialen, ja Individuellen etwas der Menschheit überhaupt Zuständiges herausgeleitet. Dieser Epoche kann man ein edles, reines, kluges Bestreben nicht absprechen, sie genügt aber mehr dem einzelnen wohlbegabten Menschen als ganzen Völkern" (ibid.).

[34] "Anstatt verständig zu belehren und ruhig einzuwirken, streut man willkürlich Samen und Unkraut zugleich nach allen Seiten; kein Mittelpunkt, auf den hingeschaut werde, ist mehr gegeben, jeder einzelne tritt als Lehrer und Führer hervor und gibt seine vollkommene Torheit für ein vollendetes Ganzes. Und so wird denn auch der Wert eines jeden Geheimnisses zerstört, der Volksglaube selbst entweiht" (ibid., 300).

For in Hegel we have the perfect representative of that age which will insist on analyzing what defies analysis and systematizing what eludes the system. And in Nietzsche we have our first indication of the costs awaiting us when the voice of the truly sacred is drowned out by the droning hum of the Prosaic Age, for it is the acidic power of the Prosaic Age to destroy all the sacredness of the past in its corrosive revenge for having been robbed of its patrimony. The prominent interpreter of German culture Erich Heller has perfectly described this rapid declension from Goethe (who tried to keep alive the Age of Poetry), past Hegel (the best representative of the Age of Philosophy), and on to Nietzsche (the prophet of the Prosaic Age):

> The all-too radical attempt of the Age of Philosophy at a "humanization" and rationalization of the mysterious ends in a perverted miracle. The mystery, cheated of its rightful place, goes underground, reverting to its primeval, unholy and barbarous stage. The human spirit, agitated by historical catastrophes, leaps backward over all hurdles which the guidance of reason has erected, clinging here and there to remnants of tradition, scattered residues of many incompatible beliefs, then plunges headlong into pools of insipid mythologies, bringing to the top the muddy poetry of the depths and proclaiming it as the creed of the age.[35]

b. Hegel:

Georg Wilhelm Friedrich Hegel (1770–1831) is much more the heir of Kant than of Goethe. Only in one respect can it really be said that Hegel drew from Goethe: he, like Goethe, looked on the civilization of classical Greece as a time of untroubled harmony and sunshine ("*Heiterkeit*"—a term that regularly crops up in both Goethe and Hegel when describing ancient Greece). But Hegel is much more the scion of the Kantian tradition, though like Aristotle with Plato, he began his career as a philosopher by rejecting Kant. Or so he thought. But actually he only rejected Kant's dualism, but he accepted his so-called "Copernican" starting point in the human subject, a subject whose reasoning structure gave it the wherewithal to judge all comers. But this admission did not entail for Hegel the

---

[35] Erich Heller, "Goethe and Nietzsche," *The Disinherited Mind: Essays in Modern German Literature and Thought* (London: Bowes & Bowes, 1975/1952), 93. Heller's interpretation here is remarkably similar to Balthasar's and perhaps explains much of the latter's isolation from, and even disdain of, contemporary culture: "In such an age every belief turns into blasphemy, and the proclamation of mysteries into sacrilege. Elements, once evolving naturally one from the other, are now interlocked in perpetual strife. It is the return of the *tohu-we-bohu*; yet a chaos not fertile as the first, but so deadening that not even God could create from it a world worthy of Himself" (ibid.).

strict and overly rationalistic dualism of Kant that contrasted duty to pleasure and reason to revelation. There had to be a way to unite them, and an analysis of the unhappy state of the human subject was the place to begin.[36] In fact, it was Hegel and not the later atheistic materialists who took the decisive step of relating the concept of God to the social circumstances out of which it arose—perhaps the most influential move ever taken in German thought. And from this "genetic" perspective Hegel came to the following important conclusion, that the idea of a perfect Creator God who was also the source of the moral law is socially corre-lated to the dehumanization of man that followed the collapse of the Greek city-state and the ascendancy of the Roman Empire:

> Thus the despotism of the Roman emperors had chased the hu-man spirit from the earth and spread a misery which compelled men to seek and expect happiness in heaven; now robbed of freedom, their spirit, their eternal and absolute element, was forced to take flight to the deity. God's objectivity is thus a counterpart to the corruption and slavery of man, and it is strictly speaking only a revelation, a manifestation, of the spirit of the age. . . . God was put into another world where we had no part, to which we contributed nothing by our activity, but into which, at best, we could beg or conjure our way.[37]

The validity of this insight depends on a large number of assumptions, rarely acknowledged by Hegel and never defended: the historical origins of monotheism in the Roman Empire, the cheerful rationality of pre-Alexandrine Greece, and above all the inherent connection between the historical origins of a doctrine and its philosophical or theological valid-ity.[38] This latter might seem like an elementary distinction, but it is one

---

[36] "It is a commonplace that Hegel started out from Kant, which is true. But it needs to be added that he did not start from the *Critique of Pure Reason* [but with] Kant's *Religion Within the Bounds of Reason Alone*. . . . Like Schiller, Hegel had not been satisfied with Kant's book on religion. He was convinced by it that religion must not contain anything that goes against reason, but he wanted something more full-blooded than Kant's purely rational religion. His imagination was nourished on the Greeks . . . and he felt that morality was a matter of humanity, of being humane, and could not be divorced from feeling, art and literature" (Kaufmann, *Discovering the Mind*, 205).

[37] Hegel, "The Positivity of the Christian Religion," II, 2, in *Early Theological Writings*, tr. T. M. Knox and R. Kroner (Chicago: University of Chicago Press, 1948), 162–163.

[38] James Collins in his magisterial *God in Modern Philosophy* has effectively summarized the implicit assumptions lurking in Hegel's philosophy of God in this way: "Hegel's method of claiming special insight into the spirit of an age and then judging a philosophical or religious doctrine by its association with that age eludes the effort to apply the ordinary canons of historical evidence. He imagines a Greek life conformable to his social ideal and then, by way of dialectical opposition, envisages Christianity as the counterpart of the

clearly foreign to Hegel's outlook, so much so that he can even say in one of his notebooks: "In Swabia people say of something that took place a long time ago: 'It happened so long ago that soon it won't be true any longer.' And Christ died for our sins so long ago that soon it won't be true any more either."[39]

The only way to preserve, therefore, the truth of Christ's death for sinners, given its ever-receding echo which will soon die out, would be to "retrieve" it for philosophy. In other words, true to his Kantian heritage, Hegel must absorb the truth of religion as an aspect of the wider truth of philosophy, a position that puts him at complete odds with Goethe:

> Hegel's philosophy seeks to remove the seal from the historical event of Holy Week by turning it into a "speculative Good Friday," making of Christian dogmatics a philosophy of religion, which identifies Christian suffering with the idea of the highest freedom, and Christian theology with philosophy. Goethe objected to this association from the ground up. Precisely because he knows how to honor the Christian cross "as a man and as a poet," he finds the detour of the philosopher repugnant, doing honor neither to the Christian faith nor to the reason of man.[40]

And perhaps nowhere is the contrast between Balthasar and Hegel made more evident than in Hegel's casual remark that "no matter how excellent we continue to find the Greek images of the gods, no matter how estimable and perfect we continue to find the representations of God the Father, Christ, and Mary, it does not help: *we no longer bow our knees.*"[41]

c. Nietzsche:

Friedrich Nietzsche (1844–1900) is a notoriously difficult philosopher to interpret. But he is not difficult for the reason Hegel, for example, is difficult, for unlike Hegel Nietzsche wrote in a style so powerful as to rival

---

wretched conditions prevailing in the Roman period. This historicist argument does not distinguish sufficiently between the time of origin of a doctrine and the grounds of its claim to validity" ([Chicago: Henry Regnery, 1959], 205).

[39] "In Schwaben sagt man von etwas längst Geschehenem: es ist schon so lange, daß es bald nicht mehr wahr ist. So ist Christus schon so lange für unsere Sünden gestorben, daß es bald nicht mehr wahr ist" ("Aphorismen aus Hegels Wastebook," *Hegels Werke*: Bd. 2: *Jenaer Schriften: 1801–1807* [Frankfurt am Main: Suhrkamp, 1986/1803], 545).

[40] Karl Löwith, *From Hegel to Nietzsche: The Revolution in 19th Century Thought*, tr. David E. Green (New York: Holt, Rinehart and Winston, 1964/1939), 18.

[41] Hegel, *Sämtliche Werke* (second edition) XI, 132; my emphasis: "Mögen wir die griechischen Götterbilder noch so vortrefflich finden und Gott Vater, Christus, Maria noch so würdig und vollendet dargestellt sehen, es hilft nichts, unser Knie beugen wir doch nicht mehr."

Luther's and Goethe's. But although he belongs in that happy category of philosophers who write well (while Hegel does not), he nonetheless belongs to that even smaller group of those philosophers who wrote *too* well.[42] Moreover, his ideas were later adopted, to the extent they were even understood, by the Nazis (under the encouragement of his sister), further obscuring the issue.[43] But that Balthasar himself valued Nietzsche we need have no doubt: during World War II, when so many of the classics of German culture were no longer available in Germany itself, Balthasar struggled as a publisher in Basel to keep them in print—including the works of Nietzsche.[44] But much more important, according to Balthasar, Nietzsche is the one thinker who most truly understood the implications of the German myth of the End Times:

> If we wanted to come up with a formula that would express the contrast between these two eschatologies, the shortest and yet

---

[42] "There are philosophers who can write and philosophers who cannot. Most of the great philosophers belong to the first group. There are also, much more rarely, philosophers who can write too well for their own good—as philosophers. Plato wrote so dramatically that we shall never know for sure what precisely he himself thought about any number of questions. And Nietzsche furnishes a more recent and no less striking example" (Walter Kaufmann, "Introduction," *The Portable Nietzsche* [New York: Penguin, 1954], 1).

[43] "Nietzsche is ordinarily considered a difficult and dangerous writer. Yet so far as difficulty is concerned, his work is not difficult in form—he rightly prided himself on having done as much for the language of Goethe as Goethe had done for the language of Martin Luther, and he wrote a German as beautiful and as clear as any ever written—but in substance his ideas, at first glance changing and inconsistent, actually correspond to the unity of life, whose mingled order and complexity he was attempting to grasp. As for being dangerous, Nietzsche is dangerous only to those who read him in haphazard fashion, selecting what flatters their own passionate desires and thus doing violence to a tissue of living thought so delicate that it can only be appreciated if it is approached dispassionately. . . . His work is such that it must be studied as a whole, approached with the care and disinterestedness of the scientist, and, if necessary, read antagonistically" (Félix Bertaux, *A Panorama of German Literature: From 1871–1931*, tr. John J. Trounstine [New York: Cooper Square, 1970], 48). This is a judgment with which Balthasar in its essentials agrees: "Few know who Nietzsche was. To Christians he is the 'anti-Christ,' to the new pagans a welcome quarry of polemical programs and slogans, to psychologists and psychiatrists a strange 'case,' to adolescents a stimulating poison. Yet his silent summit continues to tower over all simple 'solutions' and interpretations" ("Afterword," *Vergeblichkeit*, ed. Hans Werner [Basel: Benno Schwabe Verlag,, 1942], 93). On the complicated history of Nietzsche's reception see: Steven E. Aschheim, *The Nietzsche Legacy in Germany: 1980–1990* (Berkeley: University of California Press, 1992).

[44] Soon after the outbreak of the war, Balthasar was sent to Switzerland by his Jesuit superiors where he became active as student chaplain at the University of Basel, where he also assumed the editorship of the so-called "European Series" of the "Sammlung Klosterberg" (Benno Schwabe Verlag), which Balthasar devoted to publishing "in an attractive format" (*K*, 18) the authors whom he had debated in his *Apokalypse* book. He managed to edit and publish three of Nietzsche's works, with an Afterword at the end of each volume—but interestingly enough, these volumes came out under the pseudonym of Hans Werner.

the most pregnant would be Nietzsche's: "Dionysus and the Crucified One." "Dionysian" describes not only the ultimate attitude of Nietzsche but also of the whole chain from Hamann ... to Karl Barth. It is the bass tone of the German soul that comes through is this formula.[45]

What makes Nietzsche especially hard to interpret is the difficulty in specifying his own *attitude* toward the destruction he predicted the future would see. Certainly he had nothing but contempt for Hegel's pseudodeep attempt to unite reason and faith. Nietzsche's lot was thrown entirely with what he called an "absolutely honest" atheism, which is why he poured such scorn on German philosophy—from Kant on it was merely half-cooked theology! Kant, Fichte, Schelling, Hegel (but also Feuerbach and Strauss!) are all, according to Nietzsche—and this is expressed with his usual verve—still "theologians," "priestlings," and "Church Fathers":

The Germans immediately understand what I mean when I say that philosophy has been contaminated by theological blood. The Protestant pastor is the grandfather of German philosophy, Protestantism its *peccatum originale.* ... It is only necessary to say the words "Tübingen School" to understand what German philosophy is at heart: insidious theology.[46]

What makes such polemics so hard to interpret is the way Nietzsche refuses to indulge in a naïve celebration of the implications of his atheism in the manner of today's secular humanists; in some ways Nietzsche paints a picture of the future far bleaker than anything portrayed in Goethe's description of the Prosaic Age. Or perhaps in his shrill and overheated way, he *is* celebrating the terrors of the future, and it is only in retrospect that *we* see how little there is to celebrate in his vision. In any event, when

---

For details of this activity, see Johannes Gesthuisen, *Das Nietzsche-Bild Hans Urs von Balthasars: Ein Zugang zur "Apokalypse der deutschen Seele"* (Rome: Pontifical Gregorian University Press, 1986), 35–44.

[45] A 1, 8: "Wollten wir eine Gegensatzformel für diese zwei Eschatologien, so bietet sich als die kürzeste und zugleich bedeutungsbeladenste die Nietzsches an: "Dionysus und der Gekreuzigte." "Dionysisch" ist die Letzthaltung nicht nur Nietzsches, sondern der ganzen Kette von Hamann über Schelling und die Romantiker bis zu George und—Karl Barth. Es ist der Orgelpunkt der deutschen Seele, der in diesem Worte hörbar wird."

[46] Nietzsche, *Der Antichrist, Sämtliche Werke,* ed. Giorgio Colli and Mazzino Montinari (Berlin: de Gruyter, 1988), 6: 176: "Unter Deutschen versteht man sofort, wenn ich sage, dass die Philosophie durch Theologen-Blut verderbt ist. Der protestantische Pfarrer ist Grossvater der deutschen Philosophie, der Protestantismus selbst ihr peccatum originale. Definition der Protestantismus: die halbseitige Lähmung des Christenthums—und der Vernunft. Man hat nur das Wort 'Tübinger Stift' auszusprechen, um zu begreifen, was die deutsche Philosophie ist—eine hinterlistige Theologie."

looking at German culture from Kant and Goethe through Hegel and on to Nietzsche, what we can see is *the culmination of the collapse of the distinction between God and the world:* by the time Nietzsche began writing, God has been so identified with the human spirit that Nietzsche could contemptuously dismiss the outer husk of Hegel's pseudo-spirituality as empty posturing and see ahead only the hollowness of our insipid civilization:

> I know my lot. One day a memory shall attach to my name, the memory of a crisis the like of which there never was on earth, of a profound collision of consciences, of a decision demanded against everything that had previously been believed, required, sanctified. I am not a human being, I am dynamite. . . . I oppose as has never been opposed, and am nevertheless the opposite of a negative spirit . . . With all that, I am of necessity also a man of destiny. For when truth enters the lists against the lie of millennia, we shall have convulsions, a spasm of earthquakes . . . the like of which has never been dreamed. Then the concept of politics will be completely dissolved in a war between spirit, all authority structures of the old society will be blown into the air—one and all, they rest upon a lie; there will be wars the like of which has never existed on earth. From my time forward earth will see Great Politics.[47]

II

What has Balthasar drawn from all this? What is it about Goethe, for example, that prompts Balthasar to separate himself from Rahner and indeed from the whole Kantian stream in German thought? Why is Ger-

---

[47] Nietzsche, *Ecce Homo*, in *Sämtliche Werke*, Kritische Studienausgabe, ed Giorgio Colli and Mazzino Montinari (Berlin: de Gruyter, 1988), Vol. 6: 364–365: "Ich kenne mein Loos. Es wird sich einmal an meinen Namen die Erinnerung an etwas Ungeheures anknüpfen,—an eine Krisis, wie es keine auf Erden gab, an die tiefste Gewissens-Collision, an eine Entscheidung heraufbeschworen gegen Alles, was bis dahin geglaubt, gefordert, geheiligt worden war. Ich bin kein Mensch, ich bin Dynamit.— Und mit Alledem ist Nichts in mir von einem Religionsstifter—Religionen sind Pöbel—Affairen, ich habe nöthig, mir die Hände nach der Berührung mit religiösen Menschen zu waschen. . . . Mein Loos will, dass ich der erste anständige Mensch sein muss, dass ich mich gegen die Verlogenheit von Jahrtausenden im Gegensatz weiss. . . . Mit Alledem bin ich nothwendig auch der Mensch des Verhängnisses. Denn wenn die Wahrheit mit der Lüge von Jahrtausenden in Kampf tritt, werden wir Erschütterungen haben, einen Krampf von Erdbeben, eine Versetzung von Berg und Thal, wie dergleichen nie geträumt worden ist. Der Begriff Politik ist dann gänzlich in einen Geisterkrieg aufgegangen, alle Machtgebilde der alten Gesellschaft sind in die Luft gesprengt—sie ruhen allesamt auf der Lüge: es wird Kriege geben, wie es noch keine auf Erden gegeben hat. Erst von mir an giebt es auf Erden *grosse* Politik."

man thought, according to Balthasar, so relentlessly eschatological and yet also so torn between Hebrew and Hellenic eschatologies, the Dionysian and that of the Crucified One? Why is alienation so big a theme and why does it issue so readily into Utopian visions—which so quickly turn into nightmares? And how do the answers to these questions emerge out of his "mythical" analysis? In answering these questions we shall take up, in turn, Balthasar's interpretation of Goethe, Hegel and Nietzsche.[48]

a. Goethe:
There is a remarkable affinity between Balthasar's method and Goethe's, perhaps the pithiest description of which comes from Simmel's formulation: "The decisive characteristic of [Goethe's] world view that absolutely separates him from Kant is the fact that he seeks for the unity of the subjective and objective principle, of nature and the spirit, *within the appearance itself.*"[49] The center of gravity of Balthasar's theology, then, is not on the question that is so often asked in fundamental theology: what kind of conditions must obtain in the structure of human nature for revelation to take place? Balthasar's outlook is literally that: an *out*-look, that is, a look outward to the appearing phenomenon which, in manifesting itself, manifests its own power to explain and to unite. To understand how these two different starting points can affect one's theology, we shall cite Balthasar's own understanding of these differences:

> Rahner is the theological exponent of the Catholic school of thought that follows . . . German Idealism from Kant to Hegel.

[48.] We shall subsume Kant under his more influential successor, the man who inherited his Idealist mantel, Hegel. But we shall also deal with Kant more directly at the beginning of Part II, because Balthasar conceives his trilogy, especially in its order, as a response to Kant's three Critiques.

[49.] Simmel, *Kant und Goethe*, 20–21: "Der entscheidende und ihn von Kant absolute scheidende Grundzug seiner Weltanschauung ist der, daß er die Einheit des subjektiven und des objektiven Prinzips, der Natur und des Geistes, innerhalb ihrer *Erscheinung selbst* sucht." We get some idea of the extraordinary lengths to which Goethe took his objectivism (and his hostility to the Kantian turn toward the subject) in this revealing confession: "I hereby confess that the great duty 'know thyself' which sounds so important has always seemed to me to be suspect, like a trick of priests in secret conspiracy, who would like to confuse man through unfulfillable demands and lead him always from his proper activity in the external world to a false interior contemplation. A man knows himself insofar as he knows the world, which he perceives only within himself, and himself only within it. Every new object, properly examined, reveals a new organ within us," (Goethe, "Bedeutende Fördernis durch ein einziges gestreichtes Wort," *Sämtliche Werke* [Cotta Edition] 40: 444): "Hierbei bekenn' ich, daß mir von jeher die große und so bedeutend klingende Aufgabe: *erkenne dich selbst*, immer verdächtig vorkam, als eine List geheim verbündeter Priester, die den Menschen durch unerreichbare Forderungen verwirren und von der Tätigkeit gegen die Außenwelt zu einer innern falschen Beschaulichkeit verleiten wollten. Der Mensch kennt nur sich selbst, insofern er die Welt kennt, die er nur in sich und sich nur in ihr gewahr wird. Jeder neue Gegenstand, wohl beschaut, schließt ein neues Organ in uns auf."

Rahner . . . abides by the slogan *"Nicht hinter Kant zurück"* (no regression to the pre-Kantian). . . . It is not easy to summarize Rahner's widespread concerns. I might attempt it as follows: because it was God's intention from the beginning to surrender himself totally to his creatures, man—the final project of natural evolution—is from the outset projected beyond himself toward a union of God and man, a union that came into existence in the person of Christ. Anthropology thus becomes inchoate or deficient Christology. And because all the truths of revelation have their center and their foundation in Christ, there is in man a potential that corresponds to every dogma. . . . Rahner's principal objective is pastoral. He sees the people of our time as estranged from biblical truths and, stressing the essentially transcendent nature of man, he seeks to demonstrate how closely Christian truth conforms to the profoundest and boldest hopes and expectations of humankind.[50]

Balthasar finds difficulty with this entire school of thought, from Kant onwards (and so his quarrel includes many more figures than Rahner: for example, Joseph Maréchal and to some extent Bernard Lonergan). His main fear is that "this turn toward the subject" subtly implies that revelation can be recognized as true *because* it fulfills our highest expectations; and from there it is but a short step to saying that revelation is *meant* to fulfill what is highest and most "transcendent" in us:

My main argument—not only against Rahner but against the entire transcendental school which already existed before him and spread alongside him—is this: It might be true that from the very beginning man was created to be disposed toward God's revelation, so that with God's grace even the sinner can accept all revelation. *Gratia supponit naturam.* But when God sends his own living Word to his creatures, he does so, not to instruct them about the mysteries of the world, nor primarily to fulfill their deepest needs and yearnings. Rather he communicates and actively demonstrates such unheard-of things that man feels not satisfied but awestruck by a love which he never could have hoped to experience. For who would have dared describe God as love, without having first received the revelation of the Trinity in the acceptance of the cross by the Son?[51]

In other words, the truth of revelation must be allowed to testify to itself, and this can only happen when we effect the *real* Copernican revolu-

---

[50] "Current Trends in Catholic Theology," *Communio* 5/1 (1978): 77–85; here 79.
[51] "Current Trends," 80.

tion by no longer assuming that what is not verified in the human subject cannot be true. The real blow to our epistemological narcissism would be a turn away from the subject and move on to the manifesting object![52] But in both Goethe's and Balthasar's view, this is no sterile objectivism that denies the existential realities of the subject in some proposition-ridden exercise in pseudo-scholastic objectivity. It is rather an objectivity mediated by reverence (Balthasar's "kneeling" theology). A "reverent objectivity" might be the best term for describing what Balthasar learned from Goethe, as we can see in this extraordinary passage of appreciation:

> It is here that [Goethe] once again stands alone, and never more lonely, against his age and contemporaries, experiencing not without bitterness their lack of understanding. His aim was to combine the cool precision of scientific research with a constant awareness of the totality apparent only to the eye of reverence, the poetic-religious eye, the ancient sense for the cosmos. But the scientists had gone over to his arch-enemy Newton, the Idealists preferred to deduce Nature as an *a priori* system, or, if they were Romantics, to feel a vague irrational feeling of the whole. Goethe was just as much a lone fighter in his age as Thomas Aquinas had been when he sought to combine exact research and intellectual work with a reverentially pious perception of the divine presence in the cosmos. For without a union of the two, there can be no attitude objective enough to do justice to existence. (*GL* 5, 362–363)

---

[52] A serious rupture between Rahner and Balthasar eventually became inevitable, I think, a rupture which Rowan Williams notices with an admirable perspicuity: "The publication in 1966 of *Cordula oder der Ernstfall* made it abundantly clear that Balthasar and Rahner had arrived at a serious parting of the ways. This fiercely worded tract reproached Rahner and his school on several counts: for his reduction of the love of God to mere philanthropy, for his idea of a systematic 'hiddenness' of grace, for his idea of the natural aptitude of human beings for a 'transcendental' revelation in and through the structures of their own spiritual dynamism: everything, in short, summed up in the Rahnerian picture of the 'anonymous Christian' outside the visible Church, the person who, even if a theoretical atheist, lives by faith, hope and love. A good deal of Balthasar's work in the 60's and early 70's is marked by a similar animus: even where Rahner is not named, we find a sharp polemical insistence on the *particularity* of revealed love and thus on the particularity of Christian response, nourished by a concrete image, characterized by specific and unique marks. Balthasar is not, he assures us, attempting to force theology back into a narrow ecclesiasticism, denying the existence of God's grace beyond the frontiers of the Church. ... But he is insistent that in so far as Christian action is *significant* action, it requires a normative and generative focus. ... The beauty of God incarnate can never be determined in advance by a theological *a priori*. It appears as a phenomenon whose necessity is internal to itself, and thus as a manifestation of freedom. No outer condition or plastic force dictates the form of beauty: it cannot be other than it is, simply because of the logic of its own inner balance and inner adequacy, even 'comprehensiveness'" (Rowan Williams, "Balthasar and Rahner,"

Now this is not a case of "baptizing" Goethe for the cause. Balthasar is not claiming that Goethe's "reverence" or his "poetic-religious eye" are confessionally Christian. In fact, one of Goethe's most frequently cited sayings proves that his mind was too protean for any received dogma: "With all the manifold facets of my being, just one way of thinking is not sufficient for me. As a poet and artist I am a polytheist, but a pantheist as a student of nature, and either belief I hold with equal firmness. And if I need a divinity for my personal being, for my moral existence—why, that need too is promptly assuaged."[53] But what Balthasar admires in Goethe is his refusal to take his "pantheism" so seriously that he thereby collapses the analogical distinction between God and the world.[54] On the contrary, even as early as the *Westösterlicher Divan* he refused, as he put it, "to take refuge in the doctrine of absolute unity; for therein Gain merely equals Loss, and what is left at the end? the consolation of a disconsolate zero."[55]

But even more than admiring such a refusal to yield to the distinction-obliterating faith of pantheism, Balthasar drew from Goethe the great

---

in: *The Analogy of Beauty: The Theology of Hans Urs von Balthasar,* ed. John Riches [Edinburgh: T. & T. Clark, 1986]: 11–34; here, 12–14).

[53] Goethe, Letter to Jacobi, 6 January 1813. Heller's is perhaps the most judicious assessment of the complicated issue of Goethe's religiosity: "There is no creed to be elicited from Goethe's writings. Put together systematically as articulate opinions, his convictions would appear very inconsistent and at times self-contradictory. Yet it is neither his opinions nor their inconsistencies that matter in this context. What matters is the level on which his convictions are formed, or the pressure of spiritual energy by which they are sustained; and the quality and direction of his beliefs are most clearly revealed through Goethe's critique of his age. For there is little doubt that the mature Goethe would have put his contemporary world, in spite of occasional outbursts of optimism, into a rather shadowy place on his map of the world's historical epochs, at some removes, in any case, from the Age of Poetry and the Age of the Holy, and considerably nearer those grey stretches where history writes its most atrocious prose passages. And he would certainly not have discovered in it many glimpses of that radiance which emanates from 'epochs of belief,'" (*Disinherited Mind,* 97–98). I would only like to add the further "elective affinity" of Goethe and Balthasar both being able to sustain their positions "against the grain," that is, in loneliness and isolation from their times.

[54] Despite Goethe's professed admiration for Spinoza: ("This philosopher does not prove the being *of* God; God *is* being. And if others, because of this, blame him as an atheist, then I feel like praising him as *theissimum,* indeed *christianissimum.*"). For as he admitted on another occasion, his reading in Spinoza was sporadic and certainly non-philosophical: ("My way of living and thinking does not permit it. But whenever I glance into his books, I believe I understand him, that is, he never seems to be self-contradictory, and I can derive from him something that affects my own feelings" [Letter to Jacobi, 9 June 1785]). See also Ulrich Simon's perceptive remark that "Balthasar stresses Goethe's freedom from the taint of pantheism, despite Spinoza's influence" (Ulrich Simon, "Balthasar on Goethe," in: *The Analogy of Beauty: The Theology of Hans Urs von Balthasar,* ed. John Riches [Edinburgh: T. & T. Clark, 1986]: 60–76; here, 63).

[55] Goethe, *Westösterlicher Divan,* in *Sämtliche Werke* (Artemis Gedenkausgabe) 3: 452.

insight that "Beauty is the manifestation of secret laws of nature which, were it not for their being revealed through beauty, would have remained unknown forever."[56] Beauty for Goethe was the innate attractiveness of reality that draws the subject out of himself and into the splendor of what is, thereby giving us the freedom to revere what is greater than ourselves: "Freedom lies not in refusing to acknowledge anything above us, but on the contrary in revering something that is above us."[57] Which prompted Balthasar to call Goethe unquestionably one of the "last secular manifestations of the heritage of 'glory' which the history of Western metaphysics has bequeathed to us" (GL 5, 340).

b. Hegel:

But not Hegel! For nothing was more alien to Hegel's philosophy than to "revere something that is above us." According to his historical and genetic analysis of the origins of monotheism, Hegel is required to interpret the theistic account of God and man as a master-slave doctrine. For him, then, there will always be a denigration of humanity, a life-choking estrangement in *any* position which accepts God and man as irreducibly distinct beings, however intimate their union in grace.[58] This is why Hegel could not admit a Last Judgment: "[God] cannot judge the world; He can only have pity on it."[59] But this is merely the theological implication of his earlier philosophical starting point that "between man and God, between spirit and spirit, this gap of objectivity does not obtain: the one is—even in relation to the other—still only one, and is other only by knowing the other."[60]

For if what he says is true, then he will inevitably feel a tremendous resentment against the people who have borne the revelation of God's otherness and transcendence, as Balthasar well realizes:

> [In Hegel] the reconciliation of the Greek spirit with the Gospel has one precondition: the complete elimination of the Jewish

---

[56] Goethe, *Sämtliche Werke* (Jubiläumsausgabe) 35: 505.

[57] Goethe, *Conversations with Eckermann,* 18 January 1827.

[58] Such a position led Hegel to some extremely eccentric historical judgments: "[For Hegel] the Jew knows the infinite Creator, not *as* Creator but only as transcendent Lord; hence he knows himself as simply finite only, not as created in the divine image" (Emil L. Fackenheim, *The Religious Dimension in Hegel's Thought* [Chicago: University of Chicago Press, 1967], 136). Balthasar will echo these same criticisms, as we shall see immediately below.

[59] Hegel, *Dokumente zu Hegels Entwicklung,* ed. Johannes Hoffmeister (1936), 349: "Er kann sie nicht richten, er kann sich ihrer nur erbarmen." Cited in GL 5, 477.

[60] Hegel, *Der Geist des Christentums und sein Schicksal,* in *Werke,* Vol. 1: *Frühe Schriften* (Frankfurt: Suhrkamp, 1971/1800) 1:381: "Aber zwischen Mensch und Gott, zwischen Geist und Geist ist diese Kluft der Objektivität nicht; einer ist dem andern nur einer und ein anderer darin, daß er ihn erkennt."

dimension. In his insatiable and hateful polemic against the Old Testament, Hegel pursues the one element for which he has no use in his otherwise all-reconciling system: the sovereign and lordly elevation of God above the world, who acts, elects and rejects in complete freedom of will. And thus he has no use either for the distinctively Old Testament forms of the divine glory: the *kabod.* It was precisely this kind of anti-Semitism which necessarily had to appear at the end of our history of the spirit, in which the elevation of God above the world—first in terms of classical antiquity and then of Christianity—is reduced step by step until it becomes a structure [of Hegelian logic].[61]

For Balthasar the subsequent career of German thought, if not history, becomes inevitable: a Utopianism that splits off into right and left wings, and an aesthetics that so distorts biblical glory and (ironically enough) the classical view that the Prosaic Age was bound to follow. For when the distinction between God and the world collapses, not only is an anti-Semitic resentment fostered that makes the Jews the antitype for all that is regarded as harmonious in human culture, but the State also comes to assume the aura that belongs to God. There is an immense irony at work here, for according to Hegel, monotheism first arose as the expression of the unhappy consciousness trapped in an oppressive imperial polity, where the only real relationship was of master and slave. And yet by the time we get to the end of the Hegelian system, we see it fostering, *in* its very collapsing of the distinction between God and world, the very polity it criticized. This at any rate is Balthasar's view:

> If one considers that Hegel's earliest concern was the concrete (that is, national) spirit of the people which mediates between total Spirit and the monad, and that this indeterminate spirit appeared to him later as the formed spirit of the state, then it is clear that Hegel had to become the intellectual point of departure for the later socialism of the Left and of the Right, both of which in their own way have gathered the glory of absolute being into the absolute claims of their own "party." (*GL* 5, 590)

c. Nietzsche:

What most characterizes Balthasar's attitude toward Nietzsche may perhaps be summed up in one word: fascination. For in Nietzsche's case we

---

[61] *GL* 5, 580. As Hellenic culture is pure sunshine and *Heiterkeit,* so Judaism is for Hegel all clouds, and darkness: "A people who despise all foreign gods must bear the hatred of the whole of the human race in their hearts. . . . Hegel thus strikes a note of invective which is fully equal to that of Nietzsche against Christianity" (580, 582).

see lived out in the most glaring way the consequences of German thought the previous 100 years, so much so that he forms the link between the Idealism of Kant and Hegel, and the existentialism and vitalistic philosophies of the 20th century.[62] This is why Balthasar uses for the title of his second volume of the *Apokalypse* the rubric of Nietzsche himself, titling it *Im Zeichen Nietzsches* (though the main treatment of him occurs in the first volume, while he explicitly appears in the second volume only as a foil to Dostoyevsky).

One of the most telling indications of this fascination, as we have seen, is his efforts to keep Nietzsche's writings in print during World War II.[63] These selections themselves, together with their accompanying Afterwords, are an important clue to what Balthasar finds so fascinating about Nietzsche. What particularly emerges in these volumes is Balthasar's stress on Nietzsche's loneliness and on his aristocratic spirit. But most importantly of all, there is the Nietzsche who in his madness signed himself "the crucified one"—the man, that is, who so fully lived out the contradictions of the German soul that he was *himself* that "unveiling" or "apocalypse" that Balthasar set out to display in his own study of German eschatology:

> In the fading night of "the twilight of the gods," this alarm [that God is dead] cries out over the weary paths of Ahasuerus. Fires ignite in the night. From the 'grandiose edifice' of the Hegelian system a blaze breaks out. . . . From the pallid, venal and petrified world of Prometheus a strange, never-before-seen glow burns: Dionysus-Loki. A fire in the night, itself dark, not like Schelling's flame caught in the chimney-flue of the spirit, not the lovely glow of the center, a light from above and within: but an

---

[62] "Nietzsche is especially significant for Balthasar here as an 'existence-indicator.' For he experienced in himself the abysses of existence, the ultimate depths of man and through his life exposed and made them visible. At the same time, he was a 'flame-existence': he summons us to clear decisions of life, and so has a prophetic influence in the face of a nihilistic future" (Gesthuisen, 177: "Besonders Nietzsche wird ihm hier bedeutsam als 'Zeichen-Existenz,' sofern er in sich selbst die Abgründe der Existenz, die letzten Tiefen des Menschen erfährt und durch sein Leben bloßlegt und sichtbar macht. Zugleich ruft er als 'Flammen-Existenz' zu klaren Entscheidungen des Lebens auf und wirkt dabei prophetisch angesichts einer nihilistischen Zukunft").

[63] "When Balthasar also edited three small volumes of Nietzsche selections under the series of selections that came out from his editorship, this must mean that Nietzsche was able to perform for him a decisive contribution to the strenuous task that he had set for himself with this entire series. Nietzsche belongs to the great figures of the spiritual tradition who can give fruitful impulses to every period in history. For that reason the three volumes of Nietzsche selections are, along with the *Apokalypse,* a further important witness for the meaning that Nietzsche had at the time for Balthasar" (Gesthuisen, 38).

earthly and dangerously hovering glow, incalculable, blowing where it will. What should it *not* consume?[64]

But however much he can enter into Nietzsche's extraordinary pathos, Balthasar never loses sight of its roots, and what it means theologically. And this above all is what he "unveils." This is Nietzsche's true significance: from being the example *par excellence* of "the hybris of self-experimentation" (*TD* 1, 235), he ends up displaying what Balthasar will see as the tragedy of highest riches being stripped of itself into a kind of "poverty unto poverty" in a kind of unwilling, though formal living-out of the tragedy of Christ.[65] And this is the source and ground of Balthasar's deep appreciation of and sympathy for the figure of Nietzsche: "a great sign of fire erected in the darkness of the mid-19th century: a man on fire, struck to his depths with the flames of both heaven and hell."[66]

---

[64] *A* 1, 695: "In die fahle Nacht der 'Götterdämmerung,' über die müden Wege Ahasvers schreit dieser Alarm. Feuer flammen auf in der Nacht. Aus dem 'grandiosen Gebäude' des hegelschen Systems bricht eine Lohe aus. . . . Aus der Lüge gewordenen, dürren, verholzten Prometheuswelt zuckt eine fremde, nie gesehene Glut: Dionysus—Loki. Ein Nachtfeuer, selber dunkel und nicht wie das Schellings, in Rauchfänge des Geistes gefangen, nicht schöne Glut der Mitte, Licht von oben und innen: sondern irdische, gefährlich schwiefende Glut, unberrechenbar, wehend wohin sie will. Was sollte sie *nicht* verzehren?"

[65] In this formulation I am relying on Gesthuisen's analysis: "Even though Nietzsche interprets himself, as his life proceeds, as a tragic self-contradiction (which Balthasar will use against him as a general argument in his later writings), yet Balthasar will see this same life as the tragedy of highest riches being stripped of itself into a kind of 'poverty unto poverty,' that is, as a formal 'cooperation' with the tragedy of Christ. For the Christian mystery is that God demands on the Cross poverty and 'ephemerality,' in order to redeem man" (Gesthuisen, 172).

[66] *A* 1, 733: "Flammenzeichen, aufgerichtet im Dunkel der Jahrhundertmitte: Brennender Mensch als Ineinsschlagen von Höllenflamme und Himmelsflamme."

· 4 ·

Balthasar and the Church Fathers

Let heathen sing thy heathen praise,
Fall'n Greece! the thought of holier days
    In my sad heart abides;
For sons of thine in Truth's first hour
Were tongues and weapons of His power
Born of the Spirit's fiery shower,
    Our fathers and our guides.

From thee the glorious preacher came,
With soul of zeal and lips of flame,
    A court's stern martyr-guest;
And thine, O inexhaustive race!
Was Nazianzen's heaven-taught grace;
And royal-hearted Athanase,
    With Paul's own mantle blest.

John Henry Newman
"The Greek Fathers"

Patristics today is caught in a paradox. On the one hand, never has there been such an explosion of knowledge about the Church Fathers, such a plethora of critical editions of their works, such a discovery of new manuscripts, such advanced techniques of investigation (all of the Latin Fathers, for example, are now on CD-ROM disks for easy retrieval on personal computers), as in the twentieth century; and yet never has that knowledge been so confined to such a small coterie in the Church and academia. On the first prong of the dilemma, we notice how conferences of patrologists and historians of early Christianity attract an international clientele of prominent scholars; but at the other prong of the fork, we are forced to admit that their work is read for the most part only by their fellow specialists, rarely forming an essential part of contemporary systematic theology, and even less of a preacher's preaching or biblical scholar's exegesis (Vatican II's directive that exegetes bear in mind the biblical commentaries of the Church Fathers in their work [*Dei Verbum* 23] is virtually a dead letter). And the situation is even bleaker in the culture at large, once largely Christian and therefore saturated with the spiritual vision of the Fathers, and now unmoored so radically from its own past. This situation is now bleak enough that it has drawn a very poignant response from Robert Payne, Lenin's biographer and himself an amateur historian of the patristic writings:

> Today they seem to have faded into the distance, those Fathers of another time. It was not always so. St. Thomas Aquinas once said he would give all Paris for a homily written by St. John Chrysostom, and is forever quoting from the Eastern Fathers. John Donne from his pulpit at St. Paul's quotes from them endlessly, assuming in his audience a knowledge of them almost as extensive as his own. There was a time in the fourteenth century when English poetry was saturated with a visionary quality derived from Dionysius the Areopagite, whose real name no one knows.[1]

But today the general rule is that most biblical scholars do their work independent of the influence of the Church Fathers, and systematic theologians for the most part concern themselves with correlating the Bible to contemporary world views, only rarely considering how patristics might serve as a crucial resource in their work.[2] In Hans Urs von Balthasar, however, we have not only a theologian whose command of the field of patristics is unrivalled but also one who has himself done important and pioneering work in the field, both by seeing into print previously unpublished or untranslated manuscripts[3] and also by contributing to important textual studies of other manuscripts.[4]

---

[1] Robert Payne, *The Holy Fire: The Story of the Fathers of the Eastern Church* (New York: Harper & Row, 1957), xiii.

[2] A perfect example of this insouciance is the opening paragraph of Kümmel's famous history of New Testament scholarship: "It is impossible to speak of a scientific view of the New Testament until the New Testament became the object of investigation as an independent body of literature with historical interest, as a collection of writings that could be considered apart from the Old Testament and without dogmatic or creedal bias. Since such a view began to prevail only during the course of the 18th century, earlier discussion of the New Testament can only be referred to as the prehistory of New Testament scholarship" (Werner Georg Kümmel, *The New Testament: The History of the Investigation of its Problems*, tr. S. McLean Gilmour and Howard C. Kee [Nashville: Abingdon, 1972], 13).

[3] See, for example, the texts of Maximus the Confessor published in the appendix to *Kosmische Liturgie: Das Weltbild Maximus' des Bekenners* (Einsiedeln: Johannes Verlag, 1961), 363–481; abbreviated as *KL*.

[4] See, for example, his essay "Das Scholienwerk des Johannes von Scythopolis," *Scholastik* 15 (1940): 16–38; also reprinted in *KL*, 644–672, which also contains an important textual and philological study of Maximus' *Gnostic Centuries* (*KL*, 482–643).

In a book wishing to give but an introduction to his work as a whole and not just to his patristics, it would take us too far afield to discuss these technical issues in any detail. But a discussion of Balthasar's patristic scholarship is nonetheless crucial to the project of introducing his work as a whole—not simply because of the technical mastery so evident in his publications on many of the Fathers but more crucially because of their direct influence on his own thought. No one can really understand Balthasar's theology without first seeing how he was able to confront the vision that animated the first several centuries of the Church and critically incorporate it into his own project. Indeed it is the judgment of one eminent patristic scholar that "the Swiss theologian's most original contribution to the study of the Church Fathers results precisely in releasing this study from its marginal status in the field of theological research."[5]

But as Balthasar recognizes, this marginalization of patristics is the result of much more than the ineluctable factor of specialization. What made John Donne's congregations so sensitive to the cadences of patristic theology was the very pervasiveness of the Christian presuppositions that animated Elizabethan and Jacobin England—a situation that now no longer obtains. And *that,* as Balthasar realizes, is the central fact behind the marginalization of the Fathers:

> We are living in a time of collapsing images of gods and idols. The spiritual and cultural traditions of the West have become questionable. Indeed it goes well beyond that, for they have been liquidated—quickly and relatively painlessly. Just as the tree in the autumn drops its leaves, without pain or regret, in order to gather once more new strength from within, to renew its powers in hibernian peace, so too the tree of culture is being stripped of its leaves. Of course as autumn moves into winter, the leaves lie thickly under our feet—and the books thickly in the book stores—, but we aren't deceived for a moment about that. This colorful yellow and red swarm of leaves still comes to life, at most, because of the wind, not because there is any life left in the leaves themselves. A small regret might well be permitted us here, just as autumn is the time of the elegiac lyric, but who would want on that account to huddle up in an eschatological pathos! We trust the powers of nature, her wise economy and the laws of her renewal.[6]

---

[5] Charles Kannengiesser, "Listening to the Fathers," *L&W,* 59.

[6] "Patristik, Scholastik, und wir," *Theologie der Zeit* 3 (1939): 65–109; here, 65: "Wir leben in einem Zeitalter stürzender Götter-und Götzenbilder. Die geistigen und kulturellen Traditionen des abendländischen Raumes sind fragwürdig geworden, ja, mehr noch, sie werden rasch und verhältnismäßig schmerzlos liquidiert. Wie der Baum im Herbst ohne Schmerz und Bedauern seine Blätter fallen läßt, um sich innerlich wieder zu sammeln, seine

The tone of this passage is quite extraordinary, so ambivalent as almost to defy interpretation: wistful, yet hopeful; resigned (and even braced for perhaps worse to come), yet prepared for better things if the seasons suddenly change and a new spring comes upon us; sardonic about the popularity of the academic study of religion, with books lying about as thickly as dead leaves in autumn, yet recognizing that this too could serve as mulch for a later renewal. Despite, however, the poetic and therefore elusive tone of his analysis, the image of the seasons is still meant to convey a basic hope, but one that emerges only after the winter has passed—after, that is, the seriousness of the challenge of secularization has been faced:

> Under this falling bower many a Christian leaf can also be found. In the course of its two-thousand year history, Christianity has created for itself a wide variety of expressions, [drawing from the various] forms of the West's cultural life. Indeed it has had an important part in bringing forth and developing these forms. In a labile and constantly changing relationship, it has transformed these priceless works of art of the spirit and made them into its dwelling places, transforming its forms of expression and making them its vesture—indeed it has almost made them a part of its very body. So it is almost obvious that today, where these dwellings seem to have become dilapidated, indeed where the worldly "body" of the Church seems to be wasting away, Christianity is being placed before the same question that secular culture must face: what is its living essence and core? But at the same time, to ask that question—that is, to recognize a core as

---

Kräfte zu erneuern in winterlicher Ruhe, so entlaubt sich der Baum der Kultur. Freilich liegen im Spätherbst die Blätter dicht unter unseren Füßen—und die Bücher dicht in den Buchhandlungen—, aber wir täuschen uns keinen Augenblick darüber, daß dieses bunte, gelbe, rote Gewimmel höchstens noch vom Winde, nicht mehr vom Leben selbst beseelt wird. Eine kleine Trauer mag da wohl erlaubt sein, so wie der Herbst eben die Zeit der elegischen Lyrik ist, aber wer wollte sich deswegen in ein eschatologisches Pathos hüllen! Wir vertrauen den Kräften der Natur, ihrer weisen Ökonomie und den Gesetzen ihrer Erneuerung." This important essay, published in a German journal just before the outbreak of World War II, was never reprinted in any of Balthasar's books of collected essays, making it especially hard to track down. For this reason, as well as its importance as a summary of Balthasar's views of the contribution of patristic thought in its relations to medieval Scholasticism and modern theology, I shall be drawing extensively on this essay (cited henceforth as "PSW"), rather than treating Balthasar's individual interpretation of various Fathers. Readers interested in the specifics of these interpretations should consult Werner Löser's magisterial *Im Geiste des Origenes: Hans Urs von Balthasar als Interpret der Kirchenväter*, Frankfurter Theologische Studien 23 (Frankfurt: Josef Knecht, 1976).

the creative ground of those forms—means that we cannot identify *it* with *them*.[7]

One of the great ironies of the contemporary interest in patristics is
that it is, for Balthasar at any rate, a *product* of this very nostalgia he has
so wistfully described. If all that lies about us are the encrustations of
dead leaves, is there not some way we can tap beneath the dead crust and
drop our plumb line into the wellspring from which the life of the Church
originally flowed? And this view of things leads by an almost direct logic
to the period of the Fathers:

> The embodiment of the Church in the regions of secular culture
> almost seems like a progressive decline from her living essence.
> If we look, for example, at the periods of the so-called Renais-
> sance and Baroque Scholasticism, it might well appear to us as
> almost a corrupt product of medieval High Scholasticism, pro-
> duced only by mere epigones. And thus, in taking a bird's-eye
> view (and not that of the frog), we will certainly ascribe that
> much less creative power to the thought of the 19th and 20th
> centuries. But was not Scholasticism itself already a false path
> with its "rationalization" of dogma, its dialectic hair-splitting
> and its all-too naïve use of secular logic?[8]

In other words, the deeper we go digging through the leaf pile, the more
we seem to be turning up ever more dead leaves, but with the Fathers
perhaps we are nearing a new taproot: here we can finally read those
Christians who still heard the oral tradition in their churches and from

---

[7] "PSW," 65: "Unter dem fallenden Laube befindet sich manches christliche Blatt. Das
Christentum hat im Verlauf seiner zweitausandjährigen Geschichte sich mannigfachen Aus-
druck in den Formen abendländischen Geisteslebens geschaffen, ja es hat an der
Hervorbringung und Entwicklung dieser Formen den bedeutendsten Anteil gehabt. In einem
labilen, stets wechselnden Verhältnis hat es diese kostbaren Kunstwerke des Geistes zu seinen
Wohnstätten, Ausdrucksformen, Kleidern, ja oft beinahe zu seinem Leib gemacht. So ist es
fast selbstverständlich, daß heute, wo diese Wohnungen baufällig zu werden scheint, das
Christentum in gleicher Weise wie die weltliche Kultur selbst vor die Frage nach seinem
lebendigen Wesen und Kern gestellt wird, der als schöpferischer Grund jener Formen mit
ihnen aber nicht identisch sein kann."

[8] "PSW," 66: "Die Verleiblichung der Kirche in den Räumen der weltlichen Kultur
erscheint fast als ein progressiver Abfall von ihrem lebendigen Wesen. Wenn wir etwa die
Periode der sogenannten Renaissance-und Barockscholastik betrachten, so mag sie uns fast
wie ein epigogenhaftes Verfallsprodukt der mittelalterlichen Hochscholastik erscheinen, und
dem Denken des 19. und 20. Jahrhunderts werden wir, in Vogel-und nicht in Froschperspek-
tive gesehen, gewiß noch weniger schöpferische Kraft zugestehen. Aber ist nicht die Scholastik selbst schon ein Irrweg gewesen, mit ihrer 'Rationalisierung' des Dogmas, ihren
dialektischen Spitzfindigkeiten und seiner allzu naiven Verwendung weltlicher Denkformen?"

whom we could reconstruct the entire text of the Bible from their writings alone if, in some science-fiction scenario, all our original texts had disappeared, so much did they quote and live from the Bible. And it is the Eastern branch of patristics that seems to be especially inviting in this regard, at least to the nostalgic mind:

> The wide world of the Church Fathers that is thus opened up to us leads back to the very wellspring of early Christianity, of the Apostles and of the Gospel itself. And so it presents itself to us, by definition, as *the* region of the sources, the unadulterated fountain, the primitive tradition which had not yet been covered over, much less distorted, by any rationalization. Moreover, this patristic period possesses a structure unique to itself that can make it appear, precisely for us, particularly contemporary and fruitful: it is marked, especially in its Greek branches (which is by far the more important and fruitful branch, to which indeed the Latin Jerome, Ambrose, Augustine owed virtually everything they were), by an open world-transcendence which avoided contact with the [day-to-day responsibilities] of the State more fully than [the West did].[9]

But how realistic is this view? There is, first of all, the objection of Protestantism that the Fathers themselves represent a false path; they too have gone down the wrong road! Only Scripture is the source, the true well-spring from which the living waters of faith will flow. This view emerged in Protestantism as early as Luther;[10] but it received its most

---

[9] "PSW," 66: "Die weite Welt der Kirchenväter, die sich uns damit eröffnet, und die nach rückwärts unmittelbar in die Periode des Urchristentums, der Apostel und des Evangeliums selbst ausmündet, gibt sich uns von vornherein als die Region der Ursprünge, der unverfälschten Quellen, der Urtradition, die noch durch keine Rationalisierung verdeckt oder gar verbogen ist. Und weiterhin: diese patristische Periode besitzt eine eigentümliche Gesetzlichkeit, die sie gerade für uns besonders zeitnah und fruchtbar erscheinen läßt: sie ist, zumal in ihrem griechischen Zweige (dem bei weitem wichtigeren und fruchtbaren, dem ja der lateinische Hieronymus, Ambrosius, Augustin so gut wie alles verdankt), von einer entschlossenen Welttranszendenz, welche den Kontakt mit der Sphäre des Staatlichen so völlig vermied, als es anging."

[10] For example, one time while expostulating at the dinner table, Luther said of Augustine: "At first, I devoured Augustine. But when the door was opened for me in Paul, so that I understood what justification by faith is, it was all over with Augustine. The books of his *Confessions* teach nothing; they only incite the reader; they are made up merely of examples, but do not instruct" (Luther, *Tischreden,* in *Werke* Vol. 40 [Weimar: Böhlau, 1883-], listed by citation number, then page: no. 347, p. 49). If this could be his attitude to Augustine, to whose order he once belonged and from whose writings he drew so much of his theology of grace, one need scarcely imagine what he thought of the other Church Fathers: "Jerome can be read for the sake of history, but he has nothing at all to say about faith and the teaching of true religion. I have no use for Chrysostom either, for he is only a gossip. Basil

scholarly defense in Adolf Harnack, who averred that the Fathers injected the fateful elixir of Hellenization into the life blood of the Church, weakening the faith with a foreign substance and distorting the Christian world-view by force-feeding it with Plato's abstract terminology of essence and (static) being.

Roman Catholics, of course, reject such an analysis, at least if it is arrived at as the conclusion to the *a priori* premise of *sola Scriptura*. But are Roman Catholics or Eastern Orthodox believers any different, formally speaking, when they extend the era of fidelity by just a few centuries, and then place the fateful turn down the wrong road a bit later? Are we really served by romanticizing the time of the Fathers? Part of the problem with such roseate nostalgia, besides its sheer irrealism, is that it shunts the study of the Fathers off into Coterie-Land, so that either one decides to devote one's life to the necessary technical skills required to gain direct access to the literature of the first eight centuries of the Church, or one contents oneself with substitutes, supplementing one's deficiencies with the very nostalgia that motivated interest in the Fathers in the first place. No wonder the time of the early Church comes to seem like a lost Atlantis![11]

What we discover in all these Protean forms of nostalgia, whether the Protestant version with its idealization of the New Testament Church, or the more "Catholic" version of longing for the era of the Fathers, is the implicit distinction Balthasar mentioned earlier between the content of revelation and the forms it takes. By its very longing to recover lost times, nostalgia seems to recognize that the *forms* with which the Church in each age has expressed revelation cannot be the same thing as that revelation itself. For it is our very glance back through history that manifests to us the many, many forms of expression that the Church has adopted in her historical career. And the search for a norm, Protestant or Catholic, to judge those myriad forms completes the distinction. And especially when that glance backward is accompanied by a wistful feeling that things were better "back then," the distinction between content and form takes on a special pathos.

In other words, as soon as we make this distinction, we admit the provisional status of all expressive forms throughout history. But one of the key methodological presuppositions of Balthasar's theology is that content and form can in fact never be neatly separated out from each

---

doesn't amount to a thing; he was a monk after all, and I wouldn't give a penny for him. Philip [Melanchthon]'s *Apology* is superior to all the doctors of the Church, even to Augustine himself" (ibid., no. 252, p. 33). From Luther to Kümmel is not a very long journey.

[11] "Indeed patristics not seldom resembles a lost paradise: only the very few get to see it with their own eyes: the well-ordered battle array of Abbé Migne's volumes presents an all-too frightening visage. One gets to know the Fathers through hear-say, from compendia or brief translations" ("PSW," 67).

other. He resists the nostalgic view that would elevate any period of Church history—the first century included—as the one that was quintessentially faithful, with all subsequent eras representing a decline, precisely because form and content cannot be that so easily distinguished.

But this radical distinction between content and form is in fact one of the key presuppositions of Platonic philosophy that was carried over *by* the Fathers and was almost assumed by them as a matter of course—the very view that Balthasar's aesthetics will want to struggle against! This gives to his theology a startlingly anti-patristic polemic, a feature of his thought rarely noted among his commentators.[12] Not that he will go to the opposite extreme and so identify form and content that a change in one means an entirely new identity in the other, for then there would be no continuity in the historical career of Christianity at all as the Church seeks to give new expression to the received tradition. This difficult balancing act will give to Balthasar's interpretation of the patristic era a peculiar subtlety and nuance that must be kept in mind throughout his analysis. On the one hand, he will admit the legitimacy of the distinction between form and content but he will not make that distinction so radical that we can use it to dismiss out of hand any particular period in Church history:

> [We must] press on past all external and superficial features of each epoch to its innermost structural law and measure each era according to the structural law of what is essentially Christian as we encounter this norm in the Gospels. We are not claiming of course that this latter hovers like some abstract universal law over history and its changes. Nonetheless, [this essential element] expresses itself in the level of history in ever new forms without our being able thereby to call any one of these forms the absolute one. . . . Therefore we must isolate the meaning of the great epochs as well as try to understand them in their context. Under the first rubric we will uncover the unique and thus also the lasting element of each epoch's meaning and exemplary status; and under the second we shall disclose an ordered arrangement in the total context of world history, thereby stressing the perishability and provisionality of each historical period.[13]

---

[12] Because of the influence of Werner Löser's *Im Geiste des Origenes* and because of Balthasar's own pioneering work in patristic scholarship, his rather sharp critique of the Fathers tends to be slighted in almost all of the secondary literature. I offer my own views to balance the picture—not to contradict Löser's thesis so much as to supplement it.

[13] "PSW," 68, 69. To avoid a double negative in the second sentence, I have not translated this passage literally. The original reads: "Es gilt durch all äußerlichen und nebensächlichen Eigenschaften jeder Epoche zu ihrem innersten Strukturgesetz durchzustoßen und dieses am Strukturgesetz des Christlichen wie es uns im Evangelium entgegentritt, zu messen. Kein

So it is legitimate to pose this question of each era of the Church: how much are the spiritual and intellectual presuppositions that govern its thought in conformity with the Gospel? But Balthasar does not go about answering this difficult question with the *a priori* assumption that the New Testament Church represents the ideal and that all later history must necessarily demonstrate a falling away from this ideal. The facts of the case are much more complicated than that, and part of that complexity is the subtle interplay between form and content.

Nonetheless, because the question is itself legitimate, we must have some working notion of what the essence ("content") of the Gospel is over against which we may then judge all subsequent periods in Church history. And this Balthasar provides in what is I believe the first summary he ever provided in writing of what he considered to be, in Harnack's perhaps unfortunate phrase, "the essence of Christianity"—formulating his views in a way that is obviously heavily indebted to Barth:

> The deepest longing of man is to ascend to God, to become like God, indeed to become equal to God. Whereas daily life chains and constricts him in the narrow confines of everyday life on this earth, a pressure ignites within man to tear away the chains of this slavery and to break through to the mysterious depths that lurk behind this world, to a world in which he can be free, whole, wise and immortal—free of the limitations of his narrow ego and holding dominion over the total context of events, superior to fate and death. In all peoples an estate, a class, a caste, has formed that was meant to give visible, representative and, as it were, sacramental expression to this general longing. But we know that the snake got a hold of this very innermost drive of man to press on to God, and poisoned it. Original sin does not sit somewhere on the periphery of human nature. Rather, the very promise *"eritis sicut dii"* [you shall be like gods] is the perversion of the original core of this nature itself. Not in the way the Protestants interpret this, as if this innermost center of human nature had been totally annihilated by original guilt, but it *has* been "tinged," "saturated," "distorted" by sin.[14]

Zweifel freilich, daß dieses letzte nicht wie ein abstraktes Allgemeingesetz über der Geschichte und ihren Wandlungen schwebt, sondern sich in der Ebene der Geschichte in immer neuen Formen ausprägt, ohne daß man eine dieser Formen als die absolute ansprechen könnte. . . . Dies gilt schon darum, weil alle Geschichte ein Geschehen ist, eine Tendenz besitzt. Wir müssen also den Sinn der großen Epochen sowohl isoliert als in ihrem Zusammenhang zu verstehen versuchen. Im ersten Aspekt werden wir das Einmalige und damit auch Bleibende ihres Sinnes und ihrer Vorbildlichkeit entdecken, im zweiten ihre Einordnung in einen Gesamtzusammenhang und damit ihre Übergänglichkeit und Vorläufigkeit."

[14] "PSW," 69: "Des Menschen tiefste Sehnsucht ist es, zum Göttlichen aufzusteigen, Gott ähnlich, ja Gott gleich zu werden. Während das tägliche Leben ihn in die Kleinwelt des

We have already seen in the chapter on Karl Barth how both thinkers struggled with this issue of how nature could still exist and yet be in rebellion against God (and thereby rebelling at the same time against its own creaturely status). But however that dispute be settled, what is crucial to realize with both Barth and Balthasar is how much sin affects *above all* the highest religious aspirations of the human spirit:

> The religious ideal of man after his expulsion from paradise—to become "spirit," "sage," "mystic," "perfected" (to name but the purest and worthiest ideals)—always means *at the same time* that this genuinely religious impulse will contain a revolt against the Creator, a disowning of the nature in which man was placed and created: the earthly, physical-psychic, communal, spatial-temporal existence. Man does not want to be man but something else (as he imagines, something "higher"); as a "religious" person, he gives, as it were, his "resignation notice" to God, saying that he will no longer do God's service. For this service consists in the simple recognition and exercise of his nature. Instead of accepting the primary fact of his creatureliness as the basis and starting point of all his religious movements and aspirations, he tries, as it were, to leap over this basis and seek for a magical way to reach, on his own, the Creator's way of being—almost as if he were trying to eat some kind of a philosophical or spiritual apple, endowed with that same charm that ensnared Adam and Eve.[15]

---

irdischen Alltags fesselt und bannt, entbrennt in ihm der Drang, die Fesseln dieser Sklaverei zu zerreißen und in die geheimnisvolle, dahinterliegende Tiefe durchzubrechen, in der er frei, ganz, weise und unsterblich sein könnte: frei von der Grenze seines engen Ich, den Gesamtzusammenhang der Ereignisse beherrschend, überlegen dem Schicksal und dem Vergehen. In allen Völkern hat sich ein Stand, eine Kaste ausgebildet, die diesem allgemeinen Sehnen sichtbaren, repräsentativen, gleichsam sakramentalen Ausdruck verleihen sollte. Aber wir wissen, daß die Schlange sich gerade dieses innersten Triebes des Menschen, zu Gott selbst vorzudringen, bemächtigt und ihn vergiftet hat. Die Erbsünde sitzt nicht irgendwie peripher im menschlichen Wesen, sondern das 'eritis sicut dii' ist die Perversion des ursprünglichen Kernes dieses Wesens selbst. Nicht als ob dieser Kern, in protestantischem Sinn, durch die Erbschuld selbst vernichtet wäre, aber er ist sündhaft 'gefärbt,' 'durchwachsen,' 'verbogen.'"

[15] "PSW," 69–70: "Das religiöse Ideal des nachparadiesischen Menschen, 'Geist,' 'Weiser,' 'Mystiker,' 'Vollendeter' zu werden (um die reinsten und ehrwürdigsten Ideale zu nennen), bedeutet immer *zugleich* mit dem Echtreligiösen, das es enthält, eine Revolte gegen den Schöpfer: eine Absage an die Natur, in die hinein der Mensch gestellt und geschaffen wurde: die irdische, leib-seelische, gemeinschaftliche, zeiträumliche Existenzweise. Der Mensch will nicht Mensch sein, sondern etwas anderes—wie er sich einbildet 'Höheres'—als 'Religiöser' kündet er Gott den Dienst. Denn dieser Dienst bestünde ja in der schlichten Anerkennung und Ausübung seiner Natur. Anstatt die Urtatsache der Kreatürlichkeit als Basis und Ausgangspunkt aller seiner religiösen Bewegungen und Aspirationen zu nehmen, überfliegt er gleich-

In true Barthian fashion, Balthasar fully admits that this infection is as debilitating of Christianity as it is of any other religion (otherwise his critique of the Church Fathers would make no sense), but he will also want to insist that this infection of original sin will also find quintessential expression in certain philosophical world views, especially in Plato's theory of the Divided Line. According to this famous schema, first outlined in *The Republic*, there is a rigid boundary between the world of reality and the world of appearance, with the first being the realm of Being and Ideas (especially the Ideas of mathematics), and the second the realm of Becoming and the material instantiation of those Ideas. The same duality runs through human nature, with the soul being part of the world of Ideas, and the body a part of matter, doomed to perish with the rest of the world of mere Becoming.

And of course, it is the world of Ideas that is by definition divine: unchanging, always existing, and pure from all taint of matter. And this is just where the sin of original sin enters the picture, for the implication is that the human soul, simply by virtue of it being a soul, shares an *essential* (natural) communion with the divine:

> Thus one finds in one's human nature a place—perhaps only a point, but this point suffices—where one can, as it were, traffic with God "religiously," on the same footing, a place where a mystical *identity* obtains between Creator and creature. Now to reach this mysterious point of identity requires all kinds of strenuous effort: the earthly and temporal now seems in this schema to be only an external husk that envelops and hides the inner kernel—a husk which must be shattered ascetically, "denied," and made transparent. The perfected and knowing exercitant looks through all this [outer husk] as mere appearance, for all non-identity with the divine is basically a non-being; and this applies as well therefore to the constricted ego and its individuality.[16]

Why is this world-view one that so quintessentially gives expression to the taint of original sin? Because original sin is the desire to be like God

---

sam diese Basis und sucht auf magische Weise—die Einverleibung irgend eines geistigen Zauberapfels—die Seinsweise des Schöpfers selbst zu erreichen."

[16] "PSW," 70: "Man findet also in seinem Menschwesen eine Stelle—vielleicht nur einen Punkt, aber dieser Punkt genügt—wo man gleichsam 'religiös' mit Gott auf gleichem Fuße verkehren darf, wo eine mystische Identität zwischen Schöpfer und Geschöpf besteht. Diesen geheimnisvollen Identitätspunkt zu erreichen, gilt nun alles 'religiöse' Bemühen: das Irdisch-Vergängliche erscheint in diesem Aspekt nur als eine äußere Schale, die den inneren Kern umhüllt und verdeckt, sie muß aszetisch durchbrochen, 'verneint,' transparent gemacht werden. Der Vollendete, der Erkennende durchschaut sie als Schein, denn alle Nichtidentität mit dem Göttlichen ist im Grunde ein Nichtsein; also auch das begrenzte Ich, die Individualität."

on one's own terms, to deny one's creaturely status and to be like God by nature and not by gift, the gift of divine grace. This is why the concept of analogy plays so crucial a role for Balthasar: because it stresses the ever-greater *dis*-similarity with God even as we come to recognize our derivation from him and thus the truth that we are made in the image and likeness of God:

> The element of original sin in human religiosity consists in this: that the similarity between Creator and creature that is given with the fact of our derivation from God, is not inscribed in the fundamental relationship of the creature's *not being God.* Everything depends on this fact. This not-being-God of the creature must be maintained as the most fundamental fact of all, ranking first above all others. That God is God: this is the most immense and absolutely *unsurpassable* thought. It says to me (if it has really struck home to me in the deepest part of my being), with an absolute evidence than can never be gainsaid, that I myself, to the very marrow of my existence, *am not God.*[17]

Only analogy, for Balthasar, can keep this insight always in view. Failure to keep it in mind is what makes the religious journey so dangerous, why Plato makes for such a deceptive ally to Christian thought, and why every "achievement" of the Christian believer must be regarded as the straw of "works-righteousness" without the saving grace of Christ. And what analogy does is remind us (admittedly, in its own abstract terms) of that fact, *that we are not God:*

> And should I ascend into eons upon eons and perfect myself there, should I lean out of the window of my very self into an infinite, loving ecstasy, and should God himself overshadow me with the gifts of his divinity—I still am not God. If ever this thought has struck me, I grasp at the same time that my fundamental not-being-God is the very truth that can never lapse into forgetfulness if I want to strive for "my truth" and my perfection. On the contrary, my whole striving to reach the divine home must be expressly built on this fundament. In other words,

---

[17] "PSW," 70: "Das Erbsündige dieser menschlichen Religiosität besteht darin, daß die Ähnlichkeit zwischen Schöpfer und Geschöpf, die mit der Tatsache der Gottesabkunft gegeben ist, nicht in das fundamentale Verhältnis des Nicht-Gott-seins des Geschöpfs hineingeschrieben wird. In der Tat hängt alles daran, daß jenes Nicht-Gott-sein des Geschöpfs als die rang-erste, eben fundamentale Tatsache festgehalten wird. Daß Gott ist, das ist der ungeheuerste und schlechthin *uneinholbare* Gedanke; er sagt mir, wenn er mich einmal im Tiefstem getroffen hat, mit einer absoluten, durch nichts überholbaren Evidenz, daß ich selbst, bis ins letzte hinein, nicht Gott bin."

in the relation between God and creature, similarity and difference do not hold the balance, but this dissimilarity is more radical.[18]

And thus, we may say that the concept of analogy will provide Balthasar with the key for unlocking the treasury of the Fathers, the Archimedean point for judging their form against the content of the Gospel, the tool for all his interpretative analysis. Again the reader must be cautioned not to misinterpret the term "analogy," with its provenance in philosophy, as if to interpret the Fathers' fidelity to the Gospel by the standard of analogy were itself to import a foreign element into the Gospel. As we have seen in both in the chapter on Przywara and in the one on Barth, the doctrine of analogy in theology is an outgrowth of the fundamental biblical insight that we are not God and that even in the gift of divine life in grace, indeed especially there, we become even more aware of that awesome fact. Perhaps, in fact, Przywara's influence on Balthasar was perhaps never more apparent than in this passage:

> And that is why, to the extent the creature comes nearer to God and becomes more "similar" to him, this dissimilarity must always appear as the more basic, as the "first truth." The more we know of God (and that always will be: the more we are "in God," since we can only know God through God), all the more do we know also that *we* are not God and that God is the One ever beyond all similarity, the ever more improbable, the ever ungraspable One. Or, as all the authentic mystics express it: the more we know God, the less we know him. If the light grows in "arithmetic" progression, the darkness simultaneously grows in "geometric" progression. And thus in approaching God the initial "intermediate space" between him and the creature will never be gradually diminished and, as it were, done away with in an infinite asymptotic approach. . . . No, on the contrary: all true approaches to God, however they might now be brought about—whether naturally, that is, more from the creature, or by

---

[18] "PSW," 70–71: "Und möge ich mich in alle Äonen der Äonen steigern und vervollkommen, und möge ich mich auch selbst in einer unendlichen, liebenden Exstase aus mir selber hinauslehne, und möge selbst Gott mich mit den Geschenken seiner Göttlichkeit überschütten, bin ich nicht Gott. Wenn mich einmal dieser Gedanke getroffen hat, begreife ich zugleich, daß mein fudamentales Nicht-Gott-sein jene Wahrheit ist, die keinesfalls in Vergessenheit geraten darf, wenn ich nach 'meiner Wahrheit' und meiner Vollendung streben will; daß vielmehr mein ganzes Streben, die göttliche Heimat zu erreichen, ausdrücklich auf diesem Fundament sich aufbauen muß. Anders ausgedrückt: im Verhältnis zwischen Gott und Geschöpf halten sich Ähnlichkeit und Verschiedenheit nicht das Gleichgewicht, sondern die Unähnlichkeit ist das Radikalere."

grace, that is, purely from God—stand by definition in this strange paradoxical relationship, that they can be constructed only on the foundation of an ever more towering distance.[19]

But the massive influence of Greek philosophy often worked against this insight. For Balthasar, the Church Fathers were in a way too successful. Their great virtue is their youth of spirit. In fact we are drawn to the study of patristics in this century precisely because they look so fresh and energetic to us who are living in the winter of our discontent.[20] But it was that very boldness that made the Fathers see the world as already conquered and culture as already prepared for the Gospel, pedagogically trained by Greek philosophy to hear the Good News. And how especially true of the Hellenistic philosophy of the Roman Empire! How could the writers and thinkers of the Church not be confident of victory with Platonism's and Stoicism's already strongly developed sense of religiosity opening out to an apparently supernatural and world-transcendent order? But that is the very difficulty of this approach:

> For it is precisely the certainty of victory with which the Fathers contemplated all the truths they encountered as being already Christian that hid the danger of an unconscious alienation of the original deposit of revelation. They therefore claimed these truths for their own, pouring the truth of the Gospel into the

---

[19] "PSW," 71: "Und darum muß auch, als im Maße das Geschöpf Gott näher kommt und ihm 'ähnlicher' wird, diese Unähnlichkeit immer mehr als das Grundlegende, als die 'erste Wahrheit' erscheinen. Je mehr wir von Gott erkennen (und das heißt doch: je mehr wir 'in Gott' sind, da wir Gott nur durch Gott erkennen können), um so mehr erkennen wir auch, daß *wir* nicht Gott sind und daß Gott, der immer weiter über alle Ähnlichkeit hinaus Erhabene, der immer Unwahrscheinlichere, immer Unfaßbarere ist. Oder, wie alle echten Mystiker es ausdrücken: je mehr wir Gott erkennen, um so weniger erkennen wir ihn. Wenn das Licht in 'arithmetischer' Progression wächst, so wächst das Dunkel zugleich in 'geometrischer.' Niemals also wird in der Näherung an Gott ein anfänglicher 'Zwischenraum' zwischen ihm und der Kreatur allmählich verringert und gleichsam in einer unendlichen Annäherung aufgehoben. Denn dies würde, in dem entwickelten Sinn, einen möglichen, wenigstens idealen Identitätspunkt zwischen beiden Polen voraussetzen. Sondern alle wahre Annäherung an Gott, wie immer sie nun auch bewerkstelligt werden mag,—ob naturhaft mehr vom Geschöpf aus oder gnadenhaft rein von Gott aus—steht von vornherein in diesem seltsamen, paradoxen Verhältnis, daß sie sich nur auf der Grundlage der immer überragenden Distanz aufbauen kann."

[20] "Greatness, depth, boldness, flexibility, certainty and a flaming love—the virtues of youth, are marks of patristic theology. Perhaps the Church will never again see the likes of such an array of larger-than-life figures such as mark the period from Irenaeus to Athanasius, Basil, Cyril, Chrysostom, Ambrose and Augustine—not to mention the army of the lesser Fathers. Life and doctrine are immediately one. Of them all it is true what Kierkegaard said of Chrysostom: 'He gesticulated with his whole existence'" ("PSW," 84–85).

language of their time: that is, into the thought forms of late Hellenism (above all, of neo-Platonism).[21]

The truth of this observation is most clearly evident in Christianity's most daring thinker of antiquity: Origen. For in Origen we have not only a doctrine of the pre-existence of souls and the subordination of the Logos to the One (both clear importations from neo-Platonism), but also an example of that unusual courage to think bold thoughts that makes not only him but his whole era attractive. Yet our admiration for his qualities must not blind us to the implications of his move nor to the (often subtle) way he influenced later thinkers who firmly and honestly believed they had repudiated him. For he is but the extreme example of a common strategy: the *spolatio Aegyptorum,* the belief that the treasures of Hellenistic philosophy lay ready and available for immediate use by Christians; and so perhaps it is fitting that this strategy is best known among the Christian apologists of the city of Alexandria, that great center of Hellenistic thought:

> The greatest and for later times the most decisive and consequential encounter [between Hellenism and Christianity] took place in Alexandria, especially in the greatest genius, next to Augustine, of the patristic era: Origen. We can no longer deny that in his case and despite his unbending will to be and to remain an authentic Christian, not only the outer words but also the basic forms of Hellenism had penetrated into the inner realm of Christianity and to a great extent established itself there from then on because of the unique influence of this giant of the spirit (a fact which has not yet been sufficiently researched and evaluated). It is not so much a question of certain individual doctrines that worked their way inside (such as, for example, the doctrine of the pre-existence of souls), which could easily be declared heretical upon their enunciation, as much more a question of the inner space of the spirit, a whole tissue of assumptions from time immemorial that are not easy to get a hold of, an atmosphere, a formal methodology.[22]

---

21 "PSW," 85: "Gerade die Siegesgewißheit, mit der die Väter alle ihnen begegnende Wahrheit als christlich betrachteten und für sich beanspruchten, mit der sie die evangelische Wahrheit in die Sprache ihrer Zeit, in die Denkformen des späten Hellenismus, vor allem des Neuplatonismus umgossen, barg die Gefahr einer unbewußten Veräußerung des ursprünglichen Offenbarungsgutes."

22 "PSW," 85: "Die größte und für die Folgezeit entscheidende und folgenreichste Begegnung vollzog sich in Alexandrien, zumal unter dem genialsten Denker der Patristik, neben Augustinus: unter Origenes. Daß bei ihm, trotz seinem ungebeugtem Willen, echter Christ zu sein und zu bleiben, nicht nur äußere Worte, sondern Grundformen des Hellenismus

This is most evident in the doctrine of the Trinity, for here almost all of the patristic writers assimilated the Plotinian and neo-Platonic doctrine of God's emanation in creation down a Great Chain of Being. In Plotinus, this scale is characterized by, in descending order, spirit, soul and matter. But among the Fathers, this emanationism began inside the Godhead itself, with the Father representing the One, the Son the Mind (*nous* or *logos*), and the Spirit a kind of vague penumbra on the boundary between the Godhead and creation.[23] Obviously, Origen's naïve assumption that the Logos is subordinate to the Father will be inevitable, and only when Arius made this same naïve assumption explicit was the Church forced to pull back—*but not to reverse course:* "The inner logic of the Platonic scheme was so compelling that one could draw the defensive walls, as it were, only with great effort. Moreover, those defensive measures could be forgotten the next moment—because of the hypnotic power of its inner architectonic, which was especially potent when one wasn't thinking explicitly on the schema."[24]

---

in den christlichen Raum eindrangen und sich, durch den einzigartigen, noch nicht genug erforschten und gewerteten Einfluß dieses Geistesriesen auf die Folgezeit, auch weitgehend festsetzten, das dürfte heute kaum mehr zu leugnen sein. Nicht so sehr einzelne bestimmte Lehren sind es, die hier eindrangen—solche konnten, wie etwa die Vorgeburtslehre, sogleich als häretisch entlarvt werden—, als vielmehr einen geistigen Raum, ein ganzes, schwer faßbares Geflecht von uralten Denkgewohnheiten, eine Atmosphäre, eine formale Methodik." One should recall that this essay was written in 1939. It is doubtful how many people would now wish to deny the thesis Balthasar is proposing here.

[23] At least until the Cappadocians, who were forced to develop a more full-blooded theology of the Holy Spirit in the wake of the Council of Nicea's declaration of the full equality of the Son with the Father. Arius, who denied this and insisted on the absolute subordination of the Son to the Father, makes perfect sense when we realize how much the neo-Platonic schema of Plotinus had influenced patristic theology. But it is interesting to note that even after Nicea and Constantinople (which declared against the heretical implications that were bound to surface with this marriage of Christian doctrine with neo-Platonic philosophy), Plotinus continued to influence Christian thought: "Here is a young convert to Christianity [Augustine] who, for the first time in his life, reads the *Enneads* [of Plotinus], and what he sees there at once is the Christian God himself, with all his essential attributes. Who is the One, if not God the Father, the first person of the Christian Trinity? And who is the Nous, or Intellect, if not the second person of the Trinity, that is, the Word, exactly as he appears at the beginning of the Gospel of St. John? ... In short, as soon as Augustine read the *Enneads,* he found there the three essentially Christian notions of God the Father, of God the Word, and of the creation" (Étienne Gilson, *God and Philosophy* [New Haven: Yale University Press, 1941], 48–49). Note how attenuated Augustine's theology of the Holy Spirit is in this scheme, so much so that Gilson does not even deem it necessary to mention the Spirit in this summary (which Augustine admittedly corrected later in his life when he wrote the *De Trinitate*).

[24] "PSW," 87: "Aber die innere Logik des platonischen Schemas war eine so zwingende, daß man abweichende Linien gleichsam nur mit einer bewußten Anstrengung ziehen konnte und daß—durch die hypnotisierende Kraft der inneren Architektonik—die Abweichung im Augenblick wieder vergessen werden konnte, wo sie nicht mehr thematisch im Blickfeld stand."

For Balthasar, this hypnotic power explains why so many doctrinal controversies beset the Church of the Roman Empire, from Arianism all the way to the *filioque* controversy, as well as throws light on the ascetical legacy of the early Church. For example, according to Balthasar, the *filioque* controversy need never have arisen had the Trinity not been interpreted under the rubric of the neo-Platonic schema:

> A first sign for this [hypnotic power of neo-Platonism] is the fact that, in spite of constantly repeated assurances to the contrary, the schema of descent was not all that far from the dogmatics of the Trinity, even in post-Nicene theology. Although now the abstract and formal statements on the Trinity are correct, the schema of descent stands before the vision of Greek theology like some kind of accompanying phantasm. This is probably the real reason why the *filioque* could never find a home in the Greek Church: a view of the Holy Spirit that posits the Spirit as the substantial love "between" Father and Son contradicts too openly the first conceptual schema of Platonism.[25]

A further indication of this malign influence is the attenuated role that Trinitarian piety played in the life of the Church, especially among the monks.[26] But this neo-Platonic schema was most influential of all in the

---

[25] "PSW," 87: "Eine erste Anzeige dafür ist, daß (trotz immer wiederholter gegenteiliger Versicherungen) auch aus der postnikänischen Theologie das Abstiegsschema nicht ganz aus der Trinitätsdogmatik zu entfernen war. Obwohl nun die abstrakten und formalen Aussagen über die Dreifaltigkeit korrekt sind, steht vor dem Blick des griechischen Theologen gleichsam als begleitendes Phantasma das Abstiegsschema. Dies ist wohl der wahre Grund dafür, daß das Filioque in der griechischen Kirche nie heimisch werden konnte: eine Auffassung des Heiligen Geistes, die diesen als die substantielle Liebe 'zwischen' Vater und Sohn stellt, widerspricht zu offen dem ersten Denkschema des Platonismus."

[26] "A second indication for this is the fact that despite the formally orthodox post-Nicene view of the Trinity no corresponding trinitarian piety and mysticism seemed inclined to develop. For example, in the mystical writings of Gregory of Nyssa one can almost touch the fact that the loveliest trinitarian and dogmatic passages remains almost without influence and context with the actual mystical parties, who were striving in the ascent to God not to the trinitarian God but to the absolutely simple "essence" of God that stands on the summit of the Platonic pyramid. This tendency to a strict monotheism thus also completely wins the palm of victory in the grandiose and resounding clarion call of the Greek Fathers: in Dionysius the Areopagite and Maximus the Confessor, where the formally available confession of the Trinity plays almost no role whatever in the living-out of the Christian life. In fact what Maximus does is to get past the Cappadocians and Nicea and consciously link up with the Origenistic schema of Logos theology" ("PSW," 87). There is some modification of this judgment in Balthasar's book on Maximus, which came out two years later (1941; revised 1961), but I would maintain it was never entirely retracted. Nonetheless, there he stresses much more Maximus' originality: "Gegen die gesamtgriechische Tendenz einer Überordnung des Gegenstandes über das Subjekt unterstreicht er ihre Gleichberechtigung auf allen Stufen des Seins. Dieses Denkmotiv hält sich weiterhin durch in der Ontologie

attitude that the early Church took toward the incarnation and the resurrection of the flesh. It is almost as if Hellenized Christians were back at the Areopagus with St. Paul on his preaching mission to Athens: and when he came to the part about the resurrection of the flesh, his listeners mocked him (Acts 17: 32), find the notion incredible:

> Closely bound up with this is their version of the incarnation, which despite the Antiochenes and Nestorius, constantly was inclined to a docetic and Eutychian view. The incarnation is consequently thought of as the most extreme point of the "egression" of God from himself. The self-emptying (*kenosis*) appears as God's self-alienation in the service of fetching the world back home to the Godhead. The incarnation is almost looked on by the Alexandrines as a "distortion" of the purely spiritual into its polar opposite, matter, a distortion that was necessary for pedagogical and salvation-historical reasons in order to capture the distance of the material world from God and gradually lead it back to the realm of the spiritual and divine by a reverse movement. Origen's myth of the pre-existence of souls and his idea that the material world is a consequence of the fall of sin shows this conceptual schema (that in many places is muffled and only latently present) in its most bare-faced and, as such, in its most heterodox form. But even where the myth is lacking, as in Clement, Athanasius, Gregory of Nyssa, Maximus, the direction their thought takes toward this schema is still present. In this schema the incarnation must appear as something provisional and transitional. The resurrection of the flesh, formally confessed and maintained, appears like a disturbance of the systematic lines and usually was subtilized in one or another form.[27]

---

von Geist und Stoff. Um ihretwillen kommt Maximus im Chor der christlichen Denker ein Sonderplatz zu" (*KL*, 169).

[27] "PSW," 87–88: "Eng damit zusammen hängt die Auffassung von der Menschwerdung, die, trotz Antiochien und Nestorius, stets zu einer doketisch-eutychianischen Fassung neigt. Die Inkarnation ist folgerichtig als der äußerste Punkt des 'Ausgangs' Gottes aus sich selbst gedacht, die Selbstentäußerung (kenosis) erscheint als eine Selbstentfremdung Gottes im Dienste der Heimholung der Welt in die Gottheit. Sie wird von den Alexandrinern beihahe als eine 'Verstellung' des rein Geistigen in dessen Gegenpol, in der Materie, aufgefaßt, eine Verstellung, die aus pädagogisch-heilsgeschichtlichen Gründen nötig war, um die Gottferne der materiellen Welt einzufangen und in allmählicher Rückbewegung in den Bereich des Geistig-Göttlichen heimzuführen. Der Vorgeburtsmythus des Origenes und seine Idee, daß die materielle Welt eine Folge des Sündenfalls ist, zeigt dieses Denkschema, das vielerorts gedämpft und latent vorhanden ist, in seiner unverhülltesten und als solches heterodoxen Form. Aber auch wo der Mythus fehlt, bei Clemens, Athanasius, Gregor von Nyssa, Maximus, ist die Denkrichtung doch gegenwärtig. In diesem Schema muß die Menschwerdung als

This often unacknowledged but barely disguised discomfort with the incarnation and resurrection of the flesh had, of course, immense implications for the practice of the Christian life, especially in the area of asceticism; for it is in this area of asceticism that the full practical impact of the Plotinian schema was felt with such overwhelming force:

> But what is the most decisive outcome of this strategy is the total effect it had on the tendency of the Christian life, the direction of its ideal: its asceticism and mysticism. This direction proceeds, in consequence of the movement of the ascending, step-by-step return of the world potencies into God, unambiguously away from the material to the spiritual. Spiritualization, presented in a thousand different colorations, is the basic tendency of the patristic epoch. Early monasticism with its extremely ascetical experiments, its training in denial of the body, its Encratite traits, its individualism, shows this most clearly: along with its extraordinarily splendid sides, this brand of monasticism clearly shows the peril of this movement.[28]

One emerges from reading this analysis rather stunned at the negative view Balthasar takes of patristic development, almost to the point of harshness; and he fully admits the critical nature of his interpretation ("Of course, in the preceding we have first painted a strongly negative picture"[29]). But I think such a stress is useful in this chapter because of a superficial impression readers often get of Balthasar because of his extraordinary competence and range of publications in patristics: almost as if he is one of the Church Fathers come back to life. In fact, one hears from time to time phrases like "in him there breathes the spirit of the Fathers," or the like; and then there is the title of Werner Löser's book, *Im Geiste des Origenes* (*In the Spirit of Origen*). All of which is to some extent true. But we must also not forget the truth of the observation of

---

etwas Vorläufiges und Vorübergehendes erscheinen. Die Auferstehung des Fleisches, formell bekannt und festgehalten, erscheint wie eine Störung der systematischen Linien und wird zumeist in der einen oder anderen Form subtilisiert."

[28] "PSW," 88: "Das Entscheidendste aber, das sich daraus ergibt, ist die Gesamttendenz des christlichen Lebens, die Richtung seines Ideals, seiner Aszese und Mystik. Diese Richtung geht, folgerichtig zur Bewegung des aufsteigenden, stufenweisen Wiedereingehens der Weltpotenzen in Gott, eindeutig vom Materiellen weg zum Geistigen hin. Vergeistigung ist, in tausendfachen Abschattungen dargestellt, die Grundtendenz der patristischen Epoche. Das frühe Mönchtum und seine extremen aszetischen Experimente, sein Entkörperungstraining, seine enkratitischen Züge, sein Individualismus zeigt, neben herrlichen Lichtseiten, am deutlichsten die Gefährlichkeit dieser Bewegung."

[29] Ibid., 89: "Wir haben nun freilich im Vorausgehenden zunächst ein stark negatives Bild gezeichnet."

Henri de Lubac: "Without ever abdicating his freedom to criticize, he is at ease with all [the figures he studies], even those whose genius might appear most foreign to his own; but when the time comes to disagree with them he does not hesitate."[30]

And yet this chapter would have given a completely false impression if the reader got the idea that Balthasar was merely critical of the patristic turn in theology, as if he were trying to out-Harnack Harnack. On the contrary, what Balthasar recognizes, *contra* Harnack, are the essentially biblical presuppositions that operate within all of the Church Fathers, transforming—however unconsciously, in many cases—the philosophy they inherited:

> Everywhere we find that words become transparent in a deeper way than their merely denotative meaning. The whole dimension "from matter to spirit" is a *sensible image* for the dimension "from creature to God." But authentic Christianity in each period depends on how far the symbol is recognized as symbol and treated as such—how far, that is, God is not confused with the "innermost essence of the human spirit" and the "divine Pneuma" is not mistaken for that created "pneuma" that Greek anthropology counted as part of the components of man, along with his body and soul.[31]

The proof of this exoneration of the Fathers is the attitude all the Christian writers of this period take toward pantheism. For the essential implication of the Plotinian world view is pantheism (or, technically, theopanism, since Plotinus began with God as the first term): the world is essentially an emanation of God that will return at the end of time back to the Godhead, when all things will be one in the One. This ultimate eschatological obliteration of all distinctions is a direct implication of the absence of any analogical distinction in the being of God and the world. The world essentially *participates* in the being of God along a Great Chain of Being (spirit-soul-matter), and this participation is a sharing of essences. And so if the Plotinian schema had been all that controlling, the entire biblical account of creation and eschatology would have been interpreted pantheistically. But such is not the case:

> But in fact the signs of this Christian character (and thus of the symbolic distance of content and form) can be seen to be present

---

[30] Henri de Lubac, "A Witness of Christ in the Church: Hans Urs von Balthasar," *Communio* 2/3 (Fall, 1975), 231.

[31] "PSW," 89: "Überall sind Worte durchsichtig in einer tieferen als die Wortbedeutung. Die gesamte Dimension 'vom Stoff zum Geist' ist ein *Sinnbild* für die Dimension 'vom

as we gradually work our way through the texts. "Pantheism," in the sense used by the ancient Greek philosophers, is for the Fathers the worst of all gruel. Against nothing do they struggle more energetically and unambiguously. Over and again they emphasize and maintain the first basic cleft between God and creature. All "divinization" is only a participation from grace and never a fusion of nature. Even so extreme a spiritualist and fanatic of unity like Evagrius Ponticus maintains this distinction, at least formally. The corrective of a feeling of worshipping distance and the sharp sense for what grace means is precisely what the great Church Fathers like Athanasius, the Cappadocians, Cyril and Dionysius gave to us for all time in so exemplary a way.[32]

But why was that the case? Why *hadn't* the Church Fathers become so intoxicated with the Plotinian vision that they ended up pantheists *malgé eux?* For Balthasar, the answer can only be that they kept in mind, however inarticulately, the fundamental analogical distinction between God and the world:

What works against the immediate tendency to divinize creation and man is that authentic Christian shyness before the ineffable God who dwells beyond all seeing and grasping, the knowledge of God's eternal otherness and thus of his overpowering and ever-greater darkness even in the midst of his light. No one has more clearly developed the foundational doctrines of negative theology than the Greeks: the two Gregorys and Dionysius. In the wondrous mystical theology of Diadochus of Photiké, the Christian essence is so immediately effective that no trace of Hellenistic thought forms can be seen. And where could one

---

Geschöpf zu Gott.' Die jeweilige echte Christlichkeit aber hängt davon ab, inwieweit das Symbol als Symbol erkannt und als solches behandelt ist. Inwiefern also Gott nicht mit dem 'innersten Wesen des menschlichen Geistes,' das 'göttliche Pneuma' nicht mit jenem geschaffenen 'Pneuma' verwechselt wird, das die griechische Anthropologie neben Leib und Seele zu den Bestandteilen der Menschennatur zählt."

[32] "PSW," 89: "Nun aber sind die Anzeichen dieser Christlichkeit (und damit des symbolischen Abstandes von Inhalt und Form) auf Schritt und Tritt vorhanden. 'Pantheismus,' im Sinn wie altgriechische Philosophen ihn vertraten, ist den Vätern das ärgste aller Greuel. Nichts bekämpfen sie energischer und eindeutiger. Immer wird die erste grundlegende Kluft zwischen Gott und Geschöpf betont und festgehalten. Alle 'Vergottung' ist nur eine Teilnahme aus Gnade, nie eine Verschmelzung der Natur. Selbst ein so extremer Spiritualist und Einheitsfanatiker wie Evagrius Pontikus hält formell an dieser Scheidung fest. Das Korrektiv des anbetenden Abstandgefühls und der scharfe Sinn für das, was Gnade heißt, ist gerade bei den Größten, bei Athanasius, den Kappodoziern, Cyrill, Dionysius beispielhaft für alle folgende Zeiten geworden."

find examples of a more heroic fidelity to the Church than in Athanasius, Basil, Cyril and Maximus?[33]

Moreover, there is a fundamental aspect of revelation that is not only compatible with the neo-Platonic ladder of being (moving upward from matter, to soul or life, to spirit and then ultimately to God) but also almost positively demands expression in these terms—provided the schema be rightly interpreted. For it is a basic fact of revelation that matter is recalcitrant to the spirit and that the transformation and transfiguration of these fleshly bodies of ours will result in spiritual bodies (1 Cor 15:44) which are completely obedient to the dictates of the spirit, a spirit that will in turn be completely absorbed in God, so much so that rebellion against God will be literally inconceivable. And so in a much deeper sense, the Fathers took the Plotinian schema and transformed *it* by touching it with the transforming wand of revelation:

> First of all, taken in itself: every religious ascetic will have to confront the issue of the order of man's sensate instinctual drives. Augustine's basic schema: the body subordinate to the soul, the soul under God, is obligatory for all eras of Christianity. Then, understood as a symbol, this basic aspect of revelation— the dying to the world with Christ, the dynamic of life ordered toward the new eon, an age not of the gross senses but one spiritually transfigured—is the presupposition of the new Christian's life ("Your transformation is in heaven," "Your life is hidden with Christ in God"). This basic aspect of revelation can never be suppressed no matter how focused we are on the world, and it can be symbolized in the categories drawn from the world of matter and spirit. Paul and John have done this when they call God "spirit" and set up "flesh" and "spirit" as the symbolic values for the old and new eons. And so too with the Fathers: this biblical meaning [of flesh and spirit] always resonates through their use of Hellenistic terms.[34]

---

[33] "PSW," 89: "Der unmittelbaren Tendenz zur 'Vergöttlichung' wirkt entgegen jene echte christliche Scheu vor dem unnennbaren und über alles Schauen und Erfassen hinaus entrückten Gott, das Wissen um Gottes ewiges Anderssein und darum um seine mitten im Licht überwältigende, immer größere Dunkelheit. Die Grundlehren der negativen Theologie sind von niemandem klarer entwickelt worden als von Griechen: den beiden Gregor und Dionysius. In der wunderbaren mystischen Theologie des Diadochus von Photiké wirkt sich das Christliche in so unmittelbarer Weise aus, daß von hellenistischen Denkformen kaum Spuren aufzuweisen sind. Und wo fänden sich Beispiele heroischerer Kirchentreue als bei Athanasius, Basilius, Cyrill, Maximus?"

[34] "PSW," 90: "Einmal in sich selbst genommen: Jede religiöse Aszetik wird mit der Ordnung des sinnlichen Trieblebens einzusetzen haben. Das Grundschema Augustins: Leib unter Seele, Seele unter Gott, ist für alle Epochen des Christentums verpflichtend. Dann aus-

How then are we to distinguish the good from the bad, the true from the false, the underlying intent from the deceptive terminology in patristic thought? For Balthasar the key will always remain the issue of "participation." Does the human spirit automatically participate in the Spirit of God simply by virtue of being spirit? Is there some essential connection between the human spirit as emanation or ray and the divine spirit as sun or source of light?

Of course no one denies that by virtue of divine grace, we are given a share, a participation, in the divine nature; but that is precisely the issue. What the Platonic schema obscures is the *gratuity* of that participation, making it seem that it is ours by virtue of our *nature* as spirit-endowed creatures. Internal to the economy of grace, the Platonic schema can be of great pedagogical use, especially as it so usefully illuminates the path from justification to sanctification via the *askesis* from matter to the divine light of God's Spirit. This ascetical path, however, is never an achievement of nature but is itself a gift of grace.[35] And this for Balthasar is the greatest blind-spot among all the theologians of the first eight centuries of the Church, Greek and Latin alike (Augustine included!): that their theology

---

drücklich als Symbol gefaßt: Das Absterben dieser Welt mit Christus, die Dynamik des Lebens auf den neuen, nicht mehr grobsinnlichen, sondern geisthaft verklärten Äon, den das Christenleben vorauszunehmen und vorauszuleben hat ('Euer Wandel ist im Himmel,' 'Euer Leben ist verborgen mit Christus in Gott'), dieser grundlegende und in aller Weltzugewandtheit unaufhebbare Aspekt der Offenbarung läßt sich durchaus in den weltlichen Kategorien Stoff und Geist symbolisieren. Paulus und Johannes haben es selbst getan, wenn sie Gott 'Geist' nennen und 'Fleisch' und 'Pneuma' als Symbolwerte für den alten und den neuen Äon aufstellen. Und so klingt bei den Vätern auch stets diese biblische durch die hellenistische Wortbedeutung hindurch."

[35] This is in fact the main point of Balthasar's famous book on prayer. This passage in particular shows how deep Barth's influence ran: "Our praise, gratitude and worship do not spring solely from our existence—though we can never thank God enough for it; our existence itself was only given to us because of a thought in God's mind prior even to that of our existence—'before the foundation of the world.' Indeed, our whole being is immersed in the ocean of the Father's love, who creates nature and its laws to act as a foil to set off his miracles. When we contemplate the Word of God, we must let ourselves be gripped by this primary truth, namely, that the whole compact mass of created being and essence and the everyday world we are so familiar with sails like a ship over the fathomless depths of a wholly different element, the only one that is absolute and determining, the boundless love of the Father. . . . This follows, according to a logic, a system of thought and a reckoning, whose inner coherence, exactness and justice *comprise and presuppose grace* and all its accompaniments, a logic which applies even to the most formal elements of the grammar of God's language. Once we have suspected or felt the mystery of our existence, the necessity of prayer and especially of contemplative listening in prayer becomes evident. For the relation between God and creature is now seen to depend on the marvel of God's incomprehensible love, and shows him, in setting up this relation, as the Lover absolutely. Then the creature itself is seen as a sustained utterance of prayer; and man only needs to know, in some degree, what he really is, to break spontaneously into prayer" (*Prayer*, tr. A. V. Littledale [New York: Sheed & Ward, 1961], 35–36).

of the relation between nature and grace was flawed, or at least too simplistic. And it was because of this flaw that they could not hold in check the implications of the enticing Platonic schema they borrowed from their environment:

> Nevertheless, we must point out here (where what is at issue is only the most implicitly held and often painted over and corrected conceptual law of the patristic period) that the Platonic schema is what predominated. In its basic concept of "participation," this law has always hidden within itself the danger zone of a too-easy transition from the realm of the natural spirit into the gracious realm of the divine Pneuma. "Pneuma" as the place of actual participation is too dazzling: it scintillates and opalesces (just as the later Russian Sophia speculation will do, developing along the same point), hovering in an unclarified twofold unity between the divine and the created sphere. In this way the fundamental deficiency of the whole Platonic schematic is revealed: it is able to be an excellent expression of the *supernatural* relation between the God of grace and the engraced creature (to put it in Christian terms). Grace is of course essentially "participation" in the divine nature, but [the Platonic schema] is not able sufficiently to clarify the relationships of the two *natures* [divine and human] that lies at the basis of every act of grace.[36]

For Balthasar there is a quick and easy way of determining how much the terminology borrowed from Plato and Plotinus shapes the Christian message to its schema and how much it expresses what is a legitimate insight in both systems: is the creation of matter seen as a consequence of the Fall? This of course was the whole point of the struggle of the early Church with Gnosticism, and in that sense none of the Fathers would dream of equating creation with the Fall, or would think of seeing the Incarnation in docetic terms. Yet just as we saw with the incarnation, it

---

[36] "PSW," 90: "Dennoch muß hier, wo es nur um das hintergründigste und oft übermalte und korrigierte Denkgesetz der patristischen Periode geht, das platonische Schema als das überwiegende herausgestellt werden, das im grundlegenden 'Teilnahme'-Begriff immer die Gefahrzone eines gleitenden Übergangs aus dem Bereich des naturhalften Geistes in den gnadenhaften des göttlichen Pneuma in sich birgt. 'Pneuma' als der Ort der eingentlichen Teilhabe schillert (wie die im selben Punkt sich entwickelnde, spätere russische Sophiaspekulation) in einer unklärbaren Zwei-Einheit zwischen der göttlichen und der geschöpflichen Sphäre. Dabei wird der fundamentale Mangel der ganzen platonischen Schematik offenbar: sie vermag, ins Christliche übertragen, ein ausgezeichneter Ausdruck des *übernatürlichen* Verhältnis zwischen dem Gott der Gnade und dem begnadeten Geschöpf zu sein—Gnade ist ja wesenhaft 'Teilnahme' an der göttlichen Natur—, sie ist aber nicht imstande, das jeder Begnadung zugrunde liegende Verhältnis der Naturen selbst genügend zu verdeutlichen."

is possible to undervalue material creation because of the implicit influences of neo-Platonism: Just as the incarnation can be seen as intended by God for mostly pedagogical purposes but still remain metaphysically scandalous, so too it is possible to look on creation as more of a hurdle to cross to get to God than as God's loving expression of himself to the finite other. And this is what is missing for Balthasar from patristic thought when it is taken as a whole: insofar as it is good, creation is seen as something that is by definition supernatural, but insofar as it differs from God, it represents the surd of nature:

> And so it happens that in all forms of Platonic-Christian thinking creation (nature) and the Fall of sin have a secret, if often mostly unspoken, affinity. On the other side, however, the *positive* in created nature is seen as something inherently supernatural. The "pneuma" of man is directly interpreted as grace and so belongs on the other side of man's natural constitution. The Platonic schema shows the formal outline of the God-creature relationship *too simplistically* (they relate to each other according to this schema like N and-N). And from this simplification what results is ultimately, with relentless logic, all the dangers of Patristic theology and spirituality.[37]

What Balthasar has most drawn from the Fathers is their daring, but as their true son he does not flinch from applying that same daring to his criticism of them as well. This gives to his interpretation of patristics a boldness that can be disconcerting to other practitioners in the field. One can occasionally pick up in the professional literature indications of such puzzled attitudes among patrologists, as in this review of Balthasar's book on Maximus the Confessor by an expert in the field:

> My single studies on Maximus have had as their immediate scope the understanding of Maximus from within his own tradition. This is as it should be. . . . On the other hand, von Balthasar began his work in a quite different way. He is neither primarily concerned with Maximus as a *locus classicus* within the Byzantine tradition, nor with the contrast between the Byzantine and

---

[37] "PSW," 91: "So kommt es, daß in allem platonish-christlichen Denken Schöpfung (Natur) und (Sünden-) Fall eine geheime, wenn auch meist unausgesprochene Affinität besitzten und daß auf der anderen Seite das *Positive* in der erschaffenen Natur als ein Übernatürliches gesehen wird. Das als Gnade gedeutete 'Pneuma' des Menschen gehört doch anderseits mit zur naturhaften Konstitution des Menschen. Das platonische Schema zeichnet den formalen Grundriß des Gott-Geschöpf-Verhältnis zu *einfach*—(sie verhalten sich nach ihm wie N und-N)—und aus dieser Vereinfachung ergeben sich letztlich in genauer Logik alle Gefahren der patristischen Theologie und Geistigkeit."

Latin theological traditions. Rather, von Balthasar sees the task of the theologian, who, he proposes, should be audaciously creative, as that of one who would bring into coherent overall view the objective values of our post-Cartesian world that bears so deep an imprint both from German Idealism and from modern science. For this, he sees a magnificent exemplar in Origen, in Gregory of Nyssa and particularly in Maximus, who made the Chalcedonian formula the keystone of a theology embracing all in its unifying grasp. Thus are explained his frequent references to Hegel and to other German Idealists, as he leaps directly from the historical context of Maximus to a contemporary situation of the mid-20th century. More than the lack of detailed investigations, more than any want of confidence in his interpretations of Maximus on the basis of texts, is such a procedure disconcerting to many competent students of Byzantine theology, as transgressing the bounds which are habitually set to their studies.[38]

This is a fascinating remark, and deeply revealing. And no doubt, judged from the rigorous standards of a purely historical approach to patristic studies, it has a certain justification. But Balthasar's patristics is aimed at much more than merely historical clarification, what Sherwood calls "understanding Maximus [or any other figure] within his own tradition." Even in the midst of the most technically demanding work, Balthasar is not only aware of the contemporary crisis through which Christianity is now passing, he writes from that perspective and for it: his work as a theologian—and especially as a theologian who wants always to draw on the Church's patristic resources—is always directed to the apostolic end of inspiring new life into the dry bones of a long-desiccated Christianity. At no point does he hide this purpose, and indeed he opens his important study of Gregory of Nyssa with a programmatic manifesto that makes this clear from the outset:

The place of the theologian in the present world is strangely paradoxical. By vocation he is given to the study of the past where God has manifested himself, and even beyond this past to the contemplation of the eternal. Yet, by his very existence, he is rooted in a world that is shaking on its foundations and seems ready to break up. Absorbed though he be by prayer and his professional research, if he has kept enough freedom to look about him and to lift his gaze sufficiently to attempt to under-

---

[38] Dom Polycarp Sherwood, "A Survey of Recent Work on St. Maximus the Confessor," *Traditio* 20 (1964): 428–437; here 433–434.

stand what is happening, he cannot fail to realize that he belongs to an "epoch," as Péguy used to say, and not to a [mere episodic] "period"—and to an epoch where the established order still seems solid, but which has in fact decayed from within and is already deserted by a life, which at any moment may reject and, by a metamorphosis, quit that order as an empty shell, destined to pulverization at the least breath. To be sure, the contemplation of the "eternal verities" is still his; he well knows that they, at any rate, "resist" the ravages of time. But does he now realize quite as well that these eternal verities to be alive and effective— real and true, at once in the mundane as in the heavenly sense— must also be incarnate in temporal forms? And these temporal forms? Where are they to be found? The historical period that Descartes began is gone. How will the theologian be able to work at assisting at the birth and nurture of the theology that a new humanity is demanding?[39]

But far from being a drawback, or perhaps at best a charming eccentricity of the author, this approach is really the only one that is properly suited for bringing patristics out of the narrow ghetto that we described at the outset of this chapter. Accomplishments in this field of course demand a daunting array of talents and competencies, along with long training, but if such a commitment of talent and training is to bear fruit for *theology*, and not just for scholarship, it must be animated by more than merely antiquarian interest. Nor is it sufficient, on the other hand, to replace antiquarian interest with its opposite number: a vague, romantic nostalgia for a past that is seen only under the hazy glow of one's own lack of analytical power. A real assimilation of the thought of the Church Fathers entails, rather, an intensive confrontation with their texts together with a burning concern with the situation of the contemporary Church— all combined with an analytic power to see the rub of the real issue and a synthetic power to present a new vision to the Church.

What makes Balthasar so important of a challenge to contemporary theology is his ability to meet such heavy demands, which is why his achievement is so unparalleled in this century. It is in *this* respect, and not in the way so often assumed, that he is, as Werner Löser implies in the title of his book, the living heir of Origen. It is true that Balthasar writes "in the spirit of Origen," but not because he is a closet Platonist, or because he mindlessly mouths back the formulas of the Fathers, or because he timidly hearkens back to a lost paradise before the Church had to confront the acids of modernity. He is a true Origenist in his boldness,

---

[39] *Présence et Pensée: Essai sur la philosophie religieuse de Grégoire de Nysse* (Paris: Beauchesne, 1942), vii.

his powers of concentration, his synthetic hold on the true essence of the problem, his capacity for drawing on diverse sources (of which, like Origen, he has the most direct acquaintance), and—one feels sure—he is also like Origen in his destiny of shaping later generations. And so in this regard he has, once more, given us, as he did in the case of Maximus, an unconscious portrait of himself in his own sketch of Origen and his significance for today:

> It is all but impossible to overestimate Origen and his importance for the history of Christian thought. To rank him beside Augustine and Thomas simply accords him his rightful place in this history. Anyone who has given long hours to studying the Fathers will have had the same experience as a mountain climber: the slow, steady receding of the seemingly still-threatening peaks all around him, until, beyond them, the hitherto-hidden dominant central massif rises majestically before him. . . . [His] is a voice that drives straight through everything, always pushing on, without fanfare and without fatigue, almost it seems without an obvious goal, possessed almost to the point of insanity, and yet with a cool, unapproachable intellectual restraint that has never again been equaled. It is not the voice of a rhetorician (there are enough of these among the Fathers so that the difference is immediately obvious), for this voice is not even trying to persuade; nor is it the enthusiastic voice of a poet (although the images and comparisons fly up in swarms everywhere); it is too brittle, too dry and too plain for that, even to the point of poverty. . . . Everything here is unpremeditated, unforced, and expressed with a modesty that never ceases to amaze. . . . The voice of the Alexandrian is more like that glowing, rainless desert-wind that sometimes sweeps over the Nile delta, with a thoroughly unromantic passion: in pure, fiery gusts.[40]

This quintessentially Balthasarian appreciation captures perhaps more than any other passage in his writings on patristics the extraordinary verve and élan that mark his whole approach to the Fathers: it is an inner appreciation for the pathos that animated their project together with an amazing feel for the style of each author of that period. But as we have seen in the preceding analysis, this appreciation is in no sense a slavish aping of their insights. His knowledge of the Fathers comes from an in-

---

[40] *Origen: Spirit and Fire: A Thematic Anthology of his Writings*, tr. Robert J. Daly, S.J. (Washington, D.C.: Catholic University of America, 1984), 1–3. This passage concludes with a typically daring comparison: "Two names come to mind [when thinking of Origen]: Heraclitus and Nietzsche."

tense engagement with their works, but he emerges from this hard-won encounter with a sovereign freedom that can—with the benefit of hindsight, to be sure—spot weaknesses and see where further development is necessary. Even more than that, he plunges into the world of the Fathers knowing the seriousness of the issues of the present day, and that is what gives his writings on such seeming arcana such a unique sense of urgency.

But above all, from the Fathers Balthasar has been able to draw on resources that will prove crucial for his own mission as a theologian. Indeed, Part I of this book has tried to show how extraordinarily rich are the resources on which he was able to draw. Perhaps it has also given some indication of the analytic power of his mind as he wrestled with these resources, gradually building up the building blocks that would eventually come to form the towers and walls of his own grand edifice. And thus, in his slow and patient mustering of his materials and in the careful plan of construction, he has followed that evangelical prudence recommended in the Gospels. "Suppose one of you wants to build a tower," runs one of the parables of Jesus. "Will he not first sit down and estimate the cost to see if he has enough money to complete it? For if he lays the foundation and is not able to finish it, everyone who sees it will ridicule him, saying 'This fellow began to build and was unable to finish it'" (Lk 14: 28–30). But Balthasar first gathered, and then he built. And it is to the description of the edifice he built that we now turn.

Part II

THE
AESTHETICS

• • •

Therefore we thank Thee for our little light, that is
   dappled with shadow.
We thank Thee who hast moved us to building, to
   finding, to forming at the ends of our fingers and
   beams of our eyes.
And when we have built an altar to the Invisible
   Light, we may set thereon the little lights for which
   our bodily vision is made.
And we thank Thee that darkness reminds us of light.
O Light Invisible, we give Thee thanks for Thy great
   glory.

T. S. Eliot,
Choruses from "The Rock"

· 5 ·

The Splendor of Light Invisible

Our gaze is submarine, our eyes look upward
And see the light that fractures through unquiet water.
We see the light but not whence it comes.
O Light Invisible, we glorify Thee!

T. S. Eliot
Choruses from "The Rock"

The novelist George Eliot once observed that "religious ideas have the fate of melodies, which, once set afloat in the world, are taken up by all sorts of instruments, some woefully coarse, feeble or out of tune, until people are in danger of crying out that the melody itself is detestable."[1] I mention her observation because it rests on a distinction that every reader of Balthasar must also make: one simply cannot understand Balthasar's seven-volume aesthetics *at all* except as his own effort to pick up, receive and broadcast that melody. Yes, I am sure he would admit that his own perceptive and broadcasting instrument might well be as coarse and as out of tune as any other one might care to name; but that would only confirm his point: that we must concentrate on the melody and not the playing![2]

It would be difficult to exaggerate the importance of music in the construction of Balthasar's theology. The phraseology, the patterning of his sentences, his refusal to engage in either syllogistics or elenchics, the state-

---

[1] George Eliot, *Scenes of Clerical Life*, Chapter 10, (New York: Penguin, 1973/1858), 319.

[2] Balthasar's biographer, Peter Henrici, relates an eerie but strangely apposite incident from his later years: "He had the gift of perfect pitch, so that after the death of Adrienne von Speyr he was able to give away his stereo system on the grounds that he didn't need it anymore: he knew all the works of Mozart by heart and could picture the score and hear the music in his mind" (Peter Henrici, S.J, "Hans Urs von Balthasar: A Sketch of his Life," *Communio* 16/3 [Fall 1989]: 308). It does nothing to deny the first principle of Aristotelian and Thomistic epistemology (that there is nothing in the intellect that is not first in the senses) to say that music is first and above all an ideal reality—as we know from Beethoven's own life, who wrote (and conducted!) his Ninth Symphony when he was completely deaf.

liness of his pacing, the subtle interpenetration of later motifs at the outset of the work: all of these traits show the influence of his musical background, a background that was unusual for its depth and richness, as he himself once admitted in a rare autobiographical moment:

> From those first tremendous impressions of music, Schubert's Mass in E-flat (when I was about five) and Tchaikovsky's *Pathétique* (when I was about eight), I spent endless hours at the piano. At [the Benedictine-run] Engelberg *Gymnasium*, there was also the opportunity to take part in orchestral Masses and operas. However, when my friends and I transferred to [the Jesuit-run] Feldkirch for the last two and a half years of high school, we found the "music department" there to be so noisy that we lost our enjoyment in playing. My university semesters in poor, almost starving, post-war Vienna were compensated for by a superabundance of concerts, operas, orchestral masses. I had the privilege of lodging at that time with Rudolf Allers— medical doctor, philosopher, theologian, translator of St. Anselm and St. Thomas. In the evenings, more often than not, we would play an entire Mahler symphony in piano transcription. . . . [But] when I entered the Jesuits, music was automatically over and done with." (*UA*, 31)

And music was no doubt a large part of what drew Balthasar to befriend Karl Barth and what made their friendship so mutually enriching. For here was a Protestant thinker who also instinctively rejected Kierkegaard's harsh disjunction between the aesthetic and religious sphere, and did so precisely because of music, or more specifically, Mozart's music. As Balthasar explains in his own appreciation of Barth's musical sensibility:

> This refutation of Kierkegaard, already evident and fully formed in the early Barth, is attributable to a final contrast: for Kierkegaard Christianity is unworldly, ascetic, polemic; for Barth it is the immense revelation of the eternal light that radiates over all of nature and fulfills every promise; it is God's Yes and Amen to himself and his creation. Nothing is more characteristic of these two men than the way they stand in relation to Mozart. For Kierkegaard Mozart is the very quintessence of the aesthetic sphere and therefore the very contrast to a religious existence. He had no choice but to interpret him demonically, from the perspective of Don Juan. Quite different is that view of Mozart by one of his greatest devotees, Karl Barth.[3]

---

[3] *KB*, 26. As we can see in this lyrical passage in Barth's *Church Dogmatics:* "Why is it that this man [Mozart] is so incomparable? Why is it that, *for the receptive,* he has produced

And it is not merely a question of being devoted to Mozart, or to music in general; more crucial is how it stamps and affects everything he writes. He? Am I referring to Barth or Balthasar here? It doesn't matter, because what the one says of the other applies to the latter as well. As Balthasar says of Barth (and as we can say of Balthasar):

> Indeed, one will do well to keep Mozart's melodies in mind while reading Barth's *Dogmatics* and Mozart's basic style when searching for Barth's basic intention. This is the way one should read, for example, those pieces that seem like the powerful finale of a symphony: the end of Barth's doctrine of election with its absolutely masterful "concluding fugue" on Judas and Paul, or the equally radiant conclusion of his doctrine of creation in God's Yes to the world, or the three chapters on God's perfections, or that astonishing triple fugue on faith, obedience and prayer that concludes the doctrine on providence. In all of these cases, one will have to admit that the similarities with Mozart are in no way accidental or external. Indeed, we can even boldly say: *whoever is unable to hear Barth with these ears has simply not heard him.* (KB, 28–29)

This of course raises considerable difficulties for Barth's or Balthasar's interpreters. How does one verbalize a concerto? How does one capture the symphonic structure of a whole trilogy? There are no plot summaries or Cliff's Notes for works of music! But this in a way is precisely the point. I think Balthasar was drawn to a "musical" presentation of theology precisely because it is so much more resistant to systematizing, and nothing more characterizes Balthasar's thought than his consistent polemic against the potential idolatry of systematizing Christian revelation: for to arrange something in a system is to imply we have gained a kind of control over it.[4]

---

in almost every bar he conceived and composed a type of music for which 'beautiful' is not a fitting epithet: music which for the true Christian is not mere entertainment, enjoyment, edification, but food and drink; music full of comfort and counsel for his needs; music which is never a slave to its techniques nor sentimental but always 'moving,' free and liberating because wise, strong and sovereign? Why is it possible to hold that Mozart has a place in theology, especially in the doctrine of creation, but also in eschatology, although he was not a Father of the Church, does not seem to have been a particularly active Christian, and was a Roman Catholic, apparently leading what might appear to us a rather frivolous existence when not occupied with his work? . . . [Because] he had heard, and causes those who have ears to hear, even today, what we shall not see until the end of time—the whole context of Providence" (CD III/ 3, 297–298; my emphasis).

[4] J. R. Sachs also insists on this same point: that there is something about the whole structure of Balthasar's thought that eludes systematization, and without a recognition of this feature of his work, the interpreter will inevitably go astray: "At the heart of Balthasar's

Balthasar even extends this preference for the musical mode to his analysis of the human sensorium, so that in his presentation of sense-based knowledge, preference must be given to hearing over sight, at least in certain crucial respects. In a fascinating essay on the different phenomenologies involved in hearing, seeing and reading, Balthasar insists that *hearing* is above all the perceptive mode of surrender, while *sight* implies control, distance and perspective:

> The eye is the organ with which the world is possessed and dominated, the immediate reflection—in the sphere of the senses—of the rational intellect that comprehends. Through the eye, the world is *our* world, in which we are not lost; rather, it is subordinate to us as an immeasurable dwelling space with which we are familiar. The other side of this material function denotes distance, separateness. All the other senses touch their object in some direct manner, and they have at least an instinct to come as closely as possible to this object. Only the eye needs separateness, in order to see. It is not through a close encounter that it comes to terms with things but through the look from a distance that tames them—the way trainers stare down wild animals in a circus ring.[5]

But hearing is an entirely different mode of perception. Here the act of choosing what to perceive is out of the question (we can shut our eyes but never our ears!), and so our only choice is but to submit to the reality being communicated. Whereas clarity and distance are the fundamental requirements for right seeing, hearing is defenseless and necessarily open. As the practice of "modesty of the eyes" before the reigning monarch once implied, seeing establishes an equality between persons which was

---

mistrust of 'system,'" he says, "lies a keen sensitivity for the utter mystery of the divine love" (J. Randall Sachs, S.J., *Spirit and Life: The Pneumatology and Christian Spirituality of Hans Urs von Balthasar* [unpublished dissertation for the University of Tübingen, 1984], 81). Without explicitly alluding to the musical analogues that are a part of this feature of Balthasar's thought, Sachs also points out that it would be erroneous to speak of a "development" in Balthasar's thought, if that implies that at some point he changed his mind in some radical way: "Virtually everyone who has written on Balthasar agrees that one cannot really speak of a 'development,' much less of a change or break in this movement of contemplative deepening. What Balthasar once wrote about Barth could be applied to Balthasar himself: 'Least of all has Barth himself changed. While his dogmatic work has grown in fullness and depth, it has remained astonishingly true to itself'" (ibid., 29; quoting from *KB,* 392). To which I would only add that the musical analogue helps us to see why that would be so, and in both cases: Barth's and Balthasar's. Basic themes and motifs interpenetrate the entire work, for which music provides the best parallel and which precludes us from speaking in terms of "development" or "changing one's mind."

[5] "Seeing, Hearing, and Reading," *SW,* 474.

forbidden between subject and sovereign, and so in the throne room the gaze had to be cast downward. Gazing implies control, which is why we so resent it when someone is staring at us, for relentless gazing at someone is both unnerving and aggressive. But no such control is possible with hearing:

> Hearing is a wholly different, almost opposite mode of the revelation of reality. It lacks the fundamental characteristic of material relevance. It is not objects we hear—in the dark, when it is not possible to see—but their utterances and communications. Therefore it is not we ourselves who determine on our part what is heard and place it before us as an object in order to turn our attention to it when it pleases us. That which is heard comes upon us without our being informed of its coming in advance. And it lays hold of us without our being asked. We cannot look out in advance and take up our distance. It is in the highest degree symbolic that only our eyes—and not our ears—have lids. . . . The basic relationship between the one who hears and that which is heard is thus one of defenselessness on the one side and of communication on the other. . . . The equality of stance between the two is fundamentally removed; even in a dialogue between equals in rank, the one who is at the moment hearing is in the subordinate position of humble receiving. The hearer belongs to the other and obeys him. (*SW*, 475–476)

I think the import of these remarks, if rightly absorbed by theologians, would have a revolutionary impact on their discipline. For it means no less than giving the primacy to hearing when we survey the whole range of the human sensorium. Hearing is *the* central theological act of perception. Perhaps not eschatologically, where, interestingly enough, sight is the primary analogue (the "beatific vision," seeing God "face to face," etc.); but certainly here on earth we must strive above all not so much to see (which is too akin to taking possession of what is seen) as to hear (which is to submit to what has been heard). Hearing is virtuous not so much because Balthasar wishes to stress submission for its own sake as he wishes to guard against the least implication that by means of revelation we have grasped God. For the beauty of hearing sounds, especially the sounds of words and music, is that sounds always remain ever evanescent and therefore ungraspable, even as they communicate:

> The revelation of the sound and of the word communicates only the utterance, not the being itself. Every act of speaking or singing also simultaneously *conceals* the speaker or singer. An arrow speeds across and penetrates me more deeply than a look would

have been able to do, but the bow from which the arrow has flown does not itself come into my hand. No being is capable of giving total utterance to itself: even it seeks help and aims to break out of its own interior. (*SW*, 476)

These remarks are of course directly relevant as opening reflections on Balthasar's theological aesthetics, because his concern in this vast and teeming work is basically to *present* or to *display* that which faith presents to us, but this will be a display of faith that is primarily mediated by sounds, as Paul explicitly avers: "And how can they believe if they have not heard? And how can they hear without someone preaching to them? ... For it is with your heart that you believe and are justified, and it is with your mouth that you confess and are saved" (Rm 10:14,10).

There is of course a role for sight, and in a sense it must be given the primacy eschatologically, inasmuch as faith is meant to culminate in sight (1 Jn 3:2); for, as we have seen, images drawn from the world of seeing are the primary analogues of final union with God. Perhaps one way of explaining the difference between the roles of vision and hearing in the life of faith is to consider the tension in the biblical image of servant and friend, for a servant hearkens[6] to "his master's voice" while friends stand as equals in a relationship of equality. Jesus tells his disciples at one point: "I no longer call you servants, because a servant does not know his master's business. Instead, I have called you friends, for everything that I learned from my Father I have made known to you" (Jn 15:15). And yet in a Synoptic parable he makes the opposite point:

> Suppose one of you had a servant plowing or looking after the sheep. Would he say to the servant when he comes in from the field, "Come over and sit down with me to eat"? Would he not rather say, "Go and prepare my supper and wait on me while I eat and drink; after that you may eat and drink"? Would he thank the servant because he did what he was told to do? So you also, when you have done everything you were told to do, should say, "We are but unworthy servants; we have only done our duty." (Lk 17:7–10)

In other words, the tension between hearing and seeing, between subordination and equality can never be overcome: we are always both "made heirs of the promise" yet also "worthless servants" who can scarcely claim even to have done our duty, let alone be deserving of sitting at the master's table. So contemplation here on earth is an anticipation of the eschatologi-

---

[6]The etymological link between "hear" and "hearken" is a telling point in this context, a link which is even more explicit in the German *horschen* (hearken) and *gehorschen* (obey).

cal banquet, but mediated through our status as "handmaids of the Lord." Or as Balthasar puts it, "contemplation here on earth is the flashing anticipation of eschatological illumination, the presaging vision of transparent glory in the form of the servant." (*GL* 1, 39)

Besides this inevitable and irresolvable tension between seeing and hearing in the life of the faith, we must also at least allude to the irony that Balthasar must present his "musical" version of theology through the medium of his books. We gain access to the message of books, of course, through reading, that is, through sight, but what they convey is encased speech. In other words, books hover in a kind of no-man's-land of ossified speech to which we gain access only by *choosing* to read. Reading is a way of gaining control over speech, for we can freely decide to set down a book at any time, to be picked up later when we so decide.

But that is precisely the reason why we must stress the essentially *musical* nature of Balthasar's books: although they set forth for the reader as much of Christian revelation as is humanly possible to encompass in print, they are primarily meant to set things into motion in the heart of the reader and not be a reference work where one can look up the author's position on a certain topic (which his anti-systematic mode would work against in any event). In other words, his work is meant to begin a process of communication whose best analogue is that of hearing. For hearing implies movement and movement is the subject and theme of Balthasar's theology: "Thus hearing remains something intermediary and oscillating between the 'I' and 'Thou,' something that streams from the one who speaks to the one who hears."[7]

This initial phenomenology of the senses gives a fascinating new twist to Anselm's fundamental principle that the activity of theology can be summed up as: "faith seeking understanding." If that is true, then hearing maintains its primacy in the sensorium of faith, for what faith (which means the acceptance of God's Word after hearing it) does is to seek understanding (or insight) always *in terms* of faith.[8] And this means that insight must therefore always be in the service of faith. But if this be so,

---

[7] "Seeing, Hearing, Reading," *SW*, 476. This stress on movement also serves to wean vision from its desire to have control and sway over that which it sees. When vision joins in the dialectical movement of analogy, it then becomes the privileged access to Christian aesthetics: "Thus revelation itself is the foundation of a dialectic, of ever-increasing range and intensity, between event and vision, in which the element of the *tremendum,* inherent in the event itself, nevertheless overwhelms the person contemplating it and then to such a degree that he is left with no alternative except to return to simple discipleship, and this in turn brings a new sense of being overwhelmed, but at a deeper level" ("Revelation and the Beautiful," *WF*, 115).

[8] For another defense of the primacy of hearing in the life of faith, see Peter Knauer, S.J. *Der Glaube kommt vom Hören: Ökumenische Fundamentaltheologie* (Freiburg im Breisgau, 1991), 227–255; 342–352.

then the subordination of sight to hearing automatically closes off certain avenues to human speculation (and how telling is that word: *speculation!*).[9] As Balthasar says in relation to Barth:

> Faith is always obedience, even when it is seeking insight and understanding; it is never permission for us to give vent to our hunger for novelty in vain speculation. And many questions that human curiosity tends to ask of revelation are rejected by revelation, exposed as false and irrelevant. But the themes that God poses and which he reveals for our understanding cannot be pondered enough. That Barth kept to these limits, that he held such constraints to be the highest form of divine permission to be free, this constitutes the purity of his theological draftsmanship and the beauty of its execution.[10]

Now none of this is meant to imply any denigration of sight at the expense of the other senses; on the contrary, Balthasar explicitly avers that all five senses carry a theological meaning; and we know that the Bible and tradition are filled with images drawn from all of the senses ("taste and see how good the Lord is," the "odor of sanctity," etc.). Balthasar's analysis of the human sensorium is not meant to downplay any one sense at the expense of the others: "In the human spirit's own particular relationship to its object (which here in this [theological] context, means the act whereby God displays himself in the created being)," he says, "there is something that corresponds to the mode of the clear and objective act of seeing, something else that corresponds to the mode of hearing and being affected, and something else again that corresponds to the perception of smell and taste, or to the blind awareness of touch that nevertheless brings certainty and is blessed" (*SW*, 477). And of course the Church has long spoken of "contemplative" prayer, which is basically a form in interior gazing under the light and rubric of faith.[11]

---

[9] "Speculation"—and "spying," incidentally—both come from the Indo-European root **spek:* to watch, look at, gaze upon.

[10] *KB*, 29; Balthasar's frequent polemical references to nominalism and late Neo-Scholasticism is rooted in this aversion to "vain speculation." See also his aphorism: "What God has chosen once and for all not to know should also not be the object of human knowledge and research" (*W*, 37).

[11] But even here, the reality of what one contemplates overcomes the controlling aspect of sight. Normally, we do not consider the act of looking at something as demanding much effort, but because contemplative prayer is a "looking" but *not* a grasping, it is a fundamentally different kind of gazing, one that demands great effort: "Contemplative prayer is work, work done out of love for the One who 'in all created things strives and toils for my sake'" (*P*, 111; quoting the *Spiritual Exercises*, paragraph 236). Or elsewhere: "Die Kraft des betrachtenden Gebetes liegt in der Ausdauer" (*TP*, 9).

Nevertheless, Balthasar insists that the decisive attitude of the Church will be that of hearing, for faith comes from hearing.[12] Faith *gives* sight, but it *comes from* hearing:

> The listening Church stands under the Word of God like the penitent woman who stands under the flowing blood of the Cross. The obedience of this act of hearing is the form of her service and of her readiness to serve. And when she herself speaks as one who teaches and proclaims, she herself listens while she speaks the word in the commission that she has received from the Word. . . . If the act of seeing aims . . . at the encounter face to face of the highest, identical mutual gaze, the act of hearing aims upward into an ever more perfect obedience and thus into a creatureliness that distinguishes itself ever more humbly from the Creator. (*SW*, 480)

These distinctions must not of course serve to denigrate the true vision that faith gives, for as Pierre Rousselot said in his famous work *The Eyes of Faith*, "theology conceives of faith as a supernatural cognitive activity. . . . *Perception of credibility and belief in truth are identically the same act.* . . . It is the light of faith that shows that we must believe."[13] But this can be carried too far. The reason that sight is subordinate to hearing in the life of faith (that is, before death) is that faith is first and foremost an

---

[12] This judgment must be somewhat qualified by the New Testament dispensation: "If we set the sense of touch aside for the moment as being especially reserved for the experience of the Apostles, then we do not need to argue over whether precedence goes to hearing or seeing. We can only observe that hearing must be assigned particularly to imitative faith, while seeing is then more properly assigned to archetypal faith (as the word 'eyewitness' implies). Furthermore, within archetypal faith we can assign hearing . . . predominantly to the Old Testament and seeing (the Word of the flesh) predominantly to the New. Finally, in an all-inclusive view, we can ascribe hearing to earthly faith in its every form and seeing to realized 'faith' in the New Eon. But all these assignations have something precarious and inexact about them, and very often they are made on the basis of theological prejudices, the worst of which is, with Luther, to want to admit only the ear as a theological sense organ, or another prejudice . . . which would assign 'seeing' to the Greek or even the pagan religious experience in general, while 'hearing' supposedly corresponds to the biblical or the Semitic experience of God (forgetting that these two terms, biblical and Semitic, themselves denote two separate realities). There is of course some truth to all these distinctions and separations, but a good deal more that is straightforwardly misleading. But at this stage at least this one point may be made: even if sight is the chief sense and expresses man's innermost longing, nevertheless a living person is known primarily by his word. Thus the revealed religion of the living God is a religion of the Word, which does not preclude the fact that God's becoming visible remains even in the Bible . . . a fundamental human measure for the depth and integral completeness of revelation" (*GL* 1, 309–310).

[13] Pierre Rousselot, S.J. *The Eyes of Faith*, tr. Joseph Donceel, S.J. (New York: Fordham University, 1990/1910), pp. 29–31; author's emphasis.

act of obedience that *then* gives in-sight into the realities of faith, or as Balthasar puts it in his programmatic principle: "The more obediently [the Christian] thinks, the more accurately he will see" (*GL* 1, 165).

How then do we explain the "in-sight" of faith? What does Paul mean when he says that, while we are still wayfarers on earth, we yet see—even if only "through a glass darkly"? What *do* the "eyes of faith" see then, however "darkly"? And finally, we must recall that the first volume of the Aesthetics is, after all, called *Schau der Gestalt: seeing* the form. If hearing has the primacy, why not call it "Hearing the Form"?

Of course, this way of phrasing the issue already points to the absurdity of dispensing with sight, for generally we think of forms as accessible only to sight (though music, of course, has a "form," however fluid and unsystematizable). But to call vision indispensable is not yet to explain how it functions in the life of faith, and for this we must return to the primacy of *aesthetics* in the whole of the Balthasarian project. Now the word "aesthetics" is ambiguous: it comes from the general Greek word for "perception," but it has come to have a narrower meaning restricted to the appreciation of the beautiful (an appreciation which in our culture is restricted to those who are rather dismissively called "aesthetes"), but it is an ambiguity that Balthasar will wish to exploit, for it is here that we will resolve the tension between hearing and vision in the life of faith.

Recall once more *why* hearing has the primacy: because of all the senses it is the one that has the least control over what it perceives and because what it hears is merely the self-communicating word that the other *chooses* to impart. And so hearing expresses the obediential moment of faith more than any other perceptive faculty. *Hearing hands over control to the other,* all the while *receiving* what the other wishes to communicate. Vision, however, as we have seen, has things more under control . . . except in one case: beauty. If the stance of hearing is fundamentally one of assent, so too may we say the same of the inherent response to the vision of beauty: "'Is not our every encounter with the beautiful,'" says Balthasar quoting the Protestant Gerhard Nebel, "'tantamount to an assent to creation, either bestowed on us or drawn from us?'"[14]

This remark (for Balthasar's apologetic purposes so usefully made by a Protestant!) captures perhaps more than any other in Part I of the trilogy the central reason he places aesthetics as the starting point of his theology: for it is in an analysis of the nature of beauty that we see how sight and hearing can be fused into one total of assent to God's gifts of creation and revelation. For what beauty proves is that sight is not in as much control as it might first assume. Beauty by its very nature always elicits a response: one simply cannot experience a form or a phenomenon as beautiful without responding, without *assenting*. This is brought out with great

---

[14] *GL* 1, 63; quoting Gerhard Nebel, *Das Ereignis des Schönen* (Klett, 1953), 149.

loveliness by Dionysius the Areopagite in his classic work, *The Divine Names,* from which Balthasar cites this fascinating passage:

> And the divine Eros also brings rapture, not allowing them that are touched by it to belong to themselves, but only to the objects of their love. . . . And so the great Paul, constrained by the divine Eros and having received a share in its ecstatic power, says with inspired utterance: "I live, yet no longer I, but Christ lives in me." These are words of a true lover, . . . not possessing a life of his own but the life of his Beloved, a life surrounded on all sides by ardent love. And we must dare to affirm, for this is the truth, that the Creator of the universe himself is, in his beautiful and good Eros towards the universe, [also] transported outside of himself through his exceeding erotic Goodness and in his providential actions towards all things that have being, and is overcome by his own sweet spell of Goodness, Love, and Eros. . . . That is why those who know about God call him "zealous," because he is vehement in his manifold and beneficent Eros towards all beings, and he spurs them on to search for him zealously with a yearning eros of their own. . . . In short, both to possess Eros and to love erotically belong to everything Good and Beautiful, and Eros has its primal roots in the Beautiful and the Good: Eros exists and comes into being only through the Beautiful and the Good.[15]

"Not allowing them that are touched by it to belong to themselves." Here perhaps is the key that unlocks the whole point of the Aesthetics, for beauty is inherently attractive, meaning that it draws contemplators out of themselves and into a *direct* encounter with the phenomenon manifesting itself, and this beauty, the contemplator knows, testifies to itself

---

[15] *GL* 1, 122; citing Dionysius, *The Divine Names,* Book IV, section 13; tr. C. E. Rolt (London: SPCK, 1940), 105–106. Translation slightly altered, especially in word order. It should also be noted that "zealous" could also be translated as "jealous," which is not only an important biblical theme but has its roots in the aesthetic reality of creation and revelation: according to Dionysius, God creates out of a yearning that is erotic in this sense: that God is "jealous" for his creation, rightfully demanding the reciprocity of his creatures. Colm Luibheid translates "eros" as "yearning" in his edition of the Areopagite's *Complete Works* (New York: Paulist, 1987), which works well when translating the participle, as in Ignatius of Antioch's "He for whom I am yearning has been crucified," but it rather fudges the notion, essential to the Greek work *erôs,* that this "yearning" is an inevitable correlate of our response to beauty. It also defuses the sting in the word, as when Dionysius says: "So let us not fear this title of *erôs* nor be upset by what anyone has to say about these two names, for in my opinion, the sacred writers regard 'yearning' and 'love' as having one and the same meaning. They added the word 'real' to the word *erôs* regarding divine things because of the unseemly nature such a word has for men" (ibid., IV, 12; Rolt translation).

in a way that the Good and the True cannot do. Although all three transcendentals, the Beautiful, the Good, and the True, in the traditional Platonic understanding, are all inherent aspects of the nature of Being, nonetheless we may doubt, and often do, the inherent goodness and truth of the being of the world. But this, Balthasar maintains, we cannot do with beauty, once experienced:

> Most people dare not make strong affirmations about the ultimate nature of the world's essence or about the ultimate justice of human actions. But all those who have been once affected inwardly by the worldly beauty either of nature, or of a person's life, or of art, will surely not insist that they have no genuine idea of what beauty is. The beautiful brings with it a self-evidence that en-lightens *without mediation*. (GL 1, 37; my emphasis)

It is no secret in this age of rampant secularization that most people, at least in the technologically sophisticated countries of the post-industrial West, do not experience the beauty of revelation without mediation. Indeed, for most people the way to a simple affirmation of the Good News of God's salvation in Christ seems to be blocked, for any number of pastoral and cultural reasons. But surely problem is rooted in that lack of self-evidence that comes from the response to revelation when it is perceived as inherently beautiful. Balthasar asks, rhetorically of course but also almost plaintively, early in the first volume of the Aesthetics: "May we not think of the beautiful as one of the transcendental attributes of Being as such, and thereby ascribe to the Beautiful the same range of application and the same inwardly analogous form that we ascribe to the One, the True, the Good?" (GL 1,38). But as the argument builds, his voice becomes more confident and soon the author is able to show how we not only *may* think of the Beautiful as one of the transcendentals of Being, but also that *unless* we do, what is true and good in Christian revelation will become obscured.[16] For we really cannot respond to the

---

[16] Among all of Balthasar's commentators, Jeffrey Kay has best captured why the aesthetic moment is so essential: "Any theological method that fails to recognize the central role of aesthetics is doomed to be dull and unconvincing. This must be so if the object of theology is Christ, the personified love between God and man. If the task of theology is to present the truth of that relation by assisting it to reveal its own truth, the theologian's prime task is to lead others to 'see' the balance, proportion and tension within the form of Christ and then to be enraptured by the splendor. The selfless enrapturing vision of the splendor of Christ's form is the basic moment of self-verification in Christian theology. The satisfaction of human needs and expectations as a criterion of verification must be clearly subordinated to it. Verification occurs when a viewer is so fascinated that he has neither time nor desire to think about himself and what benefits he can derive from such beauty. Theology, therefore, must be concerned much less with showing man that Christ offers him what he wants and

goodness of life, of creation, and of God's action in Christ unless we are also willing to respond with joy—something that is an essential aspect of the response to beauty. Similarly, we really cannot judge the truth of the Gospel unless we can *perceive* it, and, as we have seen, only the perception of the beautiful is so direct as to banish all doubt. Beauty, then, is an essential part of both the Good and the True, and to the extent that she is treated as the neglected step-sister of the other two, the damage will redound to her two elder sisters as well:

> For the moment, the essential thing to realize is that, without aesthetic knowledge, neither theoretical nor practical reason can attain to their total completion. If the *verum* lacks that *splendor* which for Thomas is the distinctive mark of the beautiful, then the knowledge of truth remains both pragmatic and formalistic. The only concern of such knowledge will then merely be the verification of correct facts and laws, whether the latter are laws of being or laws of thought, categories and ideas. Similarly, if the *bonum* lacks the *voluptas* which for Augustine is the mark of its beauty, then the relationship to the good remains both utilitarian and hedonistic: in this case, the good will involve merely the satisfaction of a need by means of some value or object. (*GL* 1, 152)

The disengagement of aesthetics from Christian thought has indeed been a most fateful step for theology, and Balthasar devotes the entirety of the next two volumes to analyzing how that came about (the subject of our next chapter). The presentation in Volume 1, however, pretty much takes for granted that the reader will recognize the end-result of this dreary history, for it is no secret to anyone, he says, that "the word 'aesthetic' automatically flows from the pens of both Protestant and Catholic writers when they want to describe an attitude which, in the last analysis, they find to be frivolous, merely curious and self-indulgent" (*GL* 1, 51).

It would be easy to verify this insight almost at random today, but I think it much more important to see how the denigration of aesthetics in contemporary theology constitutes the hidden presupposition governing theology across the board, from liberation theology (which might be regarded as that school of theology that is governed by an overemphasis on the Good, as a theology that recommends a praxis disengaged from the

---

much more concerned with showing man that he cannot help but worship the splendor of what he sees" (Jeffrey Ames Kay, *Theological Aesthetics: The Role of Aesthetics in the Theological Method of Hans Urs von Balthasar* [Bern: Herbert Lang/ Frankfurt am Main: Peter Lang, 1975], v).

gratuity of sheer worship for its own sake, which only beauty can elicit) to the remarkable obsession with historical studies that has gripped theology since the rise of historicism in 19th-century Germany (a positivism which must surely have its roots in a hypertrophied emphasis on the True disengaged from the directness of perception that comes from a contemplative gaze upon the beautiful). This emerges especially clearly in Balthasar's shrewd and penetrating remarks on perhaps the greatest biblical critic of the 20th century, Rudolf Bultmann: "In all that Bultmann writes there is a deep seriousness which comes from his subjective sense of having been seized, in his case, of having been gripped by Christ. But this is a gravity which, alas, is full of anguish because of its total lack of imagery and form: a real dead-end for Protestantism."[17] And this pathos is not rooted simply in the particularities of Bultmann's personality but is part of the defining matrix of contemporary theology and will probably continue for quite some time after him, at least in Balthasar's rather pessimistic and bleak analysis:

> At least for the time being, Barth with his contemplation of the objective revelation has not succeeded in really shaping and transforming Protestant theology. Up to the present, and very probably for a long time to come, Protestant theology will continue in dutiful subservience to Bultmann's dualism of criticism on the one hand and existential, imageless inwardness on the other.[18]

---

[17] GL 1, 52. I would like to caution the reader that the criticism Balthasar levels at Bultmann throughout this volume does not imply any obscurantism on his part regarding biblical studies, the kind of obscurantism that was often demonstrated in the rather hysterical reactions of the anti-Modernism brigade at the turn of the century—and who still crop up from time to time. Balthasar's point is rather different, for he feels that we do not serve the cause of nuance if we see the terms of debate about biblical criticism merely as a battle between positivism and obscurantism. And indeed his own position regarding the scientific study of the Bible is itself quite nuanced: "We are entitled to expect the investigation of the 'letter' to contribute much to a future 'science of faith.' But this does not alter the fact that we have not yet begun to make use of these new insights *for* faith. In fact we may say that, as far as real theological work is concerned, we are still getting our breath back. In the interim, our task must be to draw for dogmatics whatever conclusions are possible from the new findings. At the same time, we should foster the fertile aspects of historical science, while containing its tendency to usurp lawful authority" (ibid., 76).

[18] GL 1, 56. This volume was written before historical criticism swept the Catholic world as well, which is why Kay's remarks on Balthasar's theological aesthetics are so important: "Through his emphasis on the vision of form, [Balthasar] hoped to guide Protestant theology out of, and Catholic theology away from, the continual vacillation between a blind Neo-Orthodoxy and an all-seeing liberalism. Preserving the distance of contemplation and a reverence for form prevents the reduction of man to God (theopanism) in Neo-Orthodoxy and an all-seeing reduction of God to man (pantheism) in liberalism. He counteracts their mutual tendency toward monism by demonstrating the ability of the finite to reveal the

One caution that we must register early on is this: Balthasar is not intending to supplement current schools of theology with a little bit of literary flourish, a kind of embellishment to others' scientific work. Embellishment implies adornment of façades, but Balthasar insists that revelation is itself inherently beautiful. So what he is trying to do is to draw out aspects that are already a crucial feature of theology itself but have been neglected:

> We mean a theology which does not primarily work with the extra-theological categories of a worldly philosophical aesthetics (above all poetry), but which develops its theory of beauty from the data of revelation itself with genuinely theological methods. It is, therefore, not necessary that, as generally occurs in our century, theology renounce aesthetics, whether unconsciously or consciously, whether out of weakness or forgetfulness or even a false scientific attitude. For if it were, theology would have to give up a good part—if not the best part—of herself. (*GL* 1, 117)

Nor would it be out of place here to stress another crucial feature of Balthasar's project: he is not trying to elevate the place of aesthetics *at the expense* of the other transcendentals: this is not a work that denigrates action! "Contemplation melds into action, or it is not contemplation," as he says in another context (*TP*, 10). This is no aestheticizing retreat from the real world, but a real engagement with the true nature of the Christian dispensation, and one that discovers in this engagement how much all three transcendentals interpenetrate each other, and how much a reincorporation of Beauty into the Good and the True can resolve their unhealthy isolation:

> Psychologically, the effect of beautiful forms on the soul may be described in a great variety of ways. But a true grasp of this effect will not be attained unless one brings to bear logical and ethical concepts, concepts of truth and value: in a word, concepts drawn from a comprehensive doctrine of being. The form as it appears to us is beautiful only because the delight that it arouses in us is founded upon the fact that, in it, the truth and goodness of the depths of reality itself are manifested and bestowed, and this manifestation and bestowal reveal themselves to us as being

---

infinite and by describing the beauty of that revelation. By thus establishing the unsurpassable dignity of both form and its beauty, he grounds the unsurpassable dignity of human finitude and human evidence. He prevents human evidence from either being ultimately consumed by divine evidence or ultimately consuming divine evidence. God speaks as man but neither does God become identical with man nor man with God" (Kay, v).

something infinitely and inexhaustibly valuable and fascinating. The appearance of the form, as revelation of the depths, is an indissoluble union of two things. It is the real presence *of* the depths, of the whole of reality, *and* it is a real pointing beyond itself *to* these depths.[19]

This brings us to what is perhaps the central Balthasarian doctrine of aesthetics: that form is so constituted as to be able to irradiate *from within itself* the light that illuminates its beauty. Often throughout the intellectual history of the 20th century, various schools of thought have sought to divorce form and content, most notably in the structuralism that grew out of the linguistics of Ferdinand de Saussure, which quite explicitly separates form and content, or word from meaning (or, more specifically in Saussure's case, phonology from semantics). This "great divorce," as C. S. Lewis might put it, is in fact that animating presupposition behind so much historical research.[20] And it is the ultimate reason for the split in theology between the academic study of religion and the spirituality that inspires one's life of faith. And it governs a great deal of aesthetics today that makes a distinction between the ostensive sign and what is signified by that sign. But for Balthasar,

> this dualism can be abolished only by introducing the thought-forms and categories of the beautiful. The beautiful is above all a *form,* and the light does not fall on this form from above and from outside, rather it breaks forth from the form's interior. In Beauty, *species* and *lumen* are one, provided the *species* truly merits that name (which does not designate any form whatever, but pleasing, radiant form). Visible form not only "points" to an invisible, unfathomable mystery; form *is* the apparition of this mystery, and reveals it while, naturally, at the same time protecting and veiling it. Both natural forms and the forms of art have an exterior *manifestum* which appears and an interior depth radiating through the external aspect, neither of which, however, are separable in the form itself. The content does not

---

[19] *GL* 1, 118. This same point is also made in his essay "Revelation and the Beautiful": "The light of the transcendentals, unity, truth, goodness and beauty, a light at one with the light of philosophy, can only shine if undivided. A transcendence of beauty alone is not viable. . . . This brings home to us that an apparent enthusiasm for the beautiful is mere idle talk when divorced from the sense of a divine summons to change one's life" (*WF,* 107).

[20] "In relation to the central phenomenon of revelation we can by no means speak of 'signs' which, according to their nature, point beyond themselves to something 'signified.' Jesus the Man, in his visibility, is not a sign pointing beyond himself to an invisible 'Christ of faith'—whether this view is nuanced more in a Platonizing Catholic sense or in a criticistic Protestant manner" (*GL* 1, 437).

lie behind the form but within it. Whoever is not capable of seeing and "reading" the form will, by the same token, fail to perceive the content. Whoever is not illumined by the form will see no light in the content either. (*GL* 1, 151)

Moreover, not only does the form of the beautiful elicit a proper response to itself from within its own expressive dynamism, it does so *inexhaustibly*. The most mysterious reality in every artistic expression is this inexhaustibility: why is it that with certain artists, we can return to them again and again, always finding new riches, new dimensions, new aspects that we had not noticed before—provided of course that our own appreciative powers are growing as well? Why does the work always match our perceptive powers and beckon us further, even though it has always been there for our enjoyment and contemplation? In fact before the question of a canon of "great books" or great art had become so politicized, the standard norm for judging whether a work of art was a masterpiece or not was precisely this very inexhaustibility: if a work began to cloy after a few encounters with it, it would tend not to be passed down in the canon, but if people came back to a particular work time and again, it had proved its worth and established itself in the canon—on its own power, so to speak. In any event: however the battles over the canon turn out, it still remains ineluctably true what Balthasar says of true art's inexhaustibility:

> The more a great work of art is known and grasped, the more concretely are we dazzled by its "ungraspable" genius. We never outgrow something which we acknowledge to stand above us by its very nature. And this will in no way be different for us even when we contemplate God in the beatific vision, since then we will *see* that God is forever the ever-greater.[21]

And what a fascinating analogue for God's own ever-greater inexhaustibility! St. Augustine and St. Anselm both said, famously, *si comprehendis non est Deus*: if you have grasped something, whatever it is you have got a hold of, it is not God. And this is reflected in art as well; indeed art is that outgrowth from nature and creation that is the intra-worldly expression of God's own infinity and inexhaustibility.[22] Art, in fact, is just like

---

[21] *GL* 1, 186; notice once more how aesthetics resolves the tension between hearing and seeing: what the perceiver recognizes in something beautiful is how it stands "above us by its very nature."

[22] This is a point that is easily missed in today's artistic climate, where the imitation of nature is so scorned. But if one takes the doctrine of naturalism seriously, then we must see man's works of art as true expressions of nature's own being, indeed as a rather pale imitation of what nature does so naturally. The medieval historian of philosophy, Étienne

nature in this sense: ultimately it is not only an analogue for grace but is itself, like nature, an expression of grace:

> In the luminous form of the beautiful, the being of the existent becomes perceivable as nowhere else, and this is why an aesthetic element must be associated with every act of spiritual perception as well as with all spiritual striving. The quality of "being-in-itself" which belongs to the beautiful, the demand the beautiful itself makes to be allowed to be what it is, the demand, therefore, that we renounce our attempts to control and manipulate it in order that we might thereby be able to be happy by enjoying it: all of this is, in the natural realm, the foundation and foreshadowing of what in the realm of revelation and grace will be the attitude of faith.[23]

This intimate connection between the form of the beautiful in nature and the inner attractiveness of divine revelation also serves to break down that barrier between Athens and Jerusalem that has so often served to isolate Christians (or monotheists more generally) from the innate loveliness of pagan culture and non-Christian religions. Often the doctrine of biblical revelation has been taken to mean (to some extent rightly) that Christians have been plucked out from the *massa damnata* and been given the ineffable mercy of a revelation which has not been vouchsafed to their non-believing neighbors. For revelation, if it is to mean anything, must imply that through its bestowal the believer comes to know certain things he could not find out using only his own powers of reasoning. But this can lead all too easily to the assumption that without the benefit of the light of this revelation, all is lost in darkness. This then raises insuperable problems of God's justice (why some and not others?), especially when it comes to interpreting what revelation itself means when it says that "God wills the salvation of all men" (1 Tim 2:4). But an aesthetic approach

---

Gilson, makes this point admirably: "In nature the end, the *telos*, works as every artist would wish to be able to work: in fact, as the greatest among them do work, or even the others in moments of grace when, suddenly masters of their media, they work with the rapidity and infallible sureness of nature. Such is Mozart, composing a quartet in his head while writing down its predecessor. . . . A technician, an artist who worked with the sureness of a spider weaving its web or a bird making its nest would be a more perfect artist than any of those that anyone has ever seen. Such is not the case. The most powerful and the most productive artists only summon from afar the ever-ready forces of nature which fashion the tree, and, through the tree, the fruit. That is why Aristotle says that there is more design, more good, and more beauty in the works of nature than in those of art" (Étienne Gilson, *From Aristotle to Darwin and Back Again: A Journey in Final Causality, Species and Evolution,* tr. John Lyon [Notre Dame, IN: University of Notre Dame, 1984/1971], 9–10).
[23] GL 1, 153.

that recognizes the deep affinity between the form of the beautiful and the content of revelation will see how artificial and misleading is this constantly invoked dichotomy between Athens and Jerusalem. Indeed, "we could even go so far," Balthasar says, "as to discover in the constructions of non-Christian religion, philosophy and art elements which more or less explicitly indicate an attitude of obedience toward the light of the self-revealing God" (*GL* 1, 168).

This in no way implies, of course, abandoning the claims of revelation in favor of a universalism that subordinates the particularity of revelation in favor of a generalized concept of religion under which Christianity would be subsumed (his very encounter with Barth would have prevented Balthasar from going down that route!). On the contrary, an aesthetic theology would be able to bring out the distinctively Christian dimension all the more clearly. This, as we know, is the task of apologetics—to stress the credibility and truth of the Christian dispensation in terms accessible to the culture it is addressing. But what could be more suited to this daunting task than a theology that sees revelation in terms of its inherent attractiveness? And not to see this elementary fact—that apologetics and aesthetics go together—has been ruinous to apologetics: "The central question of so-called 'apologetics' or 'fundamental theology' is thus the question of perceiving form—an aesthetic problem. To have ignored this fact has stunted the growth of this branch of theology over the past hundred years" (*GL* 1, 173).

Apologetics in this past century has in fact presented a fairly dreary visage. Its efforts certainly never reach the magnificent heights of Origen's *Contra Celsum* or Thomas Aquinas' *Summa Contra Gentiles*. But this is because apologetics has abandoned its most effective ally. Only an aesthetic approach will work:

> For fundamental theology, the heart of the matter should be the question: "How does God's revelation confront man in history? How is it perceived?" But under the influence of a modern rationalistic concept of science, the question shifted ever more from its proper center to the margin, to be restated in this manner: "Here we encounter a man who claims to be God, and who, on the basis of this claim, demands that we should believe many truths he utters which cannot be verified by reason. What basis acceptable to reason can we give to his authoritative claims?" Anyone asking the question in this way has really already forfeited an answer, because he is at once enmeshed in an insoluble dilemma. . . . How strange it is that such an apologetics does not see the form which God so conspicuously sets before us! For Christ cannot be considered one "sign" among others; . . . the

dimmest idea of what a form is should serve as a warning against such leveling. (*GL* 1, 1–174)

Apologetics, to be sure, is not to be equated with the aesthetic moment in theology, for it is a subordinate moment in theology that is taken up when theology faces the world outside of itself and faces the challenge of making its message understandable and credible to the wider world. But aesthetics *is* that message, at least under one of its three essential rubrics. A theological aesthetics recognizes that a successful presentation of the beauty of the Christian proclamation will have obvious apologetic implications—for what could benefit apologetics more than an enticing presentation of the Christian dispensation in terms of its innate attractiveness? Nonetheless, it is primarily to be pursued for its own sake, as indeed befits a mode of presentation that stresses so much the sheer gratuity of the grace of beauty.

According to Balthasar, the dynamism of the Christian *kerygma* is inherently an outward-moving one: it explodes outward by virtue of the dynamism of the Holy Spirit, who calls on Christians to go out and preach to all nations, baptizing them "in the name of the Father and the Son and the Holy Spirit" (Mt 28:19). But for this dynamism to maintain its momentum, theology must distinguish three moments, which in one essay Balthasar calls the "three faces of theology."[24] These are, respectively, the contemplative, the kerygmatic, and the dialogical. These three moments have a certain logical and chronological relationship that establishes their hierarchy in theology: contemplative theology is that prayerful gaze upon the form of Christ and his revelation that is both an anticipation of the "beatific vision" at the end of time and an exercise of the "eyes of faith" mentioned earlier; kerygmatic theology is the response to what is heard and seen in that contemplation, it is the call to proclaim to the outside world what contemplation has learned in its privileged moment; and dialogic theology is the attempt to learn what the outside world is like and to respond to what it learns with an apologetic of its own.[25]

In a sense, the contemplative moment in theology must be so absorbed in the form that it can scarcely think in terms of the credibility of what it is seeing, for, as we have seen, beauty establishes the norms of its credibility by virtue of its own beckoning power. Or rather, it beckons so effectively that talk of "norms" and "credibility" sounds rather out of

---

[24] "The Unity of the Theological Sciences," *Conv.*, 47–73.

[25] Notice that these three moments also roughly fit the flow of the Trilogy itself, with contemplation being the more specifically aesthetic moment, the response of kerygmatic theology the moment of Christian drama, and apologetics the moment for defining the logic of theology in terms of the wider world and its norms for truth. Thus we shall take up the dilemmas of apologetics more thoroughly in Part IV of this book.

place. As Balthasar quite shrewdly and rather wittily observes: "In order to 'understand' the forms of nature, the spirit must give up its own light and entrust itself to the loving intimations which only lead us with certainty when the intellect for a time renounces its argumentativeness. *Anima* begins to sing only when she feels alone and thinks that her noisy husband *Animus* has left the house" (*GL* 1, 445).

And that is why the last half of Volume 1 of the Aesthetics is dedicated to a treatment of "The Objective Evidence." For while it is perfectly legitimate, and indeed necessary, to set forth for the reader a kind of theological phenomenology of the senses (as we have just presented it here, which has covered the first section of Volume 1, "The Subjective Evidence"), the whole point of being absorbed by beauty is that this absorption leads one out of oneself and into the wonder of the form itself.

And what does this form reveal of itself? We recall from our previous considerations that, subjectively considered, we "see through a glass darkly."[26] But this has its objective correlate too, in as much as the form is always self-transcending and can never be fully grasped. This is due not simply to our limited subjective powers, but more crucially to the fact that it is God who is revealing himself in this form, a form, moreover, that is only accessible through the darkness of faith. But now the emphasis is placed much more on the *objective* reasons for this inherent obscurity: God, in order truly to be God, must remain hidden as he reveals. In a particularly helpful summary, Balthasar explains the basis for this revelation-in-obscurity:

> The form of revelation corresponding to and conditioning the biblical unity between knowledge (vision) and faith (non-vision) must, as form, span from the outset a threefold tension: 1) the inner-worldly tension between the manifestness of the body and the hiddenness of the spirit; 2) the tension, rooted in creation, between the cosmos (as image and expression of a free God who in no way is compelled to create) and God himself; and 3) the tension, rooted in the order of grace and redemption, between the sinner who has turned away from God and the God who reveals himself as redeemer in the concealment of the Cross. (*GL* 1, 441)

We shall take up each of these three issues in turn:

1) For Balthasar the best way of establishing the prior reality of "the

---

[26] Nor should we forget how genuinely salvific this obscurity is, a point Pascal never tired of stressing: "Dieu veut plus disposer la volonté que l'esprit. La clarté parfaite servirait à l'esprit et nuirait à la volonté. Abaisser la superbe" ["God wants much more to make use of the will than he does of the mind. Perfect clarity would please reason but harm the will.

hidden" that "shines through" the form is the experience of falling in love, at least provided "they [the two lovers] do not linger in the antechamber of enamored infatuation" (*GL* 1, 445). Although he speaks here in ideal terms (couples are not necessarily meant to recognize themselves in this portrait of falling in love), nonetheless *if* their relationship is to mature into true love, something like what he is saying here must be possible, and if so, then the structure of inner/outer holds true:

> if a lover sees his beloved in a wholly different way from others, [it is] because the beloved's profound interior self is manifested to him in all her utterances and appears as that which is really precious and worthy of love. Every gift, every word speaks of this, and every reply he gives contains his whole self. Exterior exchanges are only bridges by which the souls pass over into one another.[27]

Leaving aside the disappointments that ensue from illusory occasions of falling in love, it is still no less true that those who fall in love do look on their beloved in a completely different way than do their friends, family or acquaintances. And like with art itself, falling in love suggests something inexhaustible about the other person, that will not be depleted even in a lifelong relationship. Moreover, it brings with it a self-discovery that comes from precisely *leaving aside* the narcissistic search for the self:

> The lover does not give himself in order to fulfill himself or in order to become conscious of his own depths; he trusts in a nature which, to be sure, transcends him. . . . This law is at work not only in "first love" or in the sexual act; it leaves its impress on the family and everything belonging to it; in short, it characterizes all human life, which is a "play" of "representations" that are precisely most lively when, in the game of life, man assumes the most serious ethical responsibilities. (*GL* 1, 445–446)

We can see this same process at work, formally speaking, in artists as well: the truly great artists do not try to "use" their art to put across

---

Humble the proud"] (Blaise Pascal, *Pensées*, in *Oeuvres Complètes*, ed. Jacques Chevalier [Paris: Gallimard, Edition Pléiade, 1954] #596, p. 1277).

[27] *GL* 1, 445. The reciprocity between lover and beloved is much easier to convey in German, where the reflexive pronoun carries no gender marker as in English. To convey the same sense from the woman's side (also part of the passage), one would translate it as follows: "If a lover sees her beloved in a wholly different way from others, it is because the beloved's profound interior self is manifested to her in all his utterances and he appears as that which is really precious and worthy of love. Every gift, every word speaks of this, and

their own idiosyncratic views, but see themselves at the service of their vision. No more than the lover does the artist go about fashioning his creation in order to discover himself. This is why the concentration on the artist's biography carries so little weight in Balthasar's aesthetic vision.[28] Much more crucial is the vision that seizes hold of the artist and claims him for its own, demanding that *its* world-view be embodied in *his* art:

> It is this world-view, and not himself, that [the artist] wants to fashion and make worthy of belief. For this reason, the artist will conceal himself in his work as much as he will reveal himself. To be sure, insofar as he gives shape to *his* world-view, the artists reveals something of himself; but insofar as, at a deeper level, he desires to manifest the world as he has understood it, he becomes unimportant to himself and treats himself as a mere medium which as such does not strive to reach any prominence. (GL 1, 443)

2) From Plato's *Timaeus* on, a long and distinguished tradition in the West attributes the shape and form of the universe to the "artistic" work of God.[29] Here too the same interplay between interior and exterior proves to be the crucial distinction—but now taken to express the infinite qualitative difference between God and the world he created.

The major point conveyed in the Christian doctrine of creation is the world's radical contingency *vis-à-vis* God: had God so wished, he could simply never have created in the first place. This is also true, in however much more a diminished sense, of the artist as well. Though of course we speak of an artist working under the compulsion of his vision, of his "I can do no other," this however does not gainsay the fact that he is still free, and in any case his creation is radically contingent on the will of the artist (however much his own will *to him personally* is compelled by his

---

every reply she gives contains her whole self. Exterior exchanges are only bridges by which the souls pass over into one another."

[28] "With works of art we can debate whether an investigation that goes beyond the data of the work, to busy itself with the person of the artist, his biography and psychology, contributes to the aesthetic understanding of the work or, to the contrary, detracts from it, seducing us from the contemplation of art into a consideration of other areas, . . . not least because we cannot assume that the work of art is intended in its author's mind, simply, to be an expression of himself" (GL 1, 443).

[29] One of the most convincing and charming examples of this trope from a Christian in the 20th century comes from the medievalist (and mystery writer) Dorothy Sayers, whose 1941 book, *The Mind of the Maker* (San Francisco: Harper & Row, 1941/1987) is a brilliant example of comparing the artistic creativity of a playwright, actor and audience with the Christian Trinity—a theme to which we will return in our treatment of Balthasar's Theodramatics.

muse). But just as all manner of rummaging about the biographical and psychological data of the artist contributes little to the understanding of the work itself (which remains to be judged on its own terms), and conversely just as a full appreciation of the work cannot directly tell us anything much about the creator (except that he was gifted), so too with God:

> Thus all contingency does indeed reveal him unmistakably as the free Creator, but also conceals him to a deeper degree precisely on account of the fact that we can nowhere make any firm deduction. Natural theology can only take the form of allowing all creaturely being to become an indicative utterance about God (since everything derives from him and may thus bear his image and trace). But this positive, cataphatic theology must finally lead to a comprehensive negative, apophatic theology. (*GL* 1, 448)

One other point must be noted here: these statements apply to *all* of creation: "you have hated nothing you have made." And because creation is utterly gratuitous and its gratuity extends throughout the whole of creation, there is no part of it that is not affected by God's saving will, no part that does not indicate his majesty, righteousness and justice (Rm 1:20).[30] This means not only that the boundary between the grace of nature and the grace of redemption will be hard to draw but indeed, for man, will be impossible to draw: "We will never be able to determine exactly the extent to which this splendor, given with creation itself, coincides objectively with what Christian theology calls 'supernatural revelation,' which, at least for Adam, was not yet a specifically distinct revelation given in the form of words" (*GL* 1, 449). All we can say is that so rooted are we in this grace of creation that to rebel against it is to violate our very natures:

> We should not pass over [this] creaturely phase too quickly in our haste to reach the phase of the revelation of grace and the Word, which is higher and, therefore, alone supposed to be important. It is as creature that man first comes to know the evergreater and, thus, ever-more-hidden God as his Lord. This unique relationship of revelation and concealment is inscribed in his very being. For man, this is not a positive law from whose opacity he could appeal to the order of Being itself. If he rebels

---

[30] "Created being would not be an image and 'outflow' (as Thomas Aquinas puts it) of the sovereign and living God if its transcendentals were static properties, clear and evident to our view, or if, despite their immanence in all contingent beings, they did not have something of the freedom and mysterious depths of God's decision to reveal himself" ("Revelation and the Beautiful," *WF,* 111).

against it, he will attack only himself. To be sure, the revelation of the Word is much more than just the awakening of an order of being which had been forgotten due to sin. But it is always this in part, and therefore it always points to a zone of necessity behind which the creature cannot reach. Consequently, in the particular non-evidence of Christian faith there always emerges something which, with the necessary qualifications, may be called the evidence of the Creator who reveals himself in concealment as the beginning and end of all the world's paths. (*GL* 1, 449–450)

3) So there is always an inner and an outer dimension to every form: dimensions which, moreover, are so intimately bound to each other that they cannot be separated out but must simply be acknowledged from the nature of the phenomena—art, universe, love, etc.—that we are investigating. But God's obscurity in relation to the world is due to more than just the fact that creation would be overwhelmed if it were to be fully bathed in the light of God's splendor: his presence in the world is also obscured by sin. And yet that same God who was "rejected of men" responded by redeeming the world in the concealment of the Cross, whereby the darkness that invaded the world with sin has now been assumed by God and absorbed into his very Godhead.

This will be the theme of later chapters, but we need to say at the outset of this theme that, once more, we can speak in aesthetic terms of this new form of concealment caused by the blight of sin (now so intensified because of its repellent degradation) because of the analogues which the world (and the world of art) make available to us:

If the Cross radically puts an end to all worldly aesthetics, then precisely this end marks the decisive emergence of the divine aesthetic, but in saying this we must not forget that even worldly aesthetics cannot exclude the element of the ugly, of the tragically fragmented, of the demonic, but must come to terms with these. Every aesthetic which simply seeks to ignore these nocturnal sides of existence can itself be ignored from the outset as a sort of aestheticism. (*GL* 1, 460)

But in today's climate, "aestheticism" is precisely the accusation that this kind of theology often evokes. So before he can go on to show how this approach can be made fruitful for theology, Balthasar must first do a kind of archaeological dig throughout the history of theology, to see how and why what the ancients took for granted—the innate attractiveness of revelation—has lost its power to draw our sad race of men to come nigh and worship the Lord. What the 17th-century Metaphysical poet George

Herbert could so take for granted has now for us become extremely difficult, and to explain why will be the task of the next section of the Aesthetics. But for Herbert, the whole world radiated the splendor of light invisible:

> A man that looks on glass,
> On it may stay his eye;
> Or if he pleaseth, through it pass,
> And then the heavens espy.
>   "The Elixir"

To the extent that this is no longer possible for us, we must ask why—and this brings us to Balthasar's "archaeology of alienated beauty." What happened in either the history of Christian thought or in the West's intellectual career for us to feel so cut off and unable to look through the glass and "the heavens espy"?

· 6 ·

The Archaeology
of Alienated Beauty

Nos patriae finis et dulcia linquimus arva.
Nos patriam fugimus.
(We are leaving our country with its sweet fields.
We fly our native land.)

Vergil
Bucolica

O dark, dark, dark. They all go into the dark,
The vacant interstellar spaces, the vacant into the vacant,
The captains, merchant bankers, eminent men of letters,
The generous patrons of art, the statesmen and the rulers,
Distinguished civil servants, chairmen of many committees,
Industrial lords and petty contractors, all go into the dark. . . .

And we all go with them, into the silent funeral,
Nobody's funeral, for there is no one to bury.

T. S. Eliot
"East Coker," *The Four Quartets*

We know too much, and are convinced of too little. Our literature is a substitute for religion, and so is our religion.

T. S. Eliot
"A Dialogue on Dramatic Poetry"

Hans Urs von Balthasar is a theologian who has often been pigeon-holed as a "conservative." But however shopworn such catch-words as "liberal" and "conservative" remain, the label of conservative nonetheless captures a real feature of his thought—*provided* we first understand that rather inaccurate term with sufficient care. And in the neo-conservative journal *Commentary*, as it happens, the sociologists Bri-

gitte and Peter Berger have provided us with precisely the typology we
need for understanding how we might understand that all-too vague a
word—a typology I shall make use of to explain how Balthasar too might
be appropriately understood as a "conservative."[1]

Conservatives, of course, want to conserve. That is, they see the past
as valuable, as a repository of wisdom which it is the duty of later generations to assimilate and hand down. Whether by temperament or conviction, they see the threat that the future represents to the past, and thus
they take protective measures to preserve the past from the potentially
acidic effect of the present and future. So-called "progressives," on the
other hand, see the hope represented in the future and feel much more
the burden of the past and advocate that we progress beyond the obscurantism and weight of history into a more hopeful future. Perhaps these
are two fundamental orientations of the human personality, impervious
to empirical confirmation or refutation.[2]

Conservatives, in other words, are by temperament open to the myth
of the Golden Age, while progressives are more animated by the myth of
the future Millennium. One group sees history as providing an example
of the Lost Paradise, which is our duty to restore, while the other looks
for the heavenly Jerusalem to descend into the ambiguities of history at
some point in the future—and which our committed action must try to
bring about.

Now if we put things in this way, we immediately see that both temperaments contradict Christian revelation, for it explicitly places *both* protology and eschatology beyond the reach of mere history: it is in fact a heresy
to say that the Lost Paradise was located in history anywhere else but in
the Garden of Eden (a trans-historical "place").[3] But it is also a heresy to

---

[1] Brigitte and Peter L. Berger, "Our Conservatism and Theirs," *Commentary* 89/10 (October 1986): 62–67.

[2] Certainly Sir. W. S. Gilbert (of Gilbert and Sullivan fame) thought so:

> I often think it comical
> How nature always does contrive
> That every boy and every gal
> That's born into the world alive
> Is either a little Liberal,
> Or else a little Conservative!
> (William Schwenk Gilbert, *Iolanthe,* Act II).

[3] We might perhaps excuse earlier Christians for assuming that Adam and Eve initiated
history rather than serving as symbols for its initial constituents, but after the discovery by
geology of the vast age of the earth and by paleontology of the extended history of man,
this is no longer possible. But we must be careful not to read into the past the naïve views
of 19th-and 20th-century fundamentalists. As W. D. Davies explains in his fascinating study
of Paul's Rabbinic background, "the Old Testament term Adam was used [in Rabbinic
exegesis] generically for all mankind" (W. D. Davies, *Paul and Rabbinic Judaism* [Philadel-

expect the Second Coming to be but one episode in history which would then continue on: eschatology represents the *end* of history, not an occasion for its amelioration.

But if there are heretical exaggerations of these two fundamental attitudes there are also more muted versions of them that affect the orthodox mind too, and it is perhaps their ultimate roots in the pre-given structure of personality that accounts for the continued tension in the Church between liberal and conservative factions, with some people looking back to an age of lost innocence and others looking forward to a restoration of all things. And perhaps it will ever be such.

In any event, it is this framework that can explain, I think, the different varieties of conservatism in the world today. For whether or not conservatives go to the extreme of identifying their lost Golden Age with all of the features that mark the life of prelapsarian Adam and Eve, the point is that they tend to locate their Golden Age at different moments of past *history*. And yet there are differences here as well, primarily centering on where this Lost Paradise is located: while they all in some way or other look on history as a decline from a past that used to be more glorious and more harmonious but which at some point went wrong, conservatives differ quite markedly in where they place this initiating catastrophe.

Catholic traditionalists in the Hilaire Belloc and G. K. Chesterton school, for example, often point to the Middle Ages, especially the 13th century, as the high point from which all later history has been mostly a dismal decline. T. S. Eliot represents an Anglo-Catholic subspecies of this category: he located the Golden Age in the 17th century, the period of the Metaphysical Poets John Donne and George Herbert, an age when churchmen like Lancelot Andrewes and Archbishop Laud governed an Established Church of dignity and majestic worship. After that came the curse of the Romantic Personality, tediously fixated on its own emotional woes. This was a period of cultural narcissism that introduced into Western letters what Eliot called, in a frequently cited phrase, "the dissociation of sensibility," that is, a time when the objectivity of religion could no longer be harmonized with the surge of a person's self-regarding life.

---

phia: Fortress, 1980], 57, note 4). And so, despite the ancients' reputation for naïveté, the real point of the story of the Garden of Eden was lost neither on the rabbis nor on the early Christians: "The fact that all men are derived from one ancestor Adam means that in him all men are one. There is a real unity of all men in him; all belong to each and each belongs to all" (53). There is, in addition, a charming Rabbinic midrash to the effect that God made Adam out of dust gathered from all over the earth, and "later speculation claimed that his head was formed from the earth of the Holy Land, the trunk of his body from Babylonian soil and his various members from the soil of different countries" (54). On this same point also see the chapter called "The 'Adamic' Myth and the 'Eschatological' Vision of History" in: Paul Ricoeur, *The Symbolism of Evil*, tr. Emerson Buchanan (Boston: Beacon Press, 1967), 232–278.

But then there are whole other versions of conservatism, non-religious ones, such as the libertarians of today, who locate the Lost Kingdom in the free-wheeling and harshly competitive world of 19th-century laissez-faire capitalism, or, once more, the neo-conservatives of *Commentary*, who have made their peace with the Modernism of Ezra Pound, Sigmund Freud and D. H. Lawrence—intellectuals who positively celebrate the formal innovations of James Joyce's *Ulysses* and *Finnegans Wake*, whose sly mocking of epic heroism and sacred texts was seen by them as a genuine advance over the realism of most 19th-century art.[4] But then came the late 1960's with its Dionysian revels such as Woodstock and the Broadway musical *Hair*, and with that ethos there crept into the cultural atmosphere an anti-Americanism and a naïveté about the tyranny of Communism that was hard for these erstwhile liberals to counter, because politics for the New Left had degenerated from the High Seriousness of moral commitment (always essential if the Eschaton is to be brought down into history!) to empty guerrilla theater and bacchanalian free love.

This variety in the conservative movement hides within itself a considerable amount of (often unacknowledged) tension, as the Bergers point out rather amusingly: "No wonder that traditionalist conservatives perceive [neo-conservatives] as Johnny-come-latelies: The neo-conservatives are late by anything from one to six centuries, at the very least."[5]

These remarks are relevant here because they help place Balthasar in the spectrum of contemporary theology; but more specifically they highlight how jejune and unhelpful this catch-all term "conservative" can be. For one thing, there is the matter of his eschatology (a point that will be the focus of the final chapter), which is teeming with optimism and hope, and probably constitutes his single greatest innovation in theology. Conservative Christians, at least on the farther reaches of the right, are not noted for their desire to see an overly crowded heaven; and ever since the condemnation of Origenism in the fifth century, the Christian Church has pretty much taken it for granted, at least in the West (which has lived so much under the shadow cast by that giant of the spirit, St. Augustine), that hell is rather more populated than heaven. If Origen is "left" and Augustine is "right," then Balthasar definitely leans, *at least in hope*, toward the left. And we have already seen how sharply he criticizes the Church Fathers.

Nonetheless, Balthasar is hardly a "liberal" theologian either. Again we must admit at the outset the terminal vagueness of the label; but to counteract this ambiguity, I shall define "liberal" inside this chapter as a stance

---

[4] *Ulysses*, of course, is universally recognized as an epic of the anti-hero, but perhaps it is not sufficiently recognized how *Finnegans Wake* tries to create the formal equivalent of a sacred text requiring an almost religious devotion from its interpreters.

[5] Berger and Berger, 63.

that is willing to elevate the achievements of the Enlightenment to a governing methodological principle. And in this sense, Balthasar is most definitely, even fiercely, anti-liberal.

Moreover, it is that side of him that colors all of the positions of his that have given rise to his reputation as a conservative. As Medard Kehl, in a wonderfully lucid introductory essay on his thought, observes:

> The name Hans Urs von Balthasar carries with it a particular tone in today's Church. Some, who judge him predominantly from his great theological and historical works, see him—transcending all preliminary labels—as one of the most significant figures in theology today. Many others, however, who know him only from some smaller controversial works, paperbacks, and newspaper articles, content themselves with placing him—approvingly or disapprovingly—on the "conservative side" of the Church. There are certainly grounds enough for this. For many years he has done battle with a sharp tongue against certain post-conciliar "trends" in the Church in order to uncover in them numerous hidden ambiguities and inclinations which would "lighten the ballast of what is Christian." Examples of this would be: the "trend" to the Bible (with a neglect of the whole subsequent tradition), to the liturgy (which frequently dissolves into spiritual managing and community self-satisfaction), to the ecumenical movement (at the price of leveling one's own tradition), to the "secular world" (with a simultaneous devaluation of the "sacred," the "mystical," and the "monastic").[6]

None of these issues need detain us here, but much more to the point of this chapter is Balthasar's approach to the history of the tradition, for that is our immediate concern here. Of all of the great theologians of this century: Barth, Bultmann, Pannenberg, Rahner, Tillich, etc., perhaps Balthasar is most distinctive here: in his full use of the sources that comprise the Great Tradition; and in that sense, we may describe him as a "conservative" in the true sense of the term:

> The *sources* of his theological thinking and speaking lie not only—as is quite common today—in Sacred Scripture, modern

[6] Medard Kehl, S.J., "Hans Urs von Balthasar: A Portrait," *The von Balthasar Reader*, ed. Medard Kehl, S.J and Werner Löser, S.J., tr. Robert J. Daly, S.J. and Fred Lawrence (New York: Crossroad, 1982), 4. This list, of course, could be extended, and in fact Kehl does not fail to mention Balthasar's conservative position on obligatory celibacy or women's ordination, the cult of theological pluralism, the primacy of contemplation over action, his deep reservations about liberation theology, his curt dismissal of sociology of religion as a

philosophy, modern theological movements and investigations of the human sciences, but above all in the great tradition of the Church. The writings of the Church Fathers and the great saints and spiritual masters of the Church are for him more than a presupposed background of this theology. As the decisive milestones in the "*Wirkungsgeschichte*" of the Old and New Testaments, they provide him with a living and always richly available basis of argument from which to approach the theological questions of the present. This tradition-conscious starting point makes him today subject (subconsciously or openly expressed) to the occasional complaint that, with all this knowledge of modern intellectual history, he still has basically no proper understanding of the modern age and its changed problematic. The symbolic and holistic understanding of the Fathers of the Church and not the critical-analytic reflection of the moderns is what forms the real horizon of his thought.[7]

And this is why I wanted to spend at least a few pages on the varieties of conservatism at the outset of this chapter, for Balthasar too sees the history of theology in terms of a Golden Age from which modern theology has been a history of painful declension. But his location for this Fall is unique among traditionalists, who if they are Roman Catholic tend to look on the thirteenth century as the "greatest of centuries," to quote one famous title of a book very much in the Chesterbelloc school of historiography. Balthasar, however, locates this decline as occurring *with* the thirteenth century!

In his mind, the history of theology should be divided into two eras: the first is the era of "clerical" styles, during which the first Platonic transcendental, the form of beauty itself, had an *official* place in the Church; the second is the era of "lay" styles, during which those in love with the holiness and spontaneous Eros of Beauty felt (and still feel) *exiled* from the official ("clerical") Church. This now becomes an era, ironically enough, when the Church takes on that "clerical" aspect that people are

---

helpful coadjutor to theology, and perhaps above all, his fierce defense of the papacy against what he calls an "anti-Roman complex."

[7] Kehl, "A Portrait," 5. Louis Dupré seconds this judgment when he tartly notes that "one may call his attitude 'conservative' in the sense that he attempts to 'conserve' a tradition which he, unlike many who claim the title, thoroughly knows" (Louis Dupré, "Hans Urs von Balthasar's Theology of Aesthetic Form," *Theological Studies* 49 [1988]: 315). But Dupré is also quite aware how Balthasar eludes snap judgments and easy labelling: "Nor is Balthasar simply a traditionalist. His views on Augustine's theology of damnation, on Dante's hell ('the *reductio ad absurdum* of scholastic theology'), on Christ's descent into hell to suffer the pain of the damned and to liberate the captive souls, move from the center of the tradition" (ibid.).

bound to find so suffocating of their inner freedom and personal harmony. Nonetheless, says the author, "the dividing line between the two volumes which occurs about 1300 is not meant in any polemical way. It simply corresponds to an unfortunate but incontestable fact: the great upholders of Christian spirituality now feel themselves to be, and behave like, representatives of an ecclesiastical 'opposition' and have to take on themselves the corresponding fate of the exiled, the misunderstood, the outlawed" (*GL* 2, 15).

Thus the next two volumes of *The Glory of the Lord* will be titled, respectively, *Clerical Styles* and *Lay Styles*. This terminology might strike some readers as idiosyncratic and offputting, and to some extent I suppose the point can be granted; but it is important to see what Balthasar is driving at here. As we will see in later chapters, the distinction between the lay and clerical states plays a crucial role at certain junctures in his theology and never more so than here. And so it is especially crucial, here of all places, not to misunderstand him. For one thing, Balthasar is *not* trying to revive a long-lost era of "clericalism." On the contrary, as we have already seen, what normally passes for clericalism in ordinary usage only began when the official Church hardened in aspect and became self-conscious about her institutional structure: when the Church is innately attractive on her own terms, it is hard to imagine clericalism becoming that burning of an issue.

But the place of office in the Church is a matter of great importance in his ecclesiology, and it is a matter of great pastoral concern to him to figure out why official, institutional Christianity drives people away in droves today. The causes for this go deep, and are not merely attributable to that vaguely invoked term "secularization." More is at issue than merely the growth of the natural sciences, the recession of the "God of the gaps" in explanatory natural philosophy, the Enlightenment critique against the alleged obscurantism of the doctrine of revelation, etc. The causes are also, and perhaps even primarily, internal: they stem from a split in theology that began in the Middle Ages, a split that first marks the divorce between theology proper and spirituality, or more precisely, between "scientific" and "devotional" theologies (one hesitates even to use the terms—as they seem to convey, in the very bewitchment of their language, the split they signify).

While the threat of this split has always lurked in Christian thought, and while there has always been a danger that curiosity about purely speculative issues will overcome a sense that theology must be rooted in the direct covenantal encounter with God, the danger represented by this split sharpened and *became institutionalized* in the Middle Ages when monastery and university went their separate ways:

> This unique synthesis [between theology and spirituality] extends from Gregory and Bede to the school of St. Victor and its

contemporaries, and whose center and pinnacle are the works of Bernard. It is important that the breadth and openness to the world not be lacking (the monks, after all, saved the philosophy of literature of antiquity), and yet the steep summit of this theology lies in the Song of Songs as the central mystery of creation and covenant, of Church and soul, in which *eros* sublimates itself entirely in *caritas*. . . . Not without reason did Anselm perceive Roscelin, as Bernard saw Abelard, as innovators (*novitates*) and a threat to theology at its very roots.[8]

One way this found expression was in the severance of *lectio divina* (reading Scripture as a moment of prayer and for direct contact with God) from the way Scripture was presented in the university classroom.[9] This led to what soon became a distinctively mendicant (as opposed to monastic) approach to the Scriptures, and one that soon came—with that monk-Reformer, Martin Luther—around to undermining the entire monastic approach to the Bible.

Now once again it absolutely must be stressed that Balthasar is not engaging in polemics here: this examination of the career of theology is no hand-wringing exercise, and no prophet-of-doom spirit reigns here! On the contrary, I cannot help but detect moment of sly humor in his analysis, as when he points out the irony of the Protestant attack on medieval exegesis: ironic because they can now be seen to be indulging in the same four-fold method of interpreting Scriptures! If that strikes the reader as highly implausible, not to say eccentric, I will simply defer to Balthasar's analysis directly:

> The four senses of Scripture are celebrating a hidden resurrection in the most modern Protestant theology, where the "literal sense" appears as the "historical-critical" sense, to be reached by research, the "spiritual" as the "kerygmatic," the "tropological" as the "existential," and the "anagogical" as the "eschato-

---

[8] "Unity of Theology and Spirituality," *Conv.*, 32–33.

[9] Balthasar only alludes to the process in the opening pages of *Clerical Styles* and in his essay on this same theme, "The Unity of Theology and Spirituality," but it has been richly demonstrated by Beryl Smalley: "The spiritual exposition, however much it was practiced in the pulpit and in the schools, derived its vitality from religious experience in the cloister. It drew its sap through the roots of *lectio divina* from the soil of the old monastic tradition. . . . The abbot of Clairvaux was truly the last of the Fathers. . . . This in itself signifies a change of attitude. A new conception of the spiritual life and of the place of *lectio divina* in that life was leading to a decline in the spiritual exposition. . . . On the one hand, *lectio divina* becomes more intellectual. . . . On the other hand, the technique of devotion is changing. It is systematized" (Beryl Smalley, *The Bible in the Middle Ages* [Notre Dame, IN: University of Notre Dame Press, 1964/1952], 281–282).

logical" sense. (For Bultmann, moreover, as for Origen, the existential and eschatological senses are nothing but a nearer characterization of the kerygmatic sense.)[10]

In other words, there is no escaping history, so we might as well get acquainted with it, to see how we have come to the pass we have. And that is the purpose and intent of *Clerical* and *Lay Styles:* to discover, through a set of truly extraordinary monographs on twelve theologians[11] who have expressed the beauty of revelation in an especially striking way, how we have come to the point where those theologians most attuned to the beauty of the Christian religion have come to feel alienated from it.

It is perhaps the volume on "lay" styles that most displays how Balthasar's aesthetics actually encompasses within itself the most burning concerns of all the contemporary theologies concerned with action and relevance. For every figure discussed in this volume—Dante, John of the Cross, Pascal, Hopkins, Péguy and others—in fact qualifies for treatment under the aegis of "lay styles" because of the way each one actively resisted scholastic theology and its clericalization. These men are all "protesting against a narrowing-down of Christian theology merely to the training of pastors or to academic specialization and the timeless pursuit of the schools; [they are] demanding an understanding of revelation in the context of the history of the world and the actual present" (*GL* 2, 15).

The chapter on Dante, in fact, has an amazingly eloquent denunciation of church evils during the Middle Ages, and in summarizing Dante's voice, Balthasar almost seems to be joining his own to the chorus of Dante and Beatrice: "Dante's criticisms of the worldliness of the Church are unending; from heaven Beatrice and Peter pour out their reproaches on the decadent Church, and in a terrible image, the poet sees the transfigured Peter suddenly become incandescent with wrath, fulminating against the 'atrocious' Boniface VIII. . . . Peter reproaches the Popes for their ambition and their passion for pomp, which divide the Church, and for their abuse of the power of the keys for the purposes of earthly warfare and of excommunication for political ends. . . . Later the decadence of the religious orders is bemoaned and there is a denunciation of the wretched sermons that no longer expound the Gospel so that 'the poor sheep that know nothing return from pasture fed on wind.'"[12]

There can of course be no question of summarizing each of these mono-

---

[10] "Unity of Theology and Spirituality," *Conv.*, 30.

[11] Or, more generically, twelve writers, since not all of them would normally be considered "theologians" (Hopkins, Péguy, etc.).

[12] *GL* 3, 22–23. And lest one think that Balthasar is merely paraphrasing Dante here, his essay on the theme of the sinful Church, "Casta Meretrix" should be consulted in *SW,* 193–288.

graphs. Rather, since what we are faced with is fundamentally a musical work, I shall merely isolate a few of the key motifs of this fascinating work and show how the situation in theology and in the cultural history of the West has led us to the point where one of our most pressing needs—did we but know it!—is a truly theological aesthetics.

And perhaps in fact that *is* the best way to begin our entry into these rather intimidating two volumes: through a frank recognition of what we have lost. Perhaps a sense of our desperation will then make us hunger to know all the more how we got to this impasse and how Balthasar's work might effect some kind of healing. It is, however, one of the peculiarities of this work that it ends rather abruptly with Péguy and thus contains no sustained treatment of the aesthetic situation in the twentieth century. I think the omission of Eliot in this regard is rather unfortunate, as it would be interesting to see how he would deal not only with a "conservative" who places the "Fall" at a later time, and from an Anglo-Catholic perspective, but also one who managed to touch the popular imagination of our time more than most any "High Poet" one might care to name. Not only has it been said that the sun never sets on a seminar on *The Waste Land* going on somewhere on the globe but also Eliot was a great fan of vaudeville and other forms of "low" entertainment and had an uncanny knack for capturing the popular imagination (as the long-running musical *Cats* so amply demonstrates).

Also one of the reviewers of *Lay Styles* mentioned the lack of women in this work, a rather startling omission, considering not only its rubric but also its thesis of alienation from the official Church.[13] But the author openly admits that this section of the Aesthetics is somewhat arbitrarily chosen, and other confirming examples are possible,[14] among whom he explicitly mentions Hildegard of Bingen and Mechthild of Magdeburg. In retrospect, I think it is unfortunate that some of the women writers he treats elsewhere were not incorporated into the structure of *Lay Styles,* but we shall have occasion to remedy this lacuna when we take up his theology of the sexes in Chapter 10.

In any event, one of the most signal contributions that Balthasar has

---

[13] "Women, unfortunately, seem missing from these studies, and it is difficult to understand why. For Balthasar surely does not ignore women in his other 'occasional' writings (think of his studies of St. Thérèse de Lisieux and Elisabeth of Dijon), and he has said that it is nearly impossible to separate his own thoughts from those of Adrienne von Speyr. Can one say that the study on Péguy, at least, surfaces the contribution of women to the Christ-symphony in its attention to the Joan of Arc drama and the great poem on Eve, for example?" (Review by William M. Thompson, *Theological Studies* 48 [1987]: 574).

[14] "This is naturally not to deny that, between these twelve figures picked out as typical, there is not a host of others who could have clarified the intellectual and historical relations and transitions between them and would in themselves also have been worthy of presentation" (*GL* 2, 20).

made to theology has been his ability to spot this alienation of beauty from the official Church and to see where its roots lay.[15] And there certainly can be no question of the facts of the case, as he points out in a book, *The God Question and Modern Man,* that might well be interpreted as the missing last chapter in *Lay Styles* (the chapter on the twentieth century):

> Before the dawn of the technical age it was easier to create genuine culture from genuine recollection. Life was more peaceful, man's surroundings expressed eternal values more directly. Moreover, the requirements of average education at school level did not overtax the intellectual capacities of young people as they do today. All this cannot be left out of account. How immediately a landscape from which men are absent can unite us to God, for example high mountains, a large forest or a freely flowing river! The handwriting of the Creator can easily be read in them; even those who have forgotten how to pray will once more learn, with deep joy, to listen to the sound of the sources of existence. In the cities, however, only man's handwriting is everywhere visible, and much more so in the modern than in the ancient ones that were still built according to human measurements. Concrete and glass do not speak of God; they only point to man who is practically glorified in them. The cities do not

---

[15] I cannot help but think, however, that of all the diagnoses for this neglect of beauty, Carol Harrison's has come the closest: "In Dostoevski's *The Idiot* the saintly Prince Myshkin is mocked for having suggested that the world will be saved by beauty. . . . Put this claim to a theologian and he will probably be as baffled as those who heard Prince Myshkin—a measure of how much theological tradition has neglected the category of the beautiful. And yet it is an idea that attracts; one cannot read it and then pass on to the next sentence without giving it a second thought. . . . What if Prince Myshkin, the holy fool, were right? What would it mean? If he had said, 'the world will be saved by the truth,' or 'the world will be saved by goodness,' we would have had an inkling of what he meant: we have heard it before and are used to thinking in such terms. Why then is 'beauty' such a strange idea to put in this context? In Christian tradition, at least, I would suggest that it is because it is such an ambivalent concept. Whereas truth and goodness are unquestionably of God, beauty, which has an equal claim to be one of the transcendentals, is rather more problematic. Why? . . . Beauty allures and fallen man wants to possess it. A beautiful landscape or a beautiful piece of music may speak unambiguously of the divine source of beauty; but a beautiful painting, a beautiful woman: . . . that may provoke not just wonder but the desire to possess. . . . Moreover, they can easily be the occasion for actually turning man away from ultimate Beauty and can even be the occasion for his sin. Again, why is this? Is it because, of the three transcendentals, beauty is the most *embodied,* the most *incarnate,* the one which is virtually inseparable from matter—from the created, temporal, mutable realm?" (Carol Harrison, *Beauty and Revelation in the Thought of St. Augustine* [Oxford: Clarendon Press, 1992], 270–271; author's emphasis). Yes! But for Balthasar it is precisely *because* the Logos has been embodied and is incarnate, aesthetics is the most direct access to the revelation of that incarnation, all the risks notwithstanding.

transcend man, hence they do not guide to transcendence. Quickly and greedily they devour the surrounding countries and turn it into a dirty, defiled forecourt of cities. For some years now the Roman Campagna has ceased to exist, the Swiss landscape likewise. The Rhine has long "had it." Overnight, "nature" will be turned into a reservation; it will become a "national park" within the civilized world; and besides, in national parks— mostly crowded!—it is not very easy to pray either. (GQ, 57)

One of the great passions that animates Balthasar as a theologian is this increasing inability of Christians to pray. It is why he wishes to be known as a "kneeling theologian," a description that irks some people but which is not at all meant as a pharisaical indulgence in self-congratulation but is in fact motivated by the deepest pastoral concern for what the vanishing of prayer from the life of the Church will mean:

> Many, not to say most, within this technical world, have capitulated interiorly by giving up prayer. The Christians who are determined to persevere in it groan under the too great burden of external demands made on them if they want to compete with others who neither have nor allow time for prayer and thought. A synthesis between prayer and godless over-activity, between interior culture demanding a world of silence and external rush and ever increasing speed, is more and more becoming an extraordinary attainment of the heroic few, and even so only for a limited time; it seems an impossible demand to make on a larger number of people. (GQ, 57)

The reasons for this immensely powerful undertow are, in their deepest roots, aesthetic.[16] And that is why the archaeology of alienated beauty

---

[16] To those readers who might find such an assertion implausible on its face, I can do no better than recommend Jacques Barzun's *The Use and Abuse of Art* (Princeton: Princeton University Press, 1974), which points out how directly aesthetics affects, and is affected by, a loss of the sense of God: "To shock by inversion is of course an old device of religions. The Bible teems with examples of it. The high shall be low, the first shall be last, the rich will be beggars, the poor will be clad in gold raiment. . . . But it takes an omniscient God to bring justice out of these overturns. To a godless age, the negative part of the inversion alone remains potent. The negative perpetuates itself as a habit of thought—it becomes the highest form of self-consciousness—and it destroys everything in the most direct way, not by physical means, but by corrosion at the seat of faith and action, the human mind. That is how, today, we come to find thinkers for whom dissent is a routine, sex is a rhetoric, and violence is love. . . . Today, when you are tempted to see human representation in art . . . you are at once aware that the symbol is an angry distortion, a dismemberment and defamation of man, and not a reflection, must less a glorification, as it was from Phidias to the Pre-Raphaelites" (50–51, 55).

must sink its plumb-line so deep into the history of theology, for it is not *merely* a question of technology, or the fast pace of life, or the neurotic fear of solitude that dominates and rules the lives of so many of our contemporaries today, for these are all ultimately outcomes of how we perceive the world and God: that is, of aesthetics. Once the perception of God's innate beauty and of the inherent and self-establishing attractiveness of revelation disappears, it becomes impossible for the ordinary citizen of the world to see any value in being religious at all or to see in Christianity the very embodiment of God's condescension:

> Religion is nowadays so little in demand, natural religion is depopulated, and those who deny the whole phenomenon have an easy game. The "man in the street," too, has no difficulty. He can take refuge behind the scandal of Christendom. . . . Today as never before the sanctuary appears defiled; the old reverence has been replaced by a cynicism of incredible dimensions, and the truly "natural" religion by a brazen irreligion that pretends to be just as natural.[17]

I think Balthasar's description of the current dreary scene is obvious enough, but I wonder how many of his readers will follow him in diagnosing the "Fall" into irreligion at the juncture when theology, at least in the West, split off into two separate rivers: monastic and scholastic, spiritual and scientific, emotive and technical, devotional and scholarly—or whether they will see that split as taking place with the introduction of Aristotelian logic as the governing methodology in scholastic theology. There is in fact a hot debate among medievalists about how "alienated"

---

[17] *The God Question*, 71. This situation makes the challenge of apologetics unusually daunting: for how do we express the Gospel (especially apologetically!) except in terms that people can understand? But what if those terms are themselves a distortion of the Christian past? "Let us put this to the test and try to imagine St. Paul's speech at Athens delivered in one of our modern capitals: 'Men of Paris or Moscow,' so it would run, 'I find you in every respect religious. . . . What therefore you worship without knowing it, that I preach to you.' . . . Today his opponents would not wait till he began to speak of the resurrection of Christ, when the old sages of Athens shook their heads, but would object at the very beginning of the speech, where Paul sought to connect the Gospel with the fact of natural religion. Since then something has changed. Surely some well-instructed members of his audience would rise to tell him they objected to being called 'in every way religious,' a statement either made from ignorance or meant as an insult. They would further inform him that the whole passage about temples made with hands and human worship had nothing to do with *them* but was instead very applicable to the *Christians*, who had turned their religion into precisely that for which Paul was blaming the pagans. But worse than this, the whole address would somehow fall flat, for even those listeners who had not been specially trained in militant [atheist] 'cells' would hardly understand this point of departure" (ibid., 62–63).

the category of the beautiful became under scholastic methods,[18] with Jacques Maritain and Étienne Gilson insisting that Beauty was not downplayed or ignored in favor of strict logic,[19] while Umberto Eco and Jan Aertsen maintain the opposite.[20]

This debate need not detain us here, except to note that Balthasar himself sees his arrangement of the trilogy in explicitly un-Thomistic (though not anti-Thomistic) terms.[21]. But a close reading of *Clerical* and *Lay Styles* does bring with it a conviction that at least as far as the authors treated therein are concerned, there is no doubt that Irenaeus, Augustine, Dionysius the Areopagite, Anselm and Bonaventure (the "clericals") all took for granted the innate proportionality and loveliness of revelation and wrote from within that assumption, while Dante, John of the Cross, Pascal, Hamann, Soloviev, Hopkins and Péguy (the "laymen"!) all clearly wrote out of a pathos of misunderstanding, alienation and loneliness that one simply does not pick up in earlier theologians.[22]

It is unfortunate that an introductory book of this nature cannot examine each of these twelve monographs in detail, for they are all, each in its own way, magnificent. One need only consider the biographies of some of the great men (and all so isolated!) in the period of "lay styles": as a Jesuit, Hopkins rebelled against the school-Thomism of his training for a more full-bodied Scotism that took seriously the emergence of unique identity from unique form—and ended up under suspicion by his superiors

---

[18] For a useful overview of this literature, see: Jan A. Aertsen, "Beauty in the Middle Ages: A Forgotten Transcendental?" *Medieval Philosophy & Theology* 1 (1991): 68–97; abbreviated henceforth as "BMA."

[19] Jacques Maritain, *Art and Scholasticism*, tr. Joseph W. Evans (New York: Charles Scribner's Sons, 1962/1939); and Étienne Gilson, "The Forgotten Transcendental: *Pulchrum*," in *Elements of Christian Philosophy* (New York: Doubleday, 1960), 159–163.

[20] Umberto Eco, *Art and Beauty in the Middle Ages,* tr. Hugh Bredin (New Haven: Yale University Press, 1986), and *The Aesthetics of Thomas Aquinas,* tr. Hugh Bredin (Cambridge: Harvard University Press, 1988); for Aertsen, see "BMA" above and "Die Tranzendentalienlehre bei Thomas von Aquin in ihren historischen Hintergründen und philosophischen Motiven," in *Thomas von Aquin: Sein Leben, sein Wert und seine Zeit in der neusten Forschung,* ed. A. Zimmermann, Miscellanea Mediaevalia 19 (Berlin and New York: De Gruyter, 1988), 82–102.

[21] "Meine unthomistische Vorordnung des Pulchrum (des Seins als Wunder und des Staunens darüber) vor dem Bonum and Verum nimmt den Grundriß meiner späteren Trilogie vorweg, die mit einer Ästhetik (pulchrum) beginnt und einer Dramatik (bonum) fortfährt, um zur Theo-Logik (verum) zu gelangen" (*UA*, 82). Note here that we are speaking only of the *arrangement* of the transcendentals; in siding with Maritain and Gilson in the debate with Eco and Aersten, Balthasar will clearly have appreciative things to say about Aquinas' metaphysics, a point that will be discussed at the end of this chapter.

[22] The fact that two "clerics" (that is, priests) appear in this latter series, John of the Cross and Gerard Manley Hopkins, should serve to point out both the eccentricity of the terminology but also how little it builds on a clericalism that is in fact the bane of the book, as is apparent in his remarks on 2 Tim 2:24–25 in *TP*, 186.

and "exiled" to Ireland for his inability to conform; or there is Pascal, the greatest apologist for Christianity in modern times, on his deathbed and racked with pain, trying to convince his confessor of his orthodoxy and of his submission to the authority of the Church and Pope;[23] or Dante writing his *Divine Comedy* in decreed exile from his native Florence because of his Ghibelline (imperial) sympathies in opposition to Guelf (papal) Florence and populating his *Inferno* with assorted corrupt and power-hungry Popes;[24] or John of the Cross, dying the fate of a persecuted heretic as Rome's order of excommunication is on its way for promulgation in Spain; or Péguy, boiling over with frustration at his fellow-Catholic anti-Dreyfusards for their unthinking and purblind anti-Semitism who never realize that "the misunderstanding of the prophets by Israel is a figure of the misunderstanding of the saints by the sinful."[25]

These biographical considerations establish, I think, the justice and trenchancy of Balthasar's historiography of theology: the theologians of "lay styles" really do demonstrate how beauty has been alienated from the center of official theology; and their concern for beauty is undoubtedly a part of their own alienation from the official Church, since they could only work in her outlying precincts and never establish (with the possible exception of John of the Cross) an ongoing "school" of theology or spirituality.

And to move from the figures discussed in the immediately preceding *Clerical Styles* to these men, with their deathbed scenes that are almost invariably a death "in exile" and saturated with torment in relation to the institutional Church, is a real jolt: none of the earlier figures in *Clerical Styles* is a martyr, let alone at the hands of the Church! None writes with that painful self-consciousness that afflicts the exiled. And none considers the proportionality of revelation to be anything more than the most fitting structural correlate testifying to the fact that it *is* revelation. Take, for

---

[23] And the price for that submission was extraordinarily high: "He was urging his intelligence to commit suicide" (Morris Bishop, *Pascal: The Life of Genius* [New York: Reynal & Hitchcock, 1936], 338).

[24] Dorothy Sayers paints an even more poignant portrait of his isolation: "This was the task which Dante had set for himself—as Milton was to do some 300 years later—in the wreck of all his earthly hopes. He had lost love and youth and earthly goods and household peace and citizenship and active political usefulness and the dream of a decent world and a reign of justice. He was stripped bare. He looked outward upon the corruption of Church and Empire, and he looked inward into the corruption of the human heart; and what he saw was the vision of Hell. And, having seen it, he set himself down to write the great Comedy of Redemption and of the return of all things by the Way of Self-Knowledge and Purification, to the beatitude of the Presence of God" ("Introduction," *The Divine Comedy, 1: Hell*, tr. Dorothy Sayers [Harmondsworth: Penguin, 1949], 48–49).

[25] Charles Péguy, *Oeuvres en prose: 1909–1914*, Edition Pléiade, ed. Marcel Péguy (Paris: Gallimard, 1959), p. 551; quoted in GL 3, 416: "For Péguy, involvement in the Dreyfus affair was a holy, almost sacramental symbol of ethical purity and integrity" (415).

example, Balthasar's remarkable description of the Areopagite's relation to the Church:

> Therefore the mystics' praise of God is none other than the expression and development of the Church's praise, and is in this way also liturgy. . . . Everything lies in the circular movement between procession and return, and nothing can find fulfillment except by entering into this movement. No explanations can help those who do not see beauty; no "proof of the existence of God" can help those who cannot see *what* is manifest in the world; no apologetic can be of any use to the one for whom the truth that radiates from the center of theology is not already evident. (*GL* 2, 166)

The same even holds true for Anselm and his famous proof for the existence of God: his so-called Ontological Proof. Balthasar clearly takes the Barthian approach to this "proof," insisting *for aesthetic reasons* that Anselm did not, and could not, mean it to lead a non-believer to a belief in God independent of a prior faith in God. This is because for Anselm the term *necessitas* always refers, first and above all, to the "fittingness"— or, in his terminology, the *rectitudo*—of what is so appropriate that no other conclusion seems possible.[26] This comes out most clearly when Anselm asks why (that is, by what reason or necessity: *qua ratione vel necessitate*) God was made man, and replies that the question, though difficult, is both intelligible and delightful "on account of its usefulness and on account of the beauty of the reason [for it]."[27] And this link marks all of Anselm's argumentation:

> Anselm's slender work, radiant and perfectly balanced, realizes in the purest form the concerns of theological aesthetics. . . . [It is] the acme of Christian aesthetics. Anselm contemplates the highest inner accord (*rectitudo*) of the divine revelation in creation and redemption; he discerns its truth from the harmony, from the faultless proportions, from the way in which it must be so (*necessitas*), something at once dependent on and manifest-

---

[26] Rectitude in this aesthetic sense of the term is also the animating force behind Anselm's famous (or infamous, all depending) doctrine that Christ had to die as the incarnate God-man to "satisfy" the "demands" of God's justice. This much maligned theory of the atonement has been misunderstood almost from its inception, but it makes perfect sense aesthetically. Anselm even goes so far as to say that he would prefer to be free from sin and to bear hell innocently than to go to the Kingdom of Heaven polluted with the stain of sin (see *GL* 2, 248–249). Balthasar's own fuller defense of Anselm's theology of the atonement occurs in the Theodramatics, where we shall revisit this theme.

[27] *Cur Deus homo*, I.1.

ing the utmost freedom, and this vision reveals to him absolute beauty: God's beauty in the freely fashioned form of the world.[28]

And the same holds true for Augustine's "proofs" too. For example: "It can be said that Augustine's proof of the true Church is an aesthetic proof: anyone who cannot *see* the specific nature of this catholicity (as opposed to mere geographical extension or a syncretic, organizational unity) cannot be moved by it" (*GL* 2,102). It is almost as if theologians in the era of "clerical styles" were so infused with the refulgent beauty of revelation that they could no more conceive of their readers not seeing what they were referring to than we would if we were to point out the blue sky to someone and not expect our charge to see blue. Revelation is so obvious to them that "proofs" for them seem mostly to come down to pointing out what for them is already clearly there.[29]

To move from such writers, so inundated with the refulgence of the light of revelation, to the post-Dantean world of lay styles is indeed a jolt. Here frustration seems to mark every figure treated in this book. Take for example Hopkins: "The impatience of this breaking through to the uniquely true glory determines Hopkins' whole ethos; here lies the unity of his personality as poet and religious, that unity of which he was most sharply conscious even when it finally broke him, for neither his poet friends nor his brothers in religion had any eyes for it" (*GL* 3, 357). Or Pascal: "He belongs to the ranks of those acerbic, ardent spirits of the French Baroque, who as laymen ventured forth, daring to force the utterly impossible into the unity of a single visible form" (*GL* 3, 172). Or Péguy: "Péguy had abandoned the Church because the dogma of an eternal Hell

---

[28] *GL* 2, 211. One commentator has noted particularly well how the analogy of art leads one to see the connection between the "fitting" and the "necessary" in both aesthetics and theology: "What characterizes the great work of art is precisely the fittingness of its *Gestalt* to what is expressed: its necessity, '*rightness*,' such that no other theme or development would do here. And it is precisely this fittingness—the intimacy of ground and its appearing—which means that there is no question of passing 'beyond,' as it were, the outward form to its inner essence. The perception of the beauty, the revealed reality, glory, is certainly not just a matter of simple viewing of the object; the casual view may well fail to perceive the deeper dimensionality of the work of art, musical myth. It is only as their eyes are opened in and by the contemplation of the object itself that the beholders learn to read and understand the proportions and rightness of the form, to see the unity of ground and appearing; and it is in so doing that he is inspired to love and desire what he sees" (John Riches, "Balthasar and the Analysis of Faith," *The Analogy of Beauty: The Theology of Hans Urs von Balthasar*, ed. John Riches [Edinburgh: T. & T. Clark, 1986], 51–52).

[29] At one point, Balthasar assembles a caetena of passages from a wide variety of Augustine's books to demonstrate this point: "God's truth 'shows its face' (*faciem*), places itself 'in readiness' (*praesto*), lets itself be 'embraced' (*amplectere*), 'shows itself ' (*se ostendere*), 'knows when to show itself' (*novit illa pulchritutdo quando se ostendat*), 'shows itself when it pleases' (*quando placet sese ostendit*), 'lifts up to itself' (*sublevat*)" (*GL* 2, 111).

seemed intolerable to him, yet he turned to the Church without forswearing the least portion of his past. How did he manage this?" (*GL*, 435–436).

So what seismic jolt caused this strange irruption of alienation? Whence came this silent cataclysm that hurled some of the Church's greatest artists, writers and apologists out into the most distant orbits of her gravitational field? *What happened?* Balthasar addresses this question in the next two volumes of the Aesthetics. If *Clerical* and *Lay Styles* may be said to display the symptomatics of this alienation, the next two volumes *Metaphysics in Antiquity* and *Modernity* may be called its diagnostics, while the last two volumes *Old* and *New Covenant* attempt to offer the cure—the "prognostics," we might say.[30] These volumes on metaphysics do not simply display twelve "case studies" to demonstrate to the reader the clear evidence of a massive shift in theological sensibility; they now delve directly into the history of philosophy to see *from within* where this shift took place, how it was justified and the principles that animate its argumentation. It is perhaps the most difficult set of books in the entire Balthasarian *oeuvre*, as it calls on virtually the whole intellectual history of the West to establish its thesis.[31] Moreover, it is, needless to say, no textbook introducing its readers to this history but a reflection upon it, and thus the prior "cultural literacy" required to understand its thesis is intimidatingly vast.

In trying to come to terms with this vast, teeming and difficult two-volume reflection on metaphysics, one would do well do keep Bultmann in mind, whose ghost seems to hover over the proceedings.[32] This is be-

---

[30] The division of these volumes in the German original makes this linkage a bit clearer, since *Clerical* and *Lay Styles* constitute together Volume II, as the two tomes on metaphysics in ancient and modern world constitute Volume III (although here this two-tome set is not just called "Volume III" but "Volume III, Part 1!), and the two tomes on Old and New Testaments make up Volume III, Part 2. Though this arrangement makes the linkage between the books more apparent, it is clearly ungainly, and the English translation numbers them consecutively (and uses Roman numerals for them all; my own abbreviations are in Arabic numbers). Nonetheless, it would always be well to keep in mind the structure of the work as set forth by the author.

[31] I am reminded in this regard of Balthasar's own remarks on his three-volume doctoral dissertation, *The Apocalypse of the German Soul*, which attempts the same kind of marshalling of vast amounts of cultural achievements (only starting with Lessing and Goethe and not Homer!): "[This work] attempted (to the ineradicable horror of all right-thinking specialists) to present a total Christian interpretation of poetry, philosophy and theology from Lessing to the present day. I readily admit that even I find this ungainly large child somewhat of a monster. I often ask myself, when I see it on the bookshelf, what its contents might be [!]. Perhaps it contains too much—but much of it was written at the time with my heart's blood" (*MW*, 13).

[32] Balthasar cites a passage from Bultmann early in Volume 4 which he considers to be the perfect expression of all that is objectionable in the latter's thought and which would never have been possible to maintain except as the final outcome of the history he will

cause of the central place that the concept of *myth* will occupy at this juncture of the argument. In other words, it needs to be stressed that by "metaphysics" Balthasar is not simply referring to "philosophy" narrowly conceived but to that total complex of views that constitute a culture, within which one may detect, however inchoately, a "metaphysics" (in the sense of a world-view). And this in fact is what makes this section of the Aesthetics so daunting: it marshals an almost unassimilable array of materials to establish its archaeology of alienated beauty.

There is also, it must be said, a certain shift of thesis, at least by implication from what Balthasar seemed to be indicating in his previous two volumes on *Clerical* and *Lay Styles* to what he now maintains in the metaphysical volumes. Earlier, he had adduced Dante as the first example of the alienated Christian artist, and attributed his alienation, as we have seen, to the split between spirituality and theology that took place with the growth of the urban university and the mendicant orders (that is, with Scholasticism). But this now seems to be merely an overture, a foreshadowing, as it were, of a split that would occur much later. For here he extends his Golden Age of an integrated aesthetics all the way to the age of Kant, who now seems to be the one who initiated the Fall from authentic unity:

> Before aesthetics was reduced in late Rationalism and in critical Idealism to a science confined to a particular area of knowledge, it was an aspect of metaphysics: metaphysics was the science concerned with the being of what exists, and . . . metaphysics was inseparable from theology. . . . This intuition survived from Homer and Pindar through Plato and Aristotle, Plotinus, the early and high Middles Ages of Christendom, up to the Renaissance and Baroque period. (*GL* 4, 19)

Now there is in fact a way of resolving this apparent contradiction, for Balthasar sees the upshot of our own contemporary situation of a desiccated and dreary secularized Christianity as the outcome of both an internal development which we have inherited from the Middle Ages and of an external one that grew up from within Europe but impinged more from the world of philosophy (broadly speaking) than from theology *per se*. So there are two issues here, internal and external, theological and

---

proceed to outline in the next two tomes: "The idea of the beautiful," says Bultmann, "is of no significance in forming the life of Christian faith, which sees in the beautiful the temptation of a false transfiguration of the world. . . . It is not art that discloses the depths of reality . . . but *suffering*. . . . The beautiful is therefore—as far as the Christian faith is concerned—always something that lies beyond this life" (Rudolf Bultmann, *Glauben und Verstehen*, 2nd ed. [1958] 2: 137; cited in *GL* 4, 27).

philosophical, with the volumes on metaphysics concentrating more on the latter (but always noticing, of course, how the two worlds intersect, often to the detriment of the Church):

> But what now [after treating clerical and lay styles] is the status of the world? The renewed anchoring of a now-unsupported theology in the foundations of antiquity [can be traced] from Nicholas of Cusa through the Renaissance, the Baroque and the Enlightenment to Goethe and Heidegger. But then where is the distinctiveness of the Christian dispensation? . . . If the (human) Spirit masters the whole of Being conceptually, the splendor of Being is extinguished and is replaced by the "sublimity" of the thinker (Kant, Schiller), which with Hegel once again becomes entrapped in the past. What then remains is only grim materialistic fatalism. . . . How can someone who is blind to Being be other than blind to God? Ought we not rather say that the Christian, as the proclaimer of God's glory today, takes upon himself as a consequence—whether he wants to or not—the burden of metaphysics? (*MW*, 84–85)

I think it is that passing reference to a "now-unsupported theology" that provides the clue to resolving the tension between the two sets of volumes, for it is clear that for Balthasar theology now had fewer resources than before (in antiquity) for meeting the challenge of a non-Christian world: "The catastrophe of nominalism robs creation of every light of God; night falls" (*MW*, 84). This remark helps clear up a potential misunderstanding that might arise from a single-minded concentration on Volumes 2 & 3: and that is the role of Thomas Aquinas in this history. When I first read these two volumes, I had the impression that Balthasar held the scholastic method of St. Thomas to blame for the onset of "lay" styles, as he is conspicuously missing from the volume on *Clerical Styles*—not to mention the fact that Dante, who was born just a few years before Thomas's death, opens the treatment of *Lay Styles*.[33] But Volume 4, *The Realm of Metaphysics in Antiquity,* concludes with a section on Thomas that makes it clear that Balthasar very much sides with the interpretation of Maritain and Gilson: that the *pulchrum* is indeed an operative transcendental in the Angelic Doctor's thought.[34]

Admittedly, this might not be obvious at first sight, and there is good reason for the scholarly dispute about Thomas's real contribution to this

---

[33] The dates for the two are c.1225–1274 and 1265–1321, respectively.

[34] *GL* 4, 393–412; there is also, by the way, an interesting section on Mechthild of Magdeburg that goes a long way to make up the lacuna of women theologians in *Clerical* and *Lay Styles.*

question, and Balthasar frankly avers that "beauty is seldom a central concern for [Thomas], and for the most part his discussion is dependent on material presented to him by the tradition."[35] But his originality for aesthetics does not lie in his explicit treatment of the subject but in his reformulation of the whole way the question of Being was treated, one of whose transcendentals is Beauty:

> [Thomas] calmly reviews the inherited material and tries to harmonize the elements that pour in upon him, . . . without, so it would seem, making an original contribution of his own to aesthetics in the strict sense. However, at another level everything is put in a new light by the fact that the doctrine of the transcendentals is interpreted in the perspective of Thomas's major creative achievement—his definition of *esse* and its relation to essences. As everything so far has shown, the material handed down was "theological" in a two-fold sense: Greek metaphysics was oriented toward the *theion* and the Christian view of reality took possession of this "natural" aesthetics in order to complete and transcend it on the basis of revelation. Now Thomas sees *esse* as the *non*-subsistent fullness and perfection of all reality and as the supreme "likeness of divine goodness," and so God *can in no way be regarded as the being of things,* except that he is their efficient, exemplary and final cause. Thus in a new and much more radical way, God is placed over and above all cosmic being, above everything that can be calculated or attained within the structures, real or ideal, of the cosmos: He is indeed the "Wholly Other." (*GL* 4, 393–394; my emphasis)

This advances the cause of theological aesthetics in a number of ways. First of all, it prevents the theologian from falling into the trap that so frequently ensnared the Fathers: that of identifying too closely worldly beauty and the divine Glory (as if the former were the emanation of the latter). Secondly, it helps to resolve a rather peculiar dispute that affected discussion of Beauty as a transcendental: in traditional neo-Platonic terms, the fundamental constituents that comprise all Being are the One, the True, the Good and the Beautiful. But earlier thought had fallen into the

---

[35] *GL* 4, 393. Thus as one scholar says: it is only through his commentaries on the Areopagite that Thomas is stimulated to a thematic handling of the question, giving up for the time being "his typical lack of interest in the question of beauty" (Francis J. Kovach, *Die Ästhetik des Thomas von Aquin* [Berlin and New York: De Gruyter, 1961], 54). Nonetheless, Balthasar will insist that "from St. Augustine Thomas adopts the emphasis on the objectivity of beauty. Something is beautiful not because it is loved; no, it is loved because it is beautiful" (*GL* 4, 399), and that is absolutely crucial.

misleading habit of referring the One, the True, and the Good back to the trinitarian causality of Father, Son, and Spirit, respectively, and thus "there seemed to be no more room in God for another transcendental"! (GL 4, 377). But this is fundamentally to misconceive the issue, and Thomas's doctrine of the Real Distinction between essence and existence resolves this difficulty in a stroke.[36] And its importance for a Christian aesthetics could hardly be overestimated:

> Thomas's doctrine of the Real Distinction between *esse* and *essentia* is a philosophical thesis but it enables us once again to make a clear differentiation between the "glory" of God and the beauty of the world; indeed, it enables us to recover the true meaning of that glory as much for the ordinary believer as for the theologian. After Thomas [however], other "images of God" emerge and dominate thought: there is, for example, the God who is found within, on the journey through selfhood; there is the God of absolute subjectivity (Eckhart) and of absolute free will (Ockham), but in neither of these roles can he really be the God of glory. . . . Thus, where our theme of glory is concerned, Thomas is a *kairos* [providential moment], more through his general ontology than his aesthetics. (GL 4, 395)

Now if this is true, it raises the interesting question why Dante would so suddenly emerge as a theologian of *lay* style, in Balthasar's definition of that term: that is, as someone who feels misunderstood and shunted aside from the central concerns of the Church *precisely because* of his concern for beauty. It is no secret that Balthasar regards the onset of nominalism as an unmitigated catastrophe for theology, but Dante precedes that development. Thus the unacknowledged tension between the two volumes on theological styles and the two volumes on metaphysics has remained unresolved (perhaps because it went unrecognized). In any event, Balthasar is certainly Thomist in his central metaphysical insights, and as the following passage makes clear, we can be sure it most definitely affects how he treats subsequent philosophy in Volume 5 (on modern metaphysics):

> The *elevation of God over [worldly] being,* now at last established by Thomas (over against all pantheism) secures at the same time for the concept of glory a place in metaphysics. This place was always intended and envisaged in every form of Platonism; but while [Platonism] addressed being and the other

---

[36] For a discussion of the importance of this doctrine in Balthasar's own thought, see Chapters 1 and 2 of this book.

[emanations] reposing in it directly as "names of God," the sub-limity of God was not revealed as absolute *freedom,* and so the Godhead was dragged into an unfree dialectic of in-itself and out-of-itself, hidden and revealed, resting and moved, as is always the danger in all those who tie the inner-divine trinitarian process all-too closely to the process of creation, something that later will have tragic consequences in German Idealism. (*GL* 4, 375)

Thomas in a way, then, is the hinge-point, the linchpin, around which Balthasar's treatment of the history of metaphysics will revolve, and this despite Aquinas' rather minor contributions to the topic. This is important to understand, for if readers of Balthasar approaching the Aesthetics for the first time can get this point, they will have the Archimedean fulcrum by which they might "lift" this dense and heavy work. For it is the point of Volumes 4 & 5 that prior to Aquinas metaphysics, both Christian and pagan, *fused* the Being of God and the being of the world too closely, while metaphysics after him took the distinction between God and the world too far and ended up in nominalism, so that the only connection between God and the soul could be found in faith.

This too-radical distinction is what made Luther possible, for how otherwise would he have come to insist on justification by faith *alone?* But as the arbitrariness of God became more and more apparent (and unpalatable) under the influence of Protestant orthodoxy, with fewer and fewer human beings coming to seem qualified for redemption, a great pathos entered the European soul, a pathos that could only be healed by a new naturalistic fusion of God and world (Spinoza, Goethe, the *Sturm und Drang* German Romantics, Hegel, etc.). This counter-movement had the advantage of being able to reincorporate *myth* into the fabric of man's world (the expulsion of which under the influence of mechanistic, Newtonian science had left him feeling bereft and isolated in the world that had once been home), but at a heavy price: robbing God of his freedom to create or not. Once more, creation was a necessary emanation[37] of God and not his free gift of grace.

• • •

So I think that the story Balthasar tells in these two volumes may best be summed up as: 1) myth emerges as the natural expression of man's innate sense that the world is saturated with the divine; 2) philosophy realizes the cognitive inadequacy of such myth-making and critiques it, without, however, abandoning myth's basic philosophical presupposition: that the

---

[37] But "necessary" not in Anselm's sense of what seems most graciously fitting!

world is a direct expression of the divine; 3) Christian thought gradually weans itself from this presupposition under the influence of revelation, especially the Old Testament, with its polemic against idolatry; but the process is gradual because Christians too are so overwhelmed by the beauty of revelation and of the world that they naturally cannot, in their blindness from overexposure to the light, see the radical distinction between the two forms of beauty; 4) Thomas, however, through a patient engagement with the texts of Aristotle and his own biblical commentaries, comes to formulate this important distinction for the subsequent benefit of the Church; 5) but nominalism soon undoes this achievement, and when Protestantism arrives, the European soul has but two choices: naturalism (of either the scientific or romantic variety) or fideism; 6) and in either case, the sheer openness of myth to the divine has been lost, and we then meet Bultmann waiting for us at the end of the garden path.

I must admit, I feel rather sheepish offering so rapid and casual a thumbnail sketch of this teeming work, and it leaves out some important figures who run counter to the scheme, such as Ignatius Loyola at one point, or Heidegger at another. But it seems that without some initial idea of the point of these volumes, the reader could all-too easily get lost in the thicket of this man's astonishing learning. Yet he always manages to keep his main point in the foreground:

> The beautiful guards the other [transcendentals] and sets the seal on them: there is nothing true or good, in the long term, without the light of grace of that which is freely bestowed. And a Christianity which went along with modernity and subscribed merely to the true (faith as a system of correct propositions) or merely to the good (faith as that which is most useful and healthy for the subject) would be a Christianity knocked down from its own heights. But when the saints interpreted their existence in the light of God's greater glory, they were always the guardians of the beautiful. (*GL* 2, 38–39)

· 7 ·

The Wave and the Sea

Then came, at a predetermined moment, a moment in time
    and of time,
A moment not out of time, but in time, in what we call history:
        transecting, bisecting the world of time, a moment in time
        but not like a moment of time,
A moment in time but time was made through that moment:
        for without the meaning there is no time, and that moment
        of time gave the meaning.

T. S. Eliot
Choruses from "The Rock"

A Jesuit once asked a fellow priest who had joined the secular institute
founded by Adrienne von Speyr and Hans Urs von Balthasar what
relevance his membership in the Institute had for his priesthood, and the
man replied: "Thanks to [their] work, we have learned how to contemplate God in the Scriptures and consequently how to exercise our ministry
in God."[1] I mention this remark here because the present chapter intends
to take up the issue of Balthasar's biblical hermeneutics, and it will be
well to bear in mind once more what was first said in the introduction:
that Balthasar's is a "kneeling" theology that is ultimately meant to draw
the reader closer to God. And so it shall not be surprising that in his
biblical hermeneutics this too shall be his intent: "to contemplate God in
the Scriptures and consequently exercise [one's] ministry in God."

More specifically, this chapter will treat the final two volumes of *The
Glory of the Lord*, which deal with the theme of glory in the Old and
New Testaments (while of course drawing from all of his writings that
touch on his theme, irrespective of where they are located).[2] Now the

---

[1] Quoted in Georges Chantraine, S.J., "Exegesis and Contemplation in the Work of Hans
Urs von Balthasar," *Communio* 16 (1989): 366.

[2] Especially a lecture he gave on this theme, "Why I am Still a Christian," which because
of its brevity and concision will help to establish Balthasar's framework in which he unites
Old and New Testament revelations.

theme of the connection between the two Testaments has always been an important one for theology, but today under the impact of historical criticism it has undergone so significant a revolution that our theological predecessors would scarcely be able to recognize the contemporary terrain. Standard treatments of the relationship between the Old and New Testaments in the past often used to proceed under the rubric of the so-called "argument from prophecy." This had been a conventional and regular moment in apologetics almost from the very birth of theology (it dominates, for example, the second-century dialogue of Justin Martyr with his Jewish interlocutor Trypho). Its strategy was to argue from a particular prophetic text to its fulfillment in Jesus by claiming that the prophets must have been divinely inspired for the fulfillment of their utterances to have occurred so much later in time and in so uniquely resplendent a way. But then came a more exact appreciation for the historical context of the biblical materials under the aegis of historical and form criticism, which realized that the Messianic references in the Hebrew Scriptures were determined by the contemporary horizon and had not been written consciously to predict Jesus of Nazareth. In other words, the prophetic utterances were by and large directed toward contemporary events and fulfillments or, if they were eschatologically intended, the intention was "generic," so to speak: a vaguely defined "Son of Man" would usher in a new era of God's kingdom; but who that would be and whence he would come was left to the imagination of the community.

Now what happened in the New Testament was that *after* the impact of the life, death and resurrection of Jesus made its effects felt on the disciples and early Church, certain evangelists came to write an account of those saving events (Lk 1:1–4) and *retrospectively* saw the narrative of those events in terms of the Old Testament context. The result was that the prophetic texts were adapted by the New Testament writers in such a way that the narrative was shaped *by them*, rather than the prophecies predicting, miraculously, the coming of Jesus as the Messiah.[3]

The collapse of the former approach, which used to be so fundamental

---

[3] "In the first flush of triumph it might have been expected that the Gospel message could not fail to compel belief and acceptance. The apostles quickly discovered otherwise. . . . It seems that the apostles saw themselves in a situation somewhat parallel to that of Isaiah at the beginning of his prophetic ministry and included the classic text on unbelief (Is 6:9ff.) in the intellectual armory at an early date. . . . At the same time there is a host of objections raised against the manner of Christ's death. So the passages already employed in the Passion apologetic are *worked over* to provide the answer to each particular item. The composition of the Gospel Passion narratives, in which these scriptures are constantly referred to for details, has thus been influenced *by* this apologetic" (Barnabas Lindars, *New Testament Apologetic: The Doctrinal Significance of Old Testament Quotations* [Philadelphia: The Westminster Press, 1961], 253; my emphasis).

to the standard arguments for the divinity of Christianity,[4] has introduced a real crisis into the Church, as an abundant literature will attest.[5] Indeed, I think it would not be going too far to say that the whole value and validity of Balthasar's theology for the Church in the coming millennium will hinge on the validity of his approach to the Scriptures, especially because to some extent it stands in such tension with the historical-critical method (though hardly naïvely).

He is like the historical critic in this sense: that his concentration is not so much determined by the shape and history of the text as upon the events to which the text refers. On the other hand, these "events" are not so much the events of history which the historical critic seeks to unveil as they are the events of God's saving interventions in history, especially the manifestation of his glory. And so while his approach to the bond between Old and New Tesatments is "aesthetic" in the broad sense of the term, it is nonetheless a *theological* aesthetic that he is invoking.

Perhaps at this point we should recall the methods Balthasar adopted in his study of German culture (see Chapter 3), where the text, we saw, was taken on its own terms as a world-constituting manifestation. And the Bible, then, is in this sense its own inter-textual world that must be taken on its own terms.[6] This is especially important when one considers the broadly "literary" approach that has now become so popular among scholars seeking to establish the links between the two Testaments. That is, under the influence of narrative criticism among literary critics, many

---

[4] One need only think of Pascal's *Pensées* or of Isaac Newton's retirement from natural philosophy to devote himself entirely to research into the New Testament's fulfillment of the prophecies of Old Testament (primarily the Book of Daniel). Pascal even goes so far as to say that "Moses [was] the first to teach the Trinity, original sin, the Messiah"! And for Pascal all the later prophets are equally univocal: "If a single man had written a book foretelling the time and manner of Jesus's coming and Jesus had come in conformity with these prophecies, this would carry infinite weight. But there is much more here. There is a succession of men over a period of 4,000 years, coming consistently and invariably one after the other, to foretell the same coming; there is an entire people proclaiming it" (Blaise Pascal, *Pensées*, tr. A. J. Krailsheimer [Harmondsworth: Penguin, 1966], 126, 129; Brunschvicg 752, 710; cited henceforth by these Brunschvicg numbers, abbreviated B).

[5] See in particular: James Barr, *The Bible in the Modern World* (London: SCM Press, 1973) and *Old and New in Interpretation: A Study of the Two Testaments* (London: SCM Press, 1982); Peter Stuhlmacher, *Historical Criticism and Theological Interpretation of Scripture*, tr. Roy A. Harrisville (Philadelphia: Fortress Press, 1977).

[6] There are interesting parallels between Balthasar's method and those adopted by the canon critics of the so-called "Yale school," especially the work of the distinguished Old Testament scholar Brevard Childs, whose work tries to situate Christian reading of the Bible in its total canonical context (in other words, inter-textually): "To suggest that the Christian should read the Old Testament as if he were living before the coming of Christ is an historical anachronism which also fails to take seriously the literature's present function within the Christian Bible for a practicing community of faith" (Brevard Childs, *Old Testament Theology in a Canonical Context* [Philadelphia: Fortress Press, 1985], 9).

biblical scholars notice how all texts, and not just the New Testament, compose their sentences in terms of earlier traditions, incorporating into their very phraseology open references, and more especially hidden allusions, to past texts.[7] Then systematic theologians, picking up on these studies and building on the anti-apologetic strain in Karl Barth, insist that faith means inhabiting *a narrative world of the Bible,* a world which will display its inner coherence on its own terms.

Now although Balthasar obviously draws on a considerable mastery of these literary and aesthetic studies in his whole approach to theology, and while his work bears crucial affinities with the work of textual and canonical critics,[8] it is absolutely crucial to realize that the harmony he sees obtaining between the two Testaments is primarily *extra*-textual: that is, one that is shaped much more by what Anselm termed *rectitudo* than by what literary critics mean by an integrated text. What I mean by this is: that *once one realizes how, in the way our redemption was carried out, "it had to be thus,"* the inner connections between the worlds of the Old and New Testaments will emerge into view. This is admittedly related to the position that advocates of narrative theology take, but I think it must be distinguished from theirs by its fundamentally *extra-textual* referentiality.

This is no doubt why Balthasar concentrates so much attention on the biblical theme of God's glory: not only does this term distinguish itself from its more earthly analogue, Beauty,[9] but it indicates that revelatory experience of God which transports believers out of themselves and into what God means to manifest in the text—a much different focus than a concentration on what the human author (or: his community) meant to express (which is the concentration of exegesis in the historical-critical

---

[7] See especially Robert Alter, "Allusion and Literary Expression," *The World of Biblical Literature* (New York: Basic Books, 1992), and Frank Kermode, "New Ways with Bible Stories," *Poetry, Narrative, History* (Oxford: Basil Blackwell, 1990), 29–48: "To rewrite the old in terms of a later state of affairs is an ancient Jewish practice. . . . In their manner of writing stories there was much in common between the authors of the two Bibles" (47).

[8] See: Jeffrey Kay, "Hans Urs von Balthasar—ein nachkritischer Theologe?" *Concilium* 7 (1981): 86–90.

[9] "In order to gain a more precise notion of what the concerns of a *theological aesthetics* may be, we shall have to distinguish it carefully from what at first we might be led to confuse it with, namely, an *aesthetic theology.* The word 'aesthetic' in the latter expression will inevitably be understood in the worldly, limited and therefore pejorative sense. Even a glance at the whole tenor of the Bible will confirm our suspicion not only that 'aesthetic' in this sense is not one of the supreme biblical values but that it cannot seriously be considered as a biblical value at all" (*GL* 1, 79). This of course does not mean that the commonplace contempt for aesthetics shown by so much contemporary theology is justified, for this gulf between the divine splendor and worldly beauty must serve as theology's challenge, not its fence: "May it not be that we have a real and inescapable obligation to probe the possibility of there being a genuine relationship between theological beauty and the beauty of the world?" (*GL* 1, 80).

mode). This in no way denies the legitimacy of the historical-critical mode, but it must be preliminary, at least for a theologian: in the sense that historical criticism focuses on the events of history while Balthasar's focus is on those events as manifestations of the glory of God. This, however, does not mean that he therefore shies away from the results of biblical scholars; indeed, these two volumes on Old and New Covenant are saturated in the scholarship of biblical research.[10] But this familiarity with the converging lines of biblical research is all meant to set forth the primary object of contemplation: Jesus Christ himself, in his full identity and splendor as the Lord reigning in glory:

> Closely connected to the plurality of biblical ways of access to the mystery of revelation stands the contribution made by exegesis to its understanding. Since, taken abstractly in itself, it is a neutral philological science, it can be practiced by a believing or a unbelieving scholar, but of course in a very different spirit. Jesus demands a radical Yes or No to his person and claim. What is "neither hot nor cold" is spat out. Someone who wants to "bracket" this claim "methodologically," even if he does so only provisionally, in order to wait and see if this claim had really been made and, if so, if it was made rightly, exposes himself to the danger of a neutrality which is forbidden by the object and falsifies it. (*SP*, 47)

The point, then, is not so much the text that expresses the claim, or the history of the transmission of the claim as it was being sedimented in the text of the New Testament, but *the claim on its own terms*. This is why Balthasar can quite openly "step over" the intricacies of Johannine scholarship and go straight to the strongest claims about Jesus made in the entire New Testament: his own "I am" statements in the Fourth Gospel. Note in this passage how he first admits the textual "pre-history" of this claim but then goes directly to a phenomenology *of* the claim itself:

---

[10] Although it is clear that Balthasar is more comfortable, as a theologian, with Old Testament scholarship: "For more than a century, [exegesis of the Old Testament] has enriched our understanding of the theological depths of Israel's history in an unexpected fashion. What appeared earlier as flat and two-dimensional received a hitherto unknown three-dimensionality through the distinction of sources, through chronology (e.g., the chronology of parts in a prophetic book such as Isaiah or Jeremiah) and through the contributions of archeology in the Near East" (*SP*, 51). But the New Testament raises issues for Balthasar that are different in kind and not just degree: "Whoever reads the text of the Gospels with eyes schooled in form and redaction criticism in every pericope and often in every verse runs up against gaps, seams, patchwork, artificial bracketings and 'upheavals' of geological strata. . . . Dogmatics will have to reflect on this if it does not want to build its house on sand" ("Exegese und Dogmatik," *Communio: Internationale katholische Zeitschrift 5* [1976]: 385–392, here, 385–396; partial translation in *Reader*, 127–232).

> The essence of christology may be summed up by using one of
> the later "I am" pronouncements (which Jesus presumably never
> spoke himself); they are the verbal expressions of the challenge
> that Jesus lived in his actual existence: "I am the Way." Buddha
> and Mohammed might well have asserted that they were the
> way *to* the truth which they had learned through a special revela-
> tion and were now able to point out to others. But "I *am* the
> Truth" is a very different kind of assertion. In fact, it does not
> matter which concept of truth is at stake: the Old Testament
> Semitic notion or the Greek one. What is intended is much more
> than some truth that happens to rank above all others in the
> universe; and more than the sum of all the true propositions of
> what can be asserted about everything we find in the universe.
> (2SW, 16)

As we become more familiar with the pattern (*Gestalt*) of Balthasar's
christology in the course of this chapter, it will be well to bear in mind
the triad: Provocation-Death-Resurrection. That is, as Balthasar outlines
the claim implicit in the person of Jesus (and which was made explicit in
the Gospels, and most explicit in the Gospel of John), he will insist that
this claim, as claim, is quite literally intolerable: it is so exaggerated and
bizarre that it was *bound* to lead to his death. In fact, it was a claim so
extreme that only God himself could validate it: at the Resurrection;
indeed that is what the Resurrection *means:* that Jesus was right in making
the claim.

This is why, before the time of validation, that is, during Jesus's earthly
ministry, the response to the claim (on the part of all!) could only be one
of bafflement or outrage. But because the Gospels were written in the era
of the Church, that is, in light of the validation of that claim, the narrative
text itself will inevitably be saturated with a realization of the *entire* pattern. But that must not mitigate *our* astonishment at the immensity and
preposterousness of the claim (as happens all-too easily in a naïve reading
of the Gospels).[11] To understand the triadic pattern of Provocation-Death-
Resurrection, we must first absorb the outrage of the claim itself, as if
hearing it for the first time:

---

[11] We actually gain a much richer understanding of the Gospels if we take this dual focus
into account; in other words, there are theological riches to be had in realizing how the
evangelists wrote with the benefit of hindsight, as Jürgen Moltmann often stressed: "The
past can be narrated, and every narration (just like enumeration) starts at the beginning
and then comes to the end. But from the perspective of eschatological anticipation, the last
must be first, the future goes before the past, the end opens up the beginning, and objective
time-relationships are reversed. 'History as memory' and 'history as hope' cannot contradict
each other but rather must complete each other, for 'hope in the mode of memory' *defines*
Christian faith" (Jürgen Moltmann, *The Crucified God: The Cross of Christ as the Founda-*

There is an immense provocation here which is unique in world history and seems almost absurd, coming as it does from a single individual and therefore a minute fragment of the universe with all its multitudinous ways and truths—and from an individual, too, who the very night before he died claimed the power of eternal life. If we allow the speaker to take the responsibility for what he claims, and do not put it down to the enthusiasm of the author of the Fourth Gospel; if we see his assertion as the sum total of a wholly demanding life that had persisted in refusing confinement within a fixed framework and saw itself as continuous with the great things God did in Israel, and as consummating, not contradicting, those acts; then it is obvious no human wisdom (which always tries to understand the things of this world in terms of an all-encompassing framework) would endure this kind of provocation—or has been able to stand it since its first enunciation.[12]

It is also important to realize how this provocation abruptly enters into salvation history. Balthasar's christology is very much a post-critical one in the sense that he stresses much more the discontinuities between the person of Jesus and the great figures of the Old Testament than he does the continuities in the pre-critical manner of Pascal and Newton.[13] Indeed, I think it would not be too much to say that Balthasar's entire christology is a meditation on Paul's statement that Christ crucified is "a stumbling block to Jews and a folly to Gentiles" (1 Cor 1:23):

> The Greek mind found it ridiculous that one of the products of the all-pervasive *physis* should equate itself with the generative matrix. Jewish thought found it even more incredible that a created man should predicate of himself the attributes proper to the Creator of the world and the Covenant-Lord of Israel. It is *still* nonsense, but now to a modern evolutionary world-view of any persuasion, to assert that one wave in the river that has flowed on for millions of years and will continue to flow on unthinkably for yet more millions once the wave is no more, can be identified with the river. Nonsense, too, to assert that this

---

tion and Criticism of Christian Theology, tr. R. A. Wilson and John Bowden [New York: Harper & Row, 1974], 113).

[12] *2SW,* 17–18. Balthasar of course is not referring to some putative provocation of personality: "Even those great affirmations which begin with the word 'I' are not the language of 'self-consciousness' but of mission" (*MP,* 91).

[13] "The claim was intolerable, much more intolerable than that of the earlier prophets to whose fate Jesus links his own" ("Exegese und Dogmatik," 386; *Reader,* 129).

wave has already comprehended all of that future and enclosed within itself the fullness of time and the end of time. On attempting to estimate the degree of provocation in such fantastic claims, we see clearly that any school of religious or philosophic thought must be surprised and deeply shocked by another statement in the same context: "They hated me without cause"(Jn 15:25). (2SW, 18)

How might we then understand that provocation? If indeed it is as preposterous and as outrageous as Balthasar says, how can we even understand it enough to know what we are rejecting, or in the case of faith, accepting? It is here, I believe, that Balthasar's basic aesthetic approach proves its value; for here, more than in any other area of life, we can find the best analogue for understanding how Jesus's claim might be justified. In Balthasar's view, the claim of Jesus represents what he calls the "absolute singularity." But we are able to understand and then to enter into that absolute singularity under the prior analogue of what he calls *relative singularities,* one of the most remarkable of which is aesthetic—the phenomenon of art:

Great works of art appear like inexplicable miracles and spontaneous eruptions on the stage of history. Sociologists are as unable to calculate the precise day of their origin as they are to explain in retrospect why they appeared when they did. Of course, works of art are subject to certain preconditions without which they cannot come into being: such conditions may be effective stimuli but do not provide a full explanation of the work itself. Shakespeare had his predecessors, contemporaries and models; he was surrounded by the atmosphere of the theater of his time. He could only have emerged within that context. Yet who would dare offer to prove that his emergence was inevitable? (2SW, 20)

The application of this image to biblical scholarship, I think, should immediately suggest itself: for it is one thing to examine all the necessary presuppositions and prior requirements for the emergence of a work of art (or biblical text); but it is another thing entirely to claim that one has thereby *accounted* for that work of art. This is to mistake the sudden manifestation of the phenomenon for its presuppositions (a common mental habit called "the genetic fallacy"). And this fallacy is a perennial danger for scholars who job it is to concentrate on narrating the history of origins until the story ends up at the termination point: the object itself. This narrative movement of going from beginning to end can make it seem as if the beginning accounts for the end, rather than the end representing an astonishing fulfillment and supersession of what went before. But we can only fall into that illusory trap because we are already in possession of the work and so we know how our etiological narrative will conclude. But this is to fail to come to terms with the work itself, *which must itself determine how its own past is to be interpreted:*

> At most we can point to or guess at the propitious moment— the *kairos*—but never what it is that flows into it and gives it that lasting form which, as soon as it emerges, takes control. *It speaks the word.* Its unique utterance becomes a universal language. A great work of art is never obvious and immediately intelligible in the language that lies readily available, for the new, unique language now emerging before us is its own interpreter. It is "self-explanatory." For a moment the contemporary world is taken aback, then people begin to absorb the work and to speak in the newly minted language (hence such terms as "the age of Goethe," or "age of Shakespeare," etc.) with a taken-for-granted ease as though they had invented it themselves! The unique word, however, makes itself comprehensible through its own self: and the greater a work of art, the more extensive the cultural sphere it dominates will be. (2SW, 21)

Moreover, this analogy also highlights how crucial faith is to the right understanding of the claim. For it has often been the (spoken or unspoken) presupposition of much biblical scholarship that faith is an obstruction to the neutrality of the historical-critical method: meaning both the faith of the scholar and the faith expressed in the biblical text. Faith is thus like a pair of sunglasses which irremediably tint the text being interpreted, and historical criticism explicitly doffs the glasses. In doing so, it notices how the biblical text is "layered" with the community's confession of faith; and this is a layering which of course radically affects the narrative, transforming neutral history into a confessional text (a process which historical criticism reverses). But the aesthetic analogue on the contrary teaches the inner compatibility, indeed the essential symbiosis, of what the art work intends to say and the subjective readiness of the recipient to hear that message:

> A great work of art has a certain universal comprehensibility but discloses itself more profoundly and more truly to an individual the more attuned and practiced his powers of perception are. Not everyone picks up the unique inflection of the Greek in a chorus of Sophocles, or of the German of *Faust, Part II*, or of the French in a poem of Valéry. Subjective adaptation can add something of its own, but that objective adequacy which is able

to distinguish the noble from the commonplace is more important. (2SW, 21–22)

Notice the subtlety of the analysis here: on the one hand, Balthasar
fully concedes that subjective appropriation is essential, and indeed that
the more one is attuned as recipient to the work through what Rousseau
calls a "sentimental education," the more one will be able to take in what
is being communicated; on the other hand, *the standard* for that absorp-
tive power does not lie within the subject himself but within the work,
which establishes the standards for its own longevity in terms internal
to itself.

But being only a "relative" singularity, art cannot assume the role of
an all-controlling metaphor for approaching the "absolute singularity" of
the person of Christ, for, being relative, it must take its place with other
relative singularities—the other two being, in Balthasar's schema, falling
in love and the ineluctable fact of each individual's own personal death.
For once more we are enabled to understand what an absolute singularity
might be through the point of entry of a relative singularity.[14]

"Falling in love" is something that most people who have reached adult-
hood claim to have experienced, though it may be in fact be much rarer
than people suppose: "Genuine love between persons is probably less
common than one thinks, although most people think they have had some
share in it and that they really possess it for brief moments. But it may
well be as rare as great works of art, which tower here and there above
the mass of what masquerades as art" (2SW, 22). And certainly Balthasar
is not speaking of those examples, so fascinating to the Romantic imagination, of lovers whose love brings them to the brink, and beyond, of disaster. True, the stories of such immolating love *prompt* great art (*Romeo
and Juliet, Tristan und Isolde, Wuthering Heights,* etc.), but they are portraying a "love" that is not the true analogue for the absolute singularity
of Jesus. For that kind of analogue Balthasar is looking for a love that
more resembles Pascal's wager:

> I am not thinking about the mischance of passion which, as in
> *Tristan und Isolde,* relates the whole world to this one absolutely
> fixed point, and gives itself up to disaster for it. No, I am refer-
> ring to something that is much simpler and that to succeed re-
> quires a Christian disposition: a dedication of one's whole life
> to a Thou in whom the lover sees illumined the quality of the

---

[14] Note that in this presentation of relative singularities Balthasar is moving in a direction
that becomes more and more universal: not that many people can be expected to pick of
the subtleties of Valéry's poetry, but falling in love is something somewhat more common,
while death is the most universal relative singularity of all.

absolute, which involves the whole world. Such dedication is a wager that makes sense only if it is related to an absolute venture: the apparently arbitrary choice of the God of Israel from among all other nations (Deut 7:7), and its consequence: the call of Jesus and no other. . . . Eros cannot merely offer the initial impulse, but can continue the whole way only if it allows itself to be purified into transfigurations beyond itself. (2SW, 22–23)

And note here Balthasar's implicit apologetic here: his claim that the "relative singularity" of falling in love will finally collapse into meaninglessness and nihilism *without* the absolute singularity of the validity of Jesus's claim to bring eternal life. For falling in love is essentially a defiance of death, which of course is still sitting there grinning at the end of the game, unless it can somehow be trumped: "In the eyes of the world [falling in love] always looks like folly, for the stream of life flows on. . . . [This love] sets itself deliberately and stubbornly against the current laws of life; and somehow it interprets itself eschatologically: in the midst of time this love discovers not only a 'moment' of eternity, but a lasting experience of faithfulness that towers forever above all immanence" (2SW, 23).

And finally, there is that experience that *is* accessible to everyone: the uniqueness of our own life terminating in death. Whatever else may be singular, we at least are singular to ourselves! Naturally we all, except for the most incurably solipsistic, admit that time and history continue on after our death, and so we project our ego out into the future and bargain for an ersatz immortality through our works, achievements, children, etc.[15] But that wider horizon—or ocean—of time is in fact focused, or condensed, into our own briefly allotted time—and we know it. We constitute our own little world and are our own unique (relative) singularity, so that the projections of our life-project into a future beyond our death is in fact a denial of our relative singularity:

> True time is primarily the one each individual counts from his death and judgment, whereas common world-historical time, made into a chronological continuum by bracketing off personal death, is a secondary phenomenon, because in it the whole motive that constitutes the seriousness of temporality is suspended. A philosophy of the future which takes account of the whole ethos of the human race in the time to come when the individual as such will have gone, can address each individual only as a

---

[15] The classic dissection of this desperate psychology is Ernst Becker's *The Denial of Death* (New York: Free Press, 1973); see also, James P. Carse, *Death and Existence: A Conceptual History of Human Mortality* (New York: John Wiley & Sons, 1980).

member of a species and not as a person. The problem of how
the individual person can incorporate finite time into the future
of mankind in general ultimately demands a christological answer. (2SW, 25)

Unless of course one wants to avoid that answer. Then all sorts of
illusory options are available, the kind that prompted Henry David Tho-
reau to remark in *Walden* that "the mass of men lead lives of quiet desperation" and Pascal to say: "The only thing that consoles us for our miseries
is diversion, and yet this is the greatest of our miseries. For it is this which
principally hinders us from reflecting upon ourselves, and which makes
us insensibly ruin ourselves. Without this we should be in a state of weariness, and this weariness would spur us on to seek a more solid means of
escaping from it. But diversion amuses us, and leads us, gradually and
without our ever adverting to it, to death."[16] Or more specifically, to an
unrealized death. But a directly faced death can itself be the occasion for
the encounter with this relative singularity that is our finite existence, for
death is the funnel whose focus is so relentless that it forces on us a
personal response to the christological answer:

That which is seldom achieved by love is offered as a possibility
to every human being in the moment of death, when he comes
to understand himself not merely as a transitory individual in
the ever-flowing stream of life but as a unique person who has
to carry out his own unique mandate against a finite, and not
merely a limited, horizon. It is this extreme loneliness of dying
that constitutes the individual, for unlike the animals, the individual person sees what lies ahead, conscious of his own personal
uniqueness. .... When one leaves the society of men and walks
toward the judgment of God who predestines; when one enters
that refining fire through which the individual must pass and in
which the worth of his deeds upon earth will be revealed—empty
straw or solid metal (1 Cor 3:12–15)—one walks completely
alone. . . . Death and judgment are primarily an interruption of
every horizontal, dialogic situation; all such situations derive
their meaning only from a non-dialogic situation, from one that
answers to God alone. (2SW, 23–25)

Moreover, this death will be an encounter with Christ. This claim of
course cannot be verified before the event of death itself, but can only be,
at best, established in its credibility on the basis of the triad of Jesus's

---

[16] *Pensées*, B 171.

own Claim-Death-Validation. Nonetheless, this claim includes as one of its essential moments the assertion that Christ's horizon can answer the finitude of the individual's death because of the way Christ's own existence encompasses both "primary" and "secondary" time in his own person. That is, his claim includes that of pre-existence: of already being the encompassing matrix of time even though he is also an epiphenomenal human being like all the rest. In other words, the wave *is* the sea, and the sea-bed, and the horizon . . . and the All (Col 1:15–20).

And by entering into a sacramental relation to him in faith, we anticipate that entry into his kingdom that is won for us by both his person and his work. Salvation, in other words, is effected by incorporating our time into his time, which alone can heal and resolve the desperation embedded in our finite allotment of time:

> The time-horizon of Jesus of Nazareth was obviously not that of the rest of mankind. It was part of his commission, and hence of his claim, to have completely encompassed (to have 'done with') the history of the world within the scope of his mortal life. His finite span of life hid within itself the life-span of all who had died in the past and of all who would die in the future: here, in one single instance, primary personal time has become identified with all the time that has run on in the course of history.[17]

I think it is important to dwell for a moment on the phrase I used in the preceding paragraph, "person and work." For Balthasar's christology is, among other things, an attempt to get beyond the overly ontological categories of Chalcedonian christology as well as past the overly activistic stress on the work of Christ in classical and liberal Protestantism. For Balthasar, Jesus could not effect the work he accomplished without his *being* who he was, as the Letter to the Colossians well realizes; and yet it is not simply a matter of "appearing on the stage of history" as the Incarnate One for us to "see" redemption: it had to be *effected*, brought about, realized. Jesus had to accomplish a work, and it was "fitting" that he do so, in the full Anselmian sense of that word, a work which Balthasar describes using this striking image:

> Something equally crazy follows: all that Jesus is, his life and death taken together, manifests itself as the Absolute. . . . If the

---

[17] *2SW*, 39–40. This insertion of our time into his by virtue of the fact of the resurrection also explains the confusion of the early Church about the meaning of the end-times: "The resurrection of one man, who thereby had arrived at the end of the world, in contrast to all others who would go on living in time, threw every concept of time, even the apocalyptic

claim stands, the whole truth must also possess a ballast, an absolute weight [*Schwergewicht*] that can be counterbalanced by nothing else; and because it is a question of truth, it must be able to show that it is so. The stone in the one pan of the scales must be so heavy that one can place in the other pan all the truth there is in the world, every religion, every philosophy, every complaint against God, *without counterbalancing it.* Only if that is true, is it worthwhile remaining a Christian today. (2SW, 29)

Balthasar is here circling around several important themes that will receive explicit treatment elsewhere in his work: the descent into hell, theodicy, the refusal to countenance an "exemplar christology" (whereby Jesus gave us a good example of how to suffer in solidarity with sinners but whose effectiveness as an exemplar depends on our following his example), etc. Many of these themes will reappear in the Theodramatics, which as the name implies will be explicitly devoted to the work of Christ. But what he stresses here in the Aesthetics is more the issue of relative versus absolute singularities: without Christ's plunge downward of his side of the scales to the very depths of all existence, all our relative singularities would still remain ever relative, and therefore ultimately evanescent, without point, illusory, vain, and hollow: "If there were any weight capable, ever so slightly, of raising up the Christian side of the scales and moving that absolute weight into the sphere of relativity, then being a Christian would be a matter of mere preference, and one would have to reject it unconditionally. Somehow or other it would be outflanked. To think of it as more than of historic interest would be a waste of time" (2SW, 29–30).

Now when considering the issue of the Old Testament's relationship to the New, we must also think not just of the stone dropping to the bottom of the scales of the world's suffering but also of it landing in the ocean of history in such a way that its waves ripple outward in time, concentrically: that is, just as in a pond, the ripples go outward in all directions, so too does the impact of Jesus extend in both directions of time, affecting the past as well as the future. It is this "ripple effect" that will form the core of Balthasar's interpretation of the relationship between Old and New Testaments. But to understand how the ripple effect works its way backward in time, let us first consider the outward movement toward the future:

---

one, into confusion. . . . The event certainly could not have been expected, for as things were, there was no concept available to frame the thought. This is obvious from the way in which the attempt was made immediately to adapt it to current ideas: if one man has arrived at the end of the world, that means that the end of time really *had* dawned, and the resurrection of the rest would soon follow. This interpretation proved to be a delusion" (ibid., 39).

It is enough to consider three circles in succession: the Jesus event itself; biblical revelation as a whole; the overflowing of this revelation into the whole history of mankind. . . . Are we to say that we, who live in the ambit of the third circle can see the origin only through a multiplicity of estranging media, so that we are obliged to undertake a long series of hermeneutic manipulations in order to arrive, after several transpositions and by way of conjecture, at the original meaning of the first circle? (*2SW*, 37)

No! If Christ's work of reconciliation is as effective as the Christian *kerygma* proclaims it to be, then it must be able to make that efficacy present directly to the believer, and this is the work of the Spirit (Jn 16: 12–16). There is, then, a directness of connection between the believer and the Christ-event that is unmediated by either theology or learning; it is a connection to which the simple and the unlearned have privileged access (Mt 11:25–27) but which is available to all believers independent of their hermeneutical legerdemain.[18] The connection between the event of Jesus and the life of the believer must be, in some sense, *direct:*

The claim to be the overpowering weight on the scales—for all times and in all places, along with the whole scandal it contains—must be powerful enough (and this power is the Holy Spirit) to make itself intelligible "always, even until the end of the world" and "to all nations." This is not to deny the part played by hermeneutics ("you will be my witnesses" and "teach them to observe all things," which presumably includes teaching them to understand). But the claim, if justifiably upheld, is not dependent on hermeneutical acuity. (*2SW*, 37–38)

This kind of directness is of course unavailable to the men and women who preceded Christ (this is why Christian imagery depicts Christ descending into hell: in order, as one of his missions, to rescue the great righteous figures of the Old Testament from the shadow of Hades, for their access to Christ in history was purely one of hope, which they were robbed of in death); and so the ripple effect works differently in this case. And the same applies to how the Old Testament is fulfilled in the New: "The fulfillment which is posited in the fact of Jesus is not simply one new stage added in this process of transcendence. It belongs to a wholly different order. Compared with it, everything that came earlier stands at

---

[18] The defense of the faith of the "simple" (Mt 16:17; 18:1–7; 19:13–15) is an important theme in Balthasar's writings, especially in his shorter works; see especially: *Unless You Become Like This Child,* tr. Erasmo Leiva-Merikakis (San Francisco: Ignatius Press, 1988).

the proper distance to what is in process of historical development, while it establishes itself on the far side of this boundary line as an eschatological event" (*GL* 6, 407).

Old Testament images, then, are like fragments, or iron filings, which coalesce around their intended center and converge into a form only with the appearance *of* that Form—Jesus Christ—who is their magnetic attraction, as it were, without whom they have no coherence. But like the "saints" of the Old Testament, the images and roles inherited from this time must remain open and expectant, and do not carry within themselves the ultimate meaning of their referent. *They find fulfillment only retroactively.* On this basis, Balthasar can then propose three rules by which a theologian may formulate a new *argumentum ex prophetia,* one that will hold up as valid in face of the historical-critical method:

1. The individual forms which Israel established in the course of her history converge together upon a point that remains open and that cannot be calculated ahead of time on the basis of their convergence or their mutual relationship, especially since they stand in opposition to one another so often.
2. The midpoint is occupied in the fullness of time by one who *lives* this midpoint, although his primary mission is not to construct and conceive of his existence as the fulfillment of the various (and hitherto irreconcilable) individual forms of Israel.
3. When this midpoint is interpreted subsequently, one sees, in this later stage of reflection, that the midpoint retains its place as midpoint *through the crystallization of the periphery around it,* and that it is only through this crystallization that the periphery acquires its point of reference that gives it form (see *GL* 6, 403–404).

One of the great tensions that affects any attempt to construct a "theology of the Old Testament" is the conflicting nature of the images that cluster around the vaguely formulated hopes for the future as expressed by the prophets and narrators of the Old Testament, leaving what Gerhard von Rad calls "an extremely odd theological vacuum."[19] No line drawn from one image leads naturally into another but remains hovering in an unpatterned confusion, so that "the Messianic idea does not adjoin the idea of the Son of Man, nor does the idea of the Son of Man lead naturally to that of the Suffering Servant, etc" (*GL* 6, 404). But this only becomes obvious and clear *ex post facto:*

---

[19] Gerhard von Rad, *Old Testament Theology,* tr. D. M. G. Stalker (New York: Harper & Row, 1965) 2:349.

The type of "Isaac's sacrifice" or "Job's night of abandonment by God" or "Elisha's multiplication of bread" or "the Passover Lamb" or the "Suffering Servant," etc., is in each case in the same immediate relationship to the antitype [Christ] as is every other type. This naturally does not mean that the images can be abstracted from their context in salvation history and taken as something existing in themselves. For they bear their meaning only as [part of the] history that has happened between God and Israel, and it is only thus that they form an analogy to the definitive event of Christ. But precisely as types, they stand in a time of promise which is qualitatively different from the time of fulfillment.[20]

In Christopher Morse's lapidary phrase, "one may say that the personal identity of God as Promisor is 'one and the same' but that the keeping of a promise adds something new to the making of it."[21] And in Christ this is supereminently true, for he treats the cluster of Old Testament expectations with a sovereign freedom that fulfills these expectations pre-

---

[20] *GL* 6, 407–408. Consider the case of Jeremiah: "One thing stands out—both the passages in which Jeremiah holds converse with God and those in which he alone is the speaker always shade off into darkness, the impossibility of the prophet's task. . . . One is haunted by the impression that the darkness keeps growing, and eats ever more deeply into the prophet's soul. . . . It is a darkness so terrible, it is something so absolutely new in God's dealings with Israel, that it constitutes a menace to very much more than the life of a single man: God's whole way with Israel at this point threatens to end in some kind of metaphysical abyss. For the sufferings concern not just Jeremiah unofficially, as it were, as a private individual, about experiences common to all men. In every instance these confessions grow out of his specific mission as a prophet: what lies behind them is a call to serve in a quite particular way, a relationship of particular intimacy with YHWH, and therefore they have in the highest degree a typical significance for Israel" (Gerhard von Rad, *The Message of the Prophets*, tr. D. M. G. Stalker [New York: Harper & Row], 172–174). This clearly illuminates a great deal about the life and mission of Jesus, but it is equally illuminated by *it*, because of the retrospective light thrown on the life of Jeremiah by the nature of Jesus's own trinitarian mission. Could the following sentences ever have been written except in light of the Cross?: "If it is only with Jeremiah, and not earlier, that the earthly vessel broke, the reason is primarily that the prophetic office assumed by Jeremiah was far greater in its range and depth than that of any of his predecessors. In proportion, he also required the continuous support of God. At the same, however much we attempt to place Jeremiah in the correct historical framework of his age, and this is essential, a great deal remains that we cannot explain. It is still Jeremiah's secret how, in the face of growing skepticism about his own office, he was yet able to give an almost superhuman obedience to God and, bearing the immense strains of his calling, was yet able to follow a road which led ultimately to abandonment. . . . Again, if God brought the life of the most faithful of his ambassadors into so terrible and utterly uncomprehended a night and there to all appearances allowed him to come to utter grief, this remained God's secret" (ibid., 175).

[21] Morse, *The Logic of Promise in Moltmann's Theology* (Philadelphia: Fortress Press, 1979), 116.

cisely by going so far beyond them: "It is not his task to compete with the Old Testament images on their own level or even to pile them up to trump them. If his life is to be the breaching of the Old Testament boundary, then the event that is his life can only be, for the world, something obscure, since it is an eschatological event."[22]

What, for example, are we to make of that strangely taken-for-granted assertion throughout the New Testament that Christ died and rose from the dead "in accordance with the Scriptures" (1 Cor 15:4 and elsewhere)? Such a statement, which can be found embedded in the earliest strata of the *kerygma,* would be incomprehensible if the early Christian community had not interpreted the Christ event *first* in terms of itself and only then in terms of the preceding scriptural matrix. Such a statement, Balthasar insists, "presupposes, beyond all individual quotations, a total vision of the relationship between Old and New Covenants" (*GL* 6, 406). And it is this total vision that is the key to the New Testament understanding of that frequently invoked verbal form δεῖ ("it was necessary that ... ," "it had to be that ... "). It is, so to speak (and obviously speaking anachronistically), an "Anselmian" understanding of necessity: that is, an aesthetic one: "The necessity of what *de facto* happened ('*Must* not the Christ suffer this [kind of death] and thus enter into his glory?' [Lk 24:26]) is unfailingly deduced [by New Testament writers] from the way the formless images take on form" (*GL* 6, 406–407).

First of all, the way that Christ gives form to the unpatterned assemblage of Old Testament images is not a matter that can be adduced from a neutral examination of the evidence: Christ gives form and crystallizes the prior fragments of Old Testament imagery precisely because he stands in a *qualitatively* different relation to them, as promise to fulfillment, and so as such stands outside of deducible history: "It is, of course, only on the *theological* level—that is, with the eyes of faith—that it is possible to see this whole relationship in its objective correctness, and not with the eyes of the historian or psychologist of religion who abstracts from faith" (*GL* 6, 408).

Now what does this faith reveal? We have already noted how the Old Testament for the most part leaves the realm of the dead as an implicit, unthematized and cordoned-off "third partner" in the covenantal relationship, which therefore by definition cannot be touched by this covenantal intent by God until Christ descends into this realm. Death is for all human

---

[22] *GL* 6, 405; recall here the words of von Rad: "The realm of the dead remained an indefinable third party between YHWH and his creation. Apart from isolated questionings, it was not a subject of real interest to faith. ... Should we not see in this theological vacuum, which Israel zealously kept free from any sacral concepts, as one of the greatest theological enigmas in the Old Testament?" (*Old Testament Theology* 2: 350). This is one of the central reasons that Jesus so completely transcends Old Testament expectations and so radically reconstitutes the cluster of Old Testament images into a new pattern of redemption.

beings a shattering of life at its boundaries, but for Israel it must also be more: it is the entry into that realm of the unspoken, unthematized land of the "third partner." And yet Israel's covenantal faith is so strong that it cannot see death as the breakdown or abrogation of *God's* covenantal relation, however much it avoids a direct and thematic confrontation with the meaning of death itself:

> Everything human breaks down at its boundaries, and Israel too breaks down. But Israel's failure is of another kind: the boundary at which it breaks down is not above all the finitude of existence, but God, who has made it choose between life and death, blessing and curse (Deut 30:19). But to break down at the boundary of God and his Covenant does not mean simply to be finished and disqualified, since every two-sided covenant relationship is based on an antecedent unique election.[23]

But the same must apply, and more than merely formally, to the New Covenant: whatever failures the human partner might commit, whatever betrayals and neglect of his talents he might indulge, God is still there antecedently with his initiative, an initiative that is moreover seamless—and it is that seamlessness of salvific intent that forms the indissoluble link between Old and New Covenants, Israel and Church (Rm 9–11):

> The Church would not have been right to make such wide employment of Israel's hymns of praise for its own prayer if it had not been ready to pray the psalms of penitence, judgment and confession with Israel too. And this means knowing and feeling that she is guilty and subject to failure along with Israel too. . . . The images of the periphery have not been absorbed and dissolved in Christ as something that is superseded. The midpoint of the New Covenant retains its full historical form together with the images that fill it. Moses and Elijah appear on Mount Tabor to speak about the Passion, the twenty-four Elders before the throne are made up in equal measure of the "pillars" of the Old and New Covenants. For there are forms in the Old Covenant which cannot be left behind by the New, even when they are filled here with new contents and greater glory (2 Cor 3). (*GL* 6, 409)

---

[23] *GL* 6, 408. Balthasar adds in a footnote at this point a crucial perspective on the New Testament's interpretation of Israel's rejection of its Christ through its hardheartedness: "One must bear in mind that the commission to harden hearts which Isaiah and Ezekiel receive is primarily a *missionary* commission from God and thus cannot be anything other than a commission that brings salvation. And indeed it is precisely the text from Isaiah on

This allusion to Moses and Elijah conversing with Jesus on Mt. Tabor about the Passion is a crucial one for Balthasar when he comes to consider the dialogue with Judaism, and in his book on Martin Buber he explicitly invokes it as the central image that should govern Jewish-Christian dialogue.[24] Not only is this scene one of the Transfiguration, that is, an anticipation of the eschatological banquet where the realm of the dead no longer exists and where all are touched by the covenant, but it is also a scene explicitly devoted to the topic of Christ's Passion—for this is what will open the Covenant with Israel out into the world, what will touch the saints of the Old Testament in the realm of the dead, what will bring all the disparate images of the Old Testament into their true fulfillment in Christ: "The descent of the divine Word into the flesh will leave all 'form and beauty' behind it and force its way down into an inconceivable formlessness—which for this reason is also incapable of being seen and interpreted, since it is hidden—in order to display the lordship and glory of God even in territory which had hitherto been out of bounds" (*GL* 6, 411).

Now when Christ broke those bounds, he also ended up, historically speaking, splitting the one People of God into two: not by God's intent of course, but in effect. And the shadow he casts in history, like all shadows, is a dark one, so that Jews now, because of the darkness of Christian sin, see the very gateway through which Christ entered into this realm of

---

this point that occurs so often in the New Testament, and is in fact quoted by Jesus himself" (ibid., 408, note 13).

[24] And which he does with his usual elegance: "For anyone to embark upon a discussion of this kind will seem to most people a complete waste of time, a pointless and fruitless anachronism, fated not to arouse the smallest interest. For it can be said without the least hesitation that no subject is so carefully skirted, no issue so deserted, as the point at which the *one* Chosen People of God is related to itself as Old to New Covenant—that center point in the world's history which supplied Hegel with the idea of the dialectic of history. It is true, of course, that the discussion is carried on tirelessly in books which purport to explain the twofold Covenant, and that it has given rise to literary and theological problems of endless diversity. But the heirs to those two traditions, the individuals who represent them, have lived apart for two thousand years without ever coming face to face or trying to see what sort of a person the other might be. Yet their situation, their very existence one may say, involves them in a conversation *which it is not in their power to terminate*. . . . If it is to be a real conversation, and a fruitful one, its range must therefore be such as to reckon with heaven and earth, and so it will always hark back to the conversation held on the Mount of Transfiguration, when the Son of Man conversed with Moses and Elijah. . . . Whatever the two people say to one another will always have to preserve an echo of that conversation. . . . In *The Two Forms of Faith* Martin Buber ventured on to that deserted field and carried his lonely dialogue up to the point at which, in his opinion at least, the only intelligible attitude was silence. His final conclusion was that the two forms of faith are irreconcilable. That judgment is acceptable in the world, but it is not one that invokes the grace of God" (*MB&C*, 7–8; my emphasis). The title of the original German is, characteristically: *Einsame Zwiesprache:* "Lonely Dialogue."

the dead to touch the saints of the Old Testament as the very catalyst of their marginalization and persecution. Yet despite this, we must still say that history is one and, by God's intent, the People of God is still one (any other perspective would abandon the faith that brings all the disparate images of the Bible into coherence). Such an assertion seems to be refuted by history, with its dreary and disedifying spectacle of persecution and anti-Semitism as well as all the earlier attempts at Jewish-Christian dialogue that ran aground on fundamental misconceptions, from Justin Martyr's *Dialogue with Trypho* on down. But, for Balthasar, it is nonetheless true: "We must agree with Karl Barth when he says that there is only one People of God, consisting of Synagogue and Church together."[25] This of course in no way denies or mitigates the otherwise quite severe separation between these two segments of the one People. Balthasar is not interested in indulging in a false irenicism that papers over differences, nor is he interested in mitigating the implications of revelation out of guilt or modernistic revisions, as he clearly states in this passage:

> If we are to define the relationship of each portion [of the one People of God] to the other, it is not enough to establish areas of agreement between them (for example, that both are still journeying toward their ultimate fulfillment—for the Church also lives *in spe, non in re*: by faith and not by sight), that both are proceeding toward the same Redeemer and Judge, that both have the same Old Testament Scriptures in common, and so forth. Nor will it do to raise only secondary differences, for the purpose of promoting Jewish-Christian dialogue. The breach between the two "parts" is based on their Yes and No to what the Christian Church ultimately is, and Israel has refused to acknowledge this reality as its own fulfillment.[26]

---

[25] *TD* 3, 398; note that in the following we shall be drawing on this volume of *Theo-Drama*, where Balthasar interprets the split between Synagogue and Church as part of the dialectic of Yes/No that constitutes the drama between God and man from Adam to the present day. This anticipatory look at this section of *TD* will then permit us to devote more space in Part III to other themes in the second part of the trilogy.

[26] *TD* 3, 398. This section of *TD* 3 (341–446) is heavily indebted to Barth's *CD* II/2, Chapter VII, "The Election of God." As we proceed to examine Balthasar's rather controversial views on Synagogue and Church, I think it would be well to keep in mind what one Jewish thinker has to say about Barth's own rigorously New Testament approach, with its uncompromising insistence that the Church was, if not born, at least midwifed, by Israel's No: "Curiously enough it is his recognition of Israel's sinfulness that has influenced me very much. This is curious because Israel's sinfulness is a prominent theme in almost all of Christian theology. Why, then, did Barth's expression of this insight have particular meaning for me? I can speculate that it is his generally positive view of Israel that made the difference. The discovery of Israel's sinfulness is one thing when it comes from a Christian theologian who believes that Israel has been superseded by the Church and that Israel's sorrows are

In other words—and Balthasar does not mince words here—"the Church comes about as a result of a tragedy" (*TD* 3, 362; although he has a specifically theodramatic view of tragedy, which must be borne in mind). If we take it as axiomatic that Jesus Christ is God's form in history, whose unique form gives retrospective form to the previous unpatterned assemblage of Old Testament images that could not be reconciled on their own terms within the plane of their own horizon, then the conclusion is inevitable: "All the various concepts of Israel that developed in the course of time, both successively and concomitantly, were feeling their way toward the Church" (*TD* 3, 364). But in doing so they also underwent a complete transformation in the crucible of Christ's death and emerged "reconstituted," as it were, and it is that reconstitution that provokes the split between Israel and Church:

> This inevitably leads us back to the point where the one People of God split into two. This is the "primal rupture" that takes place at the birth of the Christian Church and confirms two things: first, Israel refuses to step over the threshold to which—from the Christian point of view—its paths had been leading (for New Testament thinking and speaking constantly presuppose and use these paths); secondly, in the form of the "remnant" it *does* actually step over the threshold, with the result that, having crossed it, it is no longer simply one with the past but genuinely enters into a "synthesis." A dividing wall has been torn down, which is none other than the wall of Israel's particularity; it was this wall that, in spite of Israel's universalist tendencies, prevented the "nations" joining Israel from becoming a homogeneous whole. (*TD* 3, 366)

The Christ-event broke that wall down, reconstituting the People of God now as *Church*, but one which necessarily must be composed of both Jews and Gentiles. Now this means two things: one, that the Church is not permitted to recognize within her own precincts a distinction (invidious or otherwise) between Jew and Gentile; and two, that the relationship of the Church to the continued presence of Israel and Synagogue in the midst of history is not simply one of continuity but also (and perhaps even above

---

the result of its obstinacy. It is something entirely different when it comes from a Christian theologian with roots in Judaism as deep as those of Barth. . . . Barth is right, of course. The history of Israel is a history of almost continuous rebellion. Most Jews do not like to talk about this. Nevertheless, it is true because the Bible says so and because we can see it with our eyes. And in spite of this, God loves the Jewish people in a special way. This is the triumph of God's grace over the obduracy of the human being" (Michael Wyschogrod, "A Jewish Perspective on Karl Barth," in: *How Karl Barth Changed My Mind*, ed. Donald K. McKim [Grand Rapids, MI: Eerdmans, 1986]: 156–161; here, 159).

all) of contrast. The sign of the barriers' collapse, in other words, is meant to be found in the reality of the one Church as composed of both Jew and Gentile, for this is the work of Christ, and the Church is the sign in history of that work and our incorporation in it (Eph 2:11–18).

This breakdown of the barrier between Jew and Gentile has, of course, different implications for the two peoples: they must each give up something different in the act of accepting the salvation that comes from Christ. And it is the difference in the gifts and "heirlooms," so to speak, that both sides must give up that goes a long way to explaining (for Balthasar) the reason for the Jews' rejection of Christ and the Gentiles' acceptance of him. For by the time Christ came, paganism had been exhausting itself in a hollow mythology that not many serious people believed anymore, and so the sacrifice required of paganism was not as demanding as what was demanded of the Jews, who had to "lose" the Messianic patterns they grew up with and see them reconstituted into an entirely unexpected and new pattern:

> The Jews were the bearers of a centuries-old election from among the Gentile nations. They had been favored with God's Torah and his prophetic word and with promises according to which Israel—*always a particular people*—was destined to become a lodestar around which everything mundane would collect and orient itself. To have to surrender these prerogatives and consider the Gentiles, neither chosen nor schooled by God, as equals in a new, third community, amounted, in purely human terms, to Christianity's making an unthinkable and therefore unacceptable demand of the Jews. For their part, the Gentiles lived in the freedom of their own concepts of God and their religious ideas which, when radicalized, increasingly tended to become a demythologized and dehistoricized idea of a godhead.[27]

This is not in any way to downplay the sacrifice entailed by the Gentiles, who had, for their part, to abandon the idea that flesh was, at best, a pale copy of the Ideas, where alone salvation was located. We live in a civilization that tends to scorn Plato's philosophy as being too ethereal, and so it would be all too easy to underestimate the cost of such a sacrifice by Hellenized pagans when they accepted the Gospel, as we can see reflected in the apparently typical response to Paul's sermon on the Areopagus by some Athenian Greeks: his listeners were able to follow along and had no problem with the gist of his sermon as long as he seemed to be saying

---

[27] "The Church of Jews and Gentiles—Today," *NE*, 62–63. This essay is a most useful summary of Balthasar's theology on this issue as found in both *GL* and *TD*.

something like "we all worship the same [essence of] God" under different manifestations (an opinion still prevalent among people today when faced with the diversity of religions). But when he said that this ever-unknown God had raised his Son *in* the flesh, they took scandal and slunk away, except for a few hardy converts (Acts 17:16–34). Moreover, as the *kerygma* always insisted, the God who raised Jesus was the same God who led his people through the Red Sea and schooled them in the land he had promised them, which meant that the Old Testament continued to be valid—always a sticking point for Gnosticizing Christians, all the way up to Bultmann:

> [Gentiles] were required not only to recognize a certain human being in his concreteness as Savior of the cosmos but also to accept his Jewish antecedents as expressly shaped by God, even though this history was just as strange, if not stranger, to their sensibilities as the national history of any other of the peoples about whom they were unconcerned. . . . For the one [group had to surrender] the particularity of an election by God himself *as* a unique people; consequently, for a Jew, to surrender this particularity had to seem like outright disavowal of his very being and of God's faithfulness. For the other, it was a universality [that had to be surrendered], which apparently would have to return to the shackles from which it had freed itself. . . . What a loss for both! What a humiliating exaction for both, to let themselves be robbed of their most precious possession! What a kenosis! (*NE*, 63–64)

Nonetheless, after the first generation, the Church ended up being composed almost entirely of Gentiles, although the "pillars" of the Church were all necessarily Jews (and that is much more crucial to the Church's constitution than any accident of sociological composition). And for Balthasar that accident of membership is of course due to the fact the Jews had more to lose than the Gentiles: "Since the Gentiles were more lost, more 'godless' (Eph 2:12) than the Jews, they opened their hearts more readily than the latter to the message of grace" (*NE*, 64). So history refutes what revelation insists upon: it shows the almost immediate rejection of the Christian *kerygma* by the vast majority of the Jews (at least of those who had come into contact with the Gospel—an important reservation), while within two generations Christianity had emerged from its Jewish chrysalis into its own as a full-fledged world religion.

What, then, is the meaning of Israel and the continuation of the Synagogue in the time after Christ's coming? For Balthasar, the answer to that question hinges on the issue of the continuation of time: the Church is a Church of Jews and Gentiles *because* she is an eschatological reality; and yet she lives in time, that is, in history, which confronts her with a different reality, where the dualism of elect and non-elect lives on. But here is the crucial difference: for Balthasar, this dualism lives on in such a way that Israel continues to enjoy the precedence of election: "Inasmuch as the Church—as eschatological entity—is composed of human beings living in time, and the dualism of Jew/Gentile, elect/non-elect belongs to a humanity set within history, Israel will always enjoy precedence of election (and of corresponding structure) on this level, without its having a privileged position in the Church on this account" (*NE*, 65).

How then can the issue of Church and Synagogue be resolved? First of all, it is absolutely crucial to admit that we are talking above all here of theological realities which persist throughout history because of their eschatological nature. For that reason, Balthasar dispenses with vague hopes that the mere invocation of "dialogue" will be the answer for intra-historical tensions that have their root in eschatology. It is "not on the basis of human efforts at dialogue, including all the requisite admissions of guilt and necessary humiliations," he says, that will bring us to the heart of the matter, but only "(as it were) on the divine level, the level of the economy of salvation itself" (*TD* 3, 367). And here the only question is whether revelation envisages Paul's outlook for the conversion of "all Israel" (Rm 11:26) as an event within history, or as a strictly eschatological event.[28]

Balthasar clearly comes down on the Barthian, eschatological side of this debate, and in fact accuses those who hope for the conversion of Israel in historical time of being naïve: "In fact those who take the contrary view, namely, that Israel is destined to be absorbed and dissolved into the Church (this is their hope, at least), betray a certain naïveté, considering the overall structure of Israel" (*TD* 3, 369). What is crucial, however, is to "attribute a role, recognizable within Christian revelation and theology, to Israel's existence in post-Christian time" (ibid.). And in recognizing that role, the Church's internal task will be to maintain her roots in Judaism against all Marcionite and Gnosticizing tendencies. Quoting Louis Bouyer, Balthasar says: "The Church failed in her mission to the Jews, but just as Jesus had failed. But 'we may assume that the Church will not attain her final form until she has rediscovered the Jewish-Christian Church.'"[29]

This of course does not mean ignoring the supersession of the Old by the New Testament. Nor, on the other hand, has the Old Testament vanished: it retains a validity that is hard to specify but nonetheless real:

---

[28] Jacques Maritain holds to the former, while Karl Barth affirms the latter alternative; for other literature on this issue, see: *TD* 3, 367–370.

[29] *TD* 3, 369, quoting Louis Bouyer, *L'Église de Dieu* (Paris: Cerf, 1976), 643.

This brings us to the difficult question of the theological meaning of the Old Testament for Christians. We say "difficult" because, in order to be able to constitute one total form with Christ, the Old Testament must participate in his singularity (and the relationship of proximity and distance between the Old and New Testament participates in this singularity), while, on the other hand, Christ's uniqueness—the qualitative newness that he brings—must stand in contrast to the Old Testament, which is thus lowered to another level of theological reality. (*GL* 1, 621)

But that does not abrogate the fundamental law for Christians: "Whoever accepts Jesus must also accept the unity of the Old and New Testaments" (*GL* 1, 620). This of course is not easy to work out, especially in matters of Old Testament Law, and Balthasar does not discuss in his work the minutiae of the issue, merely asserting in general terms that the person who accepts Jesus "must grasp the essence of the Law, not only so that he knows what he should keep to but also so that he knows what Jesus has freed him from" (*GL* 1, 620). True enough, but where and how this general statement is to be applied goes undiscussed by Balthasar.

In any event, the basic outlines are clear: for a Christian, the presence of both Church and Synagogue in history is part of the dialectic of the human Yes and No to God. This belongs to the more fundamental drama of God's initial and continuing Yes to his creation in his will to save all (1 Tim 2:4). *And this will to save knows how to remain faithful to itself even in the face of infidelity:* "If we died with him, we will also live with him; if we endure, we will also reign with him; . . . if we are faithless, he will remain faithful, for he cannot disown himself" (2 Tim 2:11–13). This fascinating chiasmus, this jolt from the normal expectations of the other clauses, points up the real issue here: God's continuing Yes in the face of the human No. This is what really constitutes the drama of salvation, and it is to the presentation of that drama that Balthasar devotes the second part of his vast theological trilogy.

Part III

THE THEODRAMATICS

• • •

According to most philosophers, God in making the world enslaved it. According to Christianity, in making it, He set it free. God had written, not so much a poem, but rather a play; a play he had planned as perfect, but which necessarily had been left to human actors and stage-managers, who have since made a great mess of it.

G. K. Chesterton
Orthodoxy

Christianity is not a doctrine, not I mean, a theory about what has happened and will happen to the human soul, but a description of something that actually takes place in human life. For "consciousness of sin" is a real event and so are despair and salvation through faith. Those who speak of such things (Bunyan, for instance) are simply describing what has happened to them, whatever gloss anyone may want to put on it . . . Within Christianity it's as though God says to men: Don't act out a tragedy. That is to say: don't enact heaven and hell on earth. Heaven and Hell are *my* affair.

Ludwig Wittgenstein,
Culture and Value

· 8 ·

The Drama of Finite
and Infinite Freedom

Yet the enchainment of past and future
Woven in the weakness of the changing body,
Protects mankind from heaven and damnation
Which flesh cannot endure.

Time past and time future
Allow but a little consciousness. . . .
Only through time time is conquered.

T. S. Eliot
"Burnt Norton," *The Four Quartets*

C hristian theology invariably shipwrecks itself when it confronts the
issue of divine and human freedom. Every time it tries to steer
through these dangerous waters, it seems either to crash against the rock
of divine omnipotence or to run aground on the shoals of human freedom
with its (alleged) ability to decide whether to accept the offer of redemption—and so determine its own salvation. So whenever theology takes up
the theme of how God's omnipotent freedom can be reconciled to man's
(admittedly paltry, blind and foolish) "freedom," it seems to crash on the
contradictions inherent in the very terms of the issue.[1] Over against God's
freedom (to create, to save, to condemn), man's seems a paltry thing
indeed.

And so the temptation has been well-nigh overwhelming for theology

---

[1] To deny human freedom seems to lead to fatalism, but to assert it seems to make God's
freedom no longer omnipotent. And so, as one historian of dogma puts it: "One horn of
the dilemma of Christian anthropology, that of responsibility, seems to be demanded by the
polemical situation [in responding to the fatalists]. Yet in the long run the other alternative,
that of inevitability, was the one to which the interpretation of Christian doctrine was
obliged to give its primary attention" (Jarolsav Pelikan *The Christian Tradition: A History
of the Development of Doctrine*, Vol. 1: *The Emergence of the Catholic Tradition: 100–600*
[Chicago: University of Chicago Press, 1971] 1:280).

to deny freedom to man altogether and to ascribe all the good that we do (which admittedly isn't much) to God alone. This is particularly tempting when one's glance is thrown back to the past: for freedom looks much more plausible when we face the future, so full of unchosen possibilities and seemingly endless alternatives. Here we seem masters and pilots of our own ships, who, despite the storms, control the rudders and guide the vessel to its pre-chosen goal. But when looking back on the past, we see how little we knew at the time, how things turned out quite otherwise than our plans had assumed, how the future in fact developed in such a way that our choices, like those of the heroes of Greek tragedy, provoked the very opposite of what they had intended. And who among us ever chooses to be born anyway? Or selects the most basic constituents of what makes a human life a life: sex, race, nationality, parents, siblings, era of history, language, etc.? Or even personality: parents often notice a personality forming in their children well before they even learn to speak.[2] And who *really* has any control over the economic and political forces of the globe?

And so too for Christians: when they look back on their own past, they also equally know how much of a role that chance circumstances played in their accepting the faith; and so when they link up these circumstances with a belief in God's providence, the language of predestination naturally rises to their lips: "Praise be to the God and Father of our Lord Jesus Christ, who has blessed us in the heavenly realms with every spiritual blessing in Christ. For he chose us in him before the creation of the world to be holy and blameless in his sight. . . . And you also were included in Christ, when you heard the word of truth, the gospel of your salvation" (Eph 1:3–14).

Predestination, then, is really the resulting realization that comes upon a believer when he reflects how graciously he has been received and how the circumstances that conspired to lead him to belief were not of his doing; it is, in other words, a doctrine that is the outcome of gratitude for a gift that came "in the fullness of time." Predestination as a doctrine really represents the convergence of several realizations in Christian life: 1) that God is eternal and his very creation is a gratuitously willed gift that did not have to be; 2) that even though man sinned, God can trump that sin and outrun the sinner; 3) that among the mass of human beings on the globe, *I*, for reasons that have nothing to do with my merit (for I did not even choose to be born, let alone where and when!), have been given the grace to know of this decision of God to outbid human sin; and 4) that the only response to this can be gratitude: "And we know that in

---

[2] "Among the possible determinants of the shape of character, the psychological equipment . . . may have been present from the beginning and independent of instinctual conflict" (David Shapiro, *Neurotic Styles* [New York: Basic Books, 1965], 9).

all things God works for the good of those who love him, who have been called according to his good purpose. For those God foreknew he also predestined. . . . And those he predestined, he also called; those he called, he also justified; those he justified, he also glorified. What, then, shall we say in response to this? If God is for us, who can be against us?" (Rm 8:28–39).

But once the glance wanders off this response of gratitude to the fate of others who seem to be not so similarly blessed and once the idle workshop of the logical mind gets to humming, the doctrine of predestination begins to cause problems on which theology has again and again run aground. For if a sense of gratitude is at the root of the Christian doctrine of predestination and if its enunciation is meant to give believers a strong sense of hope that they will persevere to the end (as is clearly the case with Paul), the smallest deflection from that gratitude and hope can derail the doctrine completely, so that it ends up leading those who hear of the doctrine, not to gratitude and hope, but rather to fear and despair.[3]

The trouble really is rooted in a too-close connection between the apparent outcomes of history and the eternal decrees of God: *since* the world is divided between believers and non-believers, and *since* one's being a Christian is due to the unmerited grace of God, and *since* some people obviously fall by the wayside and abandon their call before death, this must all be due to the eternal ordinance of God ("according to his purpose"). And so by a rapid logical declension, one arrives at the bottom of the Jansenist hill, concluding not only that one belongs to the elect oneself but, even more relentlessly, that "Christ died specifically and only for the faithful" and that "pagans, Jews, heretics, and others in like conditions receive no influence from Jesus Christ" since "sufficient grace is in fact harmful" (because it does not suffice!).[4] And so by a weird reversal

---

[3] "Man can, by misunderstanding this mystery, form for himself a more or less distorted notion of God and his relation to the creature, and therefore commit himself to presumption, despair, negligence, or an unchristian self-confidence. But St. Paul presented the doctrine of predestination to the Christians of Rome as a motive of hope. Hence, a true understanding of it should lead to a strengthening of the motives of true hope and of the vigor of the Christian life" (Dom M. John Farrelly, O.S.B., *Predestination, Grace, and Free Will* [Westminster, MD: The Newman Press, 1964], 31; cited henceforth as Farrelly). Thomas Aquinas holds that it is not fitting that the outcome of predestination be revealed, "because, if so, those who were not predested would despair; and security [in knowing one is predestined to salvation] would beget negligence in the predestined" (*ST* I, q. 23, a.1, ad 4), which rather makes it seem that exhortations to believe and to behave morally depend on a kind of "blissful (or anxious!) ignorance" of the predetermined outcome of judgment. Note here as well the lack of mutuality between divine and human freedoms in the Thomistic model: presumably, if the predestined *did* know of their ultimate fate to be saved, their subsequent negligence would not affect their fate.

[4] These are all propositions culled (allegedly) from the writings of Bishop Cornielius Jansen (1585–1638) and condemned by Innocent X as heretical in 1653 (DS. 2001–2007); after the Jansenists insisted that the condemned propositions were not to be found in Jansen's

of intent, the doctrine—originally intended to forestall pride—ends up making the believer feel set apart and better off than the *massa damnata,* from which pathetic mass he has been plucked by an apparently arbitrary decree of God.[5]

But the alternative, Pelagianism, hardly represents a workable solution either. Pelagians insist that man is equally free to choose good or evil, that no inherited inclination bends his will one way or the other, even after the entrance of sin in the world.[6] But it too runs aground on its own contradictions. First of all, there is a theoretical difficulty which holds that to make salvation contingent in any way on an individual's moral behavior and the exercise of free choice would be to make God's decision to save dependent on a finite event inside creation, which would be the equivalent of making God's intellect a passive determination susceptible to the self-determining choices of the creature. But all choice, in the Aristotelian and Thomistic framework (where this objection first arises), means to move from possibility to act; but God *is* pure Act and so cannot move from possibility to act. *Ergo:* his decisions cannot be dependent on finite choices.[7]

---

own writings and so did not apply to them, Alexander VII in 1656 condemned a further set of propositions (DS. 2301–2332), aimed more specifically at his followers, perhaps the most bizarre of which was the Jansenist insistence that one should pray to be *delivered* from sufficient grace ("Gratia sufficiens statui nostro non tam utilis, quam perniciosa est, sic, ut proinde merito possimus petere: 'A gratia sufficienti libera nos, Domine!'" [2306]). Surely a unique moment in the history of heresy: to pray to be delivered from grace!

[5] The danger of spiritual pride from an overemphasis on predestination becomes especially evident in Farrelly's formulation: "If two men are faced with the same temptation and one overcomes it, his superiority to the other man is due to grace and not to himself in any way that would nourish pride. [Nonetheless], he is *better* than the other because he has received a *greater* grace from God that came from a *greater* divine love for him, a love that gave him not only sufficient power to perform the good act but the performance of the act itself. In other words, it is God who distinguished him from the other through giving him a prevenient grace which was greater than that given to the other" (Farrelly, 34; my emphasis). It strikes me as being psychologically impossible that pride would not creep into this interpretation of God's action on the individual—indeed, a far more subtle and perverse pride, because now *God* is the one validating this so much more superior moral behavior with a so much superior divine favor. It seems unavoidable that such a logic would lead directly to what might be called a kind of "narcissism of grace," which of course undermines the whole point of grace (and predestination as well).

[6] "The effect of such an effort to increase the sense of responsibility for individual sinful acts by emphasizing the freedom in which they are committed, is to make every sinful act appear as a conscious choice of evil in defiance of a known good. . . . Pelagianism in short ascribes all sins to 'deliberate malice and pravity,' to use Calvin's phrase" (Reinhold Niebuhr, *The Nature and Destiny of Man: A Christian Interpretation,* Vol. I: *Human Nature* [New York: Charles Scribner's Sons, 1941] 1:247).

[7] Aquinas uses an all-too telling image in this context to explain God's causality working to lead his *rational* (!) creatures to their proper end: "Now if a thing cannot attain to something by the power of its nature, it must be directed thereto by another; thus, *an arrow is directed by the archer toward its mark.* Hence, properly speaking, a rational creature,

But even if one were tempted to dismiss these objections as merely speculative and overly dependent on an abstract definition of God's omnipotence, other considerations bear down heavily against a too-casual assumption that man remains free to decide his eternal fate.[8] For linked to an insistence that the will truly is free *vis-à-vis* God's offer of salvation is, often enough, an insistence that "free" means, in the words of the Jesuit Luis de Molina (1535–1600), the neutral freedom to choose between two equally poised alternatives: "That agent is said to be free which, once everything necessary for acting is given, is able to act or not to act, or to do one thing in such a way that *it could also do the contrary*."[9] But this flounders immediately on our prior knowledge of human nature: who has ever made a choice based on such even-steven neutrality? Moreover, it does nothing to explain why, given such neutrality, anyone would ever choose evil. Yet this is the real issue here, one which the Pelagians and the Molinists do little to confront.[10]

---

capable of eternal life, is led towards it, directed, as it were, by God. Now the reason of that direction pre-exists in God. . . . Hence the type of the aforesaid direction of a rational creature towards the end of life eternal is called predestination" (*ST* I, q. 23, a 1). I find this image of arrow/archer as an analogue to man/God quite misleading, as it finesses the issue of man as *rational* creature—supposedly the issue in this *questio* of the *Summa*. But as Farrelly so usefully points out, it is often the philosophical presuppositions that govern the conclusion, and not revelation: "If God wants a man to be saved, or if he wants him to perform a good act, it would detract from the divine power to say that he was prevented by man from fulfilling his will. God would not be omnipotent if he could not gain the created will's consent, for there would be something he could not do. . . . God does not, as some think, act in a necessary way with creatures of necessary action and in a contingent manner with free creatures; his action cannot be impeded even when it reaches free causes. . . . God's will is so powerful that it causes not only the act of the creature, but even the manner of its act" (Farrelly, 5–6). These statements are only possible if one assumes, first of all, that divine and human freedom are juxtaposed and thus antithetical and, secondly, that it would "detract" from the divine freedom to be influenced by the human will (or by any finite event). As our presentation of the Theodramatics unfolds, we shall see how Balthasar tries to undercut these assumptions.

  [8] "The truth is that, absurd as the classical Pauline doctrine of original sin may seem to be at first blush, its prestige as a part of the Christian truth is preserved, and perennially re-established, against the attacks of rationalists and simple moralists by its ability to throw light upon complex factors in human behavior which constantly escape the moralists, . . . [and this inspite of the fact that] the Christian doctrine of sin in its classical form offends both rationalists and moralists by maintaining the seeming absurd position that man sins inevitably and by a fateful necessity but that he is nevertheless to be held responsible for actions which are prompted by an ineluctable fate" (Niebuhr, *Nature and Destiny of Man* 1:248–249, 241).

  [9] Luis de Molina, *Liberi arbitrii cum graitae donis concordia*, ed. J. Rabeneck, S.J. (Madrid, 1953), q. 14, a. 13, d. 2, n. 3, p. 14; my emphasis.

  [10] "In the 20th century, when human beings have already killed well over one hundred million of their kind, disenchantment [with an optimistic view of human nature] set in. Two world wars, the Gulags, the Holocaust, Korea, Vietnam, the nuclear and ecological threats formed a somber litany that makes the optimism of the liberals ring hollow and naïve.

It is little wonder then the solution to these apparent antinomies seems well-nigh impossible. As one author says: "The whole problem then lies in this point of the relation between the divine permission and the evil initiative or, if you prefer, the failure of the creature. I see only two ways that are open to explain this, and each of them seems impossible to follow to the end."[11] Moreover, and more depressing yet, the past history of this debate shows that it doesn't really work to try to combine the insights of the two schools into a more overarching system: "[For] in adopting intrinsically efficacious grace and antecedent predestination from the former, [syncretists] have the Thomist's difficulty in explaining free will; and in adopting the contrary elements from Molina, they have difficulty in showing how God has infallible knowledge of man's free future acts."[12]

Now all this might seem merely a theologians' quarrel, with much heat and dust being generated and precious little light, but unfortunately this is not the case, as again the history of dogma proves. Misunderstandings on this score have caused an enormous number of pastoral problems in the Church, at least from the time of St. Augustine, down to our own day.[13] The dilemma simply cannot be avoided without harming the life of the Church, as Balthasar well realizes:

Despite technological progress, evil, far from vanishing, has only become more powerful and more fiendish. Freudian psychology and existentialist philosophy laid bare the tragic underside of the human condition. And artists like Conrad, Camus, Beckett, Golding, and Murdoch contended that because of our hearts of darkness there may be countless nice men and women but few if any genuinely good ones. In all these perspectives evil is held to be inherent, somehow structural, ingrained. And its terrible power defies explanation and solution. Paradoxically, the silver wings of science and technology, on which soared the hopes of the industrialized societies, carried the ultimate menace to the human prospect" (Stephen J. Duffy, "Our Hearts of Darkness: Original Sin Revisited," *Theological Studies* 49/4 [1988]: 606).

[11] M.-J. Nicholas, "Simple réflexions sur la doctrine thomiste de la grâce," *Revue Thomiste* 58 (1958): 649.

[12] Farrelly, 29. And in fact, the outcome of the debate was a standoff. While the exaggerations of Pelagius and Jansen can be dispatched easily enough, that scarcely resolves the issue, and the debate in modern times quickly debouched into two institutional camps, the Dominicans and the Jesuits, with Domingo Báñez (1528–1604) best representing the Dominican side of the debate and Molina the Jesuits. After the delation of Molina's writings to Rome, Clement VIII appointed an *ad hoc* "Congregatio de Auxiliis" to deal with the debate. On 19 March 1598 it reported for the first time, advising that the circulation of Molina's book be forbidden and 90 propositions extracted from it be condemned; but the Pope declined to ratify the decision. A second attempt to secure the Pope's condemnation when the number of offending propositions had been scaled down to 20 also proved unsuccessful. The next Pope, Paul V, also proved unsympathetic to the campaign and finally, on 5 September 1607, in an attempt to satisfy both sides, he decreed that the Dominicans could not be justly accused of Calvinism nor the Jesuits of Pelagianism—and that neither side could pronounce the other side heretical.

[13] And if Paul was countering more than a merely rhetorical question in Rm 6:15 ("What then? Shall we sin because we are not under the Law but under grace? By no means!"), the pastoral difficulties arose at the first enunciation of the doctrine of predestination.

Here [in the doctrine of double predestination] an ultimate basis for the alternative outcomes of human existence—eternal salvation or eternal perdition—is sought in the unfathomable abyss of divine freedom; so much so that, in spite of all exhortations, man's efforts slacken and fail as he loses all courage in the face of this mystery. For it is not a question (as before) of how finite freedom can develop within an infinite freedom: this infinite freedom, which is necessarily the final arbiter, now threatens to swallow up finite freedom" (*TD* 2, 250).[14]

So the pastoral resolution of this dilemma is in fact quite urgent. But taken on its own terms and in the traditional schema, this has proven to be an impossible task. It seems, then, that what is needed, to use a fashionable terms these days, is a "paradigm shift" that will completely alter the way we look at the problem, where all talk about arrows and archers drops out in favor of a perspective that both opens up the believer to a real confidence and hope, while preserving God's majesty and his uncompromising rejection of sin and evil.

I have rehearsed this strange history of unresolved problems (with their deleterious pastoral implications) because I think it is the best way of entering into the vasty deep of Balthasar's Theodramatics. For what he has done by foregrounding all of the theatrical and dramatic metaphors embedded in theology is to alter *in a stroke* the entire perspective out of which theologians consider this problem.[15] What Balthasar has done is really as simple as it is brilliant: dropping all talk of arrows, efficient causality, etc., he takes the metaphor of playwright, director and actor, and shows how a successful theatrical production always depends on the

---

[14] Echoed by Farrelly: "If there is a close association between the Christian's thought and life, an inadequate explanation of predestination results in an inadequate Christian life. For example, if one lives by the conviction that predestination is anterior to any knowledge God has of one's good or evil acts, an injunction to work out one's salvation in fear and trembling seems inappropriate, for it seems that if one has been predestined, one's salvation is certain; and if one has not, it is impossible. If one is simply uncertain whether such a divine intention exists or not, it seems that the foundations of hope and thus of a vigorous Christian life are to that extent weakened. If, on the other hand, one accepts the statement that predestination is consequent upon God's foreknowledge of a life lived in fidelity to him and that this grace is rendered efficacious *by* man's response, then man seems cast back upon himself and his own resources. He seems to have less reason to rely completely on God, for here he is certain that God has not already predestined him. He knows that God waits to see what the outcome will be before predestining him, and what the outcome of his response will be before his grace can be called truly efficacious" (31).

[15] Admittedly, the "stroke" has resulted in a 5–volume work, but the insight itself does come in a flash and, once grasped, leads to an immensely fruitful and heuristic way of looking at divine and human freedom. And that heuristic fertility is what really accounts for the length of this immense work.

harmonious cooperation of three freedoms, which are *not* however equal: for the director must serve the script and the actor must serve both; yet the actor simply cannot afford to be an automaton if the production is to be successful: some unnamed element (which we approximate by calling "talent" and which entails the actor's own free cooperation) must be engaged if the play is to emerge before the audience as playwright and director intended it.[16]

One of the great *theologoumena* of Christian revelation is the theme of *Deus absconditus:* the hidden God who *must* withdraw from his creation if it is to stand on its own and not be overwhelmed with the fire and light of the divine presence. And yet this withdrawal is itself, to use Kantian terminology, the "condition for the possibility" of atheism.[17] Yet faith claims, daringly, to be able to detect the traces of God in nature—and history (!). But building on the foundation he laid in the Aesthetics, Balthasar insists that this "absolute singularity" of faith has its analogues in the relative singularity of art. And this is what explains his interest in *style.* For is it not the case that we can detect the presence of an author or director by his or her style, though neither playwright nor director ever appears on the stage? Who cannot pick up, with proper training of course, the lines from a play that are distinctively Shakespearean? Who can miss the distinctive style of a Kurosawa film? Yet how absurd to expect them to show themselves on stage or screen!

---

[16] The analogy can of course be extended in any number of ways (script/Scripture, etc.), which accounts for the ability of the dramatic metaphor to present all of systematic theology under its rubric. But the core of the metaphor is the triad of playwright-actor-director as applied to the Trinity—for example, as applied to the Holy Spirit: "In another context, in an analogy with the theater, Balthasar speaks of the Holy Spirit as a kind of prompter who word-for-word, scene-for-scene, gives the actor-Son his part. The fact that the actor-Son has the responsibility to play the role given him by the author-Father, as 'whispered' to him in each moment by the prompter-Spirit, does not exclude the actor-Son's interpretative freedom. On the contrary, it assumes it and provides the material in which his freedom as an actor can become concrete. Therefore, although the author has a definite primacy with regard to the actor and the prompter (or director), it is by no means a tyrannical relationship. The author continues to be present in his work but as one who opens up the creative 'space' of the part. He will certainly influence both actor and director, but therein precisely make their creative activity possible" (J. Randall Sachs, S.J., *Spirit and Life: The Pneumatology and Christian Spirituality of Hans Urs von Balthasar* [Tübingen: University of Tübingen unpublished dissertation], 152–153).

[17] "*That God has willed to hide Himself:* If there were only one religion, God would indeed be manifest. The same would be the case if there were no martyrs but in our religion. God being thus hidden, every religion which does not affirm that God is hidden, is not true; and every religion which does not give the reason of it, is not instructive. Our religion does all this: *Vere tu es Deus absconditus.* If there were not obscurity, man would not be sensible of his corruption; if there were no light, man would not hope for a remedy. Thus, it is not only fair, but advantageous to us, that God be partly hidden and partly revealed, since it is equally dangerous to man to know God without knowing his own wretchedness, and to

Of course we know from our previous reflections that all of art, and not just drama, offers Balthasar a model for understanding the true nature of freedom, one that short-circuits the sterile debate between the Thomists and the Molinists. For he holds that any artist, no matter what the medium, is most free when, no longer trapped in a slum of infinite possibilities or caught up in the indecision of having to decide among a number of "neutral" possibilities for the execution of his work, he is finally "possessed" by the idea inspiring him and *surrenders* himself completely to its imperious and peremptory demands. Who would not account that freedom? Who would think this a degrading form of mental "indentured servitude"? It is true, artists sometimes talk as if inspiration *does* at times take on the aspect of their being expropriated and sold into slavery, but so too does the call of Christ to come follow him: it too takes on the aspect of being "owned" by him as his "slave" (1 Cor 9:16–23). Or as Balthasar says, "compulsion is the foundation of a future freedom" (*TH*, 55). But above all, it holds true preeminently of Christ himself, who stripped himself of his divinity and took on the form of a slave for our benefit (Phil 2:6–11). But this "being found in the form of a slave" is not merely a consequence of the incarnation but also has direct implications for how Christ acted *vis-à-vis* the Father and the Spirit through his earthly life:

> The Spirit who leads Jesus is the Spirit of the Father, the Spirit who as a divine person is free to "breathe where he will" (Jn 3:8) and who, precisely in that freedom, is given to the Son "without measure" (3:34). And it is hardly likely that the Son will obstruct the Spirit of the Father with any prior decisions of his own, or determine in what direction *his* inspiration shall blow, or sketch for himself the plan which the Spirit is to unfold for him. It would be better to compare him to an actor playing a part for the first time, receiving it by inspiration, as it were, scene-by-scene, word-by-word. The play does not exist in advance, but is conceived, produced and acted all in one. The incarnation is not the *n*th performance of a tragedy already lying in the archives of eternity. It is an event of total originality, as unique and untarnished as the eternally here-and-now birth of the Son from the Father. (*TH*, 33)

And it is in this event of total originality that the totally original event of creation is grounded and established. In the centuries-long debate about the reasons for the incarnation (was it decided by God only, so to speak,

---

know his own wretchedness without knowing God" (Pascal, *Pensées*, B 585–586 [Chevalier 598–599]).

ex post facto, that is, in view of Adam's sin? as the Thomists hold; or had God always determined to create *so that* his Son might become incarnate in creation? as the Scotists insist), we shall notice how much Balthasar leans to the Scotist thesis: "Just as there is a true sense in which sin caused the Cross, and Christ would not have come as Redeemer if the guilt of mankind had not called on him to make good in this way the pledge given at the creation, so in another and deeper sense the Cross is the *condition* for the possibility not only of sin but of existence and predestination itself" *(TH, 62).* In other words, the incarnation is the ground for the possibility not only of creation but is also the basis for all other dramas in world history. The reason Balthasar can so freely and so sovereignly survey the results and artifacts of world drama from the Greeks to Bertolt Brecht in the first volume of the Theodramatics and find them of such direct theological use is because he sees them as already grounded in the prior drama of salvation history established by God in his predestining love:

> Theologically speaking, the only thing that makes it possible to have history, in the deepest sense, within the space thus opened up is the fact that this space is an opening within the utter freedom of God. What could be more free, more completely unconditioned and gracious than the plan of the incarnation and its accomplishment in history? And that is why history is itself an area of freedom—the freedom of God giving space and scope to the freedom of man. Within this space man is free to make history happen. But since this space belongs to Christ, it is in no sense an empty space but one that is shaped and structured and completely conditioned by certain categories: the interior situations of his earthly existence. *Man cannot fall out of this space which is Christ's,* nor out of the structural form created by his life. *This* is that "prison" that Paul talks about in which God "has shut up all in their rebellion, only to include them all in his pardon" (Rm 9:32). . . . Each situation in the divine-human life is so infinitely rich, capable of such unlimited application, so full of meaning, that it generates an inexhaustible abundance of Christian situations. *(TH,* 66–67; my emphasis)

Meeting the unexpected thus becomes a kind of christological experience, an imitation of the kind of *ad hoc* "scripting" that is of the essence of Christian discipleship. And yet unlike Christ's life, our own life of meeting unexpected eventualities is nonetheless encompassed and surrounded by the prior drama of Christ, which determines the outcome of all secondary dramas (hence predestination) without infringing on the freedom of the actor to script his own life (hence free will). In his attempt to explain this double situation Balthasar invokes the play *Hamlet:*

> Man's freedom and choice are not infringed by the freedom of God, who for the sake of his own name and insulted honor (Ezek 36:22) provides what is done by man with a scale of reference on the divine plane, any more than the "play within the play" in *Hamlet* is deprived of its dramatic character because Hamlet and the court are watching and interpret it in terms of the events of their world. True, Hamlet is responsible for devising the play within the play and seeing that it is acted out, so that the reason and purpose of the minor tragedy lies in the major one. But this does not involve any violation of its own interior laws. (*TH*, 58)

One of the most striking aspects about the Theodramatics is that such a perspective seems never to have occurred to anyone before. And it is not as if the very terminology of theology has not always been deeply indebted to the theater, especially in the use of *persona* as applied to the individuations of the Trinity.[18] And yet one looks in vain for a systematic and thoroughgoing exploitation of these resources for theology. Perhaps the reason for this is the deep aversion of the early Church to the Roman spectacles of a Hellenistic culture that had become so decadent by the advent of Christianity, an attitude which seems to have persisted down to the early 20th century.[19]

This is itself a fascinating phenomenon, the explanation for which goes far in establishing the reasons for the neglect of this importance resource for theology and, paradoxically enough, in providing the opening for Balthasar's own particular exploitation of dramatic categories. For it seems

---

[18] As Balthasar is not slow to point out: "The derivation of *persons* from the Etruscan *phersu* is almost universally recognized today. *Phersu* evidently denoted a mask, or the wearer of a mask, at festivals in honor of P(h)ersephone. On the stage, *persona* could denote both the actor (the one who puts the mask on), or the role (hence generally the 'assignment') as well as the character being represented (Oedipus, for example), or by extension that which is essential, the personal character, that which carries meaning (the 'legal person'), or simply 'this particular one'" ("On the Concept of Person," *Communio* 13/1 (1986): 20).

[19] The 1917 Code of Canon Law (§ 140) still said: "Spectaculis, choreis et pompis quae eos dedecent, vel quibus clericos interesse scandalo sit, praesertim in publicis theatris, ne intersint." In the Synodal Statues of the Archdiocese of Paris (1902) priests are enjoined as follows: "Under pain of suspension we forbid all priests and ordained ecclesiastical persons to attend performances in public theaters, operas, balls, cabarets or at any other secular function where the presence of a cleric could give rise to scandal." And as late as 1702 the Archbishop of Toulouse forbade confessors, under threat of suspension, to absolve those who had attended the theater. These and other details of ecclesiastical opposition to the theater may be found in *TD* 1, 89–112, a history Balthasar seems to feel it necessary to rehearse before deflecting it with his own richly theatrical approach.

that there is much to be learned not just from the phenomenon of the theater itself but also from the near universal antipathy to it up until recent times, an antipathy that, as one shrewd commentator has noted, is embedded even in some of our most ordinary expressions and turns of phrase: "With infrequent exceptions, terms borrowed from the theater—*theatrical, operatic, melodramatic, stagy,* etc.—tend to be hostile or belittling. And so do a wide range of expressions drawn from theatrical activity expressly to convey disapproval: *acting, play-acting, playing up to, putting on an act, putting on a performance, making a scene, making a spectacle of oneself, playing to the gallery,* and so forth. . . . [These expressions] embody, in current idioms, the vestiges of a prejudice against the theater that goes back as far in European history as the theater itself can be traced."[20]

Behind this odd linguistic relic of past antipathy, there no doubt lurks a real anxiety, one that emerges clearly enough when one reads the criticisms of theater from Plato to, oddly enough, Bertolt Brecht (himself a playwright!): the fear of the successful liar. For what the very institution of the theater denotes is that one can adopt a role quite different from one's own identity and so convince the spectators in the audience that they quickly forget that they are not watching their neighbor but Agamemnon, or Hecuba, or Philoctetes. But if it can work on stage, why not in real life as well? Who can say what our neighbors are really like? Who is not really just "putting on an act" or just "playing a role" in everyday life as well? This anxiety might lurk underneath all the time, but theater's very existence presupposes this subtle art of lying and thus only serves to remind us of how fragile our identities are to begin with.

This leads Balthasar into his own analysis of the tension and interplay between *role* and *mission* (the subject of the last section of *TD* 1), and it is the transition from the first to the second that constitutes for Balthasar that movement whereby the individual is directly and consciously inserted into the divine drama of salvation that culminated in Christ but which continues on to the end of time. Now "role" is primarily a social function: it is what one does in and for society and is the "face" and identity one projects before others. But as the very institution of the theater indicates, roles can be adopted at will and hover over the person's real sense of self in ways that will always be disjunctive, leading to what the sociologist Peter Berger (building on the work of Erving Goffman) calls "role-

---

[20] Jonas Barish, *The Anti-Theatrical Prejudice* (Berkeley: University of California Press, 1981), 1–2. And note how the same does not apply to the other arts: "Most epithets derived from the arts are laudatory when applied to the other arts, or to life. If one describes a landscape as 'poetic,' or a man's struggle with adversity as 'epic,' or a woman's beauty as 'lyric,' one is using terms of praise. . . . Similarly, terms like *musical, symphonic, graphic, sculptural* are nearly always eulogistic" (1).

distancing," that is, the playing of a role without really meaning it and with an ulterior purpose, "where the actor has established an inner distance between his consciousness and his role-playing."[21]

Now it will be Balthasar's point in the Theodramatics that the dilemma posed by role-distance can only be resolved christologically. Ethical resolution is not enough, for duty is still a constraint that acts on the self, and the freedom of the actor mostly consists in playing his part well or sullenly. This is because, to use Heideggerian language, we are all *thrown* into existence. The biggest constraint on our freedom is that none of us has chosen to be born.[22] The pre-given constraints of the roles we are forced to play are but expressions and consequences of a prior constraint of existence itself. It is the thesis of the Theodramatics that "only in Jesus Christ does it become clear how profoundly this definitive 'I'-name signifies vocation, mission. In him the 'I' and the role become uniquely and ineffably one in the reality of his mission, far beyond anything attainable by earthly means" (*TD* 1, 645–646). Because the universe was created through the Logos and because that Logos, in the eternally decreed counsels of the Trinity, "volunteered" to become flesh and take on human form, the world drama of human thrownness has been radically altered; indeed it has been turned inside out:

> By and large the actor's nature and person do not coincide with the role he has to play, and this is true not only of the stage play that, on the basis of an inborn instinct, human beings creatively set forth in image and speech, but also of the *theatrum mundi* itself. In the play that takes place on the world stage, the author, director, and producer is—in an absolute sense—God himself. True, he allows [human] freedom to act in its own part according to its nature—and this is the greatest mystery of creation and of God's direct creative power—yet ultimately the play he plays is his own. In this play there can be a tragic or comic dichotomy between the actor and the role; and this produces the comedies and tragedies of world history—and its farces too, of which we today are both spectators and actors, as we have always been. Only in the drama of the God-Man do we find identity between the sublime actor and the role he has to play.[23]

---

[21] Peter L. Berger, *Invitation to Sociology: A Humanist Perspective* (New York: Doubleday/Anchor), 135, adducing the works of Erving Goffman, *Asylums* (Garden City, NY: Doubleday/Anchor, 1961) and *The Presentation of Self in Everyday Life* (Garden City, NY: Doubleday/Anchor, 1959).

[22] Martin Heidegger, *Being and Time*, tr. John Macquarrie & Edward Robinson (New York: Harper & Row, 1962), Section 38 ("Falling and Thrownness"), 219–224.

[23] *TD* 1, 646, citing Theodor Haecker, *Was ist der Mensch?* (Leipzig: Hegner, 1934), 128–129.

And by virtue of the grace of the continuation of that drama after Christ in the mission of the Church, the individual has the chance of being inserted into that same drama. Now how that can take place will be reserved for the chapter on ecclesiology (Chapter 10), after we have seen what the action is on God's part that constitutes this drama (Chapter 9), but we can at least say, by anticipation, that it takes place through the mediating action of the Holy Spirit: "Since the Spirit who mediates between God and the incarnate Son prevents any 'heteronomy,' the same Spirit, given to men to enable them to be and to act in a God-ward manner, can close the tragic breach between person and role in mission."[24]

Although, as we said, the way this can be realized will only become clear as the "plot" progresses, Balthasar does insist that this perspective can answer the most deeply felt needs of contemporary theology, which puts so much emphasis on the "event" character of revelation, on orthopraxis and committed action, and salvation history, while still preserving the overarching initiative to God and supplementing these current trends in theology (surveyed in *TD* 1, 25–50) with some needed correctives. But what is most crucial at this juncture of his presentation is to realize how the inherently dramatic situation of human existence (expressed so often in the institution of theater itself) does not in and of itself lead to a theodramatics but must itself *await* the answer of revelation—and this insight is of crucial methodological importance for Balthasar's undertaking:

> The "theodramatics" which we would like to unfold after having concluded the primarily literary prolegomena . . . is a "theological" undertaking. This means that it considers the dramatic character of existence in the light of biblical revelation: therefore, that we have already been thinking *from* this perspective and not just *upon* it. This is made equally noticeable in the way we will develop a view of God, world and man arising not primarily from human self-understanding, but rather from the drama with the world and man already staged by God, one in which we already find ourselves co-actors. This horizon will prove itself to be the widest possible (and not the more restrictive) one if it can surpass and harmonize within itself all the possible self-definitions of man.[25]

---

[24] *TD* 1, 646. And of course it will be an inherently ecclesial encounter that the Spirit will effect: "The call of the individual Christian always takes place within the context of the community of those who are in Christ, that is, in the Church, [and so] the individual cannot in any way reflect upon himself—in the sense of *Gnothi seauton*—without encountering the Church and his fellowship in her with others" (647).

[25] *TD* 2, 9. And this of course will not be primarily a theoretical harmonization but a practical one: "One final point: in a theodramatics, what is at stake is not primarily looking

"Already staged by God." A drama in which "we already find ourselves co-actors." Here, in dramatic terminology, lurks the same issue of predestination and free will that has so exercised theology almost from its inception. For "God does not play the world drama all on his own; he makes room for man to join in the acting" (*TD* 2, 91). But how? It is well enough to say that theo-drama depends on God's initiative and that we already find ourselves in that drama. But that still leaves the connection between the two unclarified: "It is not enough for God to involve himself with the world and with man. If there is to be an integrated interplay, man too must involve himself with God's drama. In principle, he already has 'access' to it, for God has opened up the play to him, but he must go on freely to accept this fact and act on it. This is the overall situation of theological hermeneutics" (ibid.).

Revelation, then, posits two freedoms, finite and infinite freedom. Admittedly, philosophical reasoning, operating solely from its own terms, will continue to take scandal at the paradoxes of what revelation insists is in fact the case—no matter how difficult their theoretical resolution might be. Now Balthasar does not deny to reason her office of trying to clarify this paradox of finite and infinite freedom and in fact insists, in a programmatic passage, "that theology should take seriously and cherish the explicit or implicit philosophy that man employs when thinking about the meaning of the world and should pursue its own reflection upon the biblical revelation in association with this mediating philosophical reflection."[26] The only snag that hits this procedure is when philosophical reasoning is allowed to dissolve the paradox when the explanatory going gets too rough; for the paradox is primary and it establishes the terms within which all explanations must unfold: "[God] is the One responsible for the play, and yet he is not responsible when man, in freedom, acts inappropriately; all the same, he stands by his original responsibility" (*TD* 2, 195).

It is of course possible to assert the inherent incompatibility of these juxtapositions and assert, with the philosophers, the incoherence of maintaining divine and human freedom at the same time.[27] But Balthasar insists

---

on and judging, but rather playing and being able to play" (*TD* 2, 13; translation altered). This is why the saints will prove so determinative for his thought: "The closer someone comes to this identity [of role and mission], the more perfectly does he play his part. In other words, the saints are the authentic interpreters of theo-drama. Their knowledge, lived out in dramatic existence, must be regarded as setting a standard of interpretation not only for the life-drama of individuals but ultimately for the 'history of freedom' of all the nations and of all mankind" (*TD* 2, 14).

[26] *TD* 2, 192; this whole passage is italicized in the original to stress its manifesto status.

[27] The philosopher Anthony Kenny claims that he lost his faith in God by crashing on the reefs of this problem: "If God is to have infallible knowledge of future human actions, then determinism must be true. If God is to escape responsibility for human wickedness, then determinism must be false. Hence in the notion of a God who foresees all sins but is the

that the "influences unleashed upon world history as a result of the intervention of infinite freedom are irreversible" (*TD* 2, 254), and that therefore the refusal, on whatever grounds (philosophical or religious), to admit the already existing polarity of finite and infinite freedoms will itself lead to severe contradictions in society, swinging from the outright determinism of behaviorism to the antinomian voluntarism of the cultural elite. Or in the religious sphere, between Islamic fatalism and New Age karma.[28] The career of philosophy and religion thus points both to the irresolvability of this problem and yet also to its continued presence in human nature: none of the answers seems to work in the long run, yet nothing in the problem itself seems to lead to its resolution. Only the revelation of our freedom in Christ, Balthasar insists, will answer the problem:

> This barrier, this lack of reciprocity [between finite and infinite freedom], is broken down in Jesus Christ, who "penetrates all things" in quite a different way from the wisdom of "Solomon" [that is, the Old Testament dispensation]. In his being "made to be sin" and bearing the "curse," infinite freedom shows its ultimate, most extreme capability for the first time: it can be itself even in the finitude that "loses itself"—a capability which neither Jews nor Greeks could have imagined. For them it remains a stumbling block and foolishness. Yet only here, where "God's love is poured into our hearts by the Holy Spirit which has been given to us," is finite freedom driven out of its last refuge and set on the path toward infinite freedom; thus the abyss that has opened up in the Christian *factum* is clearly visible to post-Christian reflection. (*TD* 2, 244–245)

It is the great principle of Balthasar's entire Theodramatics that "the creation of finite freedom by infinite freedom is the starting point of all theo-drama" (*TD* 2, 271), but the antinomies that inevitably result from their juxtaposition can only be resolved by the "wondrous exchange" that took place when Jesus Christ was "made into sin" for our sake—the central moment in that theo-drama. This gets us close to the issue of the "plot" of the theo-drama, the subject of the next chapter, but we can at least point out, if only by anticipation, that once more Balthasar leans toward the Scotist view of the incarnation: that God had always created the world in view of the incarnation (that is, *so that* it might be a home

---

author of none, there lurks a contradiction" (Anthony Kenny, *The God of the Philosophers* [Oxford: Clarendon Press, 1979], 121).

[28] "In fact, in a Stoic or Islamic view of the world, this infinity can always be upheld, since finite freedom (that of the wise man) simply consists in making room for, or not opposing, the absolute law, or *logos*, or 'will,' which will take effect in any case" (*TD* 2, 190).

for the incarnate flesh of his Son), rather than the incarnation being (in the Thomist) view consequent on the sin of Adam.

This debate might seem the very height of academic speculation, but in fact a lot rides on it. For it will be Balthasar's point that the pastoral crux of either lassitude-and-pride or anxiety-and-despair in regard to the doctrine of predestination has come from allowing the tension between finite and infinite freedom to be debated on its own terms rather than *in view of its ultimate resolution in Christ*. In other words, unless we see how the antinomies of divine and human freedom are meant to culminate at that moment when Christ was "made into sin" and became a "curse" *for our sake,* we will forever be running aground on the dilemmas posed in the doctrine of predestination. For it is absolutely central to Balthasar's theology that, in his words, "statements about God's plan are *homogeneous* and universal. There is only one single plan, embracing everything—what precedes the eon of the world, the eon of the world and the end of time. . . . This plan always includes God's 'answer' to every word that may possibly be uttered by finite freedom" (*TD* 2, 277; author's emphasis).

Where theology went astray in this regard was *not* that it imported alien philosophical categories into Paul's statements in Scripture about this plan (Rm 8:28–39; Eph 1:3–10), for the challenge represented by Hellenistic philosophy had to be met.[29] The issue is really more subtle than that; it would be better, in Balthasar's opinion, to say that theologians have habitually forgotten that "logical truth cannot be abstracted from personal truthfulness" and that a rigid doctrine of (double) predestination arises from just such a disjunction. In his critique of this doctrine, I often keep thinking of the word "glare": it is almost as if, in Balthasar's view, Augustine and his followers were simply too blinded by the light of predestination, which only dawned with the revelation of the New Testament (*TD* 2, 243). And yet the New Testament was always dazzled by the light of God's plan as revealed in the events of Christ and not by some abstraction of itself:

> The point at which this lightning struck, the New Testament, is unacquainted with the problems that arose later. It does not speak of predestination as some neutral factor, as it were, to be taken into account but as a form of proclaiming the Good News,

---

[29] "It is foolish for theologians to reproach the Fathers and Scholastics with this and speak of an alienation and 'Hellenization' of the biblical view of God, . . . [for] in the Christian framework, the Platonic-Plotinian 'Good' and 'One' becomes the absolutely free (and thus personal) God who is under no compulsion, not even from his own nature, and who freely sends forth from himself the world of finite spirits, *created to be free*" (*TD* 2, 191; my emphasis).

with all the seriousness this implies. Nor, as yet, does the rising
sun of infinite freedom outshine and so obliterate the landscape
of finite freedom: it simply illuminates it. . . . We need to keep
ever before our eyes the way in which infinite freedom was
pleased to appear in the midst of finitude, if we are not to be
drawn into abstract (and hence falsely posed) speculative problems. (*TD* 2, 250–251)

Balthasar's answer to this is both simple and elaborate. Simply put, he
asserts, as we have seen, that "the creation of finite freedom by infinite
freedom is the starting point of all theo-drama" (*TD* 2, 271). In other
words, the refusal to posit finite freedom robs salvation history of its
point, which consistently holds open the possibility of salvation being
rejected. The elaborate answer is really the whole Theodramatics itself:
only as it is worked out in terms of the "plot" to come and the response
to that plot by those who encounter the Church's proclamation can we
really see how finite freedom has been established inside the infinite freedom of God. But this will always mean taking that plot on its own terms
and not introducing adventitious categories from philosophy that only
distort the drama that Scripture wishes to unfold. And so, we must now
turn to an examination of this plot, always aware that we will come to
know its explanatory power all the more, the more we insert ourselves in
its drama, a point noticed with his characteristic brilliance by C. S. Lewis:

Now the moment of prayer is for me . . . the awareness that this
"real world" and "real self" are very far from being rock-bottom
realities. I cannot, in the flesh, leave the stage, either to go behind
the scenes or to take my seat in the pit; but I can remember that
these regions exist. And I also remember that my apparent self—
this clown or hero or supernumerary—under his grease-paint is
a real person with an off-stage life. The dramatic person could
not tread the stage unless he concealed a real person. . . . And
in prayer this real I struggles to speak, for once, from his real
being, and to address, for once, not the other actors, but—what
shall I call Him? The Author, for He invented us all? The Pro-
ducer, for He controls all? Or the Audience, for He watches, and
will judge, the performance?[30]

---

[30] C. S. Lewis, *Letters to Malcolm*, 82–83.

· 9 ·

The Strife of Shadows:
Converging Darkness,
Exploding Light

I said to my soul, be still, and let the dark come upon you
Which shall be the darkness of God. As, in a theatre,
The lights are extinguished, for the scene to be changed.

... I said to my soul, be still, and wait without hope
For hope would be hope for the wrong thing; wait without love
For love would be love of the wrong thing; there is yet faith
But the faith and the love and the hope are all in the waiting.
Wait without thought, for you are not ready for thought:
So the darkness shall be the light, and the stillness the dancing.

T. S. Eliot
"East Coker," *The Four Quartets*

You must be ready to burn yourself in your own flame: how
could you become new, if you had not first become ashes?

Friedrich Nietzsche
Thus Spake Zarathustra

In a pleasing moment of self-deprecating humor, T. S. Eliot once said of his playwrighting: "I tried to keep in mind that in a play, from time to time, something should happen."[1] In a similar vein, we may say that in theo-drama something should also from time to time happen. Or more directly: it makes no sense to claim that theology can be transposed into dramatic terms unless at the core of the Christian proclamation is a Good News of something that *happened* between God and the human race. And

---

[1] T. S. Eliot, "Poetry and Drama," *On Poetry and Poets* (London: Faber and Faber, 1957), 85. "When the curtain rises, the audience is expecting, as it has a right to expect, that something is going to happen" (84).

so having first "set the stage," so to speak, between God and humanity as, mythologically, the juxtaposition of heaven and earth and, having analyzed, philosophically, the encounter of finite and infinite freedoms, Balthasar now sets forth in the concluding three volumes of the Theodramatics the "plot" of this divine play enacted by God for the redemption of the human race. Thus, in words drawn from Gregory Nazianzus, "our task now is to consider that problem, that part of Christian teaching, which is so often passed over in silence but which—for that very reason—I want to study with all the more eagerness. That precious and glorious divine Blood poured out for us: for what reason and to what end has such an extraordinary price been paid?"[2]

In answering this question Balthasar has reached the apex of his theological achievement, for I regard the last three volumes of the Theodramatics as the culmination and capstone of his work, where all the themes of his theology converge and are fused into a synthesis of remarkable creativity and originality, an achievement that makes him one of the great theological mind of the twentieth century. Here, more than anywhere, is where his work should be judged. But this is also the most difficult part of his work to summarize, not only because so many themes converge but also because of the way they are then, as it were, dramatically "compacted" by the descent of the dead Jesus into the realm of the dead and "reversed" by the victory of his resurrection. That is, through the density of this event, all of the previous themes of Balthasar's thought are not just intensified but also converted and upended in the "great reversal"[3] that took place between God and the dead man Jesus during the Triduum of Good Friday, Holy Saturday and Easter Sunday.

It all converges here, and to understand the implications of this great event of the Holy Triduum, one must first have mastered the terms used to describe it, which are primarily trinitarian and christological. Now the distinctions that the history of theology has generated in the past touching on the divinity and human of Jesus have always demanded a great deal of concentration and subtlety to master; and this is even more true of the trinitarian distinctions thrown up by that same history, for the Trinity is by definition more removed from our experience than is at least one term (the humanity of Jesus) in christological debate. But it all comes together here: trinitarian and christological themes all play essential roles in clarifying the Great Event of the Triduum and its saving significance. But if that were not challenge enough, in Balthasar's thought, these themes all get

---

[2] Gregory Nazianzus, *Oratio 45* (PG 36, 653A); cited in *MP*, 11.

[3] "Great reversal" is one possible translation of *admirabile commercium*, more usually translated as the "wondrous exchange" that took place between God and humanity in the death of Jesus, when the sin of the world was converted into forgiveness and the "day of salvation" dawned in human history.

transposed into dramatic terms, because, according to his interpretation, in the Triduum of Good Friday, Holy Saturday, and Easter Sunday, *something happens to God,* and this is why this part of the trilogy deserves the title *Theo-Drama* in every sense of the word, being both a subjective as well as objective prefix.

Now it is true that one must approach such a statement with considerable care and we shall not be surprised to learn that the drama that Balthasar is talking about must be analogically understood. But that makes his theology even more radical, for of course, in such analogies, the *analogatum* is even more true of God than it is of us! This of course does not lessen but heightens the difficulty of describing what exactly has happened that changed the relationship between God and the human race when Jesus died, descended and rose, so that Paul could say: "When you were dead in your sins God made you alive with Christ. . . . And having disarmed the powers and authorities, he made a public spectacle of them, triumphing over them by the cross" (Col 2:13–15).

Complicating the issue even further is the issue of *role.* Earlier we saw how Balthasar interprets the Christian life as a transition from a (socially determined) role to a (divinely bestowed) mission in the Church. But the events of the Passion all take place before the birth of the Church (to the extent that the Church may be said to be born on Pentecost Sunday), and so the human actors in this drama play their allotted *roles,* for the most part unconscious of how they are symbolizing all of salvation history.[4] Furthermore, this drama is "backgrounded," so to speak, by other hidden participants: the angels and demons, not to mention the numberless Jews and Gentiles who came before Christ and who meet him in their solidarity with him in the realm of the dead—they too are very much affected by the outcome of this enactment.

Describing so densely packed a drama—and one that moreover is shrouded over in darkness by revelation and whose presentation is thus necessarily based on extrapolation and mystical insights—is, it goes without saying, extremely difficult.[5] But it is possible to begin simply, and we shall do so. Jesus's life, we know from Part I of the Trilogy, forms a pattern, but like all historical patterns it must be perceived as a whole to be perceived rightly and that pattern is, as we saw, Claim/Death/Resurrec-

---

[4] Christ certainly calls certain individuals out of their allotted roles (such as fisherman, tax collector, etc.) to take on a mission as one sent by him; but the transition from role to mission was nearly always undermined by the disciples' lack of comprehension (an important theme throughout the Gospels). And so in the Passion, they act much more out of their *roles* (this is especially true of Peter, who is the model of the transition from role to mission under the influence and impact of Pentecost).

[5] Note that as the volumes of the Theodramatics progress, the citations from the writings of Adrienne von Speyr grow more frequent (in the last volume she is cited, it seems, on almost every page).

tion. But take that same triadic pattern and conceive it in dramatic terms: now the claim sweeps Jesus and his fate into an enveloping tunnel from which he will emerge having burst through the walls of death, opening an aperture that leaves, *in perceivable history,* only the traces of a crater.[6] It is, in other words, one thing to say that the claim Jesus made (implicitly or explicitly) during his earthly life led to his death and was only verified by the Resurrection (this was the emphasis of the Aesthetics); but this same insight takes on a much stronger dramatic force when it is explained how this verification alters God's entire relationship with the world.

Let us begin our consideration of these issues with Peter's first sermon before his fellow Jews on Pentecost Sunday,[7] a mere ten days after Jesus left them[8] and the first day of their reception of the Holy Spirit, who had, as promised (Jn 16:12–16), clarified for them (in retrospect!) the redemptive pattern that was the meaning of his life, death and resurrection. The relevant verses for our consideration are the following:

> Men of Israel, listen to this: Jesus of Nazareth was a man accredited by God to you by miracles, wonders and signs, which God

---

[6] *Einschlagstrichter* in German means both "enveloping tunnel" and "meteor crater." The ambiguity of the German word is fascinating and conjures up, in my mind at least, the image of the Big Bang, with density (through the funnel) followed by the explosive power of growth (the impact of the crater). And the task of describing this great initiating event of the Church is a bit like trying to describe the earliest universe; as one physicist said of the opening line in Genesis ("In the beginning God created the heavens and the earth"): "But no one was there to see it" (Steven Weinberg, *The First Three Minutes* [London: Fontana, 1978]). But of course the same holds true of the Big Bang too. But it happened anyway. And we are there merely to witness its effects, and indeed exist because of them. Balthasar's logic of argument is similarly *a posteriori.*

[7] My analysis here follows that of C. H. Dodd (*The Apostolic Preaching and its Development* [New York: Harper & Row, 1951) and Martin Hengel (*Acts and the History of Earliest Christianity* [Philadelphia: Fortress, 1980]).

[8] Of course the specification of the number of days between Easter and the Ascension and between the Ascension and Pentecost was fairly vague in the early Church, including in Acts (see Acts 13:31); but there is always a certain "fusion of mysteries" into a single pattern that should be kept in mind when dealing with the totality of events from Good Friday to Pentecost Sunday; see in this regard: Joseph A. Fitzmyer, S. J., "The Ascension of Christ and Pentecost," *Theological Studies* 45/3 (1984): 409–440, esp. 418–419. In any event, our concentration shall be on the total *Gestalt* portrayed in Peter's first speech, using Dodd's exegesis: "By an ingenious combination of the evidence of the speeches in Acts, 1 Peter, the letters of Paul and other parts of the New Testament, Dodd reaches the conclusion that the earliest preaching was a declaration of the mighty deeds of God in Jesus Christ, a little reminiscent of the recital of the mighty acts of God in relation to Israel, such as we find in Joshua 24 and the historical Psalms. The burden of it all is 'This is what God has *done*'— and on this follows the challenge: 'Therefore, this must *you do*.' This is the *kerygma*, the task of the herald—not to teach or to edify, but to bring *news*" (Stephen Neill and Tom Wright, *The Interpretation of the New Testament: 1861–1986* [New York: Oxford University Press, 1988], 272–273). For Balthasar's own theological interpretation of Pentecost and the Forty Days, see "The Absences of Jesus," *NE,* 46–60.

did among you through him, as you yourselves know. This man was handed over to you by God's set purpose and foreknowledge, and you—with the help of wicked men—put him to death by nailing him to the cross. But God raised him from the dead, freeing him from the torments of Hades [ᾅδου], because it was impossible for death to keep its hold on him. . . .God has raised this Jesus to life, and we are all witnesses of the fact. Exalted to the right hand of God, he has received from the Father the promised Holy Spirit and has poured out what you now see and hear. . . .Therefore, let all Israel be assured of this: God has made this Jesus, whom you crucified, both Lord and Christ. (Acts 2:22-24, 32-33, 36).[9]

To understand Balthasar's theology of the Triduum we must keep several exegetical points about this passage in mind: 1) Jesus is entirely the passive object of actions which *God* does through him, very much including the resurrection and exaltation ("God raised this Jesus to life"); 2) Jesus entered the realm of the dead at his own death and had, while there, *to be freed* (and, according to the variant reading, while there he seems to have suffered the torments of Hades, because that is what God freed him from); 3) but he was set free from this realm of the dead not out of some arbitrary largesse on the part of God but because "it was impossible for death to keep its hold on him"; 4) upon being exalted to God's right hand, he *received* the Holy Spirit, though he is also the Spirit's disburser ("Exalted to the right hand of God, he has received from the Father the promised Holy Spirit and has poured out what you now see and hear"); and 5) *therefore* God *made* Jesus "Lord" and "Christ."[10]

There is much more to be made of this passage exegetically than these brief observations could bring out, but they suffice to begin our entry into Balthasar's theology of the Triduum. Working backwards from these insights, we note how Peter, a tenacious upholder of Jewish tradition in the early Church, so readily and so unselfconsciously reverts to what we

---

[9] The reading "Hades" is from the Western text-tradition, with "death" being the more likely reading; see Bruce Metzger, *A Textual Commentary on Greek New Testament* (London/New York: United Bible Societies, 1971), p. 298. The editors speculate that the variant crept in by assimilation to the use of ᾅδην in verses 27 and 31. Because these are the verses that for reasons of space I have omitted here, I have chosen the variant reading for illustrative purposes only and not as a personal assertion of the author's original intent. But I think in the total framework of the speech, Balthasar has drawn out legitimate implications.

[10] "Lord," of course, is virtually a divine title in this context as it was the translation of choice by the Septuagint Greek Bible for the divine Hebrew name for God, YHWH; and "Christ" is simply the Greek passive participle for "anointed," a Hebrew term denoting a royal figure set apart for God's liberating purposes (see Is 45:1–5).

now recognize as trinitarian language in trying to explain what Jesus's current heavenly role is: both Lord (= divine) *and* Christ (= anointed human). Moreover, by virtue of the exaltation, Christ receives a Spirit which he then bestows on the Church, the very first day of which we are now witnessing. And we note that, while it was very much *God* who raised (an entirely passively described) Jesus from the dead, there was in his identity that about him which made it impossible for death to keep its hold on him. And finally, this all happened at God's "direction," we might say, or to use biblical language, by God's predestining foreknowledge, with the humans involved playing out their script entirely unaware of the direction they are receiving or the significance of the events they are precipitating.

I do not want to overstress the Big Bang analogies, but what we find in this passage is the first distillation, in the witness of the New Testament, of the immense reversal in God's relation to the world, a reversal of relations the explosion of which led to the birth of the Church and to the proclamation of the Good News of that reversal to the ends of the earth. And in leaving its traces here in the earliest moments of the Church's preaching, we discover, as it were, all of the elements, however embryonic they might be, of the Christian *kerygma* itself: here we find at least the first beginning signs of an *interlocked kerygmatic structure* with its various intertwining factors of Trinity, descent into Hell, and Jesus's pre-existence with God as the Son of God.[11]

Balthasar's task as a theologian has been to a great extent devoted to unfolding the implications of this initiating moment. It is of course hard to talk about one feature without keeping in mind the others (which is why we began with Acts 2, as it neatly captures all of the crucial features of the kerygma); but in the rest of the chapter we shall have to take each component of the Christian message and treat it somewhat in isolation, a method Balthasar, too, is forced to adopt, but always with due warnings of the danger it represents of distorting the whole *Gestalt* in favor of one of its aspects. We shall first begin with christology:

---

[11] I say this not so much on the basis of the Psalm Peter quotes ("The Lord said to my Lord") which Peter takes to be David speaking of Christ, but of the line in verse 24 that it was impossible for death to reign over him, which could not be true of any normally constituted human being. Balthasar's Christology, as developed in these volumes of the Theodramatics currently under consideration, is heavily reliant on the historical research of Martin Hengel, whom he frequently cites, and so perhaps it would be well to note how quickly Hengel sees New Testament christology developing: "The christological development from Jesus up to Paul took place within about eighteen years, a short space of time for such an intellectual process. In essentials *more happened in christology within these few years than in the whole subsequent seven hundred years of church history*" (Martin Hengel, "Christology and New Testament Chronology," *Between Jesus to Paul: Studies in the Earliest History of Christianity,* tr. John Bowden [Philadelphia: Fortress, 1983], 39–40; author's emphasis).

There can be no doubt that the faith of the first Christians applied ideas, concepts, titles, in varying degrees, to the phenomenon of Jesus in order to communicate it to themselves and others. The decisive question, therefore, is: Has this process articulated an original "form," identified in its significance and revealed its true outlines—or has it taken what was originally a relatively form-less core and clothed it in successive garments, which ultimately yield a plausible "form"?[12]

Balthasar feels confident in being able to answer this central question with the first alternative, that the subsequent narrative written with the benefit of hindsight, has not distorted the original events, and he claims this on both historical-critical and theological grounds. It would burst the bonds of this chapter to go into his historical-critical reasons, but suffice to say it depends on a survey of history-of-Jesus scholarship culminating in the studies of Hengel.[13] The theological reasons, of course, are more crucial to his argument and these we need to look at more closely. For what one finds embedded in all strata of the dogmatic "overlay" (that is, the application to Jesus of such titles as "Lord" and "Christ" by virtue of his resurrection) is the *pro nobis:* the proclamation that Jesus is who he is because of what he has done in his redemptive work *for us.* And then, Balthasar recommends, we should take this kerygmatic insight and apply it to the exegetical results of Jesus's apocalyptic expectations of the imminent end of the world:

As for this imminent expectation itself, strange and unique, which seems to be expressed in apocalyptic terms and yet, as [has

---

[12] *TD* 3, 64. And of course it was the conclusion of many critics, especially in the 19th century but also in the first half of the 20th that the process distorted rather than explicated the historical Jesus: "By stripping away, in the text, the levels of interpretation from the original event, [Wrede] arrived at the conclusion 'that Jesus did not, in fact, claim to be the Messiah.' This assertion is identical with that of the young Bultmann that 'the life of Jesus was unmessianic'" (*TD* 3, 67).

[13] "It is easy, from the standpoint of exegesis in its search for the historical Jesus, to regard the interpretations springing from the primitive Church's reflections—such as we find even before Paul, in him and in those who come after him, right up to John—as a dogmatic 'overlay.' But such interpretations emerged so astonishingly early that, according to Hengel, within a very few years all the fundamental decisions had been made that were to result in the christology of the great Ecumenical Councils. Anyone who regards this dogmatic 'overlay' in the New Testament as something superimposed on Jesus' supposedly straightforward human life (albeit a prophetic or super-prophetic life), citing preexisting Jewish or Hellenistic materials used in it, must ask himself whether, once the said overlay has been removed, he can still present a plausible picture of the historical Jesus. As we have shown, this is difficult and indeed impossible, because, particularly where apocalyptic terms and expressions are used, the eschatological question will not allow a rounded picture of the historical Jesus to

been] admitted, cannot be fitted in with the usual apocalyptic expectation, might it not best be explained by what post-Easter dogmatic reflection drew from it? Let us put it even more clearly. Might not Jesus' consciousness of his mission have been that he had to abolish the world's estrangement from God in its entirety—that is, to the very end—or, in Pauline and Johannine terms, deal with the sin of the whole world? In that case, *after* his earthly mission, the decisive and (humanly speaking) immeasurable part was still to come. . . . The awareness that his life is moving toward a "baptism," toward that "cup" he will have to drink . . . means that his life cannot proceed along "wisdom" lines but must follow an "apocalyptic" rhythm. His life is running toward a [crescendo] that, as man, he will only be able to survive by surrendering control of his own actions to be determined totally by the Father's will. For this surrendering of control to the Father is essential if, in this hour, the single, indivisible event that dogmatics requires is to take place: he must bear the totality of the world's sin (Jn 1:29), being "made into sin" (2 Cor 5:21), becoming "a curse" (Gal 3:13) by the all-disposing will of the Father. (*TD* 3, 110)

This now explains the immense stress that Balthasar puts on Jesus's passivity in the events of the Passion (note again how Jesus is always the recipient of actions being done to or through him in Peter's first sermon in Acts 2): his mission demanded more than could be encompassed in his earthly life.[14] And for that he was "punished," as it were. And this in two

---

be drawn. There is a residue, concerning Jesus' expectation of the imminent end, which refuses to be dissolved" (*TD* 3, 109).

[14] Perhaps the best expression of this overburdening mission is located in a relatively unknown essay of Balthasar's: "This messianic work with the Chosen People, which was not to be cut short in favor of a universal mission to all people, was not big enough for one life, especially if it was only taken up at the age of 30. But, one must ask, was it feasible at all? . . . It is unthinkable that Jesus should ever have entertained the illusion that the old Israel, which had over a thousand years of tragic history behind it and which had in any case been scattered to the winds for half a millennium and had never completely returned, could become the new Israel of God without a miracle, the miracle of an eschatological transformation. . . . [For] nothing that a mortal man can do—even if he were the Messiah—can overcome sin, death, and the Prince of this world. If this is to happen, some other work must be set in motion, beyond the bounds of what can actively be 'done.' One cannot 'do' this work—for it is beyond one's own strength—one can only suffer it. The rejection which Jesus encountered, which he actually brought out and polarized through carrying out his mission, was not something he could accept himself: it had to be laid upon him as an imposition, totally exceeding human capacity" ("The Work and Suffering of Jesus," *Faith in Christ and the Worship of Christ: New Approaches to Devotion to Christ*, ed. Leo Scheffczyk, tr. Graham Harrison [San Francisco: Ignatius Press, 1982], 17).

senses: first of all, he was punished for the claim he made, a punishment that was historically unavoidable, given the setting of first-century Judaism in Roman-occupied Palestine. But above all, he was "punished" because it was the essential moment of his mission to take on the sins of the world, to be our representative, to assume in our stead what was rightly our destiny: meaning not just death as a natural termination to organic life but death as banishment from the presence of God (which is the real meaning of hell). And this he assumed in our place. And he did so truly in *our* place:

> Jesus was truly dead, because he really became a man as we are, a son of Adam, and therefore, despite what one can sometimes read in certain theological works, he did not use the so-called "brief" time of his death for all manner of "activities" in the world beyond. In the same way that, upon earth, he was in solidarity with the living, so, in the tomb, he is in solidarity with the dead. . . . Each human being lies in his own tomb. And with this condition Jesus is in complete solidarity.[15]

This is absolutely crucial to Balthasar's thought and perhaps constitutes his single greatest innovation to the tradition.[16] For the implication of the Creeds, the iconography and the pious imagination of the past held that the verb "descended" when applied to Christ ("he descended into Hell": Apostle's Creed) was an intransitive verb in the *active* voice (as in "he descended the staircase"); whereas Balthasar insists that it must be understood passively (as in "the ball descended the staircase"). In other words, Jesus is not consciously going down some prison steps to claim what rightfully now belongs to him: the "just ones" of the Old Testament who are being "unlawfully" held by their jailer Satan. This is how the Descent into Hell is most often portrayed in the icons of the Eastern Churches, with Christ already radiant in his risen splendor lighting up the darkness of the dungeon. The radicality of Balthasar's approach is that Christ's

---

[15] *MP*, 148–149. I shall be citing this work throughout the chapter because I regard it as an integral part of the Theodramatics even though it began as an encyclopedia article for a reference work of dogmatics. In fact the editors had at first commissioned the article from someone else who had to drop out of the project, and so Balthasar was asked to fill in at the last minute. Despite this occasional provenance, however, it is the single best place to find Balthasar's fully developed theology of Holy Saturday (though in the *Theologik* he mentions how this thought has moved beyond some of his positions in *MP*: see *TL* 2, 315).

[16] Wilhelm Maas is not exaggerating in the least when he says: "Für Balthasar ist die Lehre vom Descensus nicht *ein* dogmatisches Lehrstück neben anderen, sondern es ist die Mitte und eigentlich der ganze wesentliche Inhalt seiner Theologie. Balthasar ist *der* Descensus-Theologe schlechthin" (Wilhelm Maas, *Gott und Hölle: Studien zum Descensus Christi* [Einsiedeln: Johannes Verlag, 1979], 245).

descent is, must be, totally passive, the descent of the dead to the dead. And this is what makes the drama of human history genuinely *theo-dramatic*:

> What is at stake in theodrama is this: that God acts so as to take upon himself and make his own the tragedy of human existence even to the depths of that abyss, and thus conquering it without at the same time robbing it of its sting [*verharmlosen*] or going around this tragedy externally, overtaking it by avoiding it. "No other sign will be given this generation than the sign of Jonah. For as Jonah was three days and three nights in the belly of a huge fish, so the Son of Man will be three days and three nights in the heart of the earth. . . . And now one greater than Jonah is here" (Mt 12:39–41). Jonah, however, was merely swallowed and spat out. But Jesus descends into hell and comes back again. So the whole question is this: is there some standpoint from which we can observe and report on this dramatic sequence of events? (*TD* 2, 54)

Well, "observe," no. "Report," no. But extrapolate from the logic of the events, yes.[17] This is roughly equivalent to what the Church has done in the past in developing her understanding of the role of Mary in the Church: while the New Testament is generally quite reserved about her role, with her appearing only at certain crucial moments, and even then in narratives that never concentrate on her personality or "subjectivity" as such; nonetheless the moments when she does appear are crucial, and building from the fact of her motherhood and her essential role in assenting to the incarnation, the Church in a long and developing tradition drew out new ways of extrapolating from these moments and adding a deeper understanding of Mary's role. Something similar, I hold, is true of Balthasar theology of Holy Saturday, because here too the New Testament is quite reserved:

> The more eloquently the Gospels describe the passion of the living Jesus, his death and burial, the more striking is their en-

---

[17] It is admittedly difficult to know how to fit the mystical experiences of Holy Saturday undergone by Adrienne von Speyr into this framework. What further access do they give to theologians that is not otherwise available to them from revelation and later reflection on it? I myself am cautious about attributing any direct theological content (in the sense of new revelation) to her experiences, as perhaps even she herself would agree. For she says quite explicitly that even Mary at the foot of the Cross had no access to the realm of the dead at the death of her Son: "Aber jetzt steht die Mutter bei einem Ort, der in ihrem Jawort nicht inbegriffen war" (Adrienne von Speyr, *Kreuz und Hölle*, 1. Teil: *Die Passionen* [Einsiedeln: Johannes Verlag, Privatdruck, 1966], 141). We shall need to take up this issue once more in the final chapter of this book.

tirely understandable silence when it comes to the time in between his deposition in the grave and the event of the Resurrection. We are grateful to them for this. Death calls for this silence, not only by reason of the mourning of the survivors but, even more, because of what we know of the dwelling and condition of the dead. When we ascribe to the dead [in myths and in our own imaginations] forms of activity that are new and yet prolong those of earth, we are not simply expressing our perplexity at what goes on across the Other Side of death. We are also defending ourselves against a stronger conviction which tells us what we already well realize, that death is *not* a partial event. It is an event that affects the whole person, though not necessarily to the point of entirely obliterating all traces of the human subject. It is a situation that signifies in the first place the abandonment of all spontaneous activity and so a passivity, a state in which, perhaps, the vital activity now brought to its end is mysteriously summed up.[18]

But it is important to realize that the New Testament is not totally silent on the issue, and, as with Mary, there is enough of a tradition to build on, legitimately prompting theologians to ask what the Apostles' Creed

---

[18] *MP*, 148. Perhaps this passage can answer Raymond Brown's reservations as an exegete to this approach: "No theologian has been more interested in the import of what happened on this Holy Saturday than Hans Urs von Balthasar; yet his reflections (guided by the mystical experiences of Adrienne von Speyr) have not been centered on what the canonical evangelists assign to this day" (*The Death of the Messiah* [New York: Doubleday, 1994] 2:1286–1287). Brown is certainly right about the influence of von Speyr, whose views on death are unsparingly unsentimental: "Death is the end, and as such it is a mystery. It is not the kind of end which is succeeded by a continuation, a reconstruction. It is simply *the end*, a complete cessation. God has totally changed man's relation to his life and environment, but he has not told him what he will do with him when life comes to and end. Yet man has some experience of this end: he experiences the death of his follow men, he sees them being lowered into the earth, he knows that their bodies decompose, that all human contact with them is broken off. No love, no remembrance is able to call them back. Beyond death, coming into view, as it were, in the gap that death leaves, there is only— God. God, who was before this human being existed, who created and accompanied him, who survives his death, just as he will survive my death and the death of every man and of all generations. And what God will do with his deceased creatures is a mystery. . . . The person who wants to come to God in a relationship of faith does not know what God will do with him. The only certainty he has is that this relationship cannot exempt him from the certainty of death and the uncertainty of the hour. He has no knowledge about possibilities wherein his spirit may have to remain in contact with his flesh; nor does he know whether, when his body disintegrates and returns to its constituent elements, the soul will be able to maintain its relationship with God or be sustained in it by God. Both are equally inconceivable to him" (Adrienne von Speyr, *The Mystery of Death*, tr. Graham Harrison [San Francisco: Ignatius Press, 1988], 11–13).

means when it says "And He descended into Hell." One of the great oddities of this tradition, however, is that fact that nearly all the New Testament allusions (one would scarcely want to call them explicit dogmatic statements) to the Descensus into "Hades" occur in the Petrine tradition (Acts 2:17–36; 1 Pet 3:18–22; 4:5–6; see also 2 Pet 2:4–10; 3:3–13). Paul of course openly confesses that Christ "was buried" (1 Cor 15:4a), which would be a meaningless confession if that did not imply joining the dead in the realm of the dead, but when he uses the verb "descends" of Christ it is not entirely clear whether he is referring to the descent of the Kenosis or to a further descent after his death, as when he says parenthetically of Christ's ascension: "What does 'he ascended' mean except that he also descended to the lower regions of the earth?" (Eph 4:9).[19] Nonetheless, there is still a clear Pauline warrant for this doctrine too when he exhorts the Christians in Rome to attend to the direct presence of God in their souls: "Do not say in your heart, 'Who will ascend into heaven?' (that is, to bring Christ down), or 'Who will descend into the depths?' (that is, to bring Christ up from the dead). But what does it say? 'The word is near you; it is in your mouth and in your heart'" (Rm 10:6–8).

Furthermore we know how central the message that Jesus really did die for our sins was to the New Testament because of how vigorously this fact had to be defended a generation later when Gnostics insisted that Jesus saved precisely by *not* being a man of flesh, and thus he was not subject to death. Ignatius of Antioch, together with the other sub-apostolic Fathers, firmly insisted that Jesus was fully human and thus fully subject to death, indeed to the degrading death on a cross.

So the Petrine tradition of a descent into Hades carries more theological implications that might at first seem apparent. This I think is most easily shown in the famous passage in 1 Peter: "For Christ died for our sins once for all, the righteous for the unrighteous, to bring you to God. He was put to death in the body but made alive by the Spirit, through whom he also went and preached to the spirits in prison, who disobeyed long ago . . . [He] has gone into heaven and is at God's right hand—with angels, authorities and powers in submission to him" (1 Pet 3:18–22).

Two points about this passage are noteworthy and will prove to have an immense influence on Balthasar's treatment of this mystery. Note first that Jesus is depicted as going to preach to spirits in prison who are explicitly described as having been disobedient in this life. Awaiting liberation, in other words, are the very spirits who failed to be liberated from the Flood because of their disobedience to God. And secondly we note

---

[19] For Balthasar's own exegesis of this passage, see *TD* IV, 232, with references to the literature.

that Jesus was able to "preach" to these disobedient spirits by the power of the Holy Spirit who had made him alive.

Now there is no question, I think, that, exegetically speaking, the author of this Letter means that Jesus first came back to life and *then* descended, in an active sense of that verb, to this dungeon of the dead and preached there (again actively). Thus the icons of a radiant Jesus resplendent in white robes going down and snatching up the sleeping just ones in the chamber of death have considerable scriptural warrant (which Balthasar would not wish to deny). But we are by an ineluctable necessity speaking mythologically here, and his own interpretation need not therefore necessarily conflict with this picture. But it must first be radicalized, and that Balthasar does by looking more closely at the role of the Spirit in this event, a role which can only be explained, he holds, if the entire event of the Triduum is seen as an inherently trinitarian event, a point best summarized in this pithy formulation of Aidan Nichols:

> Balthasar stresses Christ's solidarity with the dead, his passivity, his finding himself in a situation of total self-estrangement and alienation from the Father. For Balthasar, the Descent "solves" the problem of theodicy, by showing us the conditions on which God accepted our foreknown abuse of freedom: namely, his own plan to take to himself our self-damnation in Hell. It also demonstrates the costliness of our redemption: the divine Son underwent the experience of godlessness. Finally, it shows that the God revealed by the Redeemer is a Trinity. Only if the Spirit, as the *vinculum amoris* between the Father and the Son, can re-relate Father and Son in their estrangement in the Descent, can the unity of Revealed and Revealer be maintained. In this final humiliation of the *forma servi*, the glorious *forma Dei* shines forth via its lowest pitch of self-giving love.[20]

We have now come to the point where Balthasar's thought is at its most daring and speculative, where perhaps indeed many will feel left behind, where they feel his thought borders on the very speculative reverie he accuses the nominalists of indulging. How true these reservations are can perhaps emerge only from one's own encounter with his thought, but I think it should be said at the outset that, at least in my judgment, Balthasar is sticking strictly to the logic of redemption (in the Anselmian sense, of course) and is certainly breaking no more new ground theologically in the 20th century than Peter did in the 1st century, with his sudden and strange talk of Jesus being made "Lord" (!) and "Christ" and receiving from the

---

[20] Aidan Nichols, O.P., "Introduction," *MP*, 7.

"Father" the "Spirit," etc. Nothing can top *that* innovation. Balthasar's "innovations," if such they be, are merely the drawing out in a more radical way than has been done in the past of the implications of Peter's sermon on Pentecost Sunday.

But let us not deny Balthasar's astonishing leaps of imagination and theo-logic. And I mean "deny" in both senses: let us not deny him the right, which Origen too assumed, of every theologian to speculate on the truths of revelation and to draw out their implication. Nor should we deny the presence of these speculations *as* speculations: they are probes and forays into areas of Christian truth that not many venture to assay. But he has dared to leap into previously uncharted territory, and we wish both to grant him this speculative freedom and also the right of the Church to assimilate these speculations in her own good time. Private reflections and personal opinions of a theologian, especially one who bases his works so heavily on the graces of a mystic, take time.

The first issue I think that must be faced is that of tritheism. In Balthasar's discussion of the role of the Trinity in the events of the Triduum, most readers will no doubt often get the impression that there are three persons involved in the modern sense of the term: that is, centers of consciousness. And like these modern persons, the Persons of the Trinity will often seem to be at considerable odds with one another, with the Father "rejecting" the Son, the Son suffering the "loss" of the Father, and the Spirit, as their *vinculum amoris,* "reconciling" them.[21] Now how accurate this initial impression is will have to be left, I think, to the judgment of posterity. What is crucial for us at this moment to see is what led Balthasar to this language—essentially the same question as to what led Peter to invoke his own incipient trinitarian language (and let us not forget how shockingly "tritheistic" *his* language would have seemed at the time!). For trinitarian language arose in the Church's proclamation not to foist a new "doctrine" on the believing community, but solely to explain how and why the events of the death and resurrection of Jesus *were salvific.* And that is the same motivation that prompts Balthasar's own language.

It is of course easy to slip into unhelpful or even false formulations, ones that later generations will correct.[22] But the first task of the interpreter is

---

[21] Often when using such verbs, Balthasar will put them in quotation marks, helping both to mitigate their initial tritheistic impression and also to show that these words cannot be taken literally.

[22] We need only think of the Cappadocians' way of explaining how there could be three persons in one God. Consider, they said, three people: Peter, James, and John. Each of them is a particular individual but the three are all human beings: they share a common essence or substance of humanity. "This interpretation created an obvious difficulty. We would count Peter, [James,] and John as three human beings. Analogically, could we could the Father, Son, and Spirit as three Gods? Of course not, the Cappadocians replied. God is a

to look at the underlying intent, and only that can explain what Balthasar is about in his explanation of what the Trinity "does" as Jesus descends into hell. For it involves nothing less than a change in the relationship between God and the world *that affects the relations within the Godhead:* "the event of the incarnation of the second Person does not leave the inter-relationship of those Persons unaffected."[23] And this means nothing less than, in short, allowing "an 'event' into the God who is beyond the world and beyond change" (*MP*, 24). Trinitarian language, I therefore venture to say, is the consequence of admitting the possibility of *event* into the Godhead: in no other way can it be explained. Just as the Cappadocians were forced into their own explanations of the Trinity, which to us sound so bizarre, because of the unacceptable implications of Sabellian modalism, so too Balthasar (I hold) is compelled to speak of the "rejection" by the Father of the Son, the Son "losing" the Father, the Spirit "reconciling" the two *because of what it means for Jesus to descend as the Son of God into the realm of the dead.*

Underneath this language we must be ready to hear the Anselmian logic of "it had to be so." That is, it is not merely a question of God "wiping the slate clean" of our sins by a simple declaration, in the manner of the nominalists, who were forever speculating whether God could have saved the human race by merely becoming incarnate, or by the slightest act of suffering as the God-man, or even by simple *fiat*, as Jews and Muslims hold today. In the forgiveness of sins, there has to be a *fitting* forgiveness, and this demands not only, as Anselm held, an incarnation, but also a death in which Jesus shared totally with the fate of sinners and drank through to the depths what sinners must experience: "Only if we appreciate the 'weight' of the world's total sin that falls on him can we adequately explain the abyss that opens up before his eyes: it is a 'hiatus' that robs his own time of any synchronicity with any other time, including that of his disciples" (*TD* 3, 115).

---

special case" (William C. Placher, *A History of Christian Theology* [Philadelphia: Westminster Press, 1983], 78). This image of three human beings could not possibly sound more tritheistic, but it should give one pause that the essay from which this metaphor comes is called "Why There Are Not Three Gods"!

[23] *MP*, 30. But caution is always in order when interpreting such statements, which must be balanced by others such as the following: "There is a theological truth which mediates between the two irreconcilable extremes: those of, on the one hand, a 'divine immutability' for which the incarnation appears only as an external 'addition,' and, on the other, a 'divine mutability' of such a sort that, for the duration of the incarnation, the divine self-consciousness of the Son is 'alienated' in a human awareness. The truth which interposes itself between them concerns the 'Lamb slain before the foundation of the world' (Rev 13:8). Here, clearly enough, two lines meet. The 'slaying' is in no sense conceived gnostically, as a heavenly sacrifice independent of what took place on Golgotha. It designates, rather, the eternal aspect of the historic and bloody sacrifice of the Cross (Rev 5:2)—as indeed Paul everywhere supposes" (*MP*, 34).

There is, then, a logic to these events, one to which God is "bound," and that is the logic of sin in its relation to the holy God. It is true that if we insist on thinking in nominalist terms, we are restricting God's freedom by insisting that he is bound by the logic of redemptive justice, that he can do no other than forgive sins by sending his divine Son to atone for them. But this is no real restriction on God's freedom, as Anselm well knew, but is merely what we mean by calling God just; and "if this is so," says Balthasar, "then this event [of the Cross] must tell us not only that sinful man sinks into the nothingness and obscurity of death, but quite simply that God hates sin" (*MP*, 138).

Now there is no doubt that such rhetoric can easily be misunderstood, especially when it is understood in terms that are too anthropomorphic. And it is especially difficult to understand in our post-Victorian times, when preachers and divines have so successfully sentimentalized the notion of God.[24] But for Balthasar this is to misconstrue the meaning of the Bible's revelation of God's two-fold stance toward the human race:

> God cannot love moral evil, he can only hate it. Of its very nature, it stands in complete opposition to God's essence. It is the counter-image of his holy love. There is no right love without wrath, for wrath is the reverse side of love. God could not truly love the good unless he hated evil and shunned it. . . . Therefore God does not forgive unexpiated sin. A mere amnesty is an ignoring of evil, which takes sin lightly or even recognizes in it an existence as of right.[25]

---

[24] The history of this sea change, with so fateful an outcome for an understanding of the biblical God, has been brilliantly analyzed by the historian James Turner: "This change in [morals] tugged God along in the same direction. . . . The dominance of moralism induced devotees to regard God Himself as concerned first and foremost with morality. A person who believed that the best worship of God was doing good to man naturally attributed the same sentiment to God. . . . His morals, moreover, bore remarkable resemblance to human moral ideals. . . . Thus, for example, God had to be a humanitarian. His creation, perplexingly, did not always give that impression. And the Enlightenment's obsession with the theodicy problem—how could a good God create evil—reflected a puzzled insistence that God measure up to human standards. Eternal damnation and original sin in particular jarred humane sensibilities and stumped rational minds. In 1710 Daniel Whitby, rector of Salisbury Cathedral, attacked original sin on the ground that imputing Adam's malfeasance to his descendants was 'exceedingly cruel, and plainly inconsistent with the Justice, Wisdom, and Goodness of our gracious God.' The dilemma so exercised that human and enlightened man Charles Chauncy that in 1782, to the scandal of Boston's other ministers, he publicly denied the eternal sufferings of hell and pronounced in favor of universal salvation" (James Turner, *Without God, Without Creed: The Origins of Unbelief in America* [Baltimore: Johns Hopkins, 1985], 71–72).

[25] *MP*, 138–139, citing E. Riggenbach's *Das Geheimnis des Kreuzes Christi* (Stuttgart/ Basel, 1927), 16–17. Balthasar also cites in this context Franz von Baader's definition of God's negation of negation: "The negativity of God against negation is indeed nothing other

The logic animating Balthasar's theology is not only Anselmian, however, as this passage seems to imply. It also follows the patristic axiom that what has not been assumed (by the human nature of Jesus) has not been saved (by its hypostatic union with his divine nature). But he radicalizes this axiom by extending it to Jesus' solidarity with the dead *as* a dead man. And this is the basis of his critique of the various images that have collected around this mystery, as in the apocryphal *Gospel of Nicodemus*, that has Death cry out when Christ enters Sheol on Holy Saturday: "Who is it who dares to enter into my dwelling alive?"[26] But such a *mythos* of Christ entering Sheol alive denies to Jesus the very status that makes him our Savior; and so Balthasar will pointedly ask the tradition:

> But is he, we must ask, really alive? *Is* he active? Or is he not actually distinguished from all the other pilgrims into Hades, from Orpheus and Odysseus to Enoch, Jonah, Aeneas and Dante, precisely in this: that he is truly *dead?* Dead, in order to be able to be truly in the "place" and in the condition of the dead. For this is precisely the issue: being-with, being in solidarity with the dead. This solidarity does not place him, in contrast to the Orphic and apocalyptic heroes, in any kind of position to observe or recognize the dead. That is why, as the Risen One, he will not provide any report about what he has seen or done there. . . . In Sheol, in the Pit, all that reigns is the darkness of perfect loneliness. But to be without contact with God *means* to be without the inner light of faith, hope and love. . . . If Jesus has suffered through on the Cross the sin of the world to the very last truth of this sin (to be forsaken by God), then he must experience, in the solidarity with the sinners who have gone to the underworld, their (ultimately hopeless) separation from God, otherwise he would not have known all the phases and conditions of what it means for man to be unredeemed yet awaiting redemption.[27]

---

than love. For he repulses evil in creation only because this evil is the obstacle placed over against the union of the creature with him, who is the source of life" (*Werke* 13, 62).

[26] Text in Schneemelcher, *Apokryphale Evangelien* I, 349; English translation in M. R. James, *The Apocryphal New Testament* (Oxford: Oxford University Press, 1924; reprint, 1969).

[27] "Abstieg zur Hölle," *PI*, 393–395: "It is easy to see why the other interpretation became so prevalent: a purely Greek anthropology has defined the essence of death, which holds that death is nothing more than the separation of the soul (that continues to live on) from the body. But this evades the essential issue. If this be so, then the direct soteriological implication of this will be first and above all else that the vicarious experience of being dead (in the biblical sense) had to be suffered, indeed could only be suffered, more deeply by the Son of God than by any other human being, because he possessed a unique experience of being connected with God the Father and *therefore* he had a much deeper access to the

Now if this is true we must admit that it puts the entire believing community in front of a wall: for what was inaccessible to Jesus as a truly dead person (and I think that the complete absence of any tradition that Jesus spoke of what the realm of the dead was "like" is very telling in this regard) is even more true for us who still dwell on this side of death. So before this mystery we must stand utterly mute:

> Between the death of a human being, which is by definition the end from which he cannot return, and what we term "resurrection" there is no common standard of measurement. In the first place, we must take with full gravity this affirmation: in the same way that a man who undergoes death and burial is mute, no longer communicating or transmitting anything, so it is with this man Jesus, who was the very Speech, Communication, and Mediation of God. He dies, and what it was about his life that made it revelation breaks off. (*MP*, 50)

This is probably why the tradition is itself so nearly mute on this central mystery of our redemption, with just a few scattered (and ambiguous!) shards of reference to it in the New Testament and only a brief reference to it in the Apostles' Creed and which then eventually disappears from the Nicene Creed. Now it might seem at first glance that this reticence in the tradition should forbid theologians from making it too central in their own reflections.

Perhaps now we can see why Balthasar is able to set so much store by the experiences of the mystics. It is not as if they have been granted some "private revelation" that does an end-run around what has been vouchsafed us in the New Testament. Mysticism does not represent for Balthasar a special "pipeline" to God that supplements revelation with new truths that cannot be found in the Bible.[28] But in those who have been specially granted this charism, it can help to bring us up short, to keep us from too hastily gliding over exactly how high the price was that brought us so precious a redemption.[29] For what their experience repre-

---

experience of being dead and forsaken (again, in the biblical sense) than was available to a creature." Of all the theologians of the tradition, Balthasar believes that Nicholas of Cusa saw this more clearly than anyone else (see Cusa's *Excitationes*, book 10 [Basler Druck, 1565], 659).

[28] As he well admits, "everyone who knows something about this topic can confirm that we are entering here a veritable garden of errors, or better, a mine field of dangers" ("Zur Ortbestimmung christlicher Mystik," (*PI*, 298).

[29] An example here might be of help, and I cite, out of numerous possibilities, the experiences of St. Rose of Lima: "She was daily visited by the most frightful nights of the soul which . . . for hours caused her anxiety that she knew not if she were in hell. . . . She groaned beneath the dreadful burden of the darkness. . . . Her will wanted to tend to love, but was paralyzed as if petrified in ice. The memory forced itself to evoke at least the images of

sents is not a private vision but a more complete insertion into the logic of this event:

> Insofar as sin has finally and ultimately been concentrated in the crucified Son, God's final *judgment* on this sin also proceeds from the Cross. . . . This reversal [from judgment to mercy] is no extrinsicist decision of God: it is made possible *by the incorporation of godforsakenness into the trinitarian relation of love.* . . . The Holy Spirit who "embodies the unity of the two is also the Guarantor for the unity of love that perdures even in this division."[30]

And this is why Christ's death was ultimately, *and in its essence,* a victory (notice how Peter says in his first sermon: "because it was *impossible* for death to keep its hold on him"): for the bonds of love in the Trinity are ultimately stronger than the godforsakenness that God in his triune counsels freely assumed into the Godhead. "The whole New Testament is unanimous on this point" (*MP*, 189). But it is so unanimous because "with the resurrection, the End is, fundamentally, already inaugurated, and what is still to be awaited is merely its definitive entry into vigor."[31]

Balthasar is very much like Barth in this respect: he is bursting with confidence in the power and victory of grace. True, he criticizes Barth for over-confidence in the outcome of this victory,[32] but perhaps that holds

---

previous consolations, but in vain. . . . Terror and anguish took possession of her totally, and her heart, overwhelmed, cried out: 'My God, my God, why have you forsaken me?' But no one replied. . . . Yet what was worst of all in her sufferings was that these ills presented themselves as having to last eternally; that no glimpse was given of an end to the distress; and that, since a wall of bronze made all escape impossible, no exit from the labyrinth could be found" (Ida Görres, *Christliche Mystik,* II [Regensburg, 1840], 286–287).

[30] *TD* IV, 232–236; my emphasis. These sentences represent a kind of "catena" of citations from the section on the descent of the Son into hell in this section of the *TD*. The last line in quotation marks is from Adrienne von Speyr; this section shows most clearly of all Balthasar's writings how indebted he is to her experiences and writings (the whole of this section is really its own catena from her writings and is perhaps the best available place to gain an overview of her mysticism, especially for those who do not have access to the privately printed *Kreuz und Hölle*).

[31] *MP*, 198. In this context I always think of Oscar Cullmann's analogy of D-Day to V-E Day: just as when the Allies successfully landed in Normandy, sober military analysts knew that for all intents and purposes the war was over (but not the battles!), with victory virtually assured, so too with the resurrection: Satan's walls have been breached, and while the battles will yet prove to be bloody, he will never win (see: Oscar Cullmann, *Christ and Time,* tr. Floyd V. Filson [Philadelphia: Westminster Press, 1950]).

[32] "In his book on the Creed, Barth warns us of eschatological arrogance. He avers that the 'positive doctrine of the *apocatastasis* does not belong to the Creed because it would simply eviscerate it.' Internal to history, God's Word will always be a two-edged sword. 'As

true for him too. We shall have to reserve our discussion of these matters for, appropriately, the last chapter; but here we want to establish the basis of Christ's ultimate victory over sin, rebellion and death. As we noticed earlier, that basis is best expressed as the "change-over" from the Old to the New Eon. But what *that* means is best approached from what the resurrection came to mean to the first disciples of Jesus, for it is this "jolt" they received that gives us the best "template" for reading off this change-over as it gets expressed in history. Or in Balthasar's image, we come to know of the meteor from the crater it made on impact. As historical critics have come to see, the jolt to history made by the meteor of the resurrection can be analyzed in terms of "disconfirmation/confirmation." While only faith can testify to the meteor, the evidence for the *crater* lies there for all to see, as Paula Fredriksen so clearly explains:

> The disciples' experience of Jesus' resurrection stands at the heart of the early Christian movement. This fact points indisputably to its origins in the eschatological hopes of first-century Judaism, with its belief in the resurrection of the dead and vindication of the righteous when the Kingdom came. . . . [But what] they all expected when they went up to Jerusalem [before the crucifixion] was the arrival of the Kingdom [as an event of their own expectation]. Instead, abruptly and brutally, this message was disconfirmed, their leader killed by the enemy who incarnated the ungodly powers of the present order. But shortly thereafter Jesus' followers experienced an *unexpected* eschatological event: Jesus was raised.[33]

This is a point every historical critic can see and assent to: the crater is located in the experience of the early Church. But what does it mean theologically? The entire history of the early Church can be seen as a continual oscillating movement from the prior expectations of the disciples about what resurrection *should* mean ("Now will you restore the fortunes of the kingdom of Israel," ask the disciples after they encounter the Risen Jesus! [Acts 1:6]) to what they learn it *does* mean (hence the only gradually dawning realization that the "mopping-up operation" will take longer than they initially thought—compare 1 Thes 4:13–5:11 with

---

in many other cases, theology must here refrain from drawing logically consistent conclusions from its premises for the sake of its own subject matter.' Nonetheless, despite these demurrals, Barth's doctrine of election does not leave much room open for possibility. There is something inevitable and necessary in his views. What is definitive in Barth's thought is grace and blessing, and all reprobation and judgment is merely provisional" (*KB*, 186).

[33] Paula Fredriksen, *From Jesus to Christ: The Origins of the New Testament Images of Jesus* (New Haven: Yale University Press, 1988), 133–134.

2 Thes 2:1–12). This is the expression within the history of the early Church of that shift from Old to New Eon from which Balthasar draws the conclusion:

> The New Covenant is neither simply the completion of something that still is awaiting fulfillment (as the concept-pair "promise-fulfillment" could imply), nor is it the reversal of values (the way a one-sided reading of the Pauline contrast of "Law-Gospel" could lead us to suspect). Rather, it is best illumined using the contrast of fleshly and earthly foretype (1 Cor 10:11) and spiritual, eschatological truth. Thereby the foretype has just as much value in itself as it shares in the truth it anticipates. (*TD* IV, 246–247)

Perhaps the reader will recall here how much discipleship for Balthasar means facing the unexpected, how much the "script" of following Jesus is not a predetermined scenario or cue sheet but a genuine drama that brings new treasures from old storehouses. This consideration now brings us to that finite drama of Response to God's initiating drama: this is the drama of saying Yes or No to this biblical drama of the "great deeds of God" out of which the Church is born and Christ can carry on his work to the end of time. But it is also the drama that could even begin at all because of that most fundamental of all finite Yes's to God: Mary's assent to the incarnation, making her the mother of all the faithful, and it is to that drama—that of Mary, of Church, and of disciple—that we will now turn, but always realizing that we are able to find our own mission in Christ because he has become the Lord of both the living and the dead:

> So then, whether we live or whether we die, we are the Lord's. For to this end Christ died and lived again, that he might be the Lord both of the dead and of the living. (Rom 14:8–9)

· 10 ·

The Finite Yes

Because of the goodness of this Lady
And because of her loveliness, and because
She honours the Virgin in meditation,
We shine with brightness.

T. S. Eliot
"Ash Wednesday"

D rama presupposes decision, and indeed is decision's correlate: drama is constituted by decisions, and the interaction of events and decisions is what we mean by drama. Thus we may venture to call the world theodramatic only because God has freely decided both to create and to redeem the world in his foreordaining and predestining love. But as we have seen in Chapter 9, his decision to create included, and was an outcome of, his decision to create finite freedoms juxtaposed to his own, so that he might have true, though finite, covenant partners for his love. Moreover, even though his created partners went astray almost from the start, God anticipated that refusal by sending his Son in atonement for their foreseen sins and rebellions, affirming in an even more glorious way his aboriginal intent to save: "For no matter how many promises God has made, they are all Yes in Christ. . . . For the Son of God, Jesus Christ, was not Yes and No, but in him it has always been Yes" (2 Cor 1:20, 19).

But this Yes is no crushing Yes that obliterates past sin by destroying present freedom. The drama of salvation is *real drama:* that is, it is co-constituted by a finite freedom that is *a real freedom.* Any other alternative would rob the drama of its dramatic character (whereas predestination in a rigid Calvinist understanding would turn the drama of salvation into a preset machine). And so the positing of a finite human freedom is essential to the theodramatic constitution of the world, the denial of which would rob it of its response-ability before God to decide how to respond to the divine initiative to save: "Behold, I set before you today life and prosperity, death and destruction. . . . Choose life, that you and your children may live" (Deut 30:15, 19).

But because of the effects of original sin (Ps 51:6), rebellion is now the implicit stance of the whole race: we humans cannot help but sense that God is now a Wholly Other in the sense of a "someone" who stands over against us and against whom—if we are to be free—we must rise up in revolt as Prometheus did against the gods. But even when we recognize the folly of such rebellion (Ps 51:1–5), our will is no longer free in the sense of being able to attain the goal God has set out for it: "I do not understand my behavior," says St. Paul. "For what I want to do, I do not do, but what I hate doing, that is what I end up doing" (Rm 7:15).[1]

This constant "misfiring" of intent, this inevitable going astray, describes the underlying and inherent pathos of the covenantal drama between God and Israel throughout the Old Testament. But because this

---

[1] I shall assume with Bultmann, Conzelmann, Fitzmyer, E. P. Sanders, and Stendahl, that the "I" speaking in Rom 7:7–25 is not Paul speaking autobiographically (at least in the psychological sense) but pre-redeemed man. Paul in other words is speaking of the failure, rooted in the essence of human nature, to respond to God in the way appropriate to his merciful initiative, a failure which very much includes those elected to join the Old Covenant, since the Law according to Paul only exacerbates that failure. Of course, as Sanders notes, Paul is in a certain sense always autobiographical, but not in the sense that Romans 7 is describing the torments of a young Luther *avant la lettre:* "I do not disagree that there is a connection in Paul's view of the law between theology and experience. The disagreement is over how to state that experience, [which] I identify as Paul's call to be apostle to the Gentiles" (*Paul, the Law, and the Jewish People* [Philadelphia: Fortress Press, 1983], 90, note 33). In other words, Paul's *mission* is the crucial determinant for establishing his perspective by which he judges the plight of unredeemed man in Rm 7. So Conzelmann is right when he says that "the theme of Chapter 7 is the unredeemed man, that of Chapter 8 the redeemed man" (Hans Conzelmann, *An Outline of the Theology of the New Testament,* tr. John Bowden [New York: Harper & Row, 1969], 229). On the other hand, no one denies that the power of Paul's rhetoric is so moving that one can easily see one's own personal moral struggles reflected in this passage, which is why Augustine, Aquinas, Luther, Barth, Althaus, Nygren (and so many untutored Christians down through the ages) have assumed that Paul is speaking here of his own experiences as a Christian confronted with regulations of his new life as a convert (see Joseph Fitzmyer, "The Letter to the Romans," *The New Jerome Biblical Commentary* [Englewood Cliffs, NJ: Prentice Hall, 1990], p. 850 [51:75]). And this raises an interesting dilemma: can an interpretation prove its exegetical validity simply by the sheer weight and fruitfulness (not to mention its apparent pastoral usefulness!) of its reading? Who would want to gainsay Barth's interpretation of this passage?: "Does not each sentence I frame require another to dissolve its meaning? And are my actions any better? . . . When my piece of work is done, do I not take leave of it sorrowfully? Woe is me, if I have unduly celebrated what I have accomplished! . . . I am unable to apprehend what I have done. What I would, I do not; what I hate, that I do. When then am I? for I stand betwixt and between, dragged here by my desires and by my hates, and there by my inability to do what I desire and by my ability to practice what I hate" (Karl Barth, *ER,* 261). But whether we take the strictly exegetical or the more open and pastoral existential approach, it is clear that any response of finite Yes to God that could even be thought as remotely adequate to his initial decision to save would also have to be created by God and not come from our own resources. How that may be conceived theologically is the focus of this chapter.

pathos is inherent to the drama of a juxtaposed finite and infinite freedom among all the children of Adam and Eve, Paul is driven to cry out: "Who then will rescue me from this body of death?" and knows the answer to be: "Thanks be to God—through Jesus Christ our Lord!" (Rm 7:24–25). Here our miserable finite Yes can find its hope for acceptance, but only here. For it is only in Christ that all of God's promises are Yes to us, even his judgment against our No.

But God so willed that this interplay between freedoms not be merely a drama of pathos but one of our genuine adoption as sons and daughters of God. In other words, this drama is no vicious circle of constantly mounting rejection overtopped with a new act of forgiveness, which then resumes the same pattern all over again. God initiates a new chapter in the history of salvation by a new inbreaking of his grace, so that Jesus enters into the world *by means of a human assent, a finite Yes* that is itself entirely an act and a creation of his grace and unmarred by the failures that affect all other responses to God's covenantal love: "There is no question," Balthasar says, "of a collective group—not even the 'faithful people'—producing the Redeemer-Messiah out of itself, in virtue of its own faith. The fact that the Church can become the 'Mother' of those who believe in Christ always presupposes that Mary conceived the Messiah and brought him to birth.[2]

Now the verb for "presuppose" in German that Balthasar is using here is *voraussetzen,* a term rich in meaning in theological German, and one that is especially crucial in Balthasar's dialogue with Barth.[3] For, in theodramatic terms, it bespeaks not only the "stage" of heaven and earth (that is, creation) on which God can enact his drama, but also all those prior events that made the climax of the coming of the Son of Man possible, such as: God's promise to Eve that from her would come someone who would crush the head of the servant (Gen 3:15); God's promise to Abraham to make his descendants as numerous as grains of sand on the seashore (Gen 17:6); his gift of the Promised Land to his people in Egypt (Ex 6:1–13); the revelation of his Law to Moses (Ex 19–31); his commissioning of the prophets to speak his warnings and console his people with the promise of a coming Messiah, etc.

Now the account of all of these "presuppositions" and prior events were eventually "sedimented" or "distilled," as it were, in the scriptures of the Old Testament, which was reaching its final canonical form at the

---

[2] *TD* 3, 291. We are circling here around the mystery of the Immaculate Conception as the acknowledgment in doctrine of God's infinite initiative incorporating into itself a finite Yes that is fully formed by his prevenient grace—the infinite initiative! And so we shall be drawing not only on the relevant sections on mariology in the *TD* (2, 365–382; 3, 283–360), but also on some of his sermons and devotional writings on this theme.

[3] For Balthasar's understanding of how this term has shaped Barth's thinking, see *KB*, 118–136 and Chapter 2 of this work.

time of the birth of Jesus; and so we may regard the Old Testament as itself one of the crucial presuppositions for Jesus' ministry and for the right interpretation of the New Covenant. But not in the sense of providing Jesus or the early Church with a "script," so to speak, which then had to be learned by heart for the right performance of Christian action. The Old Testament is less like a script to be learned than an account of all the necessary presuppositions needed for the coming of Jesus to be genuinely salvific, but not in the sense that they directly point to his coming as their direct outcome like some obvious prediction, any more than Shakespeare can be "predicted" or fully accounted for from his presuppositions in medieval and Renaissance drama, necessary as they were for his drama to flower. Scripture, too, very much belongs as one of the "presuppositions" of the drama in the same kind of way, just as every play must presuppose a script. And yet this is a script, as we have seen, that is *not* given to us merely that we might learn our lines and repeat back what has been handed to us. There is, in other words, a real *interplay* in theodrama.

These considerations have a direct bearing on one of the most crucial mysteries of God's drama with human sin and his free decision to save: the mystery of the Immaculate Conception. Often in the past, the way the debate was framed, and even the very title of the doctrine, spoke too much of the "taint" of sin and of Mary being free from its "stain," as if this mystery pertained more to the issues of Old Testament cultic purity than of God's prevenient grace. But Balthasar sees this mystery as one of the central moments that illuminate the theodramatic interaction between finite and infinite freedoms, one that brings the understanding of "presupposition" to a new level:

> Now suddenly, we see the meaning of this feast. The God who pulls down the barriers erected by men does not want to keep his own total lack of barriers to himself: he wants to bring this absolute positivity into the world, and communicate it, like rain and dew falling on the soil, to the earthly realm itself. Somewhere on earth there must ring out, in response to this word, not a half answer but a whole one, not a vague answer but an exact one. . . . By the power of heaven, the earth must accept the arrival of grace so that it can really come to earth and carry out its work of liberation. . . . [But] such a word of consent can only be given to earth from heaven's treasure house of love.[4]

Response is the key concept for understanding what this mystery is all about. First of all there is the response of creation itself, whose very

---

[4] *Crown*, 267; from "Abolishing the Boundaries," a sermon preached on the Feast of the Immaculate Conception.

existence gives praise to its Creator: (Ps 66, 104, 148). But for Balthasar, this praise that sings out from the very being of creation is essentially a "feminine" praise, for creation itself "can only be secondary, responsive, 'feminine,' *vis-à-vis* God" (*TD* 3, 287). Now what he means can easily be misunderstood, and to speak of masculine and feminine as symbols of the divine-human relationship has become a matter of intense debate and controversy in the past few years.[5] But no one denies the symbolic power of these images as applied to the God/creature relationship, and so it is important to understand what Balthasar means by his insistence that the finite response to God (in both sexes) is essentially a feminine one. There is an interesting linguistic accident in German that illustrates what he is trying to express here: in German the term for "word" is neuter (*das Wort*) but the word for "answer," "response," is feminine (*die Antwort*), in contravention of the normal rules of grammar, where the last morpheme usually determines the gender of the noun (and of course this linguistic accident is only an illustration of his point, which for him would naturally obtain in any event). And here is the lesson he draws:

> The first Adam calls nature's animals by name, and as he names them, so they are called. But no adequate response comes to him from them. Only when God forms woman from his side does nature reply ("at last!") with an appropriate word: "This at last is bone of my bones and flesh of my flesh; she shall be called Woman, because she was taken out of Man" (Gen 2:23). Thus woman is essentially an answer [*Ant-wort*] in the most fundamental sense of *ant*, which is common to all Indo-European languages and means "over against." . . . If man is the word that calls out, woman is the answer that comes to him at last. The two are related and ordered to each other. Furthermore, the second account of creation shows that the word that calls out only attains fulfillment when it is understood, accepted and given back *as* a word. This clearly shows us the way in which man can be primary and woman secondary, where the primary remains unfulfilled without the secondary. The primary needs a partner *of equal rank and dignity* for its own fulfillment. Moreover, the man is incapable of providing this answering dimension; it is latent within him—for there can be no word without an answering word—but it has to be given to him as grace. It can only come about in freedom, and only God, fundamentally, can give such freedom.[6]

---

[5] See especially Elizabeth A. Johnson, *She Who Is: The Mystery of God in Feminist Theological Discourse* (New York: Crossroad, 1992).

[6] *TD* 3, 284–285; my emphasis. I have added the italics to show that the language of "primary" and "secondary" need not—and in fact, in my opinion, does not—have any

There is, then, an essential equality of the sexes, mixed also with a symbolic ranking of masculine/feminine as an expression of the God/creature relationship. But since Adam is also a creature, he too is feminine *vis-à-vis* God. In fact, it would be theologically disastrous to equate Adam's role with that of the Creator (Adam and Eve really *are* equal!), and this perhaps more than anything shows how the *symbolic* role of the masculine-feminine dichotomy not only need not, but must not, affect the essential social equality of the sexes:

> We have already indicated that the creature can only be secondary, responsive, "feminine," *vis-à-vis* God. On the other hand, we may not in any way equate the Creator with Adam, for God does not need the creature for his fulfillment (as all pantheism assumes, whether of the static or the dynamic-evolutionist kind). In particular, God the Father is under no necessity to separate himself from the product of his fruitfulness. He does not generate the Son in order to have a vessel of himself into which to pour his richness but begets him out of the superabundant fullness of his "selfless" love, which is not stimulated to self-communication by anything outside of itself. . . . The life of the Trinity is a circle, eternally fulfilled in itself: it does not need the world. As for the act of creation, it is founded on trinitarian freedom, "selflessly" granting to needy creatures a share in this life of blessed selflessness. However, inasmuch as every creature—be it male or female in the natural order—is originally the fruit of the primary, absolute, self-giving love, there is a clear analogy to the female principle in the world. (*TD* 3, 287)

"Answer," then, is quintessentially feminine, and this is why it was so "fitting," as Thomas Aquinas says, that the consent to the incarnation come from a woman.[7] Moreover, not only was Mary predestined to be the Mother of the Savior, whose consent to the incarnation would inaugurate the drama of our redemption, she would do so entirely by the power

---

deleterious implications for the essential equality of the sexes; On the Pauline background to symbolic primacy and social equality, see Norbert Baumert, *Frau und Mann bei Paulus: Überwindung eines Mißverständnisses* (Würzburg: Echter Verlag, 1992), and *Antifeminismus bei Paulus?: Einzelstudien* (Würzburg: Echter Verlag, 1992).

7 "Non enim invite tantum beneficium praestari debebat" (*De Veritate*, q. 12, art. 10, ad 6): "For it was not right that so great a benefit be granted without consent." Although Thomas Aquinas also denied the doctrine of the Immaculate Conception, I think Protestants do not sufficiently realize how much a denial of this doctrine contradicts their own views on the necessity for prevenient grace if one is to give assent to God: far from glorifying the creature at the expense of God's grace, this doctrine is a witness to the overarching and ever-present *necessity* for grace.

of the grace of God.[8] Only this realization, enshrined in the infallibly defined dogma of the Immaculate Conception, can preserve the essential feature of our theodramatic redemption: that God has in his infinite freedom decided to save us in a way that respects our finite freedom but which also demands his infinite power of grace to fulfill:

> In the course of unfolding these implications, two difficulties were encountered that have occupied theology right up to medieval and modern times. The first arose from the realization that God's action in reconciling the world to himself in the Cross of Christ is exclusively his initiative; there is no original "collaboration" between God and the creature. But as we have already said, the creature's "femininity" possesses an original, God-given, active fruitfulness; it was essential, therefore, if God's Word willed to become incarnate in the womb of a woman, to elicit the latter's agreement and obedient consent. . . . God could not violate his creature's freedom. But where did the grace that made this consent possible come from—a consent that is adequate and therefore genuinely unlimited—if not from the work of reconciliation itself, that is, from the Cross? (And the Cross is rendered possible only through Mary's consent.) Here we have a circle—in which the effect is the cause of the cause—that has taken centuries to appreciate and formulate, resulting in the dogma of the Immaculate Conception and the exact reasoning behind it.[9]

Many of the objections of Protestantism to the so-called "innovations" of Roman Catholicism, its "departures" from the truths set forth in Scripture, would vanish with a proper understanding of this circular movement

---

[8] Which is why patristic and medieval theologians liked to contrast her free and conscious consent with Adam's sleep: "The Virgin was not visited by sleep (like Adam) but by an angel sent by God . . . to make known to her this great mystery. . . . Moreover, God wished not only that she should know of this but also that she should cooperate so that he could give his Mother the greatest privilege of honor and grace" (William of Newburgh, *Explanatio sacri Epithalamii in Matrem Sponsi,* text ed by. J. C. Gorman [Freiburg: Herder, 1960], 76–77).

[9] *TD* 3, 296–297. It is in this tangle of an effect being the cause of the cause that Aquinas went astray; but if as part of the logic, the Cross itself is made possible only through Mary's consent (which is clearly the case), then the heretical implications of a *denial* of the doctrine of the Immaculate Conception should be obvious: for it makes our salvation dependent on the power of one human creature, Mary, to say Yes to God on her own power. Denial of this dogma therefore not only leads to Pelagianism, but even makes the whole drama of salvation *hinge* on a human work! Denial of the Immaculate Conception, then, is the very apogee of the Pelagian heresy!

of understanding.[10] Marian dogmas naturally flow from theological reflection on the few (but crucial!) scenes in which Mary appears: above all, the Annunciation, the wedding at Cana, her presence at the foot of the Cross, and her fellowship with the apostles and disciples on Pentecost Sunday. These scenes, coupled with a basic reflection on the meaning of Mary's motherhood of the Savior, lead naturally to the unfolding of all of the doctrines of mariology:

> The history of Marian doctrine is highly instructive, with regard to both its development and its significance in the totality of dogma. In view of the scenes in the Gospels, particularly the infancy narratives as set forth by Matthew and Luke and the scenes at Cana and before the Cross in John, it is no surprise that there is an interest in the person and role of Mary right from the outset. Nor is it surprising that initially Mary's role was kept in the background until after Christ's role and his relationship to the Church as Redeemer was clarified (at Nicea). So the role of Mary is first of all purely christological: she is the guarantee that he is truly and fully man, "born of a woman" (Gal 4:4); but also, once the Nicene dogma is proclaimed, she is Theotokos, the God-Bearer. And yet in Justin and especially in Irenaeus, she is the "new Eve," the "type" of Christ's Church. . . . But from the beginning she is a "theological person" in her own right and has her unique and proper role to play *vis-à-vis* both Christ and the Church; the only thing necessary for the development of all the subsequent mariological insights was appropriate reflection on her place and role.[11]

This development has not always been one of steady growth and expansion of titles, despite the contrary impression often given, both by advo-

---

[10] It would be a fundamental misunderstanding to see this circle as a vicious one; it is virtuous in exactly the way Heidegger describes it in one of his most famous passages: "If we see this circle as a vicious one and look out for ways of avoiding it, even if we just 'sense' it as an inevitable imperfection, then the act of understanding has been misunderstood from the ground up. . . . *What is decisive is not to get out of the circle but to come into it in the right way.* This circle of understanding . . . is not to be reduced to the level of a vicious circle, or even of a circle that is merely tolerated. *In the circle is hidden a positive possibility of the most primordial kind of knowing*" (Martin Heidegger, *Being and Time*, tr. John Macquarrie and Edward Robinson (New York: Harper & Row, 1962), 194–195; my emphases).

[11] *TD* 3, 295–296. So Newman is quite correct when he explained to Pusey that the *veneration* of the Blessed Virgin among Catholics has grown through the centuries; but this is not true of the *doctrine:* at its core, it has remained the same from the outset ("A Letter Addressed to the Rev. E. B. Pusey on the Occasion of his Eirenicon of 1866," in *Certain Difficulties Felt by Anglicans in Catholic Teaching* [London: Longmans, 1901/1876]).

cates of a "high" mariology as well as those who wish to resist such trends. In fact, there has been considerable variation in the history, a kind of oscillation that is itself an important datum for theology. For there is always a tension in mariology that is embedded in the tension between God's all-redeeming grace in Christ (infinite freedom) and the human response to it (finite freedom): "This helps us to understand the ebb and flow throughout history of mariology's tides: a flood of lofty attributes, titles and venerations is almost necessarily followed by an ebb that restores the level; but the ebb-tide can also seep away and drain theology of important motifs, leading to a forgetfulness that is unworthy of theology" (*TD* 3, 297).

Balthasar has tried in his own mariology to resist any wild swing one way or the other, but has done so by fully admitting the tension inherent in the affirmation that the incarnation depends on a finite Yes which was, however, able to say Yes only by virtue of the grace of the incarnation that was to follow. This puts the tension in a more logical and abstract formulation, and the Church Fathers and medieval scholastics usually found more poetical paradoxes to express this tension, but the reality remains the same. But as Balthasar would surely admit, the poetic expression captures the tension much better, as in this description of Mary by St. Peter Damien (1007–1072): "source of the Living Source, origin of the Beginning."[12] And because Mary's assent to the will of God that brought forth our Savior was free of any "taint" of original sin (I prefer the expression, free of any "enticement" resulting from original sin), her assent was completely open to the future as well as being an assent that summed up of the best of the past, for it was an act of obedience that expressed what should have been at all moments the covenantal response of Israel:

> Here, in fact, we have all the elements necessary for a historical understanding of today's feast. In it, Israel's expectation of the world's transformation by God is fulfilled, and yet—as is always the case in the transition from the Old to the New Covenant—

---

[12] *Sermo* 45, *PL* 144, 740; Damien also points out that, as Christ took flesh from Mary and from his flesh the Church was born in the water and blood that flowed from his pierced side, "we see that the Church also came from Mary" (*Sermo* 65, *PL* 144, 861), a truth which led to Paul VI's declaration that Mary can be called the "Mother of the Church" (in the closing allocution at the end of the third session of Vatican II, 21 November 1964). This was done to make explicit, in title form, what the Council taught of Mary when it said in solemn assembly: "Taught by the Holy Spirit, the Catholic Church honors her with filial affection and piety as [her] most beloved mother. . . . [This sacred Synod] also wishes to describe the duties of redeemed mankind toward the Mother of God, who is mother of Christ and mother of men, particularly of the faithful" (*Lumen Gentium* # 53, 54, in *The Documents of Vatican II*, ed. Walter M. Abbott, S.J. [New York: Guild Press, 1966], 86). On this same theme, see also *TD* 3, 312–318, esp. 317, note 75.

it is outmatched and turned upside down. The salvation that comes from God is totally different, precisely because it comes from God, from what any finite human being might imagine. Where does the difference lie? Man, even the man who is devout and righteous, *sets limits*, unconsciously, automatically, because that is his original sinful nature. "Yes, but . . ." "Yes, provided that God acts as I expect a true God is supposed to act." (*C*, 266)

This of course defines sin as it exists on both sides of the Covenant, which is why the New Testament portrays Mary not only as summing up and incorporating the Yes of Israel down through the ages (Lk 1:54–55) but also why the Church prays to her to protect the faithful in future generations from the assaults of temptation. This perhaps is why the Church has perennially seen Mary's role in the Church reflected in the Woman's battle against the dragon in Revelation 12; indeed Balthasar goes so far as to say that "the best way to learn something about Mary and how she is related to our present age is to start with chapter 12 of Revelation."[13] To assert this it is not necessary to wed oneself to the traditional interpretation that the text itself intends the symbol to refer exclusively to Mary, and in fact Balthasar himself says that the Woman Clothed With the Sun crying out in pangs of birth is "without doubt first of all God's people Israel suffering the birthpangs of the Messiah" (*TD* 3, 323).

But Mary, both by virtue of her Immaculate Conception and her Assumption into Heaven, holds a "unique intermediate position between paradise and man's fallen state"[14] and for that reason is the bridge between Israel's labor pains in trying to give birth to the Messiah (birthpangs that began with Sarah's consternation and culminated in Mary's own puzzlement) and the Church's agony until the fire of the Gospel be ignited across the whole world (Lk 12:49–50). And the focal point of this transition takes place where Mary's own agony is at its greatest: at the foot of the Cross where she loses not only her Son but also her own status as Mother of the Savior in order to become, in losing him, the Mother of the faithful:

This turning point [of the Cross] is the Church's hour of birth; the Body of God's Word can now be distributed eucharistically, and from the pierced Heart there flow out the water and blood of the sacraments. Now in the midst of this great event, this Body cannot forget its origin and its connection with its Mother's body. And the body of Jesus' Mother could bear this fruit only

---

[13] *Mary For Today*, tr. Robert Nowell (San Francisco: Ignatius Press, 1988), 9.
[14] *TD* 3, 323.

because she had consented in advance to Jesus' whole mission; this is why Mary is present under the cross at the moment when God's incarnation is consummated and the Church is born. She suffers along with her Son; in her spirit she experiences his death, and the stroke of the lance that pierces the dead Jesus' heart wounds her, who must survive him, as the sword that had been promised. The disciples have already communicated in the Eucharist; sacramentally they are already Christ's Body; objectively, the Church which they constitute is already with Jesus on the cross. But subjectively, they are absent—except for the Beloved Disciple, who represents them all. (*3FG*, 102–103)

This scene constitutes what Balthasar calls "a christological constellation,"[15] and its symbolic cluster determines his whole ecclesiology.[16] For in his view "the Crucified utters a word whereby he entrusts Mary to the Beloved Disciple as her son, and this word in a way constitutes the Church's foundation document, flowing out of the midst of the suffering which gives birth to the Church as such" (*3FG*, 103). The picture that Balthasar paints here is extremely subtle and is almost as hard to describe as is his theology of what happened on Holy Saturday. For in fact what we face here is another *commercium admirabile* (wondrous exchange), but only this time brought down to a more human (or at least more ecclesiological) level. Perhaps the most concise description of the scene as

---

[15] *OP*, 136–145. As we shall be relying on this book for many of the insights to be developed in this chapter, it might be well to warn the reader of a certain tendentiousness in the translation. One does not ordinarily quote from book reviews in a work of this sort; but since many readers will be approaching Balthasar for the first time via this book, the following citation should be noted for the record: "The importance of Balthasar's theology makes it all the more regrettable that severe defects in the translation make it impossible to obtain a precise account of his thought from this publication and expose the author to criticism for positions which he does not hold. Only a few of the more than 100 [!] errors I have noted can be listed here. Balthasar's observations on the development of structure in the early Church, the factual connection of succession to Peter with the bishop of Rome, the dating of 'early Catholicism,' [and the list goes on and on] . . . have all been distorted. . . . Comments about Jesus are applied to Peter. In several places there are gratuitous insertions (e.g., 'seemingly' in a section on *Humanae vitae*) and omissions (e.g., a sentence critical of Legaut). *Kirche* is translated as 'baptism' and as 'Rome,' *paternalistisch* as 'ancestral,' *Amt* as 'church,' *Apostel* as 'pope,' *leiblicher Bruder* (of Jesus) as 'blood relative.' But I was particularly intrigued to find *antimännlich* rendered as 'feminist'" (John P. Galvin, review in *Theological Studies* 48/4 [December 1987]: 753).

[16] The influence of Adrienne von Speyr is particularly evident here; in fact, with the exception of his theology of Holy Saturday, nowhere is her influence on his thought more evident than in his mariology, a point brought out in an important article by Johann Roten, S.M, "Two Halves of the Moon: Marian Anthropological Dimensions in the Common Mission of Adrienne von Speyr and Hans Urs von Balthasar," in *L&W*, 65–86.

Balthasar has painted it can be found in the remarks of one of his translators, John Saward:

> By bequeathing [Mary] to John, Jesus unites the heavenly Church, perfected in advance, with the still struggling, earthly Church. In other words, *the visibly organized pilgrim Church on earth, in all its imperfection, has been entrusted by its Head to care for and protect the purity and the sanctity of the original, ideal Church.* John's mission is to be the link between Mary and Peter and thus between the Church as holy and immaculate, and the Church as hierarchical and infallible; between the whole Church, which, even as distinct from Christ, is greater than its members and surrounds them as a motherly presence, and that sacramentally consecrated portion, which is masculine and fatherly, the office of unity in the truth. John represents the official side of the Church, but in a special form—as uniting office and love. On Calvary John is the vicar of the absent Peter; he undertakes, in lieu of the primate, to cherish and guard Holy Mother Mary and thus Holy Mother Church, the Church as a whole, the Church as holy.[17]

And so, just as there is a constellation of certain followers of Jesus who cluster around the Cross as the Church is being born, so too is the Church thereafter "constellationally structured," so to speak, with Peter, Mary and John each representing in a real and *irrevocable* way the nature and constitution of the Church. First of all, the Church as a whole is feminine (2 Cor 11:12), open and dependent on her Bridegroom, while the male hierarchy, by contrast, is only one part, whose vocation is to serve the feminine Marian whole. The Church, Balthasar would always want to insist, existed in a woman before a single man had been called to be an apostle: "In Mary, the Church already has physical existence before it is organized in Peter."[18] Furthermore, the hierarchical Church is most definitely founded and established in the wider reality of Church prior to its consent or even its ability to give its finite Yes, as Peter's many denials so amply testify. It was Mary and not some apostle, or the Twelve assembled in a "college," who first believed and made possible, on a human level, the incarnation. And so she has the primacy in the way no "primate" or prelate could ever have:

---

[17] John Saward, *The Mysteries of March: Hans Urs von Balthasar on the Incarnation and Easter* (Washington, D.C.: Catholic University of America Press, 1990), p. 78; my emphasis.

[18] "Epilog: Die marianische Prägung der Kirche," in *Maria heute ehren*, ed. W. Beinert (Freiburg im Breisgau: Herder, 1977), 276.

Being placed in the hands of Mary at his birth and after his death is more central than being placed in the hands of office, and is in fact the presupposition of the latter. Before male office makes its entrance in the Church, the Church as woman and helpmate is already on the scene. . . . [Thus] the Marian takes precedence over the liturgical, because the incarnate Word was first entrusted to the care of his Mother at his incarnation and birth before later being placed in the care of the Church in the official and institutional sense. (*TD* III, 371, 377)

This entrusting of the incarnate Word in the womb of Mary and then later in her raising of her child foreshadows the way Jesus will entrust her, as the *Immaculata Ecclesia* (Eph 5:27), to John. But what is significant in this constellation is the glaring absence of Peter, who represents the institutional Church *par excellence*. For he is not only the Rock on which Jesus will build his Church but also the man whose very absence at the Cross represents the finite No that is entissued into the very fabric and body of the Church. How can this be explained? In his most intense meditation on this theme, an essay of masterly synthesis of so many disparate materials and called, appropriately enough "*Casta Meretrix*" ("Chaste Harlot"), Balthasar grapples with this agonizing theme:

The New Testament speaks of the safeguards granted Christ's Church, but at the same time, in harsh juxtaposition, there is the threat of abuse, the possibility of defection. Nowhere is the immaculateness of the Bride an established fact for the Bride just to accept and worry about no further. . . . Where on earth does this susceptibility of the Church-Bride come from, this curiosity and lustfulness? What makes her turn her head? Why does she heed every passer-by? Why does she not let herself be led by the apostle to her one and only Lover? Every epistle of the Apostle shakes with this fear. Apostasy and relapse are always possible. (*SW*, 208)

Nothing should prove more agonizing to a Christian than this ever-present power of sin. What happens in the saints, who are as rare as mountain peaks, should in fact be a daily experience of all Christians: "Just as the well-tuned microscope can pick up impurities in a clear drop of water that would be simply unimaginable to the naked eye, so too the spiritual person discovers how polluted, murky and impure the spiritual atmosphere is that he is inhaling with every fiber of his being. This is an experience that can often drive the saints, according to their own witness, to a kind of despair about themselves. They want to separate themselves totally from the 'monstrous corpse' they are, so that only God's own life might live within them."[19]

So even in eager response to God's infinite Yes, even when we think we have said our own meager finite Yes to the Gospel, a rebellious and stubborn No wells up within us. In the wise words of Cardinal Newman, "faith and unbelief, humbleness and pride, love and selfishness, have been from the Apostles' age united in one and the same body; nor can any means of man's device disengage the one from the other."[20] The temptation here is to admit this undeniable fact and then fall back on a doctrine of *simul justus et peccator* and "hope for the best." Unfortunately, while there is a certain sense in which this phrase expresses something true,[21] it has no real warrant in the New Testament if it leads to lassitude. Now Balthasar fully admits that rejecting lassitude and laxity can lead to its own problem of uprooting the wheat with the weeds, and he depicts the pastoral difficulties of distinguishing a true from a false sense of sin with great subtlety:

> The word sinner no longer carries much weight. Among the general public it has a slightly comic tone: it is used as a come-on to entice people to see sex films, but even there it is gradually losing its effectiveness. It is a word which comes to us from a lost world where there was a whole range of techniques designed to inculcate the delinquent's conscience with a sense of sinfulness and then to exorcise it by means of confession and imposed penances, while at the same time repeated applications of the treatment were designed to keep alive the general feeling of being a sinner and continually to bring it to a head. All this was performed in relation to a Divinity supposedly hurt in its love, efficaciously represented by an official, vicarious priesthood that possessed both the power to work on a man's conscience till he considered himself to be the "greatest living sinner" as well as the power to fish out of this murky pool of sin some magic formula to make the sinner feel endowed with the innocence of a loving child of the God of love—at least until the next fall from grace. No wonder, then, that people gradually lost patience with these hot-and-cold baths which the priests prescribed for

---

[19] *KB*, 374. In his book on St. Thérèse of Lisieux, he has the interesting remark that "it is a help simply to recognize that the saints themselves retain their weaknesses, perhaps even their sins" (*2S*, 38).

[20] John Henry Newman, "The Contest Between Truth and Falsehood in the Church," *Parochial and Plain Sermons* (San Francisco: Ignatius Press, 1987), 609.

[21] For Balthasar's reflections on this expression, see his wise and penetrating remarks in *KB*, 369–378.

them and avoided undergoing these sauna-cures by the claim that in any event one was always going to be "sinner and justified at the same time."[22]

So the current pastoral situation in the Church makes such "evasions" quite understandable: the alternative would seem only to lead to obsession, scrupulosity, and the kind of despair that led Luther to break with the whole Roman system of sacramental forgiveness. But this ends up slighting other New Testament evidence, equally compelling (Mt 25:14–46; Mk 11:12–14,20–21; 1 Cor 3:2–3,10–15; 9:24–27; 2 Cor 9:6–11).[23] Balthasar tries to resolve this tension (which is rooted in the New Testament itself) by focusing on the contrasting curse/blessing in St. Paul: "If anyone has no love for the Lord, let him be accursed" (1 Cor 16:22) and "Blessed be all who love our Lord Jesus Christ" (Eph 6:24). And from this two-sided contrast on the real essence of the Yes and No of the finite believer, he draws this important conclusion:

> Of course this "body" [of the Church] consists of sinners, that is to say those who do not love, and will therefore until the end of the world be subject to the most radical criticism. But if this criticism does not consist primarily in the example of a greater love, then it will heal no wound; the critic without love resembles rather a man who scratches himself all the more furiously, the more fiercely he itches, a process which of course can only result in exacerbating and spreading the inflammation. The great saints were reformers of the Church but they were edifying reformers. Not all the great reformers were saints, that is to say, those who truly loved; many of them destroyed more than they built up. (*El*, 186)

But who has ever loved enough? An honest answer to that question will automatically lead to the realization that the boundary line courses through each individual heart and that the uprooting must begin there. There is a No lurking in every Yes to the extent that we do not love, which is why even so tireless a worker for the Gospel as Paul himself cannot admit that the final word of judgment has been visited upon him: "With me I care very little if I am judged by you or by any human court; indeed, I do not even judge myself. My conscience is clear, but that does not make me innocent. It is the Lord who judges me" (1 Cor 4:1–5). For

---

[22] "Am I a Sinner?" *El*, 155–156.

[23] For further texts and Balthasar's interpretation of them, see "The Boundary Line," *El*, 180–182.

only the Last Judgment can reveal how deep our failures in love really have been and yet how irrevocable God's choice really is.

As Paul implies, this Last Judgment cannot be anticipated; but Balthasar will also insist that the Church is so structured here on earth that the believer will be forced into existential decisions that will be reflected in the Last Judgment, primarily because of the Church's essential structure into lay and religious states of life (or, in other contexts, lay and clerical states). His theology is deeply indebted here to the *Spiritual Exercises* of St. Ignatius, especially to those sections of the *Exercises* that are devoted to choosing a "state of life" free of inordinate attachment in the world. And out of these reflections he has brought forth one of the most remarkable books in his career, *The Christian State of Life*. It is indeed an elaborate work, astonishingly so considering how it is based on just a few short paragraphs from a spiritual handbook, the *Spiritual Exercises*.[24]

Balthasar's basic point in this book is that the distinction between the religious and lay states of life (or for others, between the clerical and the lay states) is so "enstructured" in the constitution of the Church as to force a decision in the believer, insuring that his Yes is not some vague assent to a few half-understood propositions culled from ancient Councils but a real and costly existential Yes to the Lord who calls one to a life of service and sacrifice. And for that reason, Balthasar has no difficulty in asserting that the distinction between "religious" and "lay" states goes back to Jesus himself, in this sense:

> Jesus does not hesitate to confront man with the ultimate decision. Indeed, he demands it, thereby creating for himself a multitude of enemies. He recognizes no gray area of neutral theological truths, for "I *am* the Truth" (Jn 14:6). Man's truth and falsehood, light and darkness, salvation and damnation are all judged in terms of his decision for or against Jesus (Mk 8:38). "No man can serve two masters; for either he will hate the one and love the other, or else he will stand by the one and despise the other" (Mt 6:24). . . . Jesus' mission, then, is primarily one of discernment and hence of order. . . . He wants no mass movement that will envelop the individual in anonymity, but a personal decision that each individual must make for himself alone.[25]

---

[24] Specifically, # 5, 15–16, 23, 91–100, 135–157, 165–189.

[25] *CSL*, 136–137. In this tracing of the distinction between religious and lay states back to Jesus, note that Balthasar is mostly concerned with the ineluctable demand for decision. There is, in fact, in his exegetical archaeology here a strong reliance on Martin Hengel's *Nachfolge und Charisma* (Berlin: Töpelmann, 1968); we noted a similar reliance on Hengel in his christology too. In any event, Balthasar is fully aware of the voices that are bound to object to this linkage: "Many will no doubt find it naïve that, in accordance with tradition,

The encounter with Christ always demands that one "take a stand."
Now it happens that the word for "stand" in German (*Stand*) is also the
word for "state of life," an etymological congruence that Balthasar will
exploit to the full.[26] And this is why he will also be so insistent that this
decision-demanding structure of the Church—which goes all the way back
to its foundations in Christ's demand for a decision—not be obviated by
an overly generic appeal to the Church as "the People of God," a point
which he had insisted on with ever more urgency in his later years, perhaps
never more so than in his essay on "Christology and Christian
Obedience":

> It is not even sufficient to say that the "People of God" is the
> kind of concept that only needs to be supplemented with the
> *differentia specifica* of the New Testament. For first of all, the
> Old and New Covenants are not two different types of the same
> species. God's covenant is single, and supersedes the Old Cove-
> nant as fulfillment does promise; moreover, this supersession oc-
> curs by God's reprobation of the people in his election of the
> small remnant, the little flock. Secondly, the concept of "the
> People" is ordered to the Old Testament and appears in the New
> Testament only in quotes from the Old Testament. If the Second
> Vatican Council tried to replace a certainly insufficient concept
> of the Church ... with the concept of the People of God, it
> is nonetheless a concept that hides within itself—when taken
> abstractly and absolutely—opposite dangers. Concepts are our
> fate. One cannot emphasize enough that Vatican II's Decree on
> the Church *Lumen Gentium* only introduces the concept of the
> People of God *after* it has treated the Church as Mystery. (*PI*,
> 133–134)

This is not in any way to deny the reality of the Church as the People
of God, still less to say that the "division" that Christ came to bring (Mt

---

we trace the distinctive character of the life of the evangelical counsels to Jesus, just as they
will find naïve our 'uncritical' treatment of Holy Scripture, which we have frequently cited
in support of our basic thesis. Be that as it may, we regard Holy Scripture as an inspired
whole—one that is, moreover, [to be] interpreted in the essential tradition and history of
the Church" (*CSL*, 16).

[26] *Stand* is also the German term for "estate" in the sense of a recognized class in society
(as in the expression, the "third estate," etc.), a term which the English draws from the
Latin root for "stand." The remarks of Mary Frances McCarthy, the translation of *CSL*,
are apropos in this regard: "Here and elsewhere throughout the text, von Balthasar has
opposed the dynamism of *stehen* (verb) and *Stehen* (noun) to the more static quality of
Stand. I have attempted to preserve the etymological relationship as well as the semantic
emphasis by translating these words, respectively, as 'take a stand,' 'stand' (as in the diction-
ary meaning: 'a position especially with respect to an issue'), and 'state of life' (cf. Latin

10:32–42; Lk 12:49–53) is not meant ultimately to unite ("that they may all be one, Father, just as you are in me and I am in you" [Jn 17:21]). On the contrary, all gifts and charisms are meant for the building up of the whole Temple of God. But this must not gainsay the searing uniqueness of each call, and that uniqueness cannot be faced unless it is reflected in the very constitution of the Church. But because the Church really *is* the People of God, all states of life must referred back to the People for their own good:

> By reason of Christ's mission, the Christian state of life is ultimately and essentially a communal state. It is social in nature. This may not be immediately apparent if one looks only at the personal urgency of the elective call. For why should God not also call one to serve him in a place apart? But the Christian vocation never has this character. In the first place, it is a call into the Church, which, as we have shown, antedates the vocation of the individual insofar as it is a place of community. In the second place, it is a summons to leave one's selfish and isolated self and to enter a state that is, by definition, *the end of all isolation. . . .* Because [the one called] lives henceforth in Christ, there can be for him no other concept of personhood than that which is expressed in mission, service and the renunciation of self.[27]

This is why the Church can be, and is, hurt—and hurt deeply—by the refusal of men and women in the Church to hear and respond to this overriding and imperious call (Mt 9:35–38). Because it is a finite Yes, but a free one, it can also be a finite No. And as a No it will work its havoc on both the Church and the person being called ("Once the hand is laid on the plow, no one who looks back is fit for the kingdom of God": Lk 9:62). Balthasar describes the effects on the refusing person in this way:

> There are vocations in which individuals are called into the sphere of the fire. They always demand the whole person. And such vocations are refused, though one can only speak of refusals

---

status). It is unfortunate but unavoidable that the English 'stand' more accurately conveys the meaning of German *Stehen* than of German *Stand*" (*CSL*, 11, note 3).

[27] *CSL*, 224. This work has often stressed Balthasar's isolation, but it is important to note that he makes no cult of isolation for its own sake. In fact, he holds the opposite: "Solitude: the great illusion of many who want to be chaste for God. They seek out stillness and quiet, a consecrated space, but in this stillness they find only themselves and forget that the true solitude, the solitude of Christ, is the solitude that comes from being stripped of one's rights and being defenselessly handed up to all the urgencies of human need: no protection here, no 'cloister,' but only a sailing on the high seas. This is where many of the pious have already becomes Philistines" (*W*, 48).

where one consciously resists the call (for a thousand unimportant reasons). Such refusals are more numerous than one might think. Those who have said No remain marked. They burn but they consume themselves. They become cynical and destructive, they smell each other out and hold together. . . . Anyone who has some facility in discerning spirits can recognize them. . . . In the desperate exhibition which they make of themselves, those who have rejected their call show what disappearance into pure service could have been.[28]

The Church, in other words, is so constituted as to be able to continue to bring men and women into a direct encounter with the call of Jesus, a call that in its imperiousness brooks no opposition or excuses (Mt 8:21–22; 10:37–39; 19:16–26; Lk 9:57–62). Balthasar insists that this ability to re-echo the call of Jesus down through the ages is intimately linked with the Church's hierarchical structure, as becomes clear when he describes how this same No at work in an individual Christian is also at work in the world at large: the human No to God after the coming of Christ will for Balthasar always include a loud and unequivocal No to the hierarchy of the Roman Church, and precisely because this No is encountering the Church in her divinely appointed structure:

Mankind only becomes conscious of its unity in breaking loose from, and protesting against, the claims of the Church to be the religious form of unity willed by God. This protest is wider than Protestantism in the narrow sense, but gives it some affinity with the other religions of the world, and so is bound to lead to a kind of *entente cordiale* between all non-Catholic forms of religion. "Anything but this" is the common watchword by which all non-Catholics easily understand each other. In this understanding all absolute factors are gradually leveled down. . . . Hence the religion of humanitarianism can ultimately be no better recommended and demonstrated in its inner spirit than by contrasting it with Catholicism. There is no slogan nearly so suitable for [summing up] all the forms of cultural propaganda these days as that which promises to lead men from Catholic "narrowness" into the "breadth" of natural religion. The world-wide unity of the religions is being hammered out on the anvil of Catholicism. (*GQ*, 88–89)

---

[28] "Why Do I Still Remain in the Church?" *EI*, 215–216. These same views are phrased even more sharply in *CSL*: "They have a compulsive desire for frequent association with what they have rejected. . . . They are attracted to whatever is new and interesting, especially to whatever is sensational in the field of religion, for they find therein a substitute for the

These two No's can intersect in devastating ways: both emptying the Church of needed workers in the fields of the Lord just when they are white for the harvest and yet also peopling the professional echelons of the ecclesiastic bureaucracies with men and women who want to undermine the very structure that makes the call of Jesus resound so clearly and directly to each person for whom Christ has destined a vocation.[29] And how long-lasting are these effect! In one particularly grim passage, Balthasar points to the havoc that follows down through the ages in the wake of even a single No:

> If one had accepted God's call, a vast multitude of one's fellow men might have gained access to the Lord; many who will now remain forever in their sins might have been drawn to confession; many who will now be left in ignorance might have accepted the word of God; many who will now be forever cold might have been inflamed by the fire of faith, hope and charity. As it is, a part of God's field will forever remain uncultivated. The few workers in the Lord's vineyard will be even more overwhelmed by the task that confronts them and, in consequence, will perform it less carefully and will be all the sooner exhausted. He causes untold harm who rejects God's call because his No affects not only himself but also all those who depend on his mission. (*CSL*, 497–498)

And that is why it is so important to see the Church's hierarchical structure as rooted in the will of Christ—not necessarily in the sense of a three-tiered distinction of bishop-priest-deacon being part of the consti-

---

simple greatness of the life of mission. Unable to drink from the vessel they have drained, they wallow in its dregs" (501–502).

[29] This forms the basis of his very polemical book *A Short Primer*, as he makes clear in the opening sentences: "All true Catholic Christians suffer today from the confusion within their Church. One can safely say that this unrest which followed the Council came mainly *from the clergy and religious*. By leaving their state of life in large numbers and by the secularization of the theology, catechesis and preaching that they practiced, they proved that they thoroughly misunderstood the 'opening of the Church to the world' intended by the Council. Laymen, living and engaged in the world, did not need to feel addressed by this slogan as much. the increased apostolic commitment in the political, economic and social spheres that was demanded was nothing fundamentally new for them. But the shock to the clerical world could not remain without influence on the lay world. This influence became all the more confusing as perfectly normal conciliar reforms, such as that of the liturgy, were mixed up—inextricably, for the laity—with innovations in statements of faith, catechesis, preaching and ecclesial practice which were most unworthy of belief and which the laity quickly recognized as unecclesial. These disorders were justified as legitimate by their authors in many ways, and were cemented theoretically and practically, so that calls to order by higher authorities, if they came, died away without any effect" (*SP*, 11–12).

tution of the Church directly willed by Christ with detailed instructions given to the Apostles before his death; but more in the sense that this (no less) irrevocable structure is rooted in the imperious nature of Christ's call, which would be so easy to refuse (or not even hear!) if the Church were conceived without further ado as merely "the People of God" who could themselves decide for a so-called "people's church" with ecclesiastical leaders answering the beck and call of the congregation.[30]

But it is not just a question of hierarchy, but more fundamentally for Balthasar of the vowed state: that is, married or religious life. So we must keep in mind Balthasar's distinction between the religious state (of the evangelical counsels) and the clerical state (of ordained office) and the lay state which stands in contrast to both. Both in a sense are decision-compelling structures: both demand life-time commitments ("definitiveness is inherent in self-surrender" [*CSL*, 61]), and both are direct responses to the call of the Lord. But they differ in important respects (and not merely on the gender-specificity of the clerical state). And above all, they differ in this: the religious life has priority *as a form of discipleship* over that of the clerical or priestly state.[31] And the reasons for this stem once more from the "christological constellation" clustered around Jesus on the cross:

As opposed to the lay state, the priestly and evangelical states represent a special, differentiated vocation; *the call to one of these states is the sole means by which a state of life can be established within the Church.* . . . The difference between the priestly state and the religious state, however, lies in the fact that the priestly state requires the closer following of Christ only indirectly by reason of the office it confers, whereas the evangelical state requires it directly by reason of the personal way of life it entails. Unlike John, who represents the evangelical life, Peter, who represents the official ministry, was not granted the grace of sharing in the Cross of Christ. . . . Correspondingly, the official ministry established in the New Testament seems, in one respect, to be but a continuation of the order that existed in the Old Testament, whereas the Old Testament depicts only distant images, not the actual foundation, of the evangelical state. *This state has its source wholly in the Cross of Christ and is, therefore,*

---

[30] Balthasar will often use the metaphor of a skeleton for the hierarchy: it is not life itself, but absolutely necessary *for* life, and in any event is not a feature of human anatomy that can be revoked or restructured at will.

[31] This is discussed and defended especially in *CSL*, 364–367, where Balthasar ranks the states of life with a set of arrows leading upward from the lay state at the bottom => to the priestly state in the middle => to the evangelical state at the top (365).

solely his foundation. It became possible as a way of life only
after Christ, its model, had walked the way of redemption.[32]

Furthermore, the state of the vowed life has priority over the sacerdotal
state because "the state of the counsels existed before the priestly state."[33]
Which means, above all, that the Church has authority over God's graces
only for the purpose of dispensing them; church authority is a service to
those who love so that they may grow in love." All of this is symbolized
in the christological constellation around the Cross. For according to Balthasar, "it is of the utmost significance *that John met the Lord's mother
at the foot of the Cross and nowhere else*" (CSL, 287; author's emphasis).
The reason for this is what Mary, Peter and John symbolize: "John was
himself a priest; as the virgin apostle he represented the 'religious priest'
as opposed to Peter, the married 'secular priest.'"[34] And by extension we
may also say that it is significant that Peter was *not* to be seen there, and
moreover was caught out denying the Lord three times lest he risk his

---

[32] CSL, 365–366; my emphasis. I should also mention in this context, if only in passing
(and I regret I cannot develop this important idea further) that Mary is the patron of the
lay state because, like all pious and devout women of the Old Testament, she anticipated a
life of marriage (since the "evangelical" state had not yet been born), and then in her assent
at the Annunciation became the patron of the religious state, but in a way that transcends
them both: "Although Mary's single state, in which she is at once virgin and mother,
transcends man's two states of life within the Church, it nevertheless reflects the exact
ordering of these states. *Her spiritual Yes is the cause of her bodily fecundity. . . .* Mary,
then, is not virgin and mother by equal title. She becomes a mother because she is and
remains a virgin, because she is the one totally consecrated to God. In her, the preeminence
of the state of election over the secular state is fully evidenced. On the other hand, the
purpose of her whole existence lies in her motherhood. *She is a virgin so that she may
become a mother. . . .* Consequently, there is also affirmed in her that other proposition:
that the [evangelical] state of life within the Church is not an end in itself, but is ordered
to the first [lay state] just as everything higher in the Church is higher only because it renders
greater service. . . . Never was a life more fulfilled even in a human sense than Mary's life,
on which, for the gift of her perfect Yes, God bestowed on her all the gifts of heaven"
(CSL, 204–205).

[33] CSL, 251. This does not prejudice what Balthasar said just above, that the evangelical
state was born at the Cross while the priesthood of Christ represents, to some extent, a
continuation of the Old Testament priesthood. What he means by giving the temporal priority to the life of the counsels is this: that the priest continues the sacrifice Christ made on
Calvary, whereas Christ called disciples to him in his earthly ministry in ways that are directly
related to the three vows of poverty (Mt 19:29; Lk 9:57–62), chastity (Mt 19:10–12), and
obedience (Mt 16:16–19; Lk 9:47–48; 10:16). But we may also say that the evangelical
state is born on the Cross in this sense: that its form of renunciation was unheard of in the
Old Testament and it receives its fecundity from the renunciation that John and Mary
witnessed on the Cross.

[34] CSL, 287. These of course are not exegetical judgments and Balthasar is not so naïve
as to say they are. What he means is that Mary, Peter, and John "real symbols," an interpretative model he defends in OP, 148–161.

own neck. For John, *the* Beloved Disciple *par excellence,* represents the Church of love and *agapé,* whereas Peter represents the official teaching Church that holds the power of the keys. And this means that all the scenes of the Gospels where they appear together are of the deepest significance for the later Church:

> On Easter morning, Peter and John ran together to the tomb; love, which is less encumbered than office, arrived more quickly at the goal, but did not use the nearness thus afforded it to take precedence over office. On the contrary, John waited for Peter to come up, let him enter the tomb first, and went in himself only after Peter had concluded his official inspection (Jn 20:8). ... Again, at the draft of fishes on Lake Tiberias, love was quicker than office and communicated to office its recognition of the Lord (Jn 21:6–7). (*CSL,* 283)

But these are not two Churches that stand over against one another: they must be interrelated for each other's benefit. That is why John yields to Peter at the tomb, and above all why the risen Jesus asks of Peter, painfully and embarrassingly, "Do you love me *more than these?*" and Peter can only reply with a modified affirmative: "Yes, Lord, you know I love you" (Jn 21:15), declining, one notices, the opportunity to assume the comparative:

> When it is a question of learning something from or about the Lord, Peter can no longer rely, as he has hitherto done, on John's greater love. Nor can he justify himself by claiming that the burden of office is already great enough, that he would therefore prefer to leave to John, who has been specially chosen for this purpose, the burden of love, which is an office in its own right. He must also become the embodiment of love. ... For one cannot understand anything in the realm of love unless one loves. (*CSL,* 283–284)

In his other work on these same themes, *The Office of Peter,* Balthasar extends this *Realsymbolik* to Paul and James too, and then arranges these four pillars of the Church into a cruciform foursome that illustrates all of the tensions that have marked the Church from that moment on, with James representing Jewish tradition and law, Paul our freedom in the Holy Spirit, Peter the pastoral office, and John the love that abides (*OP,* 308–358). For Balthasar this tension marks a dialectic that "will characterize the temporal course of Church history until the return of Christ."[35]

---

[35] *OP,* 322. In a revealing footnote on this same page, Balthasar points out how damaging it can be for the Church if too much weight is put on just one of the pillars; this is particularly

But it is a fruitful tension if dealt with in love—the specifically Johannine charism. And this no doubt is why he has chosen John as the patron saint of his secular institute and publishing firm, and why his own theology is so Johannine in form and charism:

> And how characteristic it is that John stands aside from this ongoing struggle to find balance in the unity of the Church! The love that "abides" does not dispute, does not enter into arguments: the most it does is repeat the one commandment of the Lord and lead people into a deeper understanding of it. . . . Then, when the brilliant convert Paul comes on the scene, John silently disappears, to set up on the sidelines that "school" of love which is also a school of obedience to the principle of office. Polycarp, Ignatius of Antioch, Irenaeus—with John's followers the Church's great theology begins to unfold. This is the model and the standard for truthfulness within the Church. (*OP*, 323)

---

damaging in the case of Paul, whose personality fairly leaps out of the page: "In practice, all great heresies or harmful one-sided judgments of the West can be traced back to Paul: the teaching of predestination of the aged Augustine, the consequences of which were devastating; the theses of the Augustinian monk, Luther, those of Calvin, Baius and of Jansenius' *Augustinus* and all its consequences. Paul, least of all, must not be isolated from the foursome of the 'pillars'" (ibid., note 24).

Part IV

THE THEOLOGIC

• • •

Be adored among men,
God, three-numberèd form;
Wring thy rebel, dogged in den,
Man's malice, with wrecking and storm.
Beyond saying sweet, past telling of tongue,
Thou art lightning and love, I found it, a winter and warm;
Father and fondler of heart thou hast wrung:
Hast thy dark descending and most art merciful then.

Gerard Manley Hopkins, S.J.
"The Wreck of the Deutschland"

· 11 ·

The Logic of God

I admire thee, master of the tides,
Of the Yore-flood, of the year's fall;
The recurb and the recovery of the gulf's sides,
The girth of it and the wharf of it and the wall;
Staunching, quenching ocean of a motionable mind;
Ground of being, and granite of it; past all
Grasp God, throned behind
Death with a sovereignty that heeds but hides, bodes but abides.
Gerard Manley Hopkins, S.J.
"The Wreck of the Deutschland"

We have finally reached the final summit of this intimidating mountain range we have been exploring and must now scale one of the most difficult issues of Balthasar's theology: his speculations on the Trinity.[1] It is, of course, an intimidation that is felt across the board by nearly anyone who familiar with Christian doctrine—and not just by theologians. Trinity Sunday in the liturgical year is notorious among priests for occasioning much hair-pulling and hand-wringing in their homily preparations and is regarded almost universally as the most difficult day of the year for the preacher. Catechists, too, resort to subterfuges and offer lame analogies. Karl Rahner even goes so far as to claim that a major part of contemporary theology could well remain unchanged had the Church no doctrine of the Trinity, since by and large theology suffers nowadays from what he calls an "anti-trinitarian timidity."[2] In an admirably lucid essay

---

[1] I have of course structured this book to follow Balthasar's own trilogy, but to avoid repetitiousness I have also tried to confine certain key themes that can be found throughout his theology to certain sections of the trilogy. Thus, it seemed best to take on the issues of the Trinity in that place where they would receive their most natural treatment, in the *Theologik,* though of course his whole work is saturated with his convictions about the Trinity, and we shall feel free to draw on all of his trinitarian writings in setting forth this chapter.

[2] Karl Rahner, *The Trinity* (New York: Herder, 1970), 13, 11.

on the Trinity, theologian Catherine LaCugna writes that this timidity extends even beyond outright critics of the doctrine to include the very people who should be most concerned with this doctrine, systematic theologians: "Even within circles sympathetic to retaining a trinitarian schema for Christian faith, many writings in christology, ecclesiology and other areas remain notably reserved about the doctrine of the triune God."[3]

Whatever mystery clings to the doctrine of the Trinity, there certainly can be no mystery about the intimidation people feel in approaching it: what on earth can it mean for God to be One and yet divisible in his self-relations? Is this not tantamount to slipping in a mythological, and hence polytheistic, view of God through the back door, as Jews and Muslims maintain? Does it not violate one of the central passages of the Old Testament, a passage that has now almost become a short-hand Credo for Jews: "Hear, O Israel, the Lord our God is One" (Deut 6:4)? Or perhaps the doctrine is, especially in the face of these objections, just a "mystery," that is, something that must be accepted "on faith," without further ado, with a shrug that this is the one part of Christian doctrine that will ever remain inaccessible to the desire of faith to seek understanding.[4]

But this clearly will not do. We have already seen in our discussion of Peter's first sermon on Pentecost Sunday (no intimidation there!) that trinitarian language is an inevitable outcome when the preacher entrusted with proclaiming the good news must speak of what God has done in Christ through his death, resurrection and ascension. There simply is no coherent way of expressing Christ's life as God's salvation *for us* except in trinitarian terms.[5] Christ clearly cannot be God *totaliter,* which would be either flagrantly mythological or would raise the awkward question of who was "minding the store" while he was walking this earth. Yet it will hardly do to go the way of the Unitarians and simply say that Jesus was

---

[3] Catherine Mowry LaCugna, "The Trinitarian Mystery of God," in *Systematic Theology: Roman Catholic Perspectives,* ed. Francis Schüssler Fiorenza and John P. Galvin (Minneapolis: Fortress Press, 1991) 1:152; henceforth: *ST:RCP.*

[4] LaCugna describes quite well the impasse to which such a surrender of the standards of reason leads: "In the recent past, theological education in Catholic seminaries often went no further than requiring students to memorize the 5–4–3–2–1 formula, a mnemonic device for retaining the essential elements of the Thomistic doctrine of the Trinity: God is 'five notions, four relations, three persons, two processions, and one nature.' When Bernard Lonergan was taught this he is reported to have added, 'and zero comprehension!'" (ibid., 153). See also recent work *God For Us: The Trinity and Christian Life* (San Francisco: Harper, 1991), which is a much more extensive presentation of the views she was only able to adumbrate in her article.

[5] See Balthasar's two article on the *pro nobis* and their trinitarian connection: "Crucifixus etiam pro nobis," *Internationale katholische Zeitschrift: Communio* 9 (1980): 26–35; and "Der sich für mich dahingegeben hat," *Geist und Leben* 53 (1980): 416–419. Unfortunately neither of these two important essays has been translated into English, nor do they appear in any of his volumes of collected essays, where they might expect future translation.

a man born of woman in the natural way of all men, who set a good example for us, and then who "rose" merely in the minds of the disciples and whose "spirit" lives on in much the same way that the spirit of Martin Luther King lives on among those committed to liberation and civil equality for African-Americans. In the case of great charismatic leaders like Socrates or King, this is an entirely appropriate scheme. But applied to Jesus? How can it do justice to the Good News of salvation wrought for us? What kind of salvation is given in mere example?

So the predicament is ineluctable: God has clearly acted in Christ in such a way as to remain fully sovereign over the universe—yet he has also acted in such a way that "through the Spirit of holiness" Christ could be "*declared* Son of God by his resurrection from the dead" (Rom 1:3): "Therefore God exalted him to the highest place and gave him the name that is above every name, that at the name of Jesus every knee should bend in heaven and on earth and under the earth, and every tongue confess that Jesus Christ is Lord to the glory of God the Father" (Phil 2:9–11). Faced with this kind of proclamation of God's great deeds in Christ, the Church instinctively knew that, in proclaiming these actions, it was thereby also saying something *about the inherent nature of God in his being and essence;* and that is why the hymn in Philippians we have just cited begins with saying that Christ Jesus was "in the very *nature* of God, but did not consider *equality* with God something to be clung to, but emptied himself, taking on the very form of a slave" (2:6–7). Moreover, the very insight into and the dawning realization of this new revelation about the nature of God takes place in the Holy Spirit: "God has revealed it to us by his Spirit. The Spirit searches all things, even the deep things of God. For who among us knows the thoughts of another except the person's own spirit within him? Similarly, no one knows the thoughts of God except the Spirit of God" (1 Cor 2:10–11).

This is why Karl Rahner's famous dictum that the economic Trinity is the immanent Trinity and vice-versa has found such a broad consensus among theologians across the confessional spectrum.[6] What he was saying here was that speculations about the inner life of the Trinity (the so-called "immanent" Trinity) had become so unmoored from our access to that triune reality via how God was acting in Christ (the so-called "economic" Trinity, that is, the Trinity that was acting in the "economy" [= dispensation] of salvation) that it was losing all relevance to Christian life (hence the trinitarian timidity he spoke of above). Basically, Balthasar agrees with this:

---

[6] Karl Rahner, *The Trinity,* 22. LaCugna mentions Congar, Kasper and Schoonenberg (*ST:RCP* 1:174–176; Kasper also includes Barth and Meyendorff (*The God of Jesus Christ,* tr. Matthew J. O'Connell [New York: Crossroad, 1984], 273–274). But all of these theologians also propose their own variants or reservations.

On the one side, we see Jesus pointing to the Father and on the other to the Spirit: and thus we discern the radiant reality of what will be formulated in terms of the divine Trinity. The Father to whom Jesus points is his Origin, but is also other than he; so too the Spirit, whom he will send from the Father after his return to him, is other than he. *In Christian faith, however, it is only on the basis of Jesus Christ's own behavior and attitude that we can distinguish such a plurality in God*. . . . We know about the Father, Son and Spirit as divine "Persons" only through the figure and disposition of Jesus Christ. Thus we can agree with the principle, often espoused today, that it is only on the basis of the economic Trinity that we can have knowledge of the immanent Trinity and dare to make statements about it.[7]

Now as is well known, the ways of explaining the mystery of this plurality in the one God move in one of two directions: either by explaining the trinity on an *interpersonal* model (always insuring of course that the substantial unity of God be protected) or on the *psychological* model (always insuring that the Persons of the Trinity not be collapsed into merely the "mental phases" of the life of God). When these two solutions veer into heresy, as they frequently do, they are referred to, respectively, as tritheism and modalism. Now speaking only generically (and in a chapter of this kind I can only paint in broad strokes), the East has favored explanations of the Trinity that often sound to Western ears tritheistic, while the West favors imagery that often strikes Eastern theologians as blandly and tautologically modalistic. Thus Gregory of Nyssa will say that God can be three persons in one nature just as Peter, James and John are three persons in one human nature.[8] Whereas Augustine will

---

[7] *TD* 3, 507–508; my emphasis. See also *TD* III, 297–305. In other words, we are trying to make clear that Balthasar's reflections on the inner exchange of life and love within the (immanent) Trinity are *not* theoretical musings or speculative reveries; rather, they are "theological meditations on the trinitarian figure of Jesus Christ as it appears in and constitutes salvation history" (J. Randall Sachs, S.J., *Spirit and Life*, 48).

[8] This surely must sound alarming, and would at first blush convince any Jew or Muslim that Christians are in fact, however *sub rosa*, tritheists. But this is a fundamental misperception, as one distinguished patristic scholar has noted: "So it might seem that [Gregory] was a tritheist after all. . . . That is how it seemed to some of [his] contemporaries; that is how it has seemed to many of [his] interpreters ever since. Nevertheless, it is a false seeming. The treatise in which Gregory discusses the example of Peter, James and John is entitled 'That we should not think of saying that there are three Gods.' Gregory was a thoroughgoing Platonist. For the Platonist the universal is more real than the particular. Strictly speaking, says Gregory, we should not speak of three men, but of three participants in the one, unique 'idea of man,' the single, real 'humanity.' So the divine *ousia* [essence] which is common to the three persons is not some abstract, conceptual notion of divinity which each has separately; it is the one, unique reality of God. It is admittedly difficult at first not to

compare the Trinity to the faculties of memory, understanding and love (with numerous variations).[9] And so the conflict has remained down to our own day, for as Wiles explains:

> It is not possible for the human mind to hold its view of the three and the one in equal focus. One can give them equal value on the written page, but the mind needs to make its approach from one side or the other. The East (with the important exception of Athanasius) tends to approach from the side of the three, the West from the side of the one. When an Easterner spoke of God he thought most naturally of the Father, with whom the Son and the Spirit must somehow be joined in one coequal godhead. When a Westerner spoke of God he thought most naturally of the one triune God, within whose being real distinctions of person must somehow be admitted. Thus while the Cappadocians could use, with careful qualification, the illustration of three men, it is not an illustration that could commend itself to Augustine. *If the word "person" were to be used in the normal human sense of God at all, declares Augustine, it would have to be used of the one rather than the three.* The use of this word to refer to the three must not be understood in such a sense.[10]

I have needed to mention all of this at the outset of this chapter because I want to head off early a potential misunderstanding: Balthasar shall be discussing the Trinity using very daring language that could be the occasion for misunderstanding. How much this misunderstanding might be his own fault is of course a legitimate question, and it is one we shall have to examine, however cursorily. But the key issue at the moment is to see how the human mind will naturally veer toward one or the other alternative, and Balthasar has certainly left the impression that he leans more toward the three than the one, especially in contrast to Rahner, who has accused him of indulging in overly gnostic speculations.[11] There is

---

read Gregory in tritheistic terms; but so to read him is to misread him" (Maurice Wiles, *The Christian Fathers* [New York: Oxford University Press, 1982/1966], 46–47).

[9] Eugène Portalié, S.J. has provided us with a list of no less than 22 variations on this theme in his essential book, *A Guide to the Thought of St. Augustine*, tr. Ralph Bastian, S.J. (Westport, CT: Greenwood Press, 1975/1960), 134–135.

[10] Wiles, *The Christian Fathers*, p. 50; my emphasis. Of course, Wiles adds that "Augustine continues to use [the term, but] only because it has become tradition and he knows of no alternative but silence" (ibid.).

[11] "If I wanted to launch a counterattack, I would say that there is a modern tendency . . . to develop a theology of the death of God that, in the last analysis, seems to me to be gnostic. One can find this in Hans Urs von Balthasar and in Adrienne von Speyr, although naturally much more marked in her than in him. It also appears in an independent form in Moltmann. To put it crudely, it does not help me to escape from my mess and mix-up and

perhaps a certain irony to this in that it is generally the speculative bent that has given rise to an insistence on the unity of God, whereas theologians who concentrate on the saving deeds of God *in history* are the ones who are drawn to trinitarian language.[12] And that is a point we will be insisting on throughout this chapter: *Balthasar develops his theology of the Trinity out of his conviction of what it meant for Jesus to become cursed for our sake and experience the condemnation of the Father in hell.* Balthasar theology of the Trinity is, so to speak, Triduum-determined.

In fact, if anything the *Theologik* intensifies this concern. In a most telling footnote in this work, he accuses himself of yielding to a "compromise" in his book *Mysterium Paschale* for merely saying that in dying Jesus showed his "solidarity with the dead," rather than coming right out and baldly asserting that Jesus also had to be tasting the condemnation and fate of the eternally damned in his descent into hell.[13] So we must always keep in mind the same intense concern that led Peter to break with traditional Jewish terminology in describing the being of God: the saving, *soteriological* significance of the death of Christ. This is not to deny the speculative concerns about the unity of God that led Augustine to be so cautious of personalist terminology, still less is it to dismiss the witness of Judaism and Islam concerning God's essential oneness. But Christians reply differently to these concerns, which they too share, simply (but crucially) because they believe that in the death of Christ the world

---

despair if God is in the same predicament. . . . It is to me a source of consolation to realize that God, when and insofar as he entered into this history as into his own, did it in a different way than I did. From the beginning I am locked into this horribleness while God— if this word continues to have any meaning at all—is in a true and authentic sense the God who does not suffer, the immutable God, and so on. In Moltmann and others I sense a theology of absolute paradox, of Patripassianism, perhaps even of a Schelling-esque projection into God of divine, conflict, godlessness and death" (*Karl Rahner in Dialogue: Conversations and Interviews, 1965–1982*, ed. Paul Imhof and Hubert Biallowons, tr. Harvey D. Egan [New York: Crossroad, 1986], 126–127). The dispute between Rahner and Balthasar in this area is so deeply rooted in metaphysical assumptions that it could be as irresolvable as the medieval debate between the realists and nominalists.

[12] "[Augustine] changed the whole approach to his subject fundamentally from that of the Greeks: his starting point was the unity of God. In this he was distinctive, as he [also] was in giving much more thought to the Trinity as a divine mystery than to the Incarnation, by which the Trinity was made known to man" (Michael O'Carroll, C.S.Sp., *Trinitas: A Theological Encyclopedia of the Holy Trinity* [Wilmington, DE: Michael Glazier, 1987], 42).

[13] I think this footnote important enough to quote in full: "Much of what is to be treated here has already been discussed in *TD* IV, 273–288 under other rubrics. Furthermore, one will notice from the previous chapter that my book *Mysterium Paschale* (which I had to write in a hurry, since at the last minute I had to substitute for an author who took sick) tried to clear a path for the more daring doctrine of Adrienne von Speyr. The concept 'solidarity with the dead' was a compromise, and it won't crop up in the following pages ever again. Instead of remaining back with the preliminary stages that I prepared the way for, the reader will henceforward have to engage her own writings directly, especially *Kreuz und Hölle*" (*TL* II, 315, note 1).

has been crucified to God, "who has bound all men over to disobedience so that he may have mercy on them all" (Rom 11:32).

Nonetheless, in some ways, despite a greater intensity and focus on the descent into hell, the Theologic also represents a move to capture the best of Western concerns of unity that are born out of more purely philosophical concerns. When juxtaposed over against the Theodramatics, the Theologic evinces a tremendous tension in Balthasar's thought to do justice both to the inherently *dramatic* nature of the intra-trinitarian relations and also to God's essential and unchangeable *eternity*. As Gerald O'Hanlon has well noted:

> What is distinctive among theologians like Balthasar is precisely the explicit attempt to combine the static with the dynamic, to preserve the category of state while being open to that of event, to avoid the rationalism of an essentialist ontology, not by giving priority to the notion of "process" but rather by retaining the ontological, without denying the abiding truth of the notion of "becoming." In Balthasar himself, then, the *Theodramatik* can never be separated from the *Theologik:* goodness and truth, with the other transcendentals of unity and beauty, must together help us to form our notion of the trinitarian God of Jesus Christ, a notion in which the philosophical elements are quite explicitly inspired by (while being able to contribute to) the theological, in that symbiosis between theology and philosophy in which Balthasar insists on the priority of the former.[14]

We are, I believe, particularly fortunate that Balthasar lived long enough that he was able to finish the last panel of his Trilogy (he was, after all, already 78 years old when he finished the last volume of the *second* panel!). For in it he is able to face more directly the issues that pertain to the tensions that have animated his thought from the beginning regarding the transcendence of God—who yet makes himself accessible to us in revelation. Now I do not mean to imply in saying this that Balthasar, in being able to finish the last panel of his triptych that the *Theologik* represents, has either departed significantly from his thought or supplemented it with previously unheard of material (though, as we have seen, he will at times try to intensify previous strains of this thought). For one thing, the first volume of the Theologic is simply the reprint of a work, *Wahrheit* (*Truth*), that he had published in 1947, several years before he began work on the opening volume of the Trilogy. So even in terms of his bibliog-

---

[14] Gerald O'Hanlon, S.J., *The Immutability of God in the Theology of Hans Urs von Balthasar* (Cambridge: Cambridge University Press, 1990), 112; henceforward: O'Hanlon, *Immutability*.

raphy, there is a circular movement at work. But this is merely the reflection of his metaphysics in any event:

> The reduction of a knowledge of the truth to a purely theoretical kind of evidence from which all living, personal, and ethical decisions have been carefully excluded entails such a palpable narrowing of the field of truth that it is already thereby robbed of its universality and thus of its own proper essence. If truth and goodness are both really transcendental properties of being, then both must interpenetrate each other and every exclusive juxtaposition of their respective realm can only lead to a distortion of their mutual essence. Correspondingly, the same also goes for the last transcendental property of being, that of beauty: she too makes a claim staked on her universal validity; she too can never be separated from her two sisters. And so the quite elementary demand for an ethic and aesthetic of truth and a knowledge of the truth naturally arises from the insight that only the three transcendental determinants of being [when taken together] reveal being's inner richness as it really is: that is, only they unveil its truth. Consequently, only a constant, living unity of theoretical, ethical and aesthetic attitudes can mediate true knowledge of being.[15]

This interpenetration of the three transcendentals might remind the reader of the Trinity and especially of the traditional doctrine of *perichoresis* (or circuminsession), of the three Persons: the doctrine that states that the Persons of the Trinity mutually interpenetrate each other so that, although each Person is distinct in *relation* to the others, nevertheless each participates fully in the *being* of the others: the being of the Godhead is thus one and indivisible. This similarity is certainly indicative, but as with any comparison drawn from worldly being, the analogy must be applied with care. Certainly, as Balthasar says, "the transcendentals that govern all being can only exist within one another."[16] But everything depends on

---

[15] *TL* I, 18. Manfred Lochbrunner claims that he can detect a "shift" or a "turning point" in Balthasar's thought which he locates somewhere between the time when he published his dissertation to the publication of *Wahrheit* in 1947, a book which to Lochbrunner represents really the opening salvo in what would become the Trilogy. I find the claim plausible, especially its implication that Balthasar had already clearly thought out the theological consequences of the three transcendentals and planned a project on that basis sometime after first meeting Adrienne von Speyr (Manfred Lochbrunner, *Analogia Caritatis: Darstellung und Deutung der Theologie Hans Urs von Balthasars*, Freiburger Theologische Studien, Vol. 124 [Freiburg im Breisgau: Herder, 1981], 82). And so my reluctance to see any radical shift in Balthasar's thought really applies only to the period that begins with the publication of *Wahrheit*.

[16] *Ep*, 52: "Die Tranzendentalien, die alles Sein durchwaltet, können nur ineinander sein."

which schema is the governing one: "Thus we may definitively conclude that the whole unabridged metaphysic of the transcendentals of being can only be unfolded under the theological light of the creation of the world in the Word of God, who ultimately expresses himself in divine freedom as a sensate-spiritual man. But in asserting this we do so without thereby saying that metaphysics itself needs to become theology."[17]

The structure of the three-volume *Theologik* respects this distinction: the first volume is called *The Truth of the World* (this volume is identical, even in pagination, with the earlier book first published in 1947, except that to it is appended an introduction to the *Theologik* and an explanation of the relevance of this volume to the whole project); the second, *The Truth of God;* and the third, *The Spirit of Truth*. Moreover, it is a distinction, I shall maintain, that is absolutely crucial for understanding his trinitarian theology.

Briefly, the distinction goes like this: while Balthasar will wish to approach the mystery of the inner-trinitarian life "negatively," that is, by denying the idea of change and suffering in God in our sense, he will nonetheless insist that the conditions for the possibility of these same realities outside God (that is, here on earth) are in fact to be found within God. This might sound dauntingly abstract and speculative, and like all trinitarian speculation, I suppose it is, but it is meant to keep two points of theology always in mind that are not easy to view together: that while the Trinity establishes within itself all of the conditions for the possibility of the world, we cannot read back the nature of God *from* the world. Balthasar speaks in this regard of a "caesura" within God between his being for himself and his decision to create the world:

Certainly we must put a caesura between the eternal Yes uttered by God's will to himself and his eternal life and the Yes which seals the decision to create. This is simply because creation is not God and hence not necessary; not even in the sense in which Plato's or Plotinus' "Good" overflows by nature beyond itself or, in Leibniz's sense, in which the idea of the best possible world "presses up" to be brought into reality. The living God does not pour himself forth by nature; *all the same, the freedom in which he determines that the world shall exist is, according to its na-*

---

[17] *Ep,* 59. Notice how each order of being is respected according to its own terms. This citation is drawn from the *Epilogue* to the whole trilogy, which is divided into three sections: "Antechamber," "Threshold," "Cathedral." The preceding two quotations come from the second section, since the transcendentals are regarded a merely the forecourt to the Holy of Holies.

ture, none other than the freedom by which he wills eternally to be what he is.[18]

From this distinction Balthasar is able to draw some astonishing conclusions. The concept of drama, we have learned, presupposes and is correlated to freedom, but our freedom is grounded in *God's* freedom, which is inherent to God's nature and does not merely arise in the caesura of his decision to create. For God is free by essence, that is, as a Trinity:

> Unlike God, the world, and finite freedom within it, will not have its ground in itself, not even in an "idea": its ground is exclusively in God's freedom, which will always distinguish its nature from that of God, even at the highest level of union between divine and created freedom. But, being totally dependent on divine freedom, the world can receive its possibility and reality nowhere else but in the eternal Son, who eternally owes his divine being to the Father's generosity. If the Son is the Father's eternal Word, the world in its totality is created by this Word (Jn 1:3), not only instrumentally but in the sense that the Word is the world's pattern and hence its goal. (*TD* 2, 261)

Because the world is contingent, it is passive in its potency to receive being; because God is necessary Being, he is entirely active in the fullness of his being (*actus purus*). But in terms of the intra-trinitarian relations (and we recall that the Persons in the Trinity have no self-subsistent substance but are definable only in terms of their mutual relations), we not only can but must speak of passivity and receptivity in God, for the Son owes his-being-Son entirely to the generating love of the Father, which he returns entirely back to the Father in Eucharistic gratitude, a responsiveness which breathes forth the Spirit, who in turn binds the love of Father and Son as their *vinculum amoris*. Even God the Father, then, is

---

[18] *TD* 2, 261; my emphasis. This caesura is of course not to be understood temporally but purely in terms of necessity and contingency, as O'Hanlon well explains: "The function of this caesura is not to introduce a temporal factor into God's being, but rather to point out that, while God's eternal inner-divine liveliness does not naturally issue in creation, nonetheless the freedom with which he creates is in accordance with his nature as love in the self-giving way that is revealed in the Trinity. Within this framework, creation is affirmed as good in its own dependent reality: it is not God, but neither is it a mere accident or appearance" (*Immutability*, 52). This same author also makes the point that the caesura between necessity in God and contingency in creation also grounds the possibility of our speaking of "liveliness" and "event" in God without prejudice to his immutability: "The dynamism of God's love, with its diverse modalities, occurs eternally, without need, and in this sense is compatible with both the perfection and the immutability of God" (ibid., 115).

"passive" in the sense of fully open to the return of the Son's love and to the binding power of the Spirit.[19]

As Balthasar himself would freely admit, one "stammers" in the attempt to speak of divine passivities within the *actus purus*.[20] For one thing, it opens up the possibility of applying feminine imagery in God, in the sense that in the act of sexual procreation, it is the woman who "passively" receives the seed and nurtures it in her womb. And because of his willingness to see a genuine passivity being ascribed to the being of God (internal to the trinitarian relations, of course), Balthasar will even speak of the "womb" of the Father:

> God is always the one who has lovingly surrendered himself in freedom, who accordingly seeks a free and loving vessel [*Raumgeben*] for his love that wants to pour itself into our hearts. He does this so that he might have created freedom by his side, that he might "make his home" (Jn 14:23) with this created freedom even alongside his own infinite freedom. For he wants to be able to "beget" and "give birth to" this freedom (Jn 1:13; 3:5; 1 Jn 3:9) from the womb of his infinite and loving surrender (of the Father to the Son in the Holy Spirit). . . . Obedience is that availability of the Spirit who *lets* himself spring forth from the Father and Son, from their entirely concrete love (as the Gospels show), and he wants also to be the Spirit of our mutual surrendering. He is first and above all the Spirit and attitude of the Father, who lets the Son spring forth from his own power of begetting and nurses him in the Spirit as in a mother's womb. In this way he becomes the prototype for our concrete love of neighbor, in which we should be father and mother to our fellow man.[21]

---

[19] "Balthasar has shown that while there is no pure potentiality or passivity in God, there is an active receptivity which is the original image of passive potency in the created realm. This can be understood as perfection when it is allowed that the omnipotence of God is primarily the absolute power of love, and thus involves the giving and receiving of trinitarian exchange and mutuality in which we too participate" (O'Hanlon, *Immutability*, 124).

[20] "Zu einer christlichen Theologie der Hoffnung," *Münchener Theologische Zeitschrift* 32 (1981): 32–102; here, 99: "Im welchem Vokabular wir von diesen Passivitäten innerhalb des *actus purus* auch immer zu stammeln versuchen, zugegeben ist, daß sie vorhanden sind, und zwar in für uns nicht vorstellbaren Ausmaßen, weil die Differenzen zwischen Vater, Sohn und Geist so unendlich sind, daß nicht einmal ein univoker (abstrakter) Personbegriff sie umfaßt."

[21] "Zur Unterscheidung der Geister," *PI*, 328–329, 334: "Vielmehr ist Gott immer schon der, der sich in Freiheit liebend hingegeben hat, der deshalb auch ein freies und liebendes Raumgeben für seine sich-ergießen-wollende Liebe sucht, um in der geschaffenen Freiheit deshalb auch mit seiner eigenen unendlichen Freiheit zu 'bewohnen' (Jn 14:23), sie aus dem *Schoß* der unendlichen Liebeshingabe (des Vaters an den Sohn im Heiligen Geist) neu 'zeugen' und '*gebären*' zu können (Jn 1:13; 3:5; 1 Jn 3:9). . . . Gehorsam ist hier zuerst jene Fügsamkeit des Geistes, der sich aus Vater und Sohn, aus ihrer ganz konkret im Evangelium bewie-

But his daring goes much farther than that: he will say that we can even attribute to God something like faith and prayer. Here the influence of Adrienne von Speyr is especially strong.[22] But so also is Péguy's, to whom Balthasar devoted an entire chapter in *Lay Styles*.[23] And this is because the infinite qualitative difference that separates the world from God and is the presupposition for prayer must itself *be grounded in God*. All attributes that inhere in us must be grounded in God: "the infinite distance between the world and God has its foundation in that original distance between God and God, within God."[24] And that even goes for sin (how daring this man is!); for God's freedom is the presupposition for man's freedom, the very ground of its possibility, including to sin; and giving man freedom must include the risk that he will abuse that freedom in sin.

Now of course, Balthasar is not saying that God wills the creature to sin, nor that the "primal image" of sin subsists in God; but he does insist that the experience of separation from God which ensues as a direct

---

senen Liebe, entspringen *läßt*, und Geist unserer gegenseitigen Hingebung sein will. Er ist zuerst Geist und Gesinnung des Vaters, der den Sohn aus seiner Zeugungskraft entspringen läßt und ihn in diesem Geist wie in einem *mütterlichen Schoße* hegt, und damit Urbild für unsere konkrete Nächstenliebe, in der wir Väter und Mütter unserer Mitmenschen sein sollen" (my emphases). For other references to the Father's womb see also *TD* 2, 262 ("Is the Father's womb not 'empty' once he has generated the entire Son?") and his radio sermon "The Communion of Saints" ("God's relation to the world is not only masculine, as *Deus faber*, but womb-like and feminine, achieving the redemption of the entire universe *through pain*") in *Crown*, 223.

[22] See *TD* 4, 83–86 ("Die Absolutheit des Gebetes"), which is almost entirely a string of quotations from her work. Most determining in this regard is her book *The World of Prayer*, tr. Graham Harrison (San Francisco: Ignatius Press, 1985), 28–74, esp.: "A person in love who is waiting for the beloved brings a fulfillment greater than the expectation. Instead of a correspondence between them, there is a relation of superabundance. Even when love knows what it may expect, namely 'more,' the 'more' of the fulfillment is not simply a replica of the expected 'more.' The Son is the Father's first expectation and his first fulfillment, and for eternity he remains what he was and is: expectation and fulfillment, expectation which, though unsurpassable, *is* surpassed by the fulfillment. ... In eternal vision and love, two things are united which in the earthly vision and love are separate, namely, *act and state*. ... In this way a rich texture arises through the interplay of fulfillment and expectation, what is present and what is yet to be discovered, state and act—an interplay that creates love's vitality and inexhaustibility. True love can never be boring; it is self-renewing" (30, 40). Or as O'Hanlon declares: "There is no boredom in heaven" (*Immutability*, 114).

[23] For example: "The whole of Péguy's art and theology flow more and more towards prayer without one ever being able to say precisely whether his prayer is his dialogue with God or his eavesdropping on God's monologue. It is a dialogue with God . . . but one which is constantly developing into a monologue of God the Father, addressed without distinction to his Son, to the humans he created and to himself. It is a form of 'theology as trinitarian conversation,' never realized prior to Péguy" (*GL* 3, 506). And in the opening volume of the Trilogy he depicts Jesus' Last Discourse on the night before he died as the "manifestation of substantial intra-divine prayer" (*GL* 1, 616).

[24] O'Hanlon, *The Immutability of God*, 54.

consequence of sin must be capable of being integrated into the trinitarian differences—otherwise there is no salvation.[25] For in the Trinity distance and separation are always positive realities; in the Trinity, and there alone, distance comes to be *because of* love: God the Father's love is so total that there is "nothing left," so to speak, when he generates his Son in love; and the Son returns that love so totally, also holding nothing back, that he too is totally "emptied." And this mutual refraction of loves, this eternal exchange and *perichoresis* of giving and receiving one's entire relational being, is itself so total that it "spirates" the Spirit (to use the tradition terminology of trinitarian theology). And that same Spirit is so much and so totally the Spirit *of* the Father and Son that he is able to bind them in loving union even when their loving self-bestowal is so total that they have "lost" themselves.[26]

One of Balthasar's most distinctive contributions to theology is his notion of "trinitarian inversion" (*Umkehrung*). By this he means that the relations that obtain within the Trinity are in a certain way "inverted" when the Word becomes flesh. What does this mean? We recall that, in terms of the immanent Trinity, the Spirit is the breathed-forth "product" of the mutual exchange of love between Father and Son and that this exchange is so total that the Spirit, proceeding from Father and Son, is constituted as his own Person, whose relational identity binds and ratifies the bond of Father and Son. Just as the Son owes his entire identity as Son to the Father's act of generation, so too does the Spirit owe his entire identity to the mutuality of love between Father and Son. And that means that as the "last" of the trinitarian Persons, the Spirit is in a special way determined by the Father and Son. But in the incarnation it is the *Son* who is "determined" by the Spirit, who (as we saw in Chapter 9) serves as the "prompter" and mediator of the Father's will:

The mysteries of the inner-divine movements *ad extra* remain for us eternally veiled. No analogy from creation or the economy

---

[25] "It is Balthasar's argument that the trinitarian personal distinctions, based on the opposition of relations, are indeed sufficiently real and infinite to embrace, without loss of unity, the kind of opposition between the Father and the Son which is involved in their common plan to overcome sin. This is so because divine love has the power freely to unfold its richness in such different modalities that the Son's experience of opposition in a hostile sense remains always a function and an aspect of his loving relationship to the Father in the Holy Spirit" (*Immutability*, 119).

[26] The texts where these views are set forth and defended are too numerous (and too prolix) to list here, but somewhat at random I will cite a fairly brief summary: "Their mutual love, which in both is, so to speak, 'exhausted,' must itself open up and demonstrate itself to be absolutely living and creative ... as the eternal fruit in God and the endless fruitfulness in the world. The 'Spirit' is this result of their mutual love, apparently an end but in truth the creative new beginning" (*GL* 7, 251); see also: *SC*, 13–50, 106–122; *PI*,331–332; *TD* 3, 505-535 (esp. 520–523); IV, 389–392; and *TL* 3, 106–119.

of salvation suffices to permit an unbroken statement about the trinitarian life. And most confusing of all is the *economic reversal of relations between Son and Spirit*. Whereas the Spirit proceeds, in the immanent Trinity, from the Father and the Son (or through the Son), the Son becomes man through the Spirit and is led by this same Spirit in his mission. As the one who placed himself under the will of the Father in the self-emptying of his divinity, he lets the Spirit made available by the Father (and who also proceeds from the Father) have power over him as a "rule" of the Father's will. He does this in order to permit this Spirit resting upon him in all fullness to stream out from himself at the end of his mission in death and resurrection (and Eucharist). And the direction of this outpouring goes both to the Father ("into your hands . . . ") as well as to the Church and world ("and so he breathed on them . . . "). (*PI*, 224; author's emphasis)

Another of Balthasar's innovations is his willingness to speak of the Spirit's *kenosis,* as well as the Son's. Indeed, it will be no surprise for the reader who has followed the argument thus far to hear that Balthasar holds that the very ability of the Son to empty himself and take on the human form of a slave is rooted and conditioned in the prior *kenosis* or emptying of each Person for the other.[27] And this holds not only of the Son, who must now follow and "obey" the promptings of the Spirit, but it also holds true of the Spirit: "Because the Spirit assumes the directing role in the incarnation (the Son *lets* himself be available) and because he presents the will of the Father (and thereby also the triune decision to save man) for the Son to follow, the Son hearkens to the Father in the Holy Spirit. And in this process the Spirit also renounces an aspect of his divine form: of being the overwhelming product of the love between Father and Son" (*PI*, 224).

Balthasar illustrates what he means by this inversion by means of a chart (he often resorts to charts, a habit he picked up from Adrienne von Speyr, whose insights into the Trinity were all intuitive—and we must recall that her own training was as a physician and that she never studied theology formally).[28] The horizontal line represents the immanent Trinity,

---

[27] We shall be applying this insight in the present context to the Spirit, but of course it hold first and primarily of the Son, as in Sachs' formulation: "The obedience of Jesus to the Father through the mediating Spirit in/over him is understood as the economic articulation of the inner-trinitarian 'obedience' of the Son, which consists in his utterly free, eternal readiness to be nothing but the perfect expression of the Father's love and will" (Sachs, *Spirit and Life*, 148).

[28] The one reproduced below can be found in *TD* 3, 191; a similar one, only with the arrows going in the reverse direction to indicate Jesus's return to the Father, is located in

and the Holy Spirit's position in the middle of the line represents the Spirit's relational identity as being the product of the interaction and love *between* Father and Son. The vertical line represents the economy of salvation, with the Father above directing the play and the Holy Spirit mediating the Father's will to the Son, who is now on the bottom of the line (the equality of the Persons is illustrated in the evenness of the horizontal line; their super-and sub-ordination in the vertical). And the kenotic movement from the immanent relations to the economic ones is symbolized by the dotted lines:

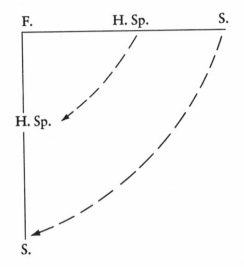

Now this chart can be misleading if the reader thinks it implies that Jesus is merely subordinate to the Spirit, for the Spirit is very definitely also his own Spirit of love for the Father. So that the Son, in descending and assuming human form, takes with himself the very Spirit of obedience that prompted him to descend in the first place. Thus, although what the superordinate Spirit presents to Jesus is often a will of the Father that is overtaxing, Jesus's obedience is always a willing and internally generated obedience, grounded in his kenotic willingness to become man.[29]

TD 3, 523; for his use of charts in other contexts, see *CSL,* 365, 368, 371, 375, 382, 385; *TL* 3, 168.

[29] "As much as Balthasar stresses that the Son does not do his *own* will, but the will of the one who sent him; as much as he describes this obedience as the unquestioning execution of an unbendable rule of law, one must always remember that the Father's will does not appear as a heteronomous command and the obedience of the Son is the expression of his divine freedom. One cannot conceive of the Incarnate Son's obedience to the Father as if he were confronted with a mission and the command to carry it out, and *then* 'decided' to obey. But the saving mission of the Son and his utterly free acceptance of this mission are one from all time" (Sachs, *Spirit and Life,* 149).

Balthasar hopes that this insight into the trinitarian inversion will help to lift the ancient *filioque* dispute out of the rut it has been in for so many centuries. For, as we have seen, in the trinitarian inversion that takes place in the economy of salvation, the Spirit has a dual role: being genuinely the Spirit *of* Jesus and yet the mediator of a will that comes at Jesus from without and which taxes him more than he can bear (Mk 14:34–36). The first role the Spirit performs as the Spirit of the *filioque* (of whom Jesus could say: "the Spirit will take what is mine and make it known to you" [Jn 16:15]): that is, it is really Jesus obeying the Father, it is really *he* performing miracles and feeling consumed by the fire of his mission (Lk 12:49–50). But the Spirit which descends upon him at his baptism, "driving" him into the desert, hurling him toward a cross he shirks, is the Spirit *a Patre procedit* (as in the famous Eastern proof-text: "the Spirit of Truth who proceeds from the Father" of Jn 15:26).[30]

The ecumenical fruitfulness of this new perspective on the Trinity will of course have to be tested by the course of time (though the Patriarch of Constantinople did bestow on him the medal of the Golden Cross of Mt. Athos,[31] which seems to indicate at least a dialogic openness to this theory on the part of the Orthodox Church). Perhaps, though, the first stage in that process will be dealing first with the classically *Western* objections to his approach, which center much more on what critics call his worrisome anthropomorphizing of the term "person" as applied to the Trinity.[32] This worry would be especially present among those theologians who, like Augustine much earlier, find that the term "person" has so radically altered as to have become downright misleading when applied to the Trinity, among whom we must certainly number Karl Rahner:

> I would like to say first of all frankly and sincerely that the term "person" in the doctrine of the Trinity seems to me to be

---

[30] "If we connect this with what we have said about Jesus as the eternal Son, it follows that the *being* of the Spirit in him—the Incarnate One—is the economic form of the *filioque;* and the Spirit who *comes down* upon him, hovers over him and drives him is the Spirit *a Patre procedit*" (TD 3, 521).

[31] On 28 March 1965, an award "established on the occasion of the Centenary Jubilee of the founding to the Greek Orthodox monastic republic, given for services to the history and theology of Orthodoxy and ecumenical dialogue" (citation from the list of "Auszeichnungen" given to Balthasar during his life, from the privately printed memorial book, or *Gedächtnisbuch,* published after his death, 142).

[32] "Nach diesem ersten Blick auf Balthasars Trinitätsdeutung wird der eine oder andere Leser sich fragen, ob man denn ohne weiteres von einem interpersonalen Dialog in Gott reden könne, oder ob es sich nicht eher um krasse Anthropomorphismen handele, mit denen Balthasar im Anschluß an A. von Speyr die Beziehungen der göttlichen Personen zueinander schildert. Man kann sich in der Tat fragen, ob er nicht eine allzustarke Differenzierung und Entgegensetzung der Personen wagt, die in seiner Deutung des Mysteriums die Einheit des Wesens zu kurz kommen läßt. Dies insbesondere dann, wenn er im Blick auf die Verschieden-

misleading or open to misunderstanding. This is not to deny that the term involves a binding linguistic usage for the Catholic theologian, for the proposition: "The one God in his one sole nature subsists in three persons," rightly understood, is correct and is a defined truth of faith. But even if this is taken for granted, the fact remains that the term "person" can be, and has constantly been, misunderstood. . . . If someone today, whether Christian or not, hears the statement that there are three persons in God, he will think instinctively of three subjects differing from one another in their subjectivity, knowledge and freedom, and wonder what kind of logic it is that permits three persons understood in this way to be simultaneously one and the same God.[33]

Balthasar clearly felt himself to be the object of these criticisms, both here and elsewhere in Rahner's writings, because he opens the final volume of the *Theodramatik* with a "Preliminary Remark" justifying his approach against these criticisms, which I think should be quoted in full:

Our theology has been characterized by Karl Rahner as "gnostic." Presumably after reading the chapter in this volume on "The Pain of God" he will find his judgment confirmed all the more. In spite of this, this assessment seems unacceptable, as an attentive reading of the last chapter of this book—which once more treats of the immutability of God, even throughout the entire economy of salvation—should clearly show. (*TD* IV, 11)

The problem really centers on the shift of meaning of "person" from the outward aspect (*persona* = mask) to the inward self-consciousness of a human being. But I have to ask myself how misleading the doctrine of the Trinity becomes simply because of this well-documented semantic shift, for, after all, the terms "Father" and "Son" must also denote centers

---

heit der Hypostasen gar von einer 'Trennung' in Gott spricht" (Thomas Rudolf Krenski, *Passio Caritatis: Trinitarische Passiologie im Werk Hans Urs von Balthasars* [Einsiedeln: Johannes Verlag, 1990], 149.

[33] Karl Rahner, "Oneness and Threefoldness of God in Discussion with Islam," *Theological Investigations*, tr. Edward Quinn (New York: Crossroad, 1983) 18: 110–111. In this same essay Rahner speaks of "some crude misunderstandings of this Christian doctrine of the Trinity" (109) which are "widespread" and "make themselves felt subcutaneously in theologies which are as such and in principle orthodox" (110). Krenski holds that whenever Rahner speaks of "subcutaneous tritheism" he has Balthasar primarily in mind: "Wenn man daher auf dem Hintergrund dieser Äußerungen Balthasars Ausführungen gegenliest, kann man sich des Eindrucks nicht erwehren, Rahners Warnung vor einem subkutanen Tritheismus als dem latenten Mißverständnis des Trinitätsdogmas sei geradezu auf Balthasars Deutung hin gesprochen und habe, was die Trinitätsspekulations des Basler Theologen angeht, ihre unbedingte Berechtigung" (Krenski, *Passio Caritatis*, 153).

of consciousness and *they* clearly conjure up the sense of "person" in the modern meaning of that term! But Balthasar takes another tack, asking how stable "personhood" really is, especially when viewed against our attempts to apply so evanescent a concept to the overwhelming power of God. In one of the most eloquent statements to be found in his writings, he says of this complicated issue:

> Can we dare to apply the concept person, personality, to the unutterable hidden ground of being from which has proceeded and continuously proceeds the mysterious multiplicity of the world in all its evolving and declining forms? These forms, of which we are one, stand out unprotected in the cold wind of existence. Perhaps from time to time we lean against each other to find a measure of support, perhaps from time to time someone else's house seems to offer us something like home and security. But how precarious such dwellings are, hurriedly erected huts in the icy wind of fate which whistles about us on all sides and which from time to time rips away the roof under which we had thought we might for a while find shelter. And if we really are so exposed to fate, and if all our insurance policies against accidents, old age, and illness are simply powerless attempts to protect ourselves against an overwhelming power, against the ultimately destructive blizzard of death, if our abandonment is really as extreme as this, no human fellowship can protect us against our loneliness, no hope for the future can alleviate the frightening situation of the world *now*. . . . Where, then, shall we find the confidence to feel ourselves truly sheltered and protected in that deeply concealed womb and ground of being from which we have been cast out without our asking and into which we will at the end fall back at the will of fate? (*El*, 26)

We must always remember that, in the use of analogies drawn from human experience as applied to God, we must ask what are the conditions for the possibility of being a person, being a center of self-consciousness, being free, etc.[34] These lay in God, but that is all we can ascertain about the manner. For we know only the fact *that* God, as Creator, establishes these possibilities out of the ground of his own eternal and necessary being, not how and in what way that being is constituted. But this cannot imply that God is therefore any less, in his reality, than what constitutes the world.

---

[34] There is a good discussion of these complexities in G. de Schrijver, *Le Merveilleux Accord de l'homme et de Dieu: Étude de l'analogie de l'être chez Hans Urs von Balthasar* (Louvain University Press, 1983).

There are two issues here, epistemological and ontological; and our way to the ontological is blocked by the epistemological, which insists that we cannot know the "what" or the "how" of God directly.[35] But the implication for ontology is therefore reduced to a "that": all we know is *that* God is the precondition for creation and all its attributes. And this above all includes the very distance between Creator and creature that blocks off access of the creature to God. As O'Hanlon says, daringly, "given that creation is a free act of God's love, its true if analogous reality must be understood to be grounded in the trinitarian Not: [that is,] *the infinite distance between the world and God has its foundation in that original distance between God and God, within God.*"[36]

Now this distance of course does not imply unbridgeable distance because it is a generated distance that emerges out of the Father's love that holds nothing back but bestows its all. And in fact the distance is infinite *because* the Father bestows all, which the Son returns, again holding nothing back from himself, and this mutuality "spirates" the Spirit who binds them together despite and because of this distance. And thus the entire created world is to be understood as the expression and gift of God according to the prior trinitarian reality of the *Son's* existence as expression and gift of the Father. And this permits both a psychological, Augustinian imaging of the Trinity, and well as an inter-personal one favored by Gregory of Nyssa: "the inter-personal model cannot touch the substantial unity of God, while the inner-personal model cannot represent the real and lasting mutuality [*Gegenüber*] of the hypostases in God" (*TL* 2, 35).

Now it would be misleading to extend "I-Thou" language to the Spirit (and in this sense Rahner is right about a modern understanding of the word "person" interfering with what Person means in the Trinity), for the Spirit is a Person in the Trinity by being the Spirit *of* the Father's and Son's mutuality. But even here, the language of relationality drawn from human communication is still appropriate:

> It is precisely in the mutual absoluteness of this relationality that the starting point lies for the procession of the Holy Spirit. Based on the human experience of an unconditioned relationality—and therefore in the "image and likeness" of a human analogy— mutual love always appears as something that transcends human understanding, as something that is always unsurpassable. Both of the loving persons experience something that goes beyond the

---

[35] "Sed quia de Deo scire non possumus quid sit, sed quid not sit, non possumus considerare de Deo quomodo sit, sed potius quomodo not sit" (Aquinas, *ST* I, 3, *prol.*). On this point see W. J. Hankey, *God in Himself: Aquinas Doctrine of God as Expounded in the "Summa Theologiae"* (Oxford: Oxford University Press, 1987), 57–80.

[36] O'Hanlon, *Immutability*, 54.

"horizon of expectation" of their surrender which is no impersonal fate but is experienced only as a miracle arising out of their personal love. Viewed from the perspective of the biblical revelation of the Spirit we can also say: it is a miracle that appears as the "personification of the mutual surrender," as their "gift in person." (*PI*, 225; see also *TL* III, 153–200)

What most determines Balthasar's trinitarian theology is the definition of God as love. Borrowing from the arguments of Richard of St. Victor (though critically), he insists that charity or love is an inherently relational concept.[37] The reason God *is* love is because the Father's act of generation is a generation entirely "motivated" by love, the return of that love is love, and the bond of their mutual love is love. The circumincession of the Persons is entirely a movement of love. Now of course that does not mean that the believer faces three different "persons" in the modern sense of the term who love him "individually," for the whole point of John's statement is that *God* is love (and the verb is singular!). That is why Balthasar is quite cautious in taking Richard's logic to its limit:

Conversely, it is mistaken to take a naïve construction of the divine mystery after the pattern of human relationships (as Richard of St. Victor attempted by way of a counterblast to Augustine) and make it absolute. For it fails to take into account the crude anthropomorphism involved in a plurality of beings. The creaturely image must be content to look in the direction of the mystery of God from its two starting points [psychological and inter-personal] at the same time; the lines of perspective meet at an invisible point, in eternity.[38]

---

[37] Actually, this argument was first advanced by Pope Gregory the Great: "There can be no charity between less than two persons. For it can be said of no one that he has charity toward himself; rather, love [*dilectio*] strives for the other in order to be able to be charity" (*In Evag.* 17, 1: *PL* 76, 1139). Richard of St. Victor paraphrases this principle almost word for word but adds the important codicil that the God who demonstrates the highest charity toward us and prescribes it to us as the highest command of discipleship must be the very definition of love, which is identical with the fullness of his goodness (Richard of St. Victor, *De Trinitate* III, 2, in: *Sources Chrétiennes* 63:1959, as cited and paraphrased in *TL* II, 37). And slightly earlier in the same work, he says: "For there to be charity, there must be a love that is directed toward another. Consequently, where there is an absence of a plurality of persons, there cannot be charity" (*De Trin.* I, 20)

[38] *TD* 3, 526–527. Thomas Aquinas objects to Richard's metaphor for another reason: "When it is said that joyous possession of good requires partnership, this holds in the case of one not having perfect goodness: hence it needs to share some other's good, in order to have the goodness of complete happiness" (*ST* I, 32, art. 1, ad 2). I cannot see how this really strikes the blow Thomas assumes: for the Father is, by definition, the Ungenerate One, while the Son is, again by definition, the Generated One; which must mean that, in relational terms, he "owes" his *relational* existence entirely to the Father's generating love.

But this meeting point, of course, meets *in* eternity, and not in time. And therefore it remains ever inaccessible to us. We are driven to various analogies and metaphors to explain the nature of the Godhead only because God's action in Christ is so clearly and manifestly a trinitarian event. But that revelation in Christ does not include giving us access to that point in eternity. God, in other words, did not cease to be God when he revealed himself in the Son. Indeed Balthasar concludes each of the three parts of the Trilogy with a final coda on the incomprehensibility of God. No doubt the temptation of any well-wrought theology is to assume that it has in some way "captured" the essence of revelation, for is that not its real purpose: to mediate revelation in a way that makes it meaningful and accessible to modern ears? And yet this is also precisely its temptation too:

> It is true that in Jesus Christ the mystery of the ground of the world burns out more brightly than anywhere. But it is also precisely in this light that for the first time and definitively we grasp the true incompressibility of God. It is here that God breaks *forever* all the "wisdom" of the world by the "folly" of his love, which chooses us without reason, by his entering into the chaos of the history of humanity, by his bearing the guilt of his lost and fallen creatures. This incomprehensible love of the God who acts in the event of Christ raises him far above all the incomprehensibilities of philosophical notions of God which consist simply in the fact of negating all statements about God, which may be ventured on the grounds of our knowledge of the world, out of regard for his total otherness. But this more power-

---

And this implies a mutual sharing, but one that is absolute on both sides: *everything* is imparted and nothing is held back, so the limitations which Thomas sees in human relationships that militate against the image do not apply to God. And as if a "psychological" interpretation is free of problems! Granted, it is much easier for us to conceive of the unity of God, together with three hypostases, using the model of the mind, for we are all acquainted with the different faculties of our mind (memory, understanding, will, etc.) and how the recognition of these faculties does not impair the essential unity of the personality (in non-pathological cases). But that hardly frees this image from all the difficulties that Augustine seems to think, and we get confirmation of that point from no less a theologian than the greatest objector to Person-language, Karl Rahner himself: "The psychological theory of the Trinity neglects the experience of the Trinity in the economy of salvation in favor of a seemingly almost gnostic speculation about what goes on in the inner life of God. In the process it really forgets that the countenance of God which turns towards us in this self-communication is, in the trinitarian nature of this encounter, the very being of God as he is in himself, and must be if indeed the divine self-communication in grace and in glory really is the communication of God in his own self to us" (Karl Rahner, S.J., *Foundations of Christian Faith: An Introduction to the Idea of Christianity,* tr. William V. Dych, S.J. [New York: Crossroad, 1978], 135).

ful incomprehensibility of the biblical God only remains in effect so long as the dogmatic formulae protect it against renewed attempts at rationalization. Like the cherubim with their fiery swords, they surround the folly of the love of God, scandalous both for Jews and Greeks, and prevent any cabbalistic or Hegelian attempts from overthrowing *agapé* with *gnosis*. (*El*, 22–23)

· · ·

At the conclusion of an interview in 1976, Balthasar was asked if he could possibly reduce the vast flood of his writings to a common denominator. As expected, he declined the opportunity, but he did say, that in its place he would like to offer the title of three of his books: *Spirit and Fire, The Whole in the Fragment,* and *Only Love is Credible.* Before moving to a final assessment of Balthasar's work in the next chapter, I would like to stress, in the spirit of his answer to the interview, how crucially he saw his own work as making a clearing for love: "No truth of revelation, from the Trinity to the Cross and Judgment, can speak of anything else than of the glory of God's poor love—which of course is something much different than what we here below imagine by the name love. No, it is Spirit and Fire. 'Whoever approaches me, approaches the Fire.'"[39] And so before we begin our assessment of his work, let us first acknowledge the core of his mission:

If you have a fire in the house, guard it well in a fireproof hearth or emberkeep. Cover it up, for if even but one spark escapes and you fail to see it, you and everything that is yours will fall victim to the flames. If you have the Lord of the World in you, in your fireproof heart, fence him in well, be careful as you carry him about, lest he begin to make demands on you and you no longer know whither he pushes you. Hold the reins tightly in your hand. Don't let go of the rudder. God is dangerous. God is a consuming fire. God intended this for you. Take heed of his words: "Whoever sets hand to the plow and looks back is not worthy of me. Whoever does not love me more than father and mother, more than beloved and country, more than even himself, is not worthy of me." Watch out: he is a good dissembler. He begins with a small love, a small flame, and before you realize it he has gotten total hold of you and you are caught. If you let yourself be caught you are lost, for heavenwards there are no limits. He is

---

[39] "Geist und Feuer," *Herder Korrespondenz* 30 (1976): 72–82; here, 82.

God—accustomed to infinity. He sucks you upwards like a cyclone, whirls you up and away like a waterspout. Look out: man is made for measure and for limits, and only in the finite does he find rest and happiness. But this God knows nothing of measure. He is a seducer of hearts. (*HW*, 117–118)

· 12 ·

Last Things

I say that we are wound
With mercy round and round
As if with air.
Gerard Manley Hopkins
"The Blessed Virgin Compared
to the Air We Breathe

It is my firm belief that an adequate assessment of the theology of Hans Urs von Balthasar is not possible at this time. For one thing, he had only just finished his Trilogy the year before his death in 1988, so there has hardly been time for the world of theology to absorb and begin to understand this immense, almost gigantic work. Furthermore, it will take some time before translations of his complete works appear in the major world languages. But the greatest hinderance in assessing his work comes from its symbiotic relation to the parallel (and equally lengthy) work of the mystic whom he baptized into the Roman Catholic Church, Adrienne von Speyr. Which means that any evaluation of him will involve a parallel evaluation of her.

It is a task I have myself been putting off for as long as possible—not from any repugnance toward her work (though I have felt nonplussed and put off more than once, which usually vanishes upon a second reading) but from the sheer gargantuan, and often repetitious, nature of her writings. Balthasar himself is certainly aware of the difficulty, for he speaks openly of the flagging energy most of her readers feel when they try to work through her books:

Faced with the quantity of her writings, many are at a loss; they struggle through two or three books and then, on account of their seeming endlessness, they lose the desire and courage to read further. For these I repeat what I said previously: something that has grown out of slow meditation is also properly absorbed only slowly and meditatively. This is especially true of the commentaries on Scripture; they are best suited as a preparation for one's own contemplative prayer. One reads the verse of Scripture, then Adrienne von Speyr's reflections on it, and uses them as "points" for meditation. (*FG,* 248)

Fair enough, but that will demand several decades before her writings take root in the life of the Church, form reactions, generate literature (both professional and lay), etc. And then at some point, the hierarchical magisterium of the Church will have to render some kind of judgment, however tentative it might be and through whatever instance seems appropriate. Until that is done, I believe it will be impossible to come to an adequate assessment of the meaning of her charism for the Church, and *a fortiori,* of Balthasar's theology.

There are, moreover, other and perhaps even more formidable obstacles to assessing her charism, simply because her story is so unusual. Balthasar's cousin, Peter Henrici, S.J., speaks of the amazement of the members of the Community of St. John (the secular institute that both Balthasar and von Speyr had founded) at the flood of graces she had received and of which they knew nothing while she was alive.[1] This is because Balthasar held back publication, until after her death, of any work of hers that indicated how intense were her mystical experiences. "Though it is impossible to draw a distinct dividing line between 'ordinary' and 'purely mystical' works," he says, "I intentionally refrained from publishing the more obviously charismatic works during the author's lifetime—it would have unnecessarily upset her life and that of her family" (*FG,* 99). But after her death they came out in a veritable cataract of print and displayed an astonishing outpouring of mystical charismata: transports, miracles, reports of the prayer life of the saints, even the stigmata.

The basic outline of this overpowering river of experiences first became clear soon after her death (on 17 September 1967) when Balthasar published his *First Glance at Adrienne von Speyr* where, among other startling revelations, we learn that Adrienne had a mysterious "encounter" with St. Ignatius of Loyola while walking up a street when she was six-years-old (!) and had a vision of Mary surrounded by angels and saints when she was 15.[2] But before her conversion to Catholicism in 1940 at the age

---

[1] "The members of the Community of St. John were amazed, one might say stunned, by the superabundance of their foundress' charismatic gifts of which, in her lifetime, they had hardly an inkling" ("Hans Urs von Balthasar: A Sketch of his Life," *L&W,* 27).

[2] And her experiences after her conversion were even more startling, one of the most remarkable of which is the following: "Eine andere für Adrienne besonders schreckhafte unverständliche und deshalb schwer zu tragende Erfahrung war die am Sarg des zwölfjährigen einzigen Kindes ihres so verehrten und geliebten Freundes Professor Merke. Sie hatte am Bett des sterbenden 'wie verrückt' gebetet, hatte sogar ihre eigenen Kinder Gott anstelle dieses einen angeboten [!]; der Knabe war gestorben, sie hatte weitergebetet, bis sich die

of 38, she had married twice and was survived by her second husband, a professor of history at the University of Basel, by several years.

I had never heard of Adrienne von Speyr until this book came out in English in 1981. I had previously first heard of Balthasar when I ran across his book on *Prayer* in the mid-1960's and found his style intoxicating and his insights extraordinarily helpful, and so learned German to read his works (the works selected by publishers for translation had been chosen at that time, it seemed, with no pattern). And so it was only through him that I came to meet her, and like most people I know to whom this has also happened, I was both put off and puzzled. In one of his last works, Balthasar shows that he is well aware of this difficulty: "In the totality of Adrienne's theological work there are individual parts that can, if taken out of context, occasionally alienate. Readers of her works are urgently requested not to lose sight of the whole of her theology on account of individual statements. The inner coherence of all the parts will become that much more obvious the more one concentrates on this whole."[3]

I have, I must admit, in spite of these warnings, kept pretty much to my original intention of devoting most of my time to an intensive study of Balthasar's work and have in my work only occasionally glanced at the mystical works of von Speyr, though I will say that based on my increased understanding of his theology I have come to have a much greater appreciation of her work, her insights and her mission and have lately increased my direct reading of her. But it's rather like those two-steps-forward, one-step-back movements, for the deeper I plunge into her writings, the more I continue to encounter moments that disconcert me. I have often heard their relationship being compared by sympathizers of their cause to the relationship of Francis of Assisi and St. Clare, or Francis de Sales and Jane Frances de Chantal, which might generically be true but still does not go very far in illuminating their actual relationship, which seems to me unprecedented. For example, one will be reading along in her posthumous works, such as *Kreuz und Hölle*, where Balthasar is taking down for posterity her reports of her "mystical descent" into hell and suddenly she will interrupt the proceedings if he seems startled or raises his eyebrow at something she has said, and she will retort: "Are you getting this? What is your education? Do you have a doctorate? There

---

Leiche bewegt und halb aufgerichtet hatte, dann kam plötzlich vom Himmel wie eine Stimme: was durchkreuzt du meinen Ratschluß? Der Tote sank zurück, die Krankenschwester mußte ihm verwundert die Hände wieder falten" (*UA*, 71).

[3] *UA*, 12–13: "Im theologischen Gesamtwerk Adriennes gibt es einzelne Teile, die, aus dem Zusammenhang gerissen, zuweilen befremden können. Leser ihrer Werke sind dringend gebeten, bei Einzelaussagen das Ganze ihrer Theologie nicht aus dem Blick zu verlieren; die inner Kohärenz aller Teile wird, je mehr man sich mit diesem Ganzen beschäftigt, desto einsichtiger." This is a remark, by the way, that applies equally as well to Balthasar and his works.

are so many imbecilic people around with doctorates!"⁴ This surely must be a *Neuigkeit in der Kirchengeschichte*.

Perhaps the fate and the career of their secular institute will prove to be the best way of judging the validity of her charism, for that is often the way the Church tests the charisms of other founders. Of course, "success" in the worldly sense cannot be the standard, but it would beg the issue to say the fate of the institute has no bearing on one's judgment of her charism. Apropos these reflections, there is a passage in *Unser Auftrag* (*Our Common Task*) where Balthasar mentions that he once told Adrienne that their foundation would end up being rather modest, a conclusion she denied:

> In early 1942 she had a conversation with an unfortunate Jesuit who told her that founders of orders have always been saints. I had to drive this idea out of her that quite rightly tormented her (for she never wanted to be mistaken for a saint), and I added: "You know, we are not going to found so splendid an order as did St. Ignatius or Francis de Sales. It will be more modest." She replied: "It will become something great, it will spread."⁵

I find this constant raising of the stakes hard to interpret. It certainly seems inevitable that one will entertain the thought that perhaps she is fooling herself, that delusions of grandeur are at work here. And I know a couple of people whose judgment I trust and who are familiar with the details of the story who believe that, when Balthasar left the Society of Jesus in 1950 because the Jesuit order refused to take responsibility, canonical or otherwise, for the secular institute, he was being led astray from his true vocation (and these are men who bear no ill will toward his theology or harbor any suspicions about his motives). Perhaps so, perhaps not. I do know that toward the end of his life, as was reported to me by one of the members of the Institute, he told the Community that they must also be open to the possibility that, having prayed the *Suscipe* (the prayer that God might accept their whole life, memory, understanding and will), they might have to be open to the possibility God might turn them down and decline the offer. Which would, I imagine, demand more

---

⁴ Adrienne von Speyr, *Kreuz und Hölle*, 1. Teil: *Die Passionen* (Einsiedeln: Johannes Verlag/ Privatdruck, 1966), 141: "Werden Sie das verstehen? Was ist Ihre Bildung? Sie sind Doktor? Es gibt so viele blöde Doktoren!"

⁵ *UA*, 41: "Im Frühjahr 1942 hat sie ein Gespräch mit einem fatalen Jesuiten, der ihr sagt, Ordensgründer seien immer Heilige gewesen. Ich muß ihr diese Idee, die sie richtig quält (weil sie nie mit einer Heiligen verwechselt werden wollte), austreiben und füge hinzu: 'wir werden ja auch keinen so großartigen Orden gründen wie der hl. Ignatius oder Franz von Sales. Er wird bescheidener sein.' Sie darauf: 'Es wird etwas Großes werden, es wird sich ausbreiten.'"

of holiness and indifference than high hopes for a future great order (and it should be noted that Ignatius of Loyola more or less backed into founding the Society of Jesus because of geo-political difficulties in getting to the Holy Land: *he* had no Grand Plans for a new order!).

But amid these uncertainties, at least this much we can say: Balthasar is absolutely right when he insists that his work and that of Adrienne von Speyr are so intricately intertwined that they cannot be separated, a point he began insisting on with increased peremptoriness as his fame grew. And this is why he wrote *Our Common Task:* "This book has been written above all with one purpose in mind: to prevent anyone after my death from trying to separate my work from that of Adrienne von Speyr. It will establish that this is in every way impossible, both as regards to [our common] theology as well as the Secular Institute that has begun [under our auspices]."[6] The further I have deepened my knowledge of and acquaintance with his thought, the more I have come to see the truth of that statement, which was even more forcefully expressed in his retrospective essay *Rechenschaft:*

> In Basel, the mission of Adrienne von Speyr . . . was decisive. What Ignatius had intended in his time meant henceforth for me "secular institute"; the hard sacrifice demanded by this transition was accompanied by the certainty of serving the same idea more exactly. It was Adrienne von Speyr who showed the way in which Ignatius is fulfilled by John and therewith laid the basis for most of what I have published since 1940. Her work and mine are neither psychologically nor philologically to be separated: two halves of a single whole, which has as its center a unique foundation.[7]

But the truth of this statement (which I do not deny) certainly does not prevent the theologian from assessing Balthasar's theology on its own

---

[6] *UA*, 11: "Dieses Buch hat vor allem einen Zweck: zu verhindern, daß mach meinem Tod der Versuch unternommen wird, mein Werk von dem Adriennes von Speyr zu trennen. Es beweist, daß dies in keiner Hinsicht möglich ist, weder was die Theologie noch was das begonnene Institut angeht."

[7] *My Work in Retrospect,* 89. Balthasar makes quite clear, however, how very painful it was for him to leave the order—for both of them: "But truly superhuman strength was demanded of her by the part she assumed in the responsibility for persuading me to leave the Jesuit Order when it became evident that it would be impossible to carry out within the framework of the Society of Jesus the mission with which we had been charged in founding the new community. Certainly I myself had more than enough proof that this mission existed and that it was to be interpreted in this and no other way. Who will deny God the possibility of expressing himself to his creature (and especially in the Church) in a way that cannot be misunderstood? For me the Society was of course a beloved homeland: the thought that one might have to 'leave all' more than once in a lifetime in order to follow the Lord, even leave

terms. It is after all a theology and must be judged as such.[8] But even here we shall find ourselves soon running into difficulties, and not just because of the sheer bulk of his writings. What makes assessing his theology particularly difficult at this time is his intention to undercut and undermine the fundamental foundations on which nearly all theology being done today rests, so that one must decide almost at the outset either to plunge into his system with him and see the rest of contemporary theology in his terms, or judge his work by the standards that are prevalent in the guild at the moment, which, to his mind at least, would be equally distorting, because of his belief that the reigning norms of rationality are precisely what are eating away at theology. And then how do we come to terms with his resolute refusal to obey the traffic laws of specialization that so dominates the profession of theology today? Who is there who has the multi-competence to assess at a single glance his patristic scholarship, his relationship to mysticism versus revelation, his trinitarian speculations, his work as a publisher and translator (of French authors primarily, but also of Maximus the Confessor and many, many others), the musical cadence to his prose, or even read all the books he has written (a man who, says his biographer, "wrote more books than a normal person can be expected to read in his lifetime"[9])?

---

an Order, had never occurred to me, and it struck me like a blow. Therefore, even though I had my own proof and took full responsibility for my own action—which I have never for a moment regretted since—still for Adrienne, through whom this call had come, her share of the responsibility was uncommonly difficult. A letter which she wrote to my provincial at that time attests to this fact" (*FG*, 43).

[8] Gerald O'Hanlon is of this opinion too, and I completely agree with his formulation: "It should be noted that this volume of the *TD* (IV) contains many quotations from and much agreement with the theology of Adrienne von Speyr, the medical doctor and woman of prayer whom Balthasar directed for so many years. . . . However cautiously one might approach the assessment of that influence in all its particularity, it is certainly true that in a general sense it is compatible with Balthasar's own understanding of the relationship between theology and prayer. And clearly also, the positions which he adopts in his theology, whatever their inspiration, must satisfy the normal criteria of theological truth and be internally consistent" (*Immutability*, 193, note 56).

[9] Henrici, "Sketch," *L&W*, 7. And to further complicate matters, Barth thought that Balthasar himself was a mystic (see Eberhard Busch, *Karl Barth: His Life from Letters and Autobiographical Texts*, tr. John Bowden [Philadelphia: Fortress Press, 1976], 409), which complicates the evaluative task even further. This very detailed biography also mentions two times when the trinity of Barth, Balthasar, and von Speyr met, and both meetings are fascinating: "During the winter the two of them [Barth and Balthasar] went on one occasion to Einsiedeln (taking along Adrienne Kaegi–von Speyr, a friend of von Balthasar) where 'we listened to records of Mozart for almost twenty-four hours. We also had the opportunity to gaze in wonder at our remarkable friend celebrating Mass in vestments in the Chapel of Grace.' Stirred up by his revived and deepened friendship with von Balthasar, Barth's love of Mozart took on a new turn. Shortly after this expedition, 'I even let myself get carried away and devoted a special excursus to Mozart.' . . . In the middle of June, 1956 Barth went with Hans Urs von Balthasar and Frau Adrienne Kaegi–von Speyr to Paris. There they

But this too we will leave aside as not the proper task and moment for this chapter. I would rather prefer, as befits a final chapter, critically to examine his eschatology. For of all the innovations that Balthasar is famous for in theology none ranks higher than his defense of his idea that "the dogma [of the Church] is that hell exists, not that people are in it."[10] And of course, purely as a matter of dogma, he is right. As the German bishops have declared in their recent catechism: "Neither Holy Scripture nor the Church's Tradition of faith asserts with certainty of any man that he is actually in hell. Hell is always held before our eyes as a real *possibility,* one connected with the offer of conversion and life."[11]

And yet whenever I think of the doctrine of *apocatastasis* (the universal restoration of all things at the end of time), I am reminded of a remark of Ludwig Wittgenstein to Maurice Drury, a former student of his. Drury had always admired Origen's vision of a final restoration of all things, including even Satan and the fallen angels, and told Wittgenstein one day of his regret that it had been declared a heresy by the Church. "Of course it was rejected," Wittgenstein shot back. "It would make nonsense of everything else. If what we do now is to make no difference in the end, then all the seriousness of life is done away with."[12] The objection to this doctrine is easy to understand: it seems so unlikely that God would condemn all those who would seem to deserve damnation under this rubric of seriousness, as Cardinal Newman notes with a certain dry wit:

> The world promises that, if we trust it, we cannot go wrong. Why? Because it is so many—there are so many men in it; they must be right. That is what it seems boldly to say: "God cannot

---

were to take part 'in the doctoral examination of a Jesuit [Père Henri Brouillard] who had written 1200 pages about me. He was cross-examined about me for five hours (at the Sorbonne), and then we celebrated in a Chinese restaurant'" (362, 421).

[10] Said in conversation with Karl Barth, when he assured Barth: "that's all right, at last we're quite alone and one can say what one thinks" (Busch, *Barth,* 362). And toward the end of his life, Balthasar had this to say about Barth's influence: "Barth's doctrine of election, this brilliant overthrow of Calvin, attracted me powerfully and lastingly; it converged with Origen's views and thus also with Adrienne's theology of Holy Saturday" (*UA,* 85).

[11] German Bishops' Conference, *The Church's Confession of Faith: A Catholic Catechism for Adults* (San Francisco: Ignatius Press, 1987), 346.

[12] Cited in Rush Rhees, ed., *Recollections of Wittgenstein* (Oxford: Oxford University Press, 1984), 161. "Your religious ideas have always seemed to me more Greek than biblical [he told Drury]. Whereas my thoughts are one hundred percent Hebraic" (ibid.). Note, however, that Wittgenstein was much more cautious about the Pauline doctrine of predestination, and for almost what seems like "theodramatic" reasons: "And yet, within his fundamentally ethical conception of religious faith, he still found the Pauline doctrine of predestination hard to embrace. For, like Origen's teaching, it seems to have the consequence that 'what we do now is to make no difference in the end.' And if this is so, how can the seriousness of life be upheld?" (cited in: Ray Monk, *Ludwig Wittgenstein: The Duty of Genius* [New York: The Free Press, 1990], 541).

punish so many." So it is, we know, in human law. The magistrate never can punish a very great number of the community at once; he is obliged to let the multitude of culprits escape him, and he makes examples; and this is what we cannot help fancying God will do. We do not allow ourselves to take in the idea that He can, and that He has said He will, punish a thousand as easily as one. What the poor and ignorant man who lives irreligiously professes, is what all really profess: he, when taxed with neglect of religion, speaks out that "he is as good as his neighbor." He speaks abruptly, but only says what multitudes feel but do not say. They think that this world is too great an evil for God to punish; or rather that therefore it is not an evil, because it is a great one. They cannot compass the idea that God should allow so great an evil to exist, as the world would be, if it is evil; and therefore, since He does allow it, it is not an evil. In vain does Scripture assure them that it *is* an evil, though God allows it. In vain does the whole Psalter, from beginning to the end, proclaim and protest that the world is against the truth, and that the saints must suffer. In vain do Apostles tell us that the world lieth in wickedness; in vain does Christ Himself declare that broad is the way that leadeth to destruction, and many there be that go thereat. In vain is the vast judgment of the Deluge; in vain the instant death of the first-born of Egypt, and of the host of Sennacherib. No, we will not believe; the words of the Tempter ring in our ears: "Ye shall surely not die!" and we stake our eternal interests on sight and reason, rather than on the revealed Word of God.[13]

So let us leave aside vain wishing and empty objections, whose hollowness becomes evident as soon they are articulated. "Salvation is not so easy a matter," as Newman kept insisting, "or so cheap a possession, as we are apt to suppose. *It is not obtained by mere wishing.*"[14] No, Balthasar would retort, it is not a matter of wishing it and having it be so, but it can be an object of our *hope*. In fact he reacts to Newman's sermons on the subject almost with a touch of sarcasm, especially when Newman considers that the sufferings of Jesus on the Cross included knowing that his sacrifice would lead to the failure of some to attain salvation: "Myriads, like herds of swine, falling headlong down the steep! O mighty God! O God of love! it is too much!" To which Balthasar

[13] John Henry Newman, "Faith and the World," *Sermons and Discourses: 1825–1839* (New York: Longmans, Green and Co., 1949), 1:289–290.

[14] "Nature and Grace," *Sermons and Discourses: 1839–1857* (New York: Longmans, Green and Co., 1949), 2:177; my emphasis.

tartly replies: "Of course it is too much."[15] What he objects to—and his objection is, in my opinion, entirely legitimate—is the claim of the advocates for an occupied hell that revelation has already told us that some have in fact died and gone to hell. Oh? asks Balthasar. But if we already *know* that, then what becomes of hope, the hope expressed in the Church's constant prayers, especially on Good Friday for the salvation of every human being ever born?[16] And for him, "it is precisely the *knowing* (about the ultimate futility of the Cross) that renders impossible this state of suspension of those on pilgrimage."[17]

Hope of course is not presumption, and just as we do not *know* the ultimate fate of anyone (except, interestingly enough, those canonized as saints), so too we do not *know* our own destiny before God. Not even St. Paul claimed to know of his own salvation: "My conscience is clear, but that does not make me innocent. It is the Lord who judges me" (1 Cor 4:4). And so we must work out our salvation with "fear and trembling" (Phil 2:12), never knowing what the judgment of the Lord will be: "But who may abide the day of his coming and who shall stand when he appeareth?" (Mal 3:2).

Balthasar also scores another direct hit against the "populated hell" school when he mentions a key point of psychology that runs right through this debate: "It can be taken as a motif running through the history of theology that, whenever one fills hell with a *massa damnata* of sinners, one also, through some kind of conscious or unconscious trick (perhaps cautiously, and yet reassuringly), places oneself on the other side" (*DWH*, 191). How convenient! But is that really the Gospel? "God, I thank thee that I am not like other men, extortionists, evildoers, adulterers—or even like this tax collector here" (Lk 18:11).

It is, I think, too little noticed how the command to hope for the salvation of all (and it *is* a command: 1 Tim 2:1–4) is intimately linked with the command to love one's enemies, and that a claim to "know" that some are destined to hell will lead, by a short but inexorable logic, to a diminution of the love one should feel for one's enemies:

> Bless those who persecute you: bless and do not curse. . . . Do not repay anyone evil for evil. Be careful to do what is right in

---

[15] *DWH*, 26; with Newman citation.

[16] And not only on Good Friday: in *DWH* Balthasar cites any number of prayers, chosen almost at random, showing that the Church in the most solemn moment of her prayer before the Lord—in the Eucharist—prays for universal salvation; for example: "Lord, accept the offering of your Church; and may what each of us offers up to the honor of your name lead to the salvation of all. For this we pray to you through Christ our Lord" (Offertory Prayer, cited on 36; others on 35–37).

[17] *DWH*, 27. A point echoed by other theologians: "Any attempt to describe the content of Christian hope shares the limitations of other attempts to describe something about the

the eyes of everyone. If it is possible, as far as it depends on you, live at peace with everyone. Do not take revenge, my friends, but leave room for God's wrath, for it is written: "It is mine to avenge; I will repay," says the Lord [Deut 32:35]. On the contrary: If your enemy is hungry, feed him; if he is thirsty, give him something to drink. In doing this, you will be "heaping burning coals on his head" [Prov 25:21–22]. Do not overcome by evil, but overcome evil with good. (Rm 12:14, 17–21)[18]

But how then to "leave room for God's wrath," as Paul recommends? The point is, there *is* a wrath to come, but because of the solidarity of the human race in Adam, it is directed at all of us; and because Christ reversed the curse of Adam on the Cross and thereby saved all men (Rm 5:15), God's grace of redemption is directed at all (Rm 11:32). What, then, of individual fate? Will not God "give to each person according to what he has done" (Rm 2:6)? Yes, definitely! But who can anticipate *for others* how that judgment will turn out—especially if even St. Paul (!) cannot anticipate his own fate before God's throne? "You, therefore, have no excuse, you who pass judgment on someone else, for at whatever point you judge the other, you are condemning yourself, because you who pass judgment do the same things. Now we know that God's judgment against those who do such things is based on truth. So when you, a mere man, pass judgment on them and yet do the same things, do you think you will escape God's judgment? Or do you show contempt for the riches of his kindness, tolerance and patience, not realizing that God's kindness leads you toward repentance?" (Rm 2:1–4).

It is fascinating to watch how far Balthasar is willing to take this insistence on the solidarity of the human race before the judgment seat of God and even trumps what has always been regarded as the Ace of Spades in this debate: what about all the monsters of human depravity that the sad history of our race has thrown up before our eyes? And with this trump card in hand, "one goes on to populate hell, according to one's taste, with all sorts of monsters: Ivan the Terrible, Stalin the Horrible, Hitler the Madman with all his cronies, which certainly results, as well, in an imposing company that one would prefer not to encounter in heaven" (*DWH,*

---

future. We do not know the future in the same way in which we know the past and present" (Monika K. Hellwig, "Eschatology," *ST:RCP*, ed. Francis Schüssler Fiorenza and John P. Galvin [Minneapolis: Fortress Press, 1991] 2:351).

[18] And what a distraction resentment is! This was Thérèse of Lisieux's recipe for distractions in prayer: "When a novice is disturbed at her many distractions, she replies: 'I have many as well, but as soon as I notice them, I pray for the people who keep coming to mind, and so my distractions are turned into blessings for them'" (*2SS,* 64–65).

190). These men are indeed a mystery, as is all evil.[19] But does that not mean they live in a separate bubble from the rest of humankind? On the contrary![20] To isolate them means also to isolate their collaborators, and whom in the final analysis would that not include?

Now this does *not* mean that there is no individual judgment, that Hitler and Stalin and the rest of the monster-menagerie will not have to answer for their crimes. Individual judgment is a doctrine of Scripture: "Because of your stubbornness and your unrepentant hearts, you are storing up wrath against yourself for the day of God's wrath, when his righteous judgment will be revealed. . . . To those who by persistence in doing good seek glory, honor and immortality, he will give eternal life. But for those who are self-seeking and who reject the truth and follow evil, there will be wrath and anger" (Rm 2:5, 7–8). And no doubt there is a reverse side to the psychology of feeling elected that Balthasar lamented in the "hell is populated" (or "Infernalist") school: yes, advocates of double

---

[19] It is remarkable how much real evil of this almost "transcendent" variety is intimately tied up with the drive for power. In other words, for Balthasar those who are so sure of the Ultimate Evil embodied in Hitler, Stalin, etc. must also examine their own consciences: "This is the most fundamental temptation [*Urversuchung*]: to want to be autonomous, 'to be like God, knowing what is good and evil' (Gen 3:5); against this fundamental sin [*Ursünde*] Jesus struggles by laying bare the sin of Phariseeism. For even if the Pharisee recognizes the law as coming from God, he has dissolved it from its origin and appropriated it for his own direction; finally he has brought God's command and prohibition into his own power. Once this point is reached, power then becomes in human history the *Instanz* that determines the content of what is ethically permitted and not permitted. And from this very real point that has determined world history so deeply we can hear the verdict of Jacob Burckhardt on power. . . . . One must let Burckhardt's entire sentence take its effects: 'Now power is in itself evil, just as is anyone who exercises it. Power is not dogged persistence [*Beharren*] but a craving and is *eo ipso* unfulfillable; thus it is unhappy by definition and must therefore makes others unhappy'" (TD III, 139). It should be noted that this is no anti-Niebuhrian lurch to the antinomian left on Balthasar's part but simply an acknowledgment of the realities of power; see this entire section (pp. 125–186) for an illuminating discussion of evil.

[20] When Balthasar mentions those who would populate hell along with "Hitler the Madmen *and all his cronies,*" how do we define cronies? Let us bear in mind the wise words of the philosopher Mary Midgley: "The objection to using the Nazis [in a book of this kind] is that mention of them may give the impression that wicked people tend to be foreigners with funny accents, and moreover—since they have already been defeated—are not very dangerous. . . . It is particularly necessary to put the Nazis in perspective because they are, in a way, too good an example. . . . We always like to think that our enemies are like this, but it cannot be guaranteed. To become too obsessed with the Nazis can therefore encourage wishful thinking. It can turn out to be yet one more way of missing their successors—who do not need to be as spiritually bankrupt to this extent to be genuinely dangerous—and of inflating mere ordinary opponents to Nazi status. . . . In general, politically wicked movements are mixed, standing also for some good, however ill-conceived, and those opposing them have to understand that good if their opposition is not to become distorted by a mindless destructive element" (Mary Midgley, *Wickedness: A Philosophical Essay* [New York: Methuen, 1984], 5).

predestination invariably assume *they* are among the elect, which is a bit of self-righteousness that speaks against the theory. But no doubt Augustine is also right when he says that, psychologically speaking, the real reason some people hold to the "unpopulated hell" school is because it gets *them* off the hook: "They are in fact moved by a human compassion which is concerned only for human beings; and in particular they are pleading their own cause, promising themselves a delusive impunity for their own disreputable lives by supposing an all-embracing mercy of God towards the human race."[21]

Let us then allow these two debating points of psychology to cancel each other out. What do we get? According to Balthasar, only the certain knowledge that we are all, while still alive, *under* the judgment of God. And because we are still under the judgment, the issue hovers in doubt as to the outcome—for all concerned. This is the root both of the hope we are enjoined to hold and the "fear and trembling" with which we seek to work out our salvation. Balthasar makes very deft use of Thomas Aquinas' theology of hope against Augustine's, which is all the more interesting because it comes from Thomas' last book—in stark contrast to Augustine, who grew more pessimistic about the fate of the human race as he grew older. In any event, in a definition that reads like it comes from a contemporary linguistic analyst, Thomas says of the word "hope" that "one has to believe of whatever one hopes that it can be attained; this is what hope adds to mere desire. Man can, namely, also have desire for things that he does not believe he can attain; but hope cannot exist in such circumstances."[22] And indeed he even goes further and adds: "It is impossible that the requests made by many do not attain their goal."[23]

What, then, of the dire warnings of Jesus? What of his saying in the Sermon on the Mount that "wide is the gate and broad is the way—and many are those who take it—that leads to perdition" (Mt 7:13)? And what of his easily interpreted parable of the Sheep and the Goats, with its solemn scene of men uncharitable in life finding out to their dismay that they have all the while been mistreating Christ and have thereby forfeited forever his kingdom (Mt 25:31–46)? According to Balthasar—and this is one of the key arguments in his eschatology—the parables of judgment in the earthly ministry of Jesus must be "back-interpreted" in the subsequent light of the cross and resurrection: "It must be said at the outset that *all the words of the Lord that point to the possibility of eternal perdition take place before Easter.*"[24]

---

[21] St. Augustine, *De Civ. Dei*, XXI, 18 (*Concerning the City of God Against the Pagans*, tr. John O'Meara [New York: Penguin, 1972], 998).

[22] Thomas Aquinas, *Compendium Theologiae*, Marietti edition (1948), Part II, c. 7.

[23] *Comp. Theol.* Part II, c. 5.

[24] *TD* IV, 253; my emphasis: "Vorweg muß angemerkt werden, daß alle Worte des Herrn, die auf die Möglichkeit eines ewigen Verlorengehens deuten, vorösterlich sind." He cites as

I am not sure how convincing this argument will prove to be among exegetes, but it seems unnecessarily simplistic, and in particular ignores the influence of post-Easter paranesis (that is, catechetical training in the faith after conversion) on the formation of the parables of judgment as we have received them in the Gospels today.[25] Not only that, Balthasar himself seems to imply that this distinction might not carry him very far, for he hedges his bets considerably in this nuanced passage:

> It is generally known that in the New Testament two series of statements run along side by side in such a way that a synthesis of both is neither permissible nor achievable: the first series speaks of being lost for all eternity; the second, of God's will, *and ability,* to save all men. Before approaching particular texts, it is necessary to consider the fact that particular words of Jesus can be attributed with a high degree of probability to the pre-Easter Jesus, because in them he uses a language and images that were familiar to the Jews of that time (which does not mean, of course, that these texts, which have been preserved by the Synoptic Evangelists, are of lesser significance to us), whereas certain reflections by Paul and John clearly look back upon all that happened to Jesus—to his life, death on the Cross and Resurrection—and, in so doing, consider and formulate this totality from a post-Easter perspective. That this distinction can be drawn only with caution, and not categorically, is obvious from the well-known fact that the Synoptics too [!] present Jesus' words and deed in the religious light shed by the post-Easter situation, from a clear awareness that all the words of Jesus that were preserved—even those that are very hard to understand—will remain relevant to the Church throughout all time. (*DWH,* 29–30)

And it is, after all, hardly the case that the post-Easter Church never held up the possibility of eternal ruin; and in fact the early Church is

---

an example Jn 9:39 ("For judgment have I come into the world") and then refers the reader to Adrienne von Speyr's commentary on John, where she says *ad loc.*: "It is one of those words of the Lord that are still spoken before the actual redemption on the Cross, at a time when the light had not yet fully penetrated the darkness" (ibid.). It seems odd to call the discourses of Jesus in John unaffected by the resurrection.

[25] This is especially true of the Parables of the Sheep and the Goats, and if Balthasar's exegetical ground is shaky there, it will prove unstable everywhere else as well. On this parable and its form-critical history see Johannes Friedrich, *Gott im Bruder? Eine methoden-kritische Untersuchung von Redaktion, Überlieferung und Traditionen in Mt 25, 31–46* (Stuttgart: Calwer Verlag, 1977); W. G. Thompson, "A Historical Perspective in the Gospel of Matthew," *Journal of Biblical Literature* 93 (1974): 243–62; and John R. Donahue, S.J.,

extremely aware of the fiduciary requirement that all Christians treat the grace of redemption they have received *as a trust* which must not only be increased, as Jesus demanded (Mt 25:14–30), but also must not be squandered, lest the very grace of redemption be the provocation leading to everlasting perdition (1 Cor 11:29; Heb 10:26–31).[26] Nor has it escaped Balthasar's richly theodramatic imagination that "the increased revelation of God's love generates increased rejection and deepened hate" (*TD* IV, 245). Cardinal Newman has, once more, put his finger on the pulse of this rebellion and in his unsparing diagnosis has found the cause:

> This is the source of the hatred which the world bears to the Church; it finds a whole catalogue of sins brought into light and denounced, which it would fain believe to be no sins at all; it finds itself, to its indignation and impatience, surrounded with sin, morning, noon and night; it finds that a stern law lies against it, where it believed that it was its own master and need not think of God; it finds guilt accumulating upon it hourly, which nothing can prevent, nothing remove, but a higher power, the grace of God. It finds itself in danger of being humbled to the earth as a rebel, instead of being allowed to indulge its self-dependence and self-complacency. Hence it takes its stand on nature, and denies or rejects divine grace. Like the proud spirit in the beginning, it wishes to find its supreme good in its own self, and nothing above it; it undertakes to be sufficient for its own happiness; *it has no desire for the supernatural, and therefore does not believe in it.* And because nature cannot rise above nature, it will not believe that the narrow way is possible; it hates those who enter upon it as if pretenders and hypocrites, or laughs at their aspirations as romance and fanaticism—lest it should have to believe in the existence of grace.[27]

"The 'Parable' of the Sheep and the Goats: A Challenge to Christian Ethics," *Theological Studies* 47/1 (1986): 3–31.

[26] It is interesting that both these texts pertain to the abuse of the Eucharist: "If, after we have been given knowledge of the truth, we should deliberately commit any sins, then there is no longer any sacrifice for them. There is left only the dreadful prospect of judgment and of the fiery wrath that is to devour your enemies. . . . You may be sure that anyone who tramples on the Son of God, and who treats the Blood of the Covenant which sanctified him as if it were not holy, and who insults the Spirit of grace, will be condemned to a far severer punishment. We are all aware who it was that said: 'Vengeance is mine; I will requite them.' And again: 'The Lord will vindicate his people.' It is a dreadful thing to fall into the hands of the living God" (Heb 10:26–27, 29–31).

[27] John Henry Newman, "Nature and Grace," *Sermons and Discourses: 1839–1857*, 1:168–169; my emphasis.

To which Balthasar has only one response left—his own last trump, so to speak, but one that is quite arresting: *if even a single human being is eternally lost by rejecting God and his holy grace, then God has lost the gamble he made with himself when he first created a universe of free beings who were made to receive that love freely.* The universe was not created, even partially, *for* damnation (this is the grotesque absurdity of double predestination, and Balthasar is quite right to condemn it outright). Even hell, though a "place," was not "created" as such. It sprang into being as an inevitable byproduct of the fallen angels' No to God, and so it never really "fits" in the created order: "For hell is the real absurdity. It is no part of a whole in which it might have a meaningful place but is a true outrage that cannot be affirmed. It is an act of violence that freedom can inflict upon itself but that is not willed by God and never can be willed."[28] Or in Balthasar's own words, "sin is essentially untruth, a lie that seeks to release from itself, once it has become personal and social, a pseudo-form of secondary 'truth' as the normal form, which is taken as valid simply as a matter of course."[29]

Now here is the real issue: how far can the finite No reach? Balthasar is quite right on both sides of the dilemma: on the one hand, *if* a soul is lost, God has also lost his "gamble" with himself when he first made the world and set free beings within it; on the other, when we fell and lost his fellowship through disobedience, he restored his friendship with us by sending his Son, *which only increased the disobedience and hatred.* Now how far can that go? Balthasar attempts to answer this question (for which he admits there is no real "answer" while we yet remain *under* judgment) in a complex and lengthy article he wrote on eschatology (called "Eschatology in Outline") for a projected Japanese series on dogmatics, in which he established the following points: first, whatever judgment will befall the human race, either collectively or individually, already resides entirely in the person of Jesus:

> The judgment is completely present in the Judge himself. First, he is judgment in the sense of a sentence that has been inflicted on the Judge by the guilty world: *he* is the one who has been put into prison by the world, condemned, spat upon, beaten, bound in chains, crowned with thorns, crucified and mocked for his impotence and godforsakenness. But behind this judgment of

---

[28] Gustave Martelet, S.J., *L'au-delà retrouvé: Christologie des fins dernières* (Paris: Desclée, 1974), 183; cited in *Dare We Hope?*, 53–54.

[29] "Eschatology in Outline," *PI*, 432; a line that is startlingly reminiscent of Newman's sermon quoted above, though, it seems, with different conclusions. It is also the opinion of C. S. Lewis: "All that are in Hell, choose it. Without that self-choice there could be no Hell" (*The Great Divorce* [New York: Macmillan, 1946], 72).

the world there appears in him the willingness to suffer everything as Son in obedience to the will of the Father; and this
means that he understands what he has been forced to undergo
as his being delivered over to the world by the Father. This has
all been taken into account beforehand in the eternal council of
the Father "from before the foundation of the world," it is already accounted for as God's own spontaneous deed: the loving
surrender and gift of his beloved Son out of love for the life of
the world (Jn 3:16; Rm 8:32). He is the Lamb slain from the
beginning of the world (Rev 13:8). (*PI*, 436)

Secondly, Balthasar insists that Jesus admits *other co-judges* to join him
in his role as Judge of the world, which include: angels ("For the Son of
Man will come in the glory of his Father, surrounded by his holy angels
and rewarding each according to his works": Mt 16:27); the Twelve Apostles ("When everything is made new again[30] and the Son of Man is seated
on the throne of his holiness, you too will sit on twelve thrones and judge
the twelve tribes of Israel": Mt 19:28); and finally all of the elect who
have passed over into the kingdom of Christ ("Do you not know that the
saints will judge the world? . . . Do you not know that we will even be
the judges of the [fallen] angels?": 1 Cor 6:2–3). Needless to say, this
assembly is not a parliament of cacophonous voices where an agreement
has to be hammered out.[31] But it does open up the possibility of an
economy of grace where intercessory prayers really count and we become
bound to each other even across the borderline of death.[32]

---

[30] *palingenesia* (rebirth): not the same word as *apokatastasis,* but an interesting syn-
onym, nonetheless.

[31] "This thought of the inseparability of Christ from his true Church even in judgment is
however self-limiting: for the image is not one of an assembly of judgment in which, as it
were, each judge has an equal say in the outcome—with the judgment coming about only
by the disparate assembly hammering out an agreement. Rather, the image implies that co-
judgment occurs by agreeing with the judgment of the one Judge. But even this needs to be
further nuanced. For there are the strong words of the Gospel about Christ that he came
'not to condemn but to save' (Lk 9:56), that 'God has not sent his Son into the world that
he might judge the world but that the world might be saved through him' (Jn 3:17): 'For I
am not come to judge the world but to save the world' (Jn 12:47). Next to these words,
however, that depict his mandate and his action, stand the words that explain the judgment
as a process that is directed *at* him but without his conscious sentencing: 'Whoever despises
me and does not accept my words has his judge; the word that I have proclaimed will judge
him on the Last Day' (Jn 12:48; similarly 3:9: 'The judgment, however, is this: the light is
come into the world, but men have preferred the darkness to the light'). Without thereby
limiting the freedom of the Judge, he is saying that his mere appearance before all beings
will separate the spirits. He and his own disciples work as catalyzers" (*PI,* 439).

[32] "The penance of one can bring about the grace of conversion of another without the
one who converts ever knowing—before Judgment Day—where this grace came from. The
basic reality of the Mystical Body of Christ is the fruitfulness of the 'theological virtues' in

And finally—and this is the most revolutionary aspect of Balthasar's eschatology—he insists that when a person is condemned to hell, Jesus is still able to meet the one condemned, for he too has been there and can meet the sinner in solidarity with him. The passage where this is set out in this essay I regard as the most crucial passage in all of Balthasar's treatment of this controversial subject,[33] and so I shall cite it in full:

> There is a final question that arises at this point but which, after all that has been said, cannot be answered. How will the Judge behave toward those who come before him as ones who have turned away, who appear in the Gospel parables and other *logia* of Jesus as the ones whom he "does not know," as the ones who have been "rejected" and "expelled" (Mt 22:13) and handed over to the powers of darkness? We do not know. We may ascribe a part of the definitive division of mankind into sheep and goats (as in Mt 25:31–46) to paranesis [catechetical pedagogy]—this is especially clear in Heb 6:4–12—and another part supposedly to the form of eschatological black-and-white painting so common in the Old Testament. But there is still an unsettling residue that cannot be interpreted away. We can only go so far as to say: as Redeemer, God also respects the freedom that God, as Creator, has given to the creature and which gives the creature the freedom to resist God's love. This "respect" means that God does not overpower, oppress, or do violence to the precarious freedom of the creature by the omnipotence of his absolute freedom. It remains, however, to consider whether it still is not open to God to encounter the sinner turned away from him in the impotent form of the crucified Brother [Christ] who has been abandoned by God, and indeed in such a way that it becomes clear to the one who has turned away from God that: this One beside me who has been forsaken by God (like myself) has been

---

the life of those who have been made holy by them: every single Christian who lets them take effect in himself without restriction will become someone, whether he knows it or not, who is letting the divine life flow into the world through himself. Even non-Christian religions have known of this mystery, although usually in a limited sense. Certain Christian denominations that broke off from the Catholic Church, however, have almost completely forgotten it out of an obsession with personal salvation. Indeed in the center of the Catholica there lives the knowledge of this buoyant, jubilant mystery whose concrete effects cannot be developed in detail: that we can 'shine like stars in the universe' (Phil 2:15) for one another" (*PI*, 440–441). This is no doubt what is behind Paul's mysterious reference to "baptism for the dead" (1 Cor 15:29)—a practice now prevalent only among the Mormons. But whatever else Paul's passing reference means, surely he saw the fate of all mankind bound up in solidarity with the event of Christ, including retroactively.

[33] It is, by the way, the passage chosen by the editors of *The von Balthasar Reader* for the section on eschatology.

abandoned by God *for my sake*. Now there can be no more talk of doing violence to freedom if God appears in the loneliness of the one who has chosen total loneliness of living only for himself (or perhaps one should say: who *thinks* that is how he has chosen) and shows himself to be as the One who is still lonelier than the sinner. In order to see this we must recall what was said at the outset, according to which the world has been founded in advance with all its freely chosen destinies in view of the mystery of the self-surrendering Son of God: whose descent is *a priori* deeper than the depths any lost person in the world can reach. Even what we call "hell"—although it is indeed the place of reprobation—is still even more a christological place.[34]

We are clearly up against what Socrates called an "aporia" (impasse) beyond which we cannot penetrate. We are before the same mystery in the face of which Job cried out, "My words have been frivolous: what can I reply? I put my hand over my mouth. I spoke once, but I have no answer—twice, but I will say no more" (Job 40:4–5). To which God replies:

> Brace yourself like a warrior, I am going to ask you the questions, and you are going to inform me! Do you really want to

---

[34] *PI*, 443–444; my emphasis. Which brings up Hitler once more in his odd role as a *theologoumenon* of this problem. While I believe it is permitted to hope that death itself would lead to a repentant encounter with God, we must not assume that it will be so. In this regard (since his name has been brought up by Balthasar in *Dare We Hope?*), I think we should be impressed with Hitler's willful defiance up to the last moment: when the Allied armies were closing in on Berlin so tightly that even his General Staff joked that to get from the Eastern to the Western front one had only to take a Berlin street car, Hitler wrote his last will and testament, blaming the outcome of the war on the international conspiracy of the Jews and promising the German *Volk* a future salvation. But *also* he ordered the complete dismantling of the infrastructure of Germany, lest the country recover from the debacle *he* enticed his country into: "In his bunker deep beneath the Reich's Chancellery, he called for a program of demolition and destruction that would result in obliteration of the German nation. When Albert Speer came to him with a memorandum of protest, he told him in icy tones: 'If the war is lost, the people must be lost also.' . . . A few days later he answered Speer's protest with the order [that] . . . wholesale destruction of the means of livelihood in Germany was to be carried out by the *Gauleiter*. . . . If the order had been carried out— and it was not—there would have been no electricity, gas, pure water, fuel or transportation in Germany. . . . The German Reich was his; he had made it, it had proved unworthy of him and now he would destroy it" (Robert Leckie, *Delivered From Evil: The Saga of World War II* [New York: Harper & Row, 1987], 900–901). What must be considered in Balthasar's proposal cited above is the accumulation of sin acting like an inertial force at death so that one is hurled, so to speak, into defiance, even in the face of an encounter with Christ in hell. One cannot afford to put off the moment of repentance: *now* is the time of salvation, not after death!

reverse my judgment, put me in the wrong and yourself in the right? Has your arm the strength of God's, can your voice thunder as loud? Come then, display your majesty and grandeur, robe yourself in splendour and glory. Let the fury of *your* wrath burst forth, humble the haughty at a glance if you can! At a glance bring down the proud and strike the wicked where they stand. Bury the lot of them in the ground, shut them up, every one, in the Dungeon. And then I shall be the first to pay you homage, since your won right hand is strong enough to save you. (Job 40: 6–14)

This is the same mystery before which Paul exclaimed (just after the verse in which he says that "God bound all men over to disobedience so that he might have mercy on them all" (Rom 11:32):

Oh how rich and deep is the knowledge and wisdom of God! How unsearchable his judgments and his paths beyond tracing out! "Who has ever known the mind of the Lord or has been his counsellor?" [Is 40:13]. "Who has ever given anything to him so that his gifts come only as a debt returned?" [Job 41:11]. Everything there is comes from him and is caused by him and exists for him. To him be glory for ever! Amen. (Rom 11:33–36)

Therefore, I suppose we are left "at a loss" (another possible translation of "aporia"). And the same must hold when we come to judge Balthasar's eschatology: where is the basis? His critics understandably fear the boldness of his hope as implying too much.[35] For it seems to weaken the motivation not to sin, as when St. Ignatius has the exercitant contemplate "how many have been lost on account of a single mortal sin, how many times I have deserved eternal damnation because of the many grievous sins I have committed . . . to obtain some grace or gift that one earnestly

---

[35] E.g.: "Magnificent and inspiring though it is, Balthasar's theology of the Descent in many ways bewilders me. Two years before his death he wrote a book to defend the orthodoxy of his views on Hell and took the trouble of obtaining an imprimatur from the Cardinal Prefect of the Holy Office [sic]. Nonetheless, despite all the painstaking and scholarly qualifications and explanations, he does give the impression to some of his readers that Christ's Descent makes universal salvation inevitable. . . . When I first read [his views on Christ's encounter with sinners in Hell] it disturbed me because it seemed to imply the possibility of a conversion taking place in the Hell of the damned. No, what he is describing is the Hound of Heaven's loving pursuit of the self-destructive soul to the very end *of this life*, revealing his presence to him in the loneliness of an earthly Hell, for no one has descended more deeply than he" (John Saward, *The Mysteries of March*, 129–130). I believe as an exegesis of Balthasar's views, this thesis will not stand up to scrutiny, but theologically Saward could have a point. Perhaps, then, the issue boils down to whether there is a possibility of conversion after death, that is, in hell. Can the Church pronounce on that possibility if revelation has not?

desires" (*Sp. Ex.*, 48, 87.3). Now I believe, as a matter of personal opinion, that this fear is unjustified, that on the contrary Balthasar has a very lively sense of sin and therefore does not fall under the spell of that psychologically determined hope that Augustine stripped away in his *City of God*.[36]

But as we have noted, there is also the opposite psychological danger—that of assuming that if human history really is divided between sheep and goats, one must therefore be accounted among the sheep (has any advocate of double predestination ever assumed otherwise?). The great advantage of Balthasar's eschatology is that it puts us in touch once more with the essential solidarity of the human race,[37] and schools us in compassion.[38] So in conclusion let me clamber down from these vast theological heights and stress simply the gracious advantages of Balthasar's defense of the theological virtue of hope. In this regard I am reminded of the remarks of an eminent psychiatrist who said in a recent work:

> Imagine this scene: three to four hundred people, strangers to each other, are told to pair up and ask their partner one single question, "What do you want?" over and over and over again. Could anything be simpler? One innocent question and its answer. And yet, time after time, I have seen this group exercise evoke unexpectedly powerful feelings. Often, within minutes, the room rocks with emotion. Men and women—and these are by no means desperate or needy but successful, well-functioning, well-dressed people who glitter as they walk—are stirred to their depths. They call out to those who are forever lost—dead or

---

[36] As an example from Balthasar's writings, I cite this passage: "In the household of the heart . . . evil reigns, possessing no nature of itself since it is anti-natural, and it piles itself high like ever-growing refuse, and does not dissolve of itself; and no worldly power . . . is able to sweep it away. In the north of France you can see factories, and next to them black mountains of slag tower ten times higher than the city's rooftops. These sinister hills that exhale a dark curse attempt in vain to form a bit of landscape. And you, Lord, want to demolish the towers and mountains of sin? You want to drink up this ocean of infallibly lethal poisons? You want to transform your sublime Heart into a purification plant for the world?" (*HW*, 104–105).

[37] John R. Sachs, S.J. in his article "Current Eschatology: Universal Salvation and the Problem of Hell," *Theological Studies* 52/2 (1991): 227–254, makes the point that this perspective can help answer the challenge posed by fundamentalism. Though this term too often serves as a journalistic shorthand for phenomena that do not have that much in common with each other, nonetheless I think it can be said that those groups within a religion that have been labeled "fundamentalist" often show an intolerance for others outside the sect, an intolerance that receives a certain theological justification from the sense of being saved from the *massa damnata* (which naturally means excluding all the outsiders).

[38] "Today we live at a time when all things conspire to draw us into a more far-reaching interpretation of the content of hope as Jesus preached it: the conversion of the world to the reign of God" (Monika Hellwig, "Eschatology," *Systematic Theology* 2:371).

absent parents, spouses, children, friends: "I want to see you again." "I want your love." "I want to know you are proud of me." "I want you to know I love you and how sorry I am I never told you." "I want you back—I am so lonely." "I want the childhood I never had." So much wanting. So much longing. And so much pain, so close the surface, only minutes deep. Destiny pain. Existence pain. Pain that is always there, whirring continuously just beneath the membrane of life.[39]

This perspective brings a very chastening and holy humility to the Christian, who can easily become all too aware of the distinctiveness of his faith as a sign of God's distinctive favor over his fellows. And this holds even for Christianity's cult of its own martyrs, a point that Balthasar does not flinch from drawing:

> Considering the immense sea of suffering that people have inflicted on one another in the history of the world—murders of individuals and entire peoples, tortures of every kind such as only the perverse human brain can concoct, planned mass extermination—it is not easy to single out the atrocities perpetrated against Christians in the last 2000 years. Is there any sense in making them the subject of a separate consideration? After all, countless other so-called innocent people have likewise been killed on account of their religious, political or moral convictions; or simply because they were in the way of someone powerful, a tyrant or an expansion-needy race or people; or because they represented an alien element in their environment, such as the Jews in Egypt or Persia, who long before the Christian era

---

[39] Irvin D. Yalom, M.D., *Love's Executioner & Other Tales of Psychotherapy* (New York: Basic Books, 1989), 3. This remarkable book recounts the stories of ten of Dr. Yalom's patients and their progress in finding healing for their pain. Perhaps the most remarkable of these tales was of Carlos, a terminally ill cancer patient who finally came to see that, as he said, "everyone has a heart." For "during the group meeting last week," he reported, "all three of the women in the group were sharing a lot of their feelings, about how hard it was being single, about loneliness, about grieving for their parents, about nightmares. I don't know why, but I suddenly saw them in a different way. They were like me! They were having the same problems of living that I was. . . . At that moment I had a vision of their naked hearts. Their chest wall vanished, just melted away leaving a square blue-red cavity with rib-bar walls and, in the center, a liver-colored, glistening heart thumping away. All week long I've been seeing everyone's heart beating, and I've been saying to myself, 'Everybody's got a heart, everybody has got a heart.' I've been seeing the heart in everyone—a misshapen hunchback who works in reception, an old lady who does the floors, even the men I work with!" (84). Although devotion to the Sacred Heart has noticeably waned since the Second Vatican Council, I have often thought that it would find new relevance if Christians could once more feel their solidarity with the hearts of all their fellow human beings.

were persecuted and partially exterminated in organized po-
groms. . . . And assuming that we were to find sufficient reason
to return in spirit to this heroic age of Christianity and make a
special reflection on the many martyrdoms of this time, would
not its entire edifying effect immediately be obliterated if we
placed on the *other* side of the scale all the outrages committed
by Christians (regardless of denomination) in every succeeding
age, against those of other faiths—heretics or Jews, for example—and against fellow Christians?

It is certainly dreadful to read that Emperor Galerius had his
soldiers barricade and set on fire a Phrygian town whose inhabit-
ants were all Christians, thus causing every man, woman and
child to burn to death. But the illustrious builder of the Hagia
Sophia, the most Christian Emperor Justinian, did the same thing
a number of times in order to eradicate certain sects, as well as
the Jews, in Asia Minor. Nor was it any different during the
Albigensian wars: the heretics were locked up in their churches
and the churches were set afire. Other highlights were the capture
of Constantinople by the Crusaders, the conquest of Latin
America by the Spanish, the Thirty Years' War, the St. Bartholo-
mew's Day Massacre, the living torches of the Inquisition and
witch-hunts and the executions of Savonarola and Giordano
Bruno. There is no end of Christian abominations: they continue
today in the tortures and prisons of South American military
states, as well as in the hardheartedness of many Christian capi-
talist entrepreneurs who unscrupulously exploit poor peoples
and nations.[40]

Underneath these Christian atrocities, I believe, can be found that same
lurking psychology of feeling the Gospel is one's personal possession that
has bedeviled (in more than one sense) the advocates of a populated hell—
especially the double-predestinarians. But even more important than that
consideration, in my opinion, is the reverse: what is *gained* by seeing the
human race in its solidarity with itself, and here Balthasar's insights converge with those of Yalom:

And how much unpretentious, unnoticed courage, even heroic
courage unto death is exercised in everyday life, not only in
oppressed countries where men, women and children have to
struggle through from one day to the next but also in the slums

---

[40] "Martyrdom and Mission," *NE*, 279–282.

of our affluent countries, in hospitals; in the lonely, seemingly meaningless life of the elderly; in the martyrdom of unhappy marriages, in which two people have to bear with one another without the support of love. No, in the immense anthill of humanity there is a prodigious amount of courage in the face of life and death. The Christian courage that makes martyrs certainly has a place here, but does it excel qualitatively to the extent that it is worthy of special notice? (*NE*, 283–284)

I am reminded here of Edith Stein, who was killed as a Jew in Auschwitz but died as a Catholic convert and Carmelite nun. When her canonization was announced, a swirl of controversy arose about its significance: technically, in canon law, a martyr is someone who is killed out of hatred for the faith, which does not exactly fit Edith Stein's case, a Catholic who was murdered for her Jewishness, not her Catholic faith. She knew that too, and died in conscious solidarity with her people and yet fully faithful to the grace of her conversion. The debate about her canonization soon degenerated to the point where Jews and Christians were accusing each other of appropriating each other's suffering—which is itself a rather disedifying display of the violation of human solidarity. Balthasar, as it happens, concluded nearly the last book he ever wrote with an extended quotation from Edith Stein, parts of which I would like to cite, especially as she was herself a victim of the very evil whose mysteries she was trying to address in this passage:

By its own power [grace] can, at best, come up to man's door but never force its way inside. And further: it can come to him without his seeking it, without his desiring it. The question is whether it can complete its work without his cooperation. It seems to us that this question has to be answered negatively. This is a weighty thing to say. For it obviously implies that God's freedom, which we call omnipotence, meets with a limit in human freedom. Grace is the Spirit of God, who descends to the soul of man. It can find no abode there if it is not freely taken in. That is a hard truth. It implies—besides the aforementioned limit to divine omnipotence—the possibility, in principle, of excluding oneself from redemption and the kingdom of grace. It does *not* imply, however, a limit to divine mercy. . . . All-merciful love can descend to everyone. We believe that it does so. Now: can we assume that there are souls that remain perpetually closed to such love? As a possibility in principle, this cannot be rejected. *In reality*, it can become infinitely improbable. . . . Seen in this way, what were described earlier as limits to divine omnipotence are also canceled out again. They exist only as long as we oppose divine and human freedom to each other and fail to consider the sphere that forms the basis of human freedom. Human freedom can be neither broken nor neutralized by divine freedom, but it may well be, so to speak, outwitted.

The descent of grace to the human soul is a free act of divine love. And there are *no limits* to how far it may extend. Now which particular means it chooses for bringing this about, why it strives to win one soul and lets another strive to win it, whether and how and when it is also active in places where our eyes perceive no effects—those are all questions that escape rational penetration. For us, there is only knowledge of the possibilities in principle and, on the basis of those possibilities in principle, an understanding of the facts that are accessible to us.[41]

And that is what Balthasar has given us in his life: simply an understanding of the facts that are accessible to us, all the while inviting us to worship the One who remains ever inaccessible.

A fitting conclusion to a great life.

---

[41] Edith Stein, *Welt und Person: Beitrag zum christlichen Wahrheitsstreben*, ed. L. Gelber and Romaeus Leuven, O.C.D. (Freiburg, 1962), pp. 158ff; cited in "Short Discourse," *Dare We Hope?*, 218–221.

Index